Recommended by Teachers
Trusted by Toppers

AF814414

All in One®

English Communicative

CBSE Class 9

Focused Theory ▪ Practice Exercise ▪ Sample Papers

Author
Parneet Kaur

arihant
SUCCESS AND NOTHING LESS

arihant
SUCCESS AND NOTHING LESS

ARIHANT PRAKASHAN

(School Division Series)

卐 ADMINISTRATIVE & PRODUCTION OFFICES

Regd. Office

'Ramchhaya' 4577/15, Agarwal Road, Darya Ganj, New Delhi -110002
Tele: 011- 47630600, 43518550; Fax: 011- 23280316

卐 *Head Office*

Kalindi, TP Nagar, Meerut (UP) - 250002, Tel: 0121-7156203, 7156204

卐 SALES & SUPPORT OFFICES

Agra, Ahmedabad, Bengaluru, Bareilly, Chennai, Delhi, Guwahati, Hyderabad, Jaipur, Jhansi, Kolkata, Lucknow, Nagpur & Pune.

PO No. : TXT-59-T064198-04-25

Published By Arihant Publications (India) Ltd.

For further information about the books published by Arihant, log on to www.arihantbooks.com or e-mail at info@arihantbooks.com

Follow us on

卐 PRICE ₹340.00

PRODUCTION TEAM

Publishing Managers
Mahendra Singh Rawat & Keshav Mohan

Cover Designer
Rakesh Rawat

Inner Designer
Ankit Tyagi

Project Head
Manju

Page Layouting
Lalit Chaprana

Proof Reader
Harsh Agarwal

Index *cum* Study Planner

SECTION A

READING SKILLS

SECTION B

WRITING SKILLS

SECTION C

GRAMMAR

Latest Course Structure

Section	Title	Total Weightage
A	Reading Skills	20
B	Writing Skills	24
C	Grammar	10
D	Literature Textbook	26
	TOTAL	80

SECTION A: READING SKILLS **(10+10=20 Marks) 40 Periods**

- The section will have two unseen passages with the maximum word limit of 600 words. The passages can be of any two types out of the following: literary / factual / discursive. Please refer to the Main Course Book.
- Objective Type Questions (including Multiple Choice Questions), and Very Short Answer type Questions will be asked to test inference, evaluation, analysis and vocabulary in context.

SECTION B: WRITING SKILLS **24 Marks** **50 Periods**

This section will have a variety of short and long writing tasks.

- Notice Writing for school assembly/ Resident Welfare Association/ School Events/ Classroom information etc. (maximum 50 words) 4 Marks
- Dialogue Writing, (maximum 100 words) 5 Marks
  Informal Letter (maximum 120 words) 7 Marks
- Paragraph on one out of two themes from the Main Course Book, based on verbal or visual cues (maximum 150 words) 8 Marks

SECTION C: GRAMMAR **10 Marks** **20 Periods**

Grammar items will be taught and assessed over a period of time.

1. Tenses
2. Modals
   1. Subject – verb concord
   2. Reported Speech
      (I) Commands and Requests (ii) Statements (iii) Questions
   3. Clauses:
      (i) Noun clauses (ii) Adverb clauses (iii) Relative clauses
   4. Determiners

The above items may be tested through test types as given below:

- Gap filling — 3 marks
- Editing or Omission — 4 marks
- Sentences Reordering or Sentence Transformation in context. — 3 marks

SECTION D: LITERATURE TEXTBOOK **26 Marks** **50 Periods**

- Two out of three extracts from prose/poetry for reference to the context. Very Short Answer Questions and Short Answer Questions will be asked to assess local and global comprehension, interpretation and analysis. — 8 marks
  (4+4)
- Six Short Answer Questions out of seven, from the Literature Reader, to test local and global comprehension of theme and ideas, analysis and evaluation
  (30-40 words each) — 2x6 = 12 Marks
- One out of two Long Answer type Questions to assess how the values inherent in the text have been brought out. Creativity, imagination and extrapolation beyond the text and across the texts will be assessed. This can also be a passage-based question taken from a situation/plot from the texts. (120 words). — 6 marks

Prescribed Books: Interact in English Series by CBSE (Available on www.cbseacademic.nic.in)

- Main Course Book (Revised Edition)
- Literature Reader (Revised Edition)
- Workbook (Revised Edition)

NOTE: Teachers are advised to

i. encourage classroom interaction among peers, students and teachers through activities such as role play, group work etc.,

ii. reduce teacher-talk time and keep it to a minimum,

iii. take up questions for discussion to encourage pupils to participate and to marshal their ideas and express and defend their views.

Assessment of Listening and Speaking Skills: 50 Periods

Guidelines for the Assessment of Listening and Speaking Skills are given at Annexure I.

SECTION A READING SKILLS

Reading Comprehension

CHAPTER 1

Let's REVISE Reading comprehension involves a thorough understanding of a given passage consisting of one or more paragraphs. It is meant to test the understanding power and intellectual skills of a student.

Reading comprehension usually includes questions that test the reader's ability to

- find the main idea or a suitable title for the passage.
- find information directly specified in the passage.
- draw inferences from the given passage.
- determine the meaning of unfamiliar words used in the passage.
- determine the author's style, mood or point of view.

In the **Class IX English Communicative** examination, two passages carrying a **total of 20 marks** will be asked from the reading section.

Both passages are either factual, discursive or literary and each passage carries 10 marks.

Types of Passages

Different types of passages given are designed to test the reading skills of students in exams. They may be of any of the kinds given below

- **Factual Passages** A factual passage includes some facts about the physical aspects of a subject. Such passages are generally taken from newspapers, magazines, brochures, reference books and encyclopaedias.
- **Discursive Passages** A discursive passage includes argumentative, interpretative and persuasive text. These passages are mostly inclusive of opinions or feedback and allow a student to arrive at a conclusion through reason and understanding.
  The sources of such passages are newspapers, magazines, reference books and blogs.
- **Literary Passages** A literary passage includes lines or an excerpt taken directly from a story or a poem. It includes extracts from fiction, drama, essay, biography, etc. The sources of such passages are-novels, short stories, dramas, biographies or any other literary books.

Types of Questions

In the examination, students are tested on a variety of questions that test their inferential and analytical skills along with their vocabulary. These types include

- Objective type questions (including Multiple Choice Questions)
- Very short answer type questions

Points to Remember

- Read the passage carefully and thoroughly to understand its content. Underline the main ideas, instances, examples and arguments supporting them.
- Underline the words you don't understand and try to guess their meaning from the context. Check the vocabulary related questions and try to find the answers from the context after thorough reading.
- Quickly go through the questions and mark the parts of the passage you feel can be the answers.
- Read the passage again to counter check your answers and write your answers briefly and to-the-point. Remember, use your own words to write the answer.
- Answers should be based on information given/inference derived from the information in the passage.
- Make sure to use the same tense in which the question has been asked.
- In Multiple Choice Questions, analyse the questions and options carefully before selecting the correct option because some of the four options are closely related.

SOLVED EXAMPLES

Factual Passages

Read the given passages carefully and answer the questions that follow.

PASSAGE 1

The first written public examinations were introduced over 1400 years ago with the establishment of the imperial examination system in 606 AD in China. By the middle of the 19th century, competitive examinations had been introduced in Britain and India to select government officials. Public examination in schools have a shorter but still considerable history.

At present, the examination systems in India are characterised by heterogeneity. They differ in their vintage organisational design, financial stability, autonomy, organisational culture and credibility. For instance, the National Institute of Open Schooling (NIOS) is unique in conducting exams through the distance mode; the Indian School Certificate Examination confines itself only to private schools; and the West Bengal Board of Madrasa Education is for Islamic educational institutions only. The Amrik Singh Report (1997) on reorganising boards wondered, 'Can there also be a system whereby it becomes possible to grade and categorise the boards in respect of how efficiently and honestly examinations are organised?'

To do so, a set of parameters was chosen to measure effectiveness, transparency and economic efficiency of the functioning of these organisations. These parameters include indicators like cost incurred per student, fees charged per student, number of examinees per employee and number of affiliated schools per employee. The functioning of a total of 20 boards was analysed in terms of 18 performance indicators in 2005. The data collected from the states shows that most boards have an operating surplus. The CBSE, along with the Maharashtra board, seem to fare the best.

Another important measure of effectiveness of the functioning of the boards is the time taken for declaration of examination results. It was found that this ranged from a mere 26 days in the case of Karnataka Secondary Education Examination Board in 2005 to 48 days for Class X in neighbouring Maharashtra. The Supreme Court has recently issued directions that results should be declared within 45 days from the end of examinations. In 2005, 10 of the 20 boards which provided this information could not declare results within 45 days.

Questions

1. When were the first written public examinations introduced?

2. The feature(s) of the examination system in our country are
(a) Organisational design
(b) Dependency
(c) Autonomy
(d) Both (a) and (c)

3. The Amrik Singh Report brought forth that
(a) the board results
(b) the need to revamp the system of boards.
(c) which board(s) fared the best
(d) the board that needs improvement

4. Which boards seem to fare the best in terms of operating surplus?

5. Substitute the underlined word/phase in the following sentence with a word/phrase from the last paragraph that means the same. **Competency Based**
The tennis star is in an upbeat mood as he won the Australian open <u>a short while ago</u>.

6. Give one feature of National Institute of Open Schooling (NIOS). **Competency Based**

7. Complete the following suitably.
The examinations are characterised by ....

8. Complete the following suitably.
West Bengal Board of Madrasa Education is for .... institutions only.
(a) Islamic educational
(b) Christian educational
(c) Co-educational
(d) Jain educational

9. Rectify the given False statement.
The time taken for the declaration of results is not an important feature of the functioning of the boards.

10. Which one of the following correctly lists the direction issued by the Supreme Court?
(a) Results should be declared within 30 days from the start of the examination.
(b) Results should be declared within 45 days from the end of the examination.
(c) Results should be declared within 45 days from the start of the examination.
(d) Results should be declared within 60 days from the end of the examination.

Answers

1. The first written public examinations were introduced with the establishment of the imperial examination system in 606 AD in China.
2. (d) Both (a) and (c)
3. (c) which board(s) fared the best
4. In terms of operating surplus, the CBSE board and Maharashtra board fare the best.
5. Recently
6. The National Institute of Open Schooling (NIOS) conducts examinations through the distance mode.
7. heterogeneity
8. (a) Islamic educational
9. The time taken for the declaration is an important feature of the functioning of the boards.
10. (b) Results should be declared within 45 days from the end of the examination.

PASSAGE 2

Environmental pollution refers to the introduction of harmful pollutants into the environment. The major types of environmental pollution are air pollution, water pollution, noise pollution, thermal pollution, soil pollution and light pollution. Deforestation and hazardous gaseous emissions also lead to environmental pollution. We all live on planet Earth which is the only planet known to have an environment where air and water are two basic things that sustain life.

Without air and water, the Earth would be like the other planets. The biosphere in which living beings have their sustenance has oxygen, nitrogen, carbon dioxide, argon and water vapour. All these are well-balanced to ensure and help a healthy growth of life in the animal world. The sources and causes of environmental pollution include the following

Industrial Activities The industries that brought prosperity made inroads in the biosphere and disturbed the ecological balance. The pall of smoke, the swirling gases, industrial effluents and the fall-out of scientific experiments became constant health hazards, polluting and contaminating both air and water. The improper disposals of industrial wastes are the sources of soil and water pollution.

Pollution by Vehicles The smoke emitted by vehicles using petrol and diesel and the cooking coal also pollutes the environment. The harmful smoke of these vehicles causes air pollution. Further, the sounds produced by these vehicles cause noise pollution.

Rapid Urbanisation and Industrialisation The urbanisation and the rapid growth of industrialisation are causing, through environmental pollution, the greatest harm to plant life which in turn harms the animal kingdom and human lives.

Population Overgrowth Due to the increase in population, there has been a surge in demand for basic food, occupation and shelter. The world has witnessed massive deforestation to expand and absorb the growing population and their demands.

There surely cannot be any radical solution, for the existing factories cannot be bodily lifted to a place far from the populated zone. However, many attempts have been made to solve the problem of environmental pollution. The government can atleast see that future factories are set up at a distant place, an industrial complex far away from the township. Deforestation should be stopped and forestry should be preserved. Discharge of factory wastes in rivers should be banned so as to make the river-water free from pollution.

Questions

1. Select the way in which deforestation can be controlled.
   (a) By launching new industries
   (b) By cutting more and more trees
   (c) By purchasing new vehicles
   (d) By planting new plants
2. How is Earth different from any other planet in our solar system?
3. How have the industries contributed to soil and water pollution?
   (a) Poor ecological balance
   (b) Encroaching the environment
   (c) Disposing wastes carelessly
   (d) Doing scientific experiments
4. What is causing the greatest harm to plant life?
5. Why is there no radical solution to the problem of pollution?
6. Substitute the underlined word in the given sentence with a word from the passage which means the same. **Competency Based**
   The constant cutting of trees had <u>damaged</u> the ecological balance.
7. Select the tone of the author in the passage.
   (a) Objective
   (b) Dejected
   (c) Didactic
   (d) Philosophical
8. Complete the sentence appropriately.
   Deforestation leads to ....
9. Complete the sentence appropriately.
   The population overgrowth causes an increase in ....
10. State whether the given assertion is True or False.
    Improper disposals of industrial wastes are the sources of soil and water pollution.

Answers

1. (d) By planting new plants
2. Earth is the only planet known to have an environment. It has what no other planet has – life, plants and an atmosphere.
3. (c) Disposing wastes carelessly
4. Urbanisation and the rapid growth of industrialisation are causing the greatest harm to plant life.
5. There is no radical solution to the problem of pollution because many factors cannot be changed in such large populations. Many factories cannot be placed very far off from populated zones.
6. disturbed
7. (a) Objective
8. environmental pollution and ecological imbalance
9. demand for basic food, occupation and shelter
10. True

Discursive Passages

Read the given passages carefully and answer the questions that follow.

PASSAGE 1

"Teenagers? Stress? You must be joking." This is probably the reaction when asked whether teenagers get fretful and apprehensive. For it is generally believed that they have no responsibilities, no worries and no duties. But that is not true.

In today's competitive world, one needs to struggle and fight to make it in this dynamic yet uncertain environment that is both stressful and anxiety inducing. Teenagers face myriad of pressures, three of which are briefly discussed here. The pressure to perform i.e. to do well academically comes principally from parents, teachers and peers.

The lack of aptitude tests or respecting the students' preferences push them into fields which may not interest them or for which they are not equipped. Apart from the pressure to perform well, they are often burdened with the pressure to conform to the norms laid down by society. Next, teenagers are pressurised to reform themselves. This is commonly experienced, especially by students in the age group of 13 to 17. Everybody is telling them when to wake up and what to do. Here's what you can do to deal with these pressures. As a result of pressure, teenagers are often found to be very anxious. A sign of anxiety is holding one's breath. The easy way out is to take deep breaths at regular intervals, trying to calm your mind.

Modern life's competitiveness and challenges put a tremendous load of work on teenagers. They need to understand that they are strong enough to handle the tough challenges in life, studying and assignments being two of them. Procrastinators i.e. people who habitually delay and postpone doing their work, need to cultivate "the art of starting" and this involves dealing with the minor discomfort experienced while beginning a task. Once a job has started, it is much easier to continue.

Some students worry about factors like social and financial status, intelligence and habits that might make them different from their peers. Effective stress management lies in having a healthy attitude towards competition, work, friends and acquaintances. It lies in taking life as it comes, doing your best and being prepared for the worst.

Questions

1. What do you mean by effective stress management?
2. Procrastinators are people who
   (a) sometimes delay and postpone doing their work
   (b) never delay or postpone doing their work
   (c) habitually delay and postpone doing their work
   (d) habitually delay and postpone someone's work
3. Teenagers can deal with pressures by
   (a) avoiding doing the task they are assigned
   (b) taking shallow breaths at regular intervals
   (c) completing the tasks on time
   (d) taking deep breaths at regular intervals
4. What kind of pressures are faced by teenagers?
5. "Teenagers? Stress? You must be joking"
   What can be inferred from the above line?
   (a) There is a lot of stress in a teenager's life.
   (b) We usually do not associate stress with teenagers .
   (c) We usually do not associate stress with adults.
   (d) Teenagers today lead a stressful life.
6. Substitute the underlined word/phrase in the following sentence with a word from Paragraph 2 that means the same. **Competency Based**
   <u>A troubled state of mind</u> is not easy to deal with.
7. Fill in the blank with one word.
   .... from the third paragraph that is synonymous with 'likings'.
8. Complete the sentence appropriately.
   The word in the last paragraph which is a synonym of 'position' is ....
9. Which of the following statements is True?
   (a) We live in a dynamic and uncertain environment these days.
   (b) We live in a static but uncertain environment these days.
   (c) We live in a dynamic but certain environment these days.
   (d) We live in a static and certain environment these days.

10. What pushes a student to choose a field for which he/she is not equipped?

(a) Lack of aptitude tests

(b) Respecting the student's preferences

(c) Not respecting the student's preferences

(d) Both (a) and (c)

Answers

1. Effective stress management means having a healthy attitude towards competition, work, friends and acquaintances, besides taking life as it comes, doing our best but being prepared for the worst.
2. (c) habitually delay and postpone doing their work.
3. (d) taking deep breaths at regular intervals
4. The pressures faced by teenagers are
   (i) pressure to perform i.e. to do well academically
   (ii) pressure to conform to the norms laid down by society
   (iii) pressure to reform themselves
5. (b) We usually do not associate stress with teenagers.
6. Anxiety
7. Preferences
8. status
9. (a) We live in a dynamic and uncertain environment these days
10. (d) Both (a) and (c)

PASSAGE 2

1. Too many parents these days can't say no. As a result, they find themselves raising children who respond greedily to the advertisements aimed right at them. Even getting what they want doesn't satisfy some kids; they only want more. Now, a growing number of psychologists, educators and parents think it's time to stop the madness and start teaching kids about what's really important: values like hard-work, contentment, honesty and compassion. The struggle to set limits has never been tougher—and the stakes have never been higher. One recent study of adults who were overindulged as children paints a discouraging picture of their future: when given too much too soon, they grow up to be adults who have difficulty coping with life's disappointments. They also have distorted sense of entitlement that gets in the way of success in the work place and in relationships.

2. Psychologists say that parents who overindulge their kids, set them up to be more vulnerable to future anxiety and depression. Today's parents themselves raised on values of thrift and self-sacrifice, grew up in a culture where 'no' was a household word. Today's kids want much more, partly because there is so much more to want. The oldest members of this generation were born in the late 1980s, just as PCs and video games were making their assault on the family room. They think of MP3 players and flat screen TV as essential utilities, and they have developed strategies to get them. One survey of teenagers found that when they crave for something new, most expect to ask nine times before their parents give in. By every measure, parents are shelling out record amounts. In the heat of this buying blitz, even parents who desperately need to say no find themselves reaching for their credit cards.

3. What parents need to find, is a balance between the advantages of an affluent society and the critical life lessons that come from waiting, saving and working hard to achieve goals. That search for balance has to start early. Children need limits on their behaviour because they feel better and more secure when they live within a secured structure.

4. Older children learn self-control by watching how others, especially parents act. Learning how to overcome challenges is essential to becoming a successful adult. Few parents ask kids to do chores. They think their kids are already overburdened by social and academic pressures. Every individual can be of service to others and life has meaning beyond one's own immediate happiness. That means parents eager to teach values have to take a long, hard look at their own.

Questions

1. What do the psychologists, educators and parents want to teach the children?

(a) To teach them about treachery.

(b) To teach them about indiscipline.

(c) To teach them about the values of life like hard-work, contentment, honesty and compassion.

(d) None of the above

2. What are the results of giving the children too much too soon? Answer in 30-40 words.

3. What is essential to become a successful adult?

(a) Values of honesty, hardwork and security

(b) Learning how to overcome challenges

(c) Learning to be satisfied with what they have

(d) Practical skills and worldly knowledge

4. What is the balance which the parents need to have in today's world?

5. How do older children learn self-control?

6. Substitute the underlined word in the given sentence with a word from the passage which means the same.

My friend's family is very <u>wealthy</u> and noble.

7. What is the drawback of giving children too much too soon?
   (a) They fail to cope with life's disappointments when they grow up.
   (b) They do not study seriously.
   (c) They become quarrelsome when they grow up.
   (d) None of the above
8. Complete the sentence appropriately.
   Children who are overindulged by their parents come out to be ....
9. State whether the given assertion is True or False.
   The children of the present are different from their parents because the children want to gain as many luxuries as the world offers while the parents follow the values of thrift and self-sacrifice.

Answers

1. (c) To teach them about the values of life like hard-work, contentment, honesty and compassion.
2. When children are given too much too soon, they grow up to be adults who have difficulty in coping with the disappointments of life. Such children may develop a distorted sense of entitlement that comes in the way of success in the work place and relationships.
3. (b) Learning how to overcome challenges.
4. Parents need to find a balance between the advantages of an affluent society and the critical lessons of life that come from waiting, saving and working hard to achieve goals in today's world.
5. Older children learn self-control by watching how others, especially elders and parents act.
6. affluent
7. (a) They fail to cope with life's disappointments when they grow up.
8. vulnerable, anxious and depressed
9. True

Literary Passages

Read the given passages carefully and answer the questions that follow.

PASSAGE 1

1. I saw 'Jaws', the popular shark movie the summer it came out, in 1975 and became paranoid about sharks. Though I kept swimming after Jaws, it was always with the vague fear that a shark's teeth could tug on my leg at any moment. Never mind that there'd been only two shark bites since 1900 on the Connecticut coast, where I lived.
2. So, when I got this assignment for the National Geographic magazine, I decided to accept and do what I'd never wanted to do: swim with the sharks. I had to go to a place in the Bahamas known as Tiger Beach and dive with tiger sharks, the species responsible for more recorded attacks on humans than any shark except the great white. It was to be my first dive after getting certified—which meant it would be my first dive anywhere other than a swimming pool or a quarry—and without a diver's cage. Most people who got wind of this plan thought I was either very brave or very stupid.
3. But I just wanted to puncture an illusion. The people who know sharks intimately tend to be the least afraid of them, and no one gets closer to sharks than divers. The divers who run operations at Tiger Beach speak lovingly of the tiger sharks the way people talk about their children or their pets. In their eyes, these sharks aren't man-eaters any more than dogs are.
4. The business of puncturing illusions is never just black and white. My fellow divers had hundreds of dives under their belt and on the two-hour boat ride to the site in the morning of our first dive, they kept saying things like "Seriously, I really can't believe this is your first dive." All this was okay with me until I reached the bottom and immediately had to fend off the first tiger shark I had ever laid eyes on. However, when I watched the other divers feeding them fish and steering them gently, it became easy to see the sharks in a very benign light.
5. I think it would be unfair not to mention that tiger sharks are apex predators. They act as a crucial balancing force in ocean ecosystems, constraining the numbers of animals like sea turtles and limit their behaviour by preventing them from overgrazing the sea grass beds. Furthermore, tiger sharks love warm water, they eat almost anything, have a huge litter and are the hardiest shark species. If the planet and its oceans continue to warm, some species will be winners and others will be losers, and tiger sharks are likely to be winners.

Questions

1. What does the use of the phrase 'benign light' suggest in the context of the writer's viewpoint about the tiger sharks?
   1. Friendly nature of sharks
   2. Baseless fear of shark
   3. Incorrect quality associated with shark
   4. Superstition related to sharks.

   (a) 1 and 2
   (b) 3 and 4
   (c) 1, 2 and 3
   (d) All of the above
2. Cite a point in evidence from the text to suggest that the writer's post-Jaws fear was not justified.

3. People thought the writer was 'either brave or very stupid'. Why did some people think that he was 'very stupid'? Answer in 30-40 words.

4. Which one of the following traits of the writer is evident from lines 5-10?

(a) Bold

(b) Adventurous

(c) Experimental

(d) All of the above

5. Why does the writer say that people who know sharks intimately tend to be least afraid of them?

6. Substitute the underlined word/phrase in the sentence with a word/phrase from the passage which means the same.

Some academicians think that reward, as a form of discipline, is a simple right or wrong issue.

7. What do the tiger sharks love?

(a) Eating turtles

(b) Harming people who bother them

(c) Warm water

(d) Sea grass

8. Complete the sentence appropriately.

The author of the given passage wants the reader to ....

9. Complete the sentence appropriately.

The writer decides to swim with the sharks because ....

Answers

1. (c) 1, 2 and 3
2. There were only two shark attacks reported from 1900 till after 1975. So, it was highly unlikely that the writer had to fear sharks.
3. Some people thought that the author was very stupid because he ignored the popular notion that tiger sharks are dangerous and was risking his life. He was walking into obvious danger without the required expertise and could be bitten by the sharks.
4. (d) All of the above
5. The writer says that the people who know sharks intimately tend to be the least afraid of them because they find them to be harmless. They find that the sharks feed on the food they offer and seem to be as docile as pets.
6. black and white
7. (c) Warm water
8. not fear sharks and to understand the ecosystem
9. he wanted to puncture the illusion that sharks are vicious man-eating animals

PASSAGE 2

The Last Will of the Tiger

By : Amit Dahiyabadshah

1. When you have stolen my skin from my entity
and removed the roar from my life
O hunter wield that skinning knife
with some grace a little skill
for I too have hunted and killed
many many many times
but every kill
was a prayer in praise of the Creator
my movements were always quick, clean, merciful
Such is the way of true believers

2. But do you now skinner slice slash and cut clean
I pray only that you leave no part of me behind
to be eaten by the jackal and the hyena
for I have ruled this forest on behalf of the creator himself
and there is no honour in a king becoming carrion
…

3. Send my claws to the young of the rich and the highborn to save them from their own nightmares
Send my teeth to Tibet that their aspirations for freedom find new teeth
Send my bones to China that they find a cure
for the fear that builds such great walls
Send my fat to Singapore
so they learn to make a balm for pain
that is mine not only in name
Send my waste to the alchemists
for that is the only substance they have not yet tried
in their efforts to invent gold.

4. Give my entrails to whoever shall take them
But hang on to my eyes you puny murderer
that your tribe might know that
you did not kill a creature beneath you
that I looked you in the eye and did not flinch
when you shot me

5. Instead I have turned away released
from the cancer of your footprint

Questions

1. What will the roar of the tiger do?

(a) Take revenge (b) Fill heaven with rage

(c) Ordained by God (d) Shabby end of the king

2. What is the advice given to the hunter by the tiger?

3. What kind of emotions are embedded in the poem?

(a) Gloomy
(b) Anger
(c) Fear
(d) Restlessness

4. How does the tiger want its bone to be used?

5. What is the tiger's wish for his eyes? Answer in 30-40 words.

6. Substitute the underlined word/phrase in the sentence with a word/phrase from the passage which means the same. **Competency Based**

The corpse of the dog was buried under the pine tree.

7. The tiger wants the tribe of the hunter to know that ....

(a) hunter is happy with the kill
(b) puny murderers don't deserve an applaud
(c) it was not afraid of dying
(d) it fell beneath the hunter

8. Rectify the given False statement.

The tiger wants to befriend the hunter and his tribesmen.

9. Complete the sentence appropriately.

The beauty in each of the tiger's kill was that ....

Answers

1. (b) Fill heaven with rage
2. The tiger advices the hunter to use some skill while skinning the tiger and to put all his body parts to good use.
3. (b) Anger
4. The tiger wants its bone to be sent to China where it can be used to find a cure for the fear that led them to build great walls.
5. The tiger wishes that the hunter keeps its eyes so that he and his tribesmen can remember that the tiger was not a creature beneath man. It fought for its life and was not afraid of dying.
6. Carrion
7. (c) it was not afraid of dying
8. The tiger wants to haunt the hunter and his tribesmen.
9. it killed in praise of the creator and its movements were always quick, clean and merciful.

REVIEW EXERCISE

Including Factual, Discursive and Literary Passages

Factual Passages

PASSAGE 1

A doll is a girl's first best friend with whom she shares every small-little thing in her mind. It is the first toy of her life which, ironically, is supposed to symbolise her own demeanour. Whether it is an innate quality or just a social construction, girls are always supposed to be as prim and proper as a doll. Perhaps this special significance of a doll in a girl's life is the reason behind the international recognition of the Doll Museum in Delhi. Established in the year 1965, Shankar's International Doll Museum is like a dreamland for children. It is, by far, the largest Doll Museum in the country spreading across an area of 5184 square feet. A noted political cartoonist by profession, K Shankar Pillai conceptualised the idea behind this museum and thus it came to be known as Shankar's Doll Museum. Today, it houses almost 6500 exhibits from a total number of 85 nations.

The museum has been divided into two halves. One half is for the collection from Europe, the US, Australia and New Zealand and the other for the Asian countries including India. The Indian contribution sums up to around 500 unique dolls dressed up in the Indian attire worn all across the country. Some dolls are also the representation of the different dance forms of India. A 'clinic' for the dolls which is needed for restoration can also be found at the museum. Shankar's Doll Museum or simply the Doll Museum, is one of the most visited destination for children's day out. Watching such a huge collection of beautiful dolls all together is a delighting experience rejoiced by the children. Not only does it bring joy to their faces but also educates about a lot many things around the world.

Questions

1. Which toy symbolises a girl's own demeanour?

2. What added on to the recognition of the Doll Museum in Delhi?

(a) The special significance of a toy in a girl's life.
(b) The special significance of a doll in a girl's life.
(c) The special significance of a doll is a child's life .
(d) The special significance of a toy in a child's life.

3. Complete the sentence appropriately.
Shankar's International Doll Museum was established in ....

4. State whether the given statement is True or False.
Shankar's International Doll Museum is also the largest Doll Museum in the country spread across 5186 square feet. **Competency Based**

5. The man who proposed the idea of a Doll Museum was
   (a) a noted columnist by profession
   (b) a famous amateur political cartoonist
   (c) an unknown political cartoonist
   (d) a famous political cartoonist

6. What are the collections in the Doll Museum? Answer in 30-40 words.

7. Which of the following statements is not True?
   (a) A girl shares ever small-little thing with a doll.
   (b) The Doll Museum is situated in New Delhi.
   (c) Some dolls in the museum are a representation of various forms of Asia.
   (d) The museum has collection of dolls from New Zealand.

8. A visit to the Doll Museum
   (a) is merely a joyous experience for children
   (b) serves no educational purpose for children
   (c) is a fretful experience for children
   (d) is both a joyous and an educational experience for children

9. Substitute the underlined word in the following sentence with a word from the first paragraph. **Competency Based**
The National Gallery of Modern Art <u>contains</u> some of the rarest antique pieces from all over India.

PASSAGE 2

Many years ago, when the art of stunting plants was quite unheard except in remote areas of India, Buddhist monks in isolated monasteries in Tibet stunted trees like the oak, orange tree, Peepal tree, watching with excitement, the tree still flowering and bearing fruit regardless of this 'deformity.' Since the trees looked so artistically beautiful, the art was learnt by some Chinese monks who taught 'Bonsai' making an art that became most sought after in China. Every garden, among plant lovers had at least half a dozen 'Bonsais'. China and India claimed rights of the art, till Japan followed, enamoured by its beauty. Today Japan leads in Bonsai making of plants and has derived new methodologies to make the plants look aesthetic and artistic. The most beautiful is the cherry blossom that is breathtakingly attractive. The Bonsai remains full if grown for even more than ten years, although it needs constant pruning, watering, shaping and correct environment. The trees can be planted in colourful containers of your choice. Innumerable schools have mushroomed where the art is taught and cultivated. Best known among them is the Indian Bonsai Association. India has great demand for Bonsai, and hotels, homes, garden houses, farm houses, restaurants, guest houses, invariably decorated lobbies, dining halls, drawing rooms with these exotic plants. It is aptly said, that 'a thing of beauty is a joy forever.' Indeed the Bonsai lasts in one's imagination long after the plant has lived its life span.

Bonsai gardeners use methods including wiring branches, extreme pruning of roots and branches, root binding, grafting, and custom soil and cinder mixtures. But perhaps the most important element of all is patience.

Instructions for achieving the 'roots over rock' effect give insight to the work of a Bonsai artist: trim the roots, place the rock, bind roots, then re-pot and wait two years. Often a Bonsai is created by many hands over the years–a highly prized tree is one where the hand and ego of the artist become invisible, as in the Zen concept of 'artless art'.

Questions

1. Who first began to stunt trees and plants?
   (a) Chinese monks in monasteries
   (b) Buddhist monks in China
   (c) Buddhist monks in Tibet
   (d) Monks in monasteries

2. Which Bonsai is breathtakingly attractive?

3. Who leads in the art of stunting today?
   (a) China (b) India
   (c) Tibet (d) Japan

4. How can we take care of Bonsai plants?

5. What is the life span of a Bonsai?
   (a) Five years
   (b) Ten years
   (c) Ten months
   (d) Ten or more than ten years

6. Where is great demand for Bonsai in India?

7. Why does the writer say 'a thing of beauty is a joy forever'?

8. Complete the sentence appropriately.
The word 'enamoured' means ....
   (a) liking something very much
   (b) disliking something very much
   (c) keeping something intact
   (d) taking care of something very much

9. Substitute the underlined word/phase in the following sentence with a word/phase from Paragraph 2 that means the same. **Competency Based**
Many new beauty salons have <u>come up</u> in my area recently.

10. What plays the most important role in creating a bonsai?
(a) Extreme pruning of roots (b) Patience
(c) Grafting (d) Root binding

PASSAGE 3

The Olive Ridley turtle has a circumtropical distribution, living in tropical and warm waters of the Pacific and Indian Oceans from India, Arabia, Japan and Micronesia, South to Southern Africa, Australia, and New Zealand. In the Atlantic Ocean, it has been observed off the Western coast of Africa and the coasts of Northern Brazil, Surinam, Guyana, French Guiana and Venezuela. Historically, this species has been widely regarded as the most abundant sea turtle in the world. More than one million Olive Ridleys were commercially harvested off the coasts of Mexico in 1968 alone.

The Chennai seacoast is a breeding ground for the endangered Olive Ridley turtles. 'The Turtle Walk' is an initiative aimed at educating the fishing community and the general public living near the beach on the need to protect the Olive Ridley turtle and its turtle nests.

During the night, under normal conditions, the sea is a brighter source of light than the land. But now with urbanisation and night time lighting, the shore is brighter than the sea at night. This distracts the Olive Ridley turtles that come ashore to lay eggs. Even the hatchlings get distracted. Instead of going in the direction of the sea, the hatchlings and adults stray towards human habitations.

The volunteers, during their walk, begin their enthusiastic search for turtles and their egg-laden nests. Some may be lucky enough to witness at close quarters, a large turtle. Turtles come ashore, dig their nests in the sand, lay eggs, cover the nest, and then walk back into the sea. The volunteers trace many such nests and dig out the turtle eggs. While newborns are prone to attack by crows and dogs, adult turtles face the threat of being run over by vehicles. Eggs are collected and carried back to the hatchery where they would be kept safely for hatching and once hatched, they are released into the sea. They also rescue lost baby turtles, which could have been hatched from one of the undiscovered nests and had strayed away on account of the distracting lights on the shore. They carry them to the sea and let them free in the water.

Questions

1. The Olive Ridley turtle is a/an .... species.
(a) enfeebled (b) danger
(c) migratory (d) endangered

2. Which place is the reproducing ground of Olive Ridley Turtles?
(a) Micronesia (b) Odisha
(c) Chennai (d) Western Coast of Africa

3. What is 'The Turtle Walk'?

4. Why do the adult turtles and hatchlings stray towards human habitations?

5. In which ocean(s) the Olive Ridley Turtles are found ?
(a) Indian Ocean (b) Atlantic Ocean
(c) Pacific Ocean (d) All of these

6. What kind of danger do the newborn turtles face?
(a) Attack from cows and crows
(b) Attack from dogs and cats
(c) Attack from dogs and crows
(d) Attack from dogs and cows

7. After rescuing lost baby turtles, what is done to them?

8. Complete the sentence appropriately.
In 1968, more than one million Olive Ridleys were harvested in ....

9. The word 'egg-laden' in the last paragraph means
(a) having no eggs
(b) containing a lot of eggs
(c) containing a lot of broken eggs
(d) having a single egg

10. Substitute the underlined phrase in the following sentence with a word/phrase from the last paragraph that means the same.
Yesterday I got a chance of watching an accident <u>from a short distance away</u>.

PASSAGE 4

The **Indian Rhinoceros** or the **Great One-Horned Rhinoceros** or the **Asian One-horned Rhinoceros** *(Rhinoceros unicornis)* is a large mammal primarily found in North-Eastern India, Nepal and parts of Bhutan.
It is confined to the tall grasslands and riversine forests in the foothills of the Himalayas.

The Indian Rhinoceros once ranged throughout the entire stretch of the Indo-Gangetic Plain but excessive hunting reduced their natural habitat drastically.

Today, about 3,000 Indian Rhinos live in the wild, 1,800 of which are found in Assam alone. In 2008, more than 400 Indian Rhinos were sighted in Nepal's Chitwan National Park.
In size, it is equal to that of the White Rhino in Africa; together they are the largest of all rhino species. The Great One-Horned Rhinoceros has a single horn; this is present in both males and females, but not on the newborn.
The nasal horn curves backwards from the nose. The horn is naturally black.

Due to the loss of habitat, the Rhinos have been forced towards cultivated land. They are mostly solitary creatures, with the exception of mothers and calves and breeding pairs, although they sometimes congregate at bathing areas.

The Indian Rhinoceros makes a wide variety of vocalisations. At least ten distinct vocalisations have been identified: snorting, honking, bleating, roaring, squeak panting, moo-grunting, shrieking, groaning, rumbling and humphing. In addition to noises, the rhino also uses olfactory communication.

Indian Rhinos are often friendly. They will often greet each other by waving or bobbing their heads, mounting flanks, nuzzling noses, or licking. Rhinos will playfully spar, run around, and play with twigs in their mouth. Adult males are the primary instigators of fights. Fight between dominant males is the most common cause of rhino mortality. Indian rhinos have few natural enemies, except for tigers.

Humans are the only other threat, hunting the rhinoceros primarily for sport or for the use of its horn. Indian Rhinos have been somewhat tamed and trained in circuses but they remain dangerous and unpredictable animals. In the nineteenth and early twentieth century, the Indian Rhinoceros was hunted relentlessly. Reports from the middle of the nineteenth century claim that some military officers in Assam individually shot more than 200 rhinos. In the early 1900s, officials became concerned about the rhinos' plummeting numbers. By 1908 in Kaziranga, one of the Rhinos' main ranges, the population had fallen to around 12 individuals. In 1910, rhino hunting in India became prohibited.

The Indian Rhino Vision 2020 (IRV 2020), launched in 2005 was an ambitious effort to obtain a wild population of at least 3,000 Great One-Horned Rhinos spread over seven protected areas in Assam by the year 2020. Various organisations like the International Rhino Foundation, Assam's Forest Department, World Wild Life Fund-India, and others collaborated towards IRV 2020.

The Indian and Nepalese Governments have taken major steps towards Indian Rhinoceros conservation with the help of the World Wild Life Fund (WWF). The Kaziranga National Park and Manas National Park in Assam, Pobitora Reserve Forest in Assam (having the highest Indian rhino density in the World), Orang National Park of Assam, Laokhowa Reserve Forest of Assam (having a very small population) and Royal Chitwan National Park in Nepal are homes to this endangered animal. The Indian Rhino is the only large species in Asia to be down-listed from endangered to vulnerable in the IUCN Red list in 2008.

MCB Theme : Environment

Questions

1. Mention any two features of the Indian Rhinoceros.

2. What is the reason for the dwindling number of Rhinoceros?

1. Loss of habitat   2. Illness
3. Poaching

(a) Only 1   (b) 2 and 3
(c) Only 3   (d) Only 2

3. What kinds of vocalisations does an Indian Rhinoceros make?

(a) Snorting   (b) Shrieking
(c) Roaring   (d) All of these

4. Mention the steps taken by the government to protect the Indian Rhinoceros.

5. Which species is the largest Rhinoceros in the world?

6. Substitute the underlined word in the sentence with the word from the passage which means the same.

The <u>harsh</u> rains destroyed the crops.

7. Which state has the largest number of Rhinoceros in India?

(a) Assam   (b) West Bengal
(c) Kerala   (d) Chattisgarh

8. Complete the following sentence appropriately.

The Rhinoceros lives in ....

9. Complete the sentence appropriately.

One-Horned Rhinoceros is also known as ....

10. Rectify the given False statement.

The Indian and Nepalese Governments have joined hands to preserve Rhinoceros.

PASSAGE 5

1. Tourism, for millennia, has been a perpetual industry. Though initially unorganised and highly chaotic, it retained a place in each nook of history. The present tourism scenario in India is on the rise, with destinations grabbing eyeballs globally and domestically. Being the youngest nation in the world, it's no wonder that the aggregate of 'millennials' spends more time and money on travel than previous generations. This could be huge for the economy of various states that rely majorly on tourism, if only it were sustainable.
2. Unsustainability prevails throughout the country in states with higher domestic tourist inflow than foreign. The Dev Bhoomi is a prime example. No matter how popular, Uttarakhand tourism is loop-holed through and through.
3. Approx. 80% of tourists arrive to complete the infrastructure of the Dham Yatra. Such unchecked tourism puts immense pressure on natural and infrastructure facilities. The extreme shortage of accommodation in correspondence with thriving footfalls has led to the construction of illegal buildings, the majority of which exist on riverbanks. With an

increasing number of tourists coming in through private vehicles to save 'transportation money', pollution levels are rising, increasing temperatures in return. With unlawful construction and pollution on riverbanks, the Ganges could cause direct harm to local species in Rishikesh and Haridwar.

4. Around 10,000 hilly areas are being convened for the construction of roads alone. We know roads are basic infrastructure but the Forest Conservation Act requires a project developer to plant trees in a non-forest /degraded forest area equal to or twice the trees it's clearing respectively, to compensate which does not happen.
5. The India State of Forest Report illustrates how Uttarakhand is losing its forest cover, which has indirect development through tourism at its core.
   The government and private tour operators may think they can deny allegations but the charts speak for themselves.
6. We, as consumers of the tourism industry, hold the power to cause a massive stir in this context. According to research conducted, Uttarakhand's mass tourism comprises people between 25-35 years of age, with higher education, out with either family or friends and enough average income to contribute to the local economy.
7. Regardless of what the figures say, if we look forward to sustainable tourism being the target market, it leaves little choice to the rest of the hierarchy.
   Consciously making efforts to be responsible tourists and thinking of how to provide for the local community/environment in a way - tiny or big, could act as a catalyst in obliterating this ruckus due to ignorance. After all, there can only ever be seven deadly sins and wanderlust isn't one of them.

Questions

1. Infer one consequence, based on your understanding of the passage, that highlights the result of the pressures of a large number of tourists. **Competency Based**

2. Select the appropriate option to fill in the blank.
From Paragraph 3, we can infer that .... is the main cause for putting pressure on infrastructural and natural resources. **Competency Based**

1. unchecked tourism
2. illegal construction
3. pollution
4. increasing temperatures
5. deforestation

Codes

(a) 1, 2 and 3 (b) 2 and 3
(c) Only 1 (d) 2 and 4

3. Complete the following analogy correctly with a word/phrase from Paragraph 6.

Movie : Viewers :: Product : ....

4. Select the correct option to complete the following sentence.
The Forest Conservation Act vouches for ....

(a) the preservation of local species of flora and fauna
(b) plantation of trees in a non-forest/degraded forest area equal to or twice the trees it's clearing
(c) construction only in the non-forest or degraded forest area
(d) All of the above

5. Based on your understanding of the passage, choose the option that lists the result of the pressures of a large number of tourists.

(a) Illegal infrastructural constructions
(b) Rise in pollution
(c) Deforestation
(d) Both (a) and (b)

6. Fill in the blank by selecting the correct option.
The unchecked tourism in Uttarakhand over the last few years has showed .... effects on the environment and infrastructure of the place.

(a) positive (b) beneficial
(c) detrimental (d) encouraging

7. Substitute the word 'illegal' with one word similar in meaning, in the following sentence from Paragraph 3.
The extreme shortage of accommodation in correspondence with thriving footfalls has led to the construction of ILLEGAL buildings, the majority of which exist on riverbanks.

8. List any two reasons to explain why unsustainability prevails in the Dev Bhoomi.
(i) ....
(ii) ....

9. What does the tourist statistics show in the region of Uttarakhand?

PASSAGE 6

Sport has rapidly become an established part of entertainment industry and the smallest detail of a sportsman's private life is exposed by the media to public scrutiny. Top professionals are often described as 'stars' and large business interests exploit their skills. Considerable profits are made out of selling sports gear which is a replica of the gear used by the professionals; newspapers sell more copies if their sports coverage is good, and substantial gains can be made out of the spectators' willingness to gamble on results. The increasing demand for new talented sportsmen serves to strengthen the popular image of professional sport as a highly glamorous occupation.

A handful of top professionals can afford a house in London, another in the country, and a third one on the French Riviera, as well as a Rolls Royce and a yacht in the Bahamas but most professional players just manage to get a bare living from their sport. Outdoor life can be delightful except when the prevalent weather conditions are rain, wind, snow, fog or ice. It's flattering to hear one's name chanted with acclaim by thousands on the terraces but crowds are fickle and soon forget once time takes its toll on muscle and mind.

Sportsmen at the height of their professional lives travel all around the world but their own social lives are disrupted and leisure hours have to be sacrificed to hard, exhausting practice. All professional sportsmen must adhere to strict training schedules to maintain their physical fitness; their lives are devoted to keeping the body in peak condition by exhausting exercise combined with a strict regime of self-discipline and moderation in food and drink.

Retirement comes at an early age and the financial rewards gained will probably not provide enough to live on for the rest of the life and the early-retired sportsman has to seek a new career. He enters the new career fifteen years later than his contemporaries and often with not enough reputation in his sport to persuade an employer to pay him a high salary. Perhaps, after all, it is better to remain a keen amateur.

Questions

1. In what ways do large business interests exploit sportsmen's skills? List any two.
2. What is the popular image of professional sport? How does the media help to keep up this image?
3. What is the attitude of the crowd towards sportsmen?
4. What sacrifices do sportsmen make in their careers? List any one.
5. Who gives out the smallest details of a sportsman's private life?
   (a) His friends
   (b) His relatives
   (c) His teammates
   (d) The media
6. Why should a sportsman stick to a strict training schedule?
   (a) To please his manager
   (b) To get more screentime
   (c) To maintain his physical fitness
   (d) To get a raise
7. How do sportsmen spend their leisure hours?
   (a) By reading the newspaper
   (b) By watching movies
   (c) By practicing their game
   (d) By sitting idle
8. Complete the sentence appropriately
   Sportsperson who are at the top of their respective sports are described as ....
9. Complete the sentence appropriately.
   Retirement for sportspersons comes ....

PASSAGE 7

'Su' means number and 'doku' means single. The game of Sudoku has many similarities to the game of life. Sudoku is a puzzle game designed for a single player, much like a crossword puzzle. The puzzle itself is nothing more than a grid of little boxes called 'cells'. They are stacked nine high and nine wide, making 81 cells in total.

The roots of the Sudoku puzzle are in Switzerland. Leonhard Euler created 'carre latin' in the 18th century which is similar to a Sudoku puzzle. The first real Sudoku was published in 1979 and was invented by Howard Garns, an American architect. The real world wide popularity started in Japan in 1986 after it was published and given the name Sudoku by Nikoli.

In life too, you start with a given set of notions and then work from there on. In Sudoku, you need to follow a set of rules to build up the grid, filling each row, column and box with numbers ranging from one to nine, so much like in life where you have to go on your way without antagonising anyone else. Respect every number (person) and things would be fine.

While playing, you never think of the end (the result); you just keep working on the numbers and the final result (fruits of action) accrues on its own. Extremely difficult puzzles may take hours. Similarly, to achieve desired results in life may take years. The game of Sudoku and the game of life are best played in a calm but focussed state.

Everything has to go in tandem in a Sudoku grid: the rows, columns and squares. Exactly as in life. Your duties towards your family, teachers, society and country all go on simultaneously. In Sudoku, the arrangement of the given numbers is symmetrical. This is instructive in life, on how to maintain steadfast faith, poise and equanimity despite situations when everything turns topsy-turvy.

There is a subtle difference between the two as well. Make a mistake and you can erase it and begin all over again in Sudoku. Not so in life. You can learn a lesson though and avoid making the same mistake in future.

Questions

1. What is Sudoku?
   (a) An outdoor game designed for a single player.
   (b) A puzzle designed for 2 players.
   (c) A puzzle game meant for a single player.
   (d) An outdoor game meant for 2 players.

2. What has the writer compared the numbers in Sudoku to?
   (a) A loving being (b) Life
   (c) A tricky situation (d) A non-living thing
3. Based on the article, write any two similarities between Sudoku and life.
4. What gets the final result?
5. Fill in the blank and complete the analogy.
   Garns : American : : Euler : ....
6. When did Sudoku became popular worldwide?
   (a) In 1976 (b) In the 18th Century
   (c) In the 19th Century (d) In 1986
7. Which word can replace the underlined word in the sentence without changing the meaning of the sentence.
   In life too, you start with a given set of notions and then work from there on.
8. Complete the sentence appropriately.
   The total number of cells in a Sudoku puzzle is ......
9. State whether the following statement is True or False.
   A cell in Sudoku can be filled with numbers ranging from zero to nine.
10. What happens when you make a mistake in life?

Discursive Passages

PASSAGE 1

On 1st June, 1937 Amelia and her navigator Fred Noonan departed from Miami, Florida for California. Their first destination was San Juan, Puerto Rico; from there, skirting the Northeast edge of South America; and then on to Africa and the Red Sea.

The flight to Karachi was another first. No one had previously flown non-stop from the Red Sea to India before. From Karachi, the Electra flew to Calcutta on 17th June onto Rangoon, Bangkok, Singapore and Bandoeng.

The monsoon prevented departure from Bandoeng for several days. Repairs were made on some of the 'long distance' instruments which had given trouble previously. It was 27th June before Amelia and Noonan were able to leave Bandoeng for Port Darwin, Australia. At Darwin, the direction finder was repaired and the parachutes were packed and shipped home as they would be of no value over the Pacific.

Amelia reached Lae in New Guinea on 29th June. At this point they had flown 22,000 miles and there were 7,000 more to go over the Pacific. Amelia cabled her last commissioned article to the Herald Tribune. Photos show her looking very tired and ill during her time at Lae.

The U.S. Coast Guard cutter, Itasca had been standing off Howland Island for some days to act as a radio contact for Amelia. Radio communications in the area were very poor as Itasca was overwhelmed with commercial radio traffic that the flight had generated.

Amelia left Lae at precisely 00:00 hours Greenwich Mean Time on 2nd July. It is believed that the Electra was loaded with 1,000 gallons of fuel, allowing for 20-21 hours of flying.

At 08:00 GMT Amelia made her last radio contact with Lae. She reported being on course for Howland Island at 12,000 feet. There is no real evidence as to the precise track of the aircraft after Nukumanu. No one saw or heard the plane fly over.

Several short transmissions were received by the Itasca with varying signal strengths but they were unable to get a fix on her location because they were too brief. At 19:30 GMT the following transmission was received from the Electra at maximum strength.

"KHAQQ calling Itasca. We must be on you but cannot see you... gas is running low..."

At 20:14 GMT, the Itasca received the last voice transmission from Amelia giving positioning data. The Itasca continued to transmit on all frequencies until 21:30 hours GMT. They determined that Amelia must have died at sea and began to implement search procedures.

It has been determined that the plane went down some 35-100 miles off the coast of Howland Island. A life raft was stowed on board but no trace was ever found of the raft. Some experts felt that the empty fuel tanks could keep the plane afloat for a period of time.

President Roosevelt authorised a search party of 9 naval ships and 66 aircrafts at an estimated cost of over $4 million. On 18th July, the search was abandoned by ships in the Howland area. George continued to seek help in the search, but by October he too abandoned all hope of finding them alive.

MCB Theme : Adventure

Questions

1. Where were Amelia and Fred Noonan heading to?
   (a) California (b) Florida
   (c) Puerto Rico (d) Africa
2. Why was the flight to Karachi another first?
3. What prevented departure from Bandoeng?
   (a) Amelia's illness
   (b) Monsoon
   (c) Problems in direction finder
   (d) Preparation for the flight

4. What did Amelia do in Darwin?
5. What happened in Lae?
6. Substitute the underlined word in the sentence with the word that means the same in the passage.
   She was engulfed with the emotions of hatred.
7. What is Electra?
   (a) Amelia's plane (b) Amelia's friend
   (c) Amelia's ship (d) Can't say
8. Complete the sentence appropriately.
   In her last contact with Lae, Amelia ....
9. Complete the sentence appropriately.
   The search for Amelia ....
10. State whether the given assertion is True or False.
    Amelia's death is a mystery for many.

PASSAGE 2

Next time you go to a store, take a minute to look at all the things that are trying to grab your attention. Whether it's convenience, good service or finding the best deals, store owners want to know what attracts you to their stores and what it takes to keep you coming back. Turns out, there's a science to all this.

With support from the Virginia based National Science Foundation, computer scientists Rajeev Sharma, Satish Mummareddy and their colleagues have developed a software that breaks down shopping behaviour much like websites do. Sharma's Pennsylvania based company, Video Mining, uses overhead cameras to put together a top down view of how people shop and what they buy. "Basically, what Video Mining does is use software along with cameras mounted on the ceiling of stores to track shoppers as they move around the store and create data that helps us understand how shoppers are shopping," explains Sharma.

The software can also tabulate how long shoppers take before that 'moment of truth' when they select an item to purchase. Cameras are positioned directly above and picture resolution is intentionally set low so that all shoppers remain anonymous. The idea is to show retailers and manufacturers the best areas in the store to place products, and how to create a comfortable place for people to shop. "By providing the data to the retailers and manufacturers," says Sharma, "they can customise and design the stores and the shelves and the products to match the shoppers' interest."

Sharma identifies trends. For example, people prefer wider aisles when they shop. Women take a lot longer to shop than men, and except in a few cases, brand loyalty is not always strong. "What we're finding is that in some categories, people are going to the store and making up their mind right there. You can see people coming in, going between brands and picking up the product based upon price or other attributes." The software is keeping an eye on the shoppers, giving businesses a scientific leg up in the rat race of figuring out how to best serve their customers and keep them coming back.

Questions

1. In the first paragraph, what does the phrase 'all this' refer to?
   (a) All the things in a store.
   (b) Store owners wanting to know what distracts customers in their stores.
   (c) Store owners wanting to know what attracts customers to their stores.
   (d) All the things not available in a store.
2. What are the two most important findings that Sharma has identified about customer behaviour?
3. After installing Sharma's software, what will store owners be able to know about designing their stores?
   (a) The best areas in the store to place products
   (b) How to create a comfortable place for people to shop
   (c) The worst areas in the store to place products
   (d) Both (a) and (b)
4. The functions that the software is not used to perform are
   (a) monitor shoppers as they move around the store
   (b) create data that helps the store owners understand how shoppers are shopping
   (c) store the card details and other information of the customers
   (d) Both (a) and (b)
5. What does the phrase 'moment of truth' refers to the 3rd Paragraph?
6. The word in the third paragraph that means 'to alter something to make it fit someone's requirements' is
   (a) tabulate (b) resolution
   (c) intentionally (d) customise
7. State whether the given statement is True or False.
   Brand loyalty plays a major role these days.
8. Substitute the underlined word in the following sentence with a word phrase from Paragraph 4, that means the same. **Competency Based**
   I was watching when the kids were playing alone in the garden.
9. Which word in the fourth paragraph is a synonym of 'tendencies'?
10. Complete the sentence appropriately.
    The title 'What Drives a Customer' would be an appropriate title for the passage because ....

PASSAGE 3

Introspect: Realise Your Potential.

Sixteen year old Shreya, a student of XI, angrily outbursts at her parents and says, "No one likes me".

She has not been able to develop an interest in any activity, be it painting, swimming, games or studying. She is not sure what types of relationships give her comfort.

She has never had a good friend. She is not clear about her choice of career.

Shreya is good-looking as well as physically healthy. During the interview, she was pre-occupied with what others think about her.

When asked to talk about her positive qualities, she thought for a long time but could not list any. Nor was she able to mention her negative aspects.

Self Awareness

Knowing your strengths and weaknesses will help you succeed.

Knowing our strengths helps us in acknowledging our success as well as appreciating our capacity to do something with or without support from others.

This gives us a sense of well-being and we are able to learn new skills and develop assets, thereby developing our confidence. Confident people attract friends and other stable relationships.

In due course, we are ready to accept various challenges with the right kind of investment of energy towards task completion.

Knowing our weaknesses helps us in accepting our limitations, and developing a willingness to take help when offered and enabling us to overcome our deficits.

This paves the way to expansion of skills and qualities which prove useful in the long run.

It is worthwhile to introspect and reflect so as to realise our potential. This helps to bring about a change in us and we are able to meet challenges.

If Shreya had introspected or had been helped by her parents or teachers to reflect on herself, she would have understood her positive and negative qualities, her likes, dislikes, strengths, weaknesses, feelings, emotions, outlook, choices, values and attitude towards life.

Self-awareness paves the way to progress with respect to relationships, academic success, professional and personal fulfillment.

Adapted from 'The Quest', The Hindu **MCB Theme : Children**

Questions

1. Why does Shreya have an angry outburst?

2. What is the problem with Shreya?
(a) She had no interests.
(b) She had no friends.
(c) She was not self-aware.
(d) She was not physically healthy.

3. What does self awareness help us to know?
1. Strengths 2. Weaknesses
3. Ailments 4. Emotions
5. Intelligence
(a) 1 and 5 (b) 1, 2 and 3
(c) 2 and 5 (d) 1 and 2

4. How does knowing our strengths help us?

5. How does knowing our strengths develop our confidence?

6. Substitute the underlined word in the line with a word that means the same from the passage.
The proof of a <u>solid</u> friendship is understanding and trust.

7. Knowing our weaknesses help us
(a) accept our flaws
(b) learn to overcome negativity
(c) garner attention
(d) expand skills

8. Complete the sentence appropriately.
Introspection is worthwhile for ....

9. Complete the sentence appropriately.
Self awareness develops our ability ....

10. State whether the given assertion is True or False.
Shreya needs to develop self awareness.

PASSAGE 4

Grandmaster Koneru Humpy: Queen of 64 Squares
Avik, a correspondent for his school magazine interviews Grandmaster Koneru Humpy. Let us read:

Interview with Koneru Humpy

Avik: Good morning, Ma'am! Congratulations on your achievements in the World Grand Prix Women's Chess Championship in Istanbul recently!

Koneru Humpy: Thank you! This is my **biggest win** in the women's circuit. This is very significant, considering that it has come in an event which had three former world champions.

Avik: Indeed! Please tell us something about yourself , Ma'am!

Koneru Humpy: I was born in Gudivada, near Vijaywada, in Andhra Pradesh on 31st March, 1987. I was originally named 'Hampi' (which means champion) by my father Mr. Koneru Ashok, who later changed the spelling to Humpy to give the name a Russian flavour. I write my family name Koneru before my given name as is the convention with the Telugu speaking people. I started playing chess when I was 5 years old.

Avik: Who introduced you to the game?

Koneru Humpy: My father acquainted me with the game. He is also my first coach. I first showed interest at the age of 6 years when I watched him play a game and suggested a move. Indeed, it was the move that actually got me into the game.

Avik: Your father left his teaching profession to make you a champion!

Koneru Humpy: Yes, when I secured the 4th position in the Indian Under 8 Championship in 1995, he decided to leave his career and dedicate his time to me.

Avik: And you have won four World Championships at a very early stage.

Koneru Humpy: Yes, the 'World Girls under-10', the 'World Girls under-12', the 'World Girls under-14' and 'World Girls Junior Championships.' I acquired my IM title in 1999 and in May 2002, I achieved my 3rd GM Norms in Elekes Memorial Grandmaster tournament in Budapest.

Avik: You held the record from 2002 to 2008 for the youngest woman ever to become a grandmaster!

Koneru Humpy: Yes, I achieved it at the age of 15 years, 1 month, 27 days, beating Judit Polgar's previous record by 3 months which was later lost in the Women's World Chess Championship in 2008 to Hou Yifan. In 2006, I participated in the Women's World Chess Championship but my campaign had to end early in the second round.

Avik: Have you also got some awards?

Koneru Humpy: Yes, Arjuna Award in 2003, Padmashri Award in 2007 and Raja-Lakshmi Award in 2008.

Avik: In India, many young chess players are ready to take a break in education and are fully focussed on chess preparations. What are your views?

Koneru Humpy: I don't think that taking up chess as a career and completely neglecting studies is necessary at an early stage. After getting to a certain level in the game, they themselves should decide their preferences, i.e., whether to play seriously or not.

Avik: How often do you exercise? Do you think daily physical exercise can help a chess player to cope with the pressure and increase the brain's ability to concentrate?

Koneru Humpy: I spend around one hour per day on physical exercise. Exercise is a must for every chess player. As the proverb says, 'a sound mind can only exist in a sound body'. Exercise has a lot of impact on the brain.

Avik: Thank you for talking to me and giving me your valuable advice.

Koneru Humpy: Thank you! **MCB Theme : Sports and Games**

Questions

1. Koneru Humpy was trained in chess by
   (a) an acquaintance (b) her father
   (c) a coach (d) her teacher
2. What does Koneru Humpy regard as her biggest achievement? Why?
3. Koneru Humpy's talent in the game of chess was identified when she
   (a) celebrated her sixth birthday
   (b) suggested a move
   (c) watched a game
   (d) played with her father
4. "Parents are teachers, guides, leaders, protectors and providers for their children." Evaluate the role of parents in the lives of chess players.
5. "A sound mind can only reside in a sound body", says Koneru Humpy. Substantiate.
6. Substitute the underlined words in the line with a word from the passage which means the same.
   She was <u>winning against</u> the Assamese player.
7. Select the personality traits of Humpy's father with reference to the extract.
   1. Ambitious 2. Selfless 3. Sacrificial
   4. Calculative 5. Manipulative
   (a) 1, 2 and 3 (b) 2, 3 and 4
   (c) 3, 4 and 5 (d) 1, 4 and 5
8. Complete the sentence appropriately.
   In 2006, Koneru Humpy participated in ....
9. Complete the sentence appropriately.
   Koneru Humpy has won ....
10. State whether the given assertion is True or False.
    Koneru Humpy's mother encouraged her to play chess.

PASSAGE 5

Ban the Bag

The Indus Valley Civilisation left beautifully crafted pottery that speaks volumes of the advances its people made. After 3,000 years if the ruins we leave behind are excavated, chances are only plastic bags would be dug up. It may sound like an exaggeration but these bags are not biodegradable. Apart from causing emissions when these are manufactured, noxious fumes are released while these are being burnt or disposed of. So, be kind to Mother Earth, the next time you go shopping for groceries, remember to carry a cloth bag with you.

What India Should Do

India has released the National Action Plan on Climate Change. Is it adequate? Is there more that the country can do? Here are some ways we can make a difference.

(a) **Solar Mission** To promote the use of solar energy through solar photovoltaic and thermal systems for power generation. To integrate other renewable energy technologies like biomass and wind.

(b) **Energy Efficiency** To mitigate GHG through sector specific and cross-cutting technology and fuel switch options. To use more LNG and biomass fuels besides seeking tech transfer.

(c) **Sustainable Habitat** To promote energy efficiency in the residential and commercial sectors through LPG use. To manage municipal solid waste and urban public transport in a better way.

(d) **Water Mission** To promote efficient water use, augment the supply in critical areas and ensure effective management of water resources. To have better management of surface and groundwater, and conserve wetlands.

(e) **Sustaining Himalayas** To enhance monitoring and conservation of the Himalayan ecosystems, empower local communities for management of ecological resources and promote sustainable tourism

(f) **Green India** To reduce fragmentation of forests, enhance public and private investments for plantation, upscale joint forestry management and promote conservation of biodiversity. Need to afforest degraded lands.

(g) **Sustainable Agriculture** To focus on four crucial areas - dry land agriculture, risk management, access to information and promoting the use of biotechnology. To develop drought-and-pest resistant varieties.

MCB Theme : Environment

Questions

1. What does the pottery made by the Indus Valley civilisation indicate?

(a) Advancement (b) Sustainability
(c) Artistry (d) All of these

2. What would the future progeny find if they dig up land 3000 years from now?

3. What happens when plastic is burned?

(a) They turn to ash.
(b) They do not burn.
(c) They emit bad fumes.
(d) They become a part of the soil.

4. What does the author want to do?

5. What is the Solar Mission?

6. Which word in the passage is a synonym of reduce?

7. What does sustainable habitat include?

(a) Use of LPG
(b) Planting trees
(c) Use renewable resources
(d) Use EVs

8. Complete the sentence given below.
Water mission functions to ensure ....

9. Complete the sentence appropriately.
.... focuses on empowering local communities for better management of ecological resources.

Competency Based

10. State whether the given assertion is True or False.
Sustainable agriculture focuses on pesticide free land.

PASSAGE 6

The Mystery of Bermuda Triangle

The potential of nature, of discovered and undiscovered elements in our world, persuades us to probe into some of her mysteries and what they may tell us. Prepare yourself then for a true odyssey of the Earth around us.

An Air France Plane went missing near Bermuda Triangle on 1st June, 2009. The Agence France-Presse reported that an Air France Airbus A330-200 wide-body jet carrying 216 passengers and 12 crew members disappeared from the radar screens on Monday somewhere off Brazil's Atlantic coast. Flight AF 447, out of Rio de Janeiro, was headed for Paris. According to the Mirror, the Agence France-Presse reported that the plane had radioed in that they were going through turbulence. They also reported that a message signalling electrical circuit malfunction was received before it disappeared. A search for the missing plane was conducted by the Brazilian Air Force. The French were also involved in the search. Another well known case of 1962, vividly brings home the need for careful behind-the-scenes probing. Once again, it involved an aircraft.

Bermuda Triangle Theories

The Bermuda triangle is a stretch over the Atlantic Ocean, measuring less than a thousand miles on any one side. The name 'Bermuda Triangle' remained a colloquial expression throughout the 1950s. By the early 1960s, it acquired the name 'The Devil's Triangle.' Bordered by Florida, Bermuda, and Puerto Rico, the location became famous on account of the strange disappearance of ships as well as aircrafts in the area. A number of supernatural explanations have been put forward with regard to the mysterious disappearances.

Many probable logical explanations for the missing vessels include hurricanes, earthquakes, as well as magnetic fields which render navigation devices worthless. However, most people do not like to accept such boring explanations and instead opt for more interesting options like alien abduction, giant squids or getting sucked into another dimension.

Supernatural Theories

Death Rays from the Atlantis Rays from the magic crystals, left from the time of Atlantis, deep down in the sea are responsible for the strange sinking of ships. However, several underwater expeditions have revealed places under the ocean that look man-made but no such crystals have been found. In fact, no real proof that the Atlantis existed has been ever found.

Sea monsters The presence of sea monsters was the most widely believed explanation especially in the earlier times when their existence was believed to be true.

Presence of a time warp People claim to be lost in the time warp while going through the region.

Alien abductions The Bermuda Triangle is a collecting station from where aliens take our people, ships, planes and other objects back to their planet to study.

Scientific Explanations

Magnetic Compass According to the scientists in the US Navy, this area is one of the only two in the world where a magnetic compass points to true north rather than magnetic North. This probably caused some navigators to go off course, which is very dangerous because many of the islands in 'The Triangle' have large areas of shallow water where vessels can run aground. Even Christopher Columbus experienced this strange phenomenon. They can also sink a long way down as some of the ocean's deepest trenches, from 19,000 to over 27,000 feet below sea level, are found here.

Unpredictable weather Since, the island is situated in the Atlantic Ocean, the weather is influenced by several factors and can change instantly. That means that at one moment, the weather is stable and at another it becomes extremely turbulent accompanied by strong currents of wind along with the hurricanes.

Formation of methane in the sea Methane can lower the density of water leading to the sinking of ships. Similarly, methane can cut out an aircraft engine, leading to crashes.

MCB Theme: Mystery

Questions

1. What message did the Agence France-Presse receive from the Flight AF 447?
   (a) That they were going through turbulence
   (b) That they had an electrical circuit malfunction
   (c) That they were going smoothly in the journey
   (d) Both (a) and (b)
2. What, according to the news, happened to the Air France Plane?
3. Bermuda Triangle is a sea space between
   (a) Florida
   (b) Bermuda
   (c) Puerto Rico
   (d) All of these
4. What made the Bermuda Triangle famous?
5. How has the theory of the death rays from the Atlantis been disapproved? Answer in 30-40 words.
6. Substitute the underlined word in the sentence with a word that means the same from the passage.
   The <u>justification</u> given by the convict was not accepted by the judge.
7. How does Methane cause the sinking of ships?
   (a) Creates a whirlpool
   (b) Due to its lower density
   (c) Changes the weather instantly
   (d) Make the water shallow
8. Complete the sentence appropriately.
   According to the US Navy, the Bermuda triangle is a place where ....
9. State whether the given assertion is True or False.
   The Bermuda Triangle is also called the 'Devils's Triangle'.

PASSAGE 7

1. Yoga in India is considered to be around 5,000 years old mental, physical and spiritual practice. It originated in ancient times when people used to meditate to transform their body and mind. Launching and celebrating 21st June as Yoga Day was an initiative taken by the Indian Prime Minister in the United Nations General Assembly. From then, the yoga day became a worldwide event celebrated by the people of all countries.
2. Yoga is essentially a spiritual discipline. It is the art and science of healthy living. It is a practice of controlled body part movements and control of breath. It is not just a physical practice but also a way to get control over mental, emotional and spiritual thoughts. It improves discipline and sense of power while providing a chance to live a healthy life without physical and mental problems.
3. Yoga is a very safe, easy and healthy way to get fit for the whole life without any problems. It can be practiced by people at any age be it childhood, teenage, adult or old age irrespective of age, religion or health circumstances. It needs only safe, slow and controlled movements of body with controlled breathing. Regular practice of yoga regularises the connection between the body, mind and soul. It enhances the functioning of all the body organs. By providing good health it fulfills our physical needs, through knowledge it fulfills our psychological needs and through inner peace it fulfills the spiritual need thus, it helps in maintaining the harmony among all.
4. Regular practice of the yoga in the morning provides outer and inner relief by keeping away from the countless ailments at the physical and mental level. Practicing postures or asana creates the feeling of well-being. It sharpens the human mind, improves intelligence and helps in achieving high level of concentration. Yoga is like a practical philosophy which develops self-discipline and self-awareness.
5. We cannot count the benefits of yoga; we can understand it only as a miracle which can be experienced by practice. It maintains physical fitness, reduces stress, controls emotions, feelings, controls negative thoughts, feelings of general well-being, improves mental clarity, enhances self-understanding and connects us to the nature.

Questions

1. Complete the following statement by choosing an appropriate option.
Yoga is basically ....
(a) a material discipline
(b) associated with material living
(c) a practice of uncontrolled body movements
(d) the art and science of healthy living

2. Comment on the writer 's reference to the kind of people who can practice yoga.

3. Pick the option that correctly lists the benefits of doing yoga.
1. Maintains physical fitness
2. Controls emotions, feelings
3. Controls negative thoughts
4. Improves mental clarity
5. Enhances self-understanding

Codes
(a) 1 and 4 (b) 2 and 6 (c) 3 and 5 (d) All of these

4. Comment on the importance of asanas in yoga?

5. How does yoga fulfill our psychological needs?

6. Substitute the underlined word in the given line with a word from the passage which means the opposite:
The lights <u>diminishes</u> the ambience of the banquet.

7. Which of the following is true for yoga?
(a) It is an art and science combined into one
(b) It is primarily spiritual in nature
(c) It is not backed by WHO
(d) Both (a) and (b)

8. Complete the given sentence with an appropriate inference with respect to the following.
Yoga enables one to get control over ....

9. Complete the sentence appropriately.
Yoga regularises the connection between ....

10. State whether the given assertion is True or False.
21st June is celebrated as Yoga Day.

Literary Passage

PASSAGE 1

When the liner had finally vanished over the horizon, I was absolutely alone in the stormy night sea. First I thought I had to swim one way, then another. It was not even midnight yet and I had no hope at all of finding my way in this terrible night time ocean. I began to feel afraid. Waves of fear rolled through me, starting from my hands and feet, attacking my heart and then reaching through my neck to my head. Waves broke over me and water went into my snorkel. I realised I would not be able to last even half an hour in such a condition.

I saw individual stars but I could not distinguish the constellations they belonged to. Then dawn came and put out all my stars and I felt my solitude more keenly. The sky was grey at first, then blue-violet shades appeared. In a few minutes, the colours became brighter with dark red strips cutting across the sky! The rising Sun came up over the ocean. I was surrounded by large waves. The clouds turned pink and swept across the sky in all directions. It was a windy day.

There was no land visible. I grew alarmed. Had I made a mistake in my calculations? Perhaps the current had carried me a long a way off the course during the night?

An hour passed, perhaps two. "Land!!!" I could not deny myself the pleasure of shouting the magic word aloud and of hearing my own voice. Perhaps it was my ghostly island of Siargao? I almost felt I had succeeded - now at least I had hope.

The Sun looked out for the last time, as if it was saying goodbye to me and hid itself away again. In a few minutes the sky was filled with all the colours of a rainbow, the bright shades changing and merging as I watched. At first the clouds became deep red and then their edges turned bright orange. A little while afterwards, the clouds turned lilac and dark violet. Darkness fell swiftly. My second lonely night in the ocean began. The stars came out unnoticed. I changed course and headed for the South-West. As it turned out, this was an unforgivable mistake.

Evening was approaching. The ocean around me was full of life; large fish often leapt out of the water and big birds flew right above my head. I could see the island distinctly now. A line of dancing palms stretched the length of its shore. The sides of the mountain were covered in many different shades of green.

An hour passed, perhaps more. It was extraordinarily quiet. Then suddenly to my horror, I discovered my island had noticeably begun to move North and was drifting further and further in that direction right before my eyes. Before I had worked out what was happening and could sharply change my course towards the North, the Southern tip of the island had appeared in front of me and, beyond that, open ocean stretched to the very horizon. I was totally at the mercy of the current and realised to my alarm that it was slowly carrying me past the land.

My third night in the ocean crept up unnoticed. This third night in the ocean was very dark, much darker than the two previous ones. I almost decided to die as I had no hope of seeing another dawn. I was suddenly aware of a quiet voice: "Swim to the sound of the breakers."

Indeed, there had been a distant rumbling for some time although I had paid no attention to it. Now, I started listening and I thought it sounded like the characteristic noise of jet aeroplanes constantly landing and taking off. The voice inside kept insisting that I should swim towards this thunder of waves.

At last I obeyed. Again I heard an approaching rumble. What I suddenly saw at a distance of about 30 or 40 metres has imprinted itself on my memory forever. It was a gigantic wave with steep, very slowly falling crests. Never in my life had I seen such an enormous wave - it even seemed to be touching the sky. It moved very slowly and was fantastically beautiful.

The wave did not break over me as I assumed it would. An irresistible force dragged me up its steep slope right to the very foot of the falling crest. Instinctively, I clutched my mask snorkel and managed to take a deep breath. The crest started to break over me and pulled me under it. For a moment, I found myself in the air under the crest as if in a cave. Then my body was in a swirling current of water; the inner power of the wave made me recover several times, twisting me in all directions before it subsided.

I realised that I had to try to keep my body on the crest and I quickly took up a horizontal position. This time the wave quickly grabbed me and carried me at great speed for quite a long distance on its crest.

I got up to the surface easily and swam in the direction the waves were heading. "Somewhere there, beyond the reef, there should be a lagoon," I hoped. Suddenly, I felt something hard under my feet. I could stand up to my chest in water! Around me I could see random currents of water, splashes of foam and phosphorescent spray, all swirling about. Before I fully came to my senses, another large wave approached and carried me some distance further. I was up to my waist in water when a new wave picked me up, taking me several metres forward. Now, the depth of the water was only up to my knees. I had enough time to take a few tentative steps, to catch my breath and look around.

I surfaced at the foot of a very tall palm tree. I left a trail of luminous water and my body glittered like some princess's ball-gown. Only now did I feel completely safe. The ocean was behind me.

MCB Theme : Adventure

Questions

1. What emotion can be associated with the narrator in the beginning of the passage?

(a) Anger (b) Fear

(c) Nervousness (d) Joy

2. At the beginning of the story, the narrator seems to be swimming alone in the stormy night sea. Why? Give reason including evidence from the story.

3. Why did the narrator feel that he would not last?

(a) He was scared.

(b) Water had entered his snorkel.

(c) He did not know where to go.

(d) Both (b) and (c)

4. Why did the narrator grow alarmed?

5. Slava Kurilov mentions one of his actions as an unforgivable mistake. Do you think it was the biggest mistake made by the narrator? Explain.

Competency Based

6. Select the most suitable replacement of the underlined word from the extract that is similar in meaning.
The organisers of the Desert Festival came across gigantic sand dunes and decided to set up camp in that vicinity.

Competency Based

7. State whether the given statement is True or False.
The narrator was certain that the enormous wave will break his hope to be onshore.

8. Complete the sentence appropriately.
The voice inside the narrator's mind indicated him to ....

9. Complete the sentence appropriately.
The narrator was horrified because ....

PASSAGE 2

1. The windless night filled our ears with unaccustomed silence and the foul dryness of our mouths aggravated the discomfort as we tried to ease the agony of our thirst. Then breathlessly, we watched the gathering clouds obscure the stars and it began to rain with a steady downpour. Slowly, the water in the pipe from the canopy ran clear and we filled our empty cans and spare plastic bags, our bellies and our mouths until we could not force down another drop. Suddenly, everything had changed from the shadow of the spectre of death to the joyful prospect of life and all by a shower of rain. We had water!
2. Douglas, lazily watching the dispersing clouds, suddenly sat up with a start, pointing excitedly. "A ship! A ship! It's a ship!" We all crowded to the door of the raft, staring in the direction of his pointing finger; a cargo vessel of about 6000 tonnes was approaching us on a course that would bring her within 3 miles of us. "Get out the flares", I said hoarsely, "and pass them to me in the dinghy. They all see us better from there."
3. Three miles was a fair distance, but on a dull day such as this, against a background of rain, they should see us easily. I clambered into the dinghy and Douglas passed me the rockets and hand flares; my hands trembled as I ripped open a parachute rocket flare and, with a mute appeal to the thing to fire, struck the igniter on the fuse. It sputtered and hissed, then roared off on a trajectory high above the raft, its pinkish magnesium flare slowly spiraling downwards leaving a trail of smoke in the sky. They couldn't fail to see it. I waited a moment or two, watching for the ship to alter course, then struck a hand flare, holding it high above my head. The blinding red light was hot to hold and I pointed it away from the wind to ease my hand, the red embers of the flare dropping into the dinghy; as it went out, I struck another, smoke from the first now arising in the sky; surely they must see that! I waited a little, my hands trembling.
4. However, the ship sailed on, slowly disappearing behind a rain shower and, when she reappeared, her hull was half obscured by the horizon. My shoulders drooped."We daren't use another", I said. "They won't see it now and we have to keep something for the next one."
5. I surveyed the empty flare cartons bitterly, and the one smoke flare which was damp and wouldn't work; then something happened to me in that instant that, for me, changed the whole aspect of our predicament. If these poor bloody seamen couldn't rescue us, then we would have to make it on our own. The word from now on was, 'survival', not 'rescue', or 'help' or dependence of any kind, just survival. We would live for three months or six months from the sea, but "We would get these boys to land" as Lyn had said, and we would do it ourselves if there was no other way.
6. Towards late afternoon, we felt an unusually hard bump on the raft floor and we found ourselves gazing at the large scaly head of a turtle. The day before I would have said, "Leave it, we can't manage that", but now things were different. "We'll have this one", I said. "Let's get it aboard the dinghy." The turtle's flippers had become entangled in the sea anchor line, so, first passing a rope from the dinghy under the raft, we made it fast to one of the back flippers, then carefully avoiding the searching beak, freed the turtle from the sea anchor rope and towed it around the raft to the Ednamair. With a bump and a thrashing of claws, the reptile lay on its back in the bottom of the dinghy.
7. I plunged the knife into the leathery skin of the neck. Deep red blood spurted into the bottom of the dinghy and gradually, the beak and flippers ceased thrashing as the beast died. Twenty-four hours previously, I would not have had the stomach for such a bloody business, but the laws of survival applied and the first principle, "The fittest survive, the weakest go to the wall", had now become our way of life. We would struggle and endure and, if our reflexes were not as swift as the animals and fish around us, we had to be cunning and improve with practice.

Questions

1. Why did the author kill the turtle?
(a) He liked to hunt
(b) He was feeling angry
(c) He was hungry and had nothing to eat
(d) He wanted to prove that he was brave

2. Why did the author's shoulders droop when the cargo ship reappeared?

3. The containers were filled with the rainwater as they
   (a) wanted to play with water.
   (b) did not have any work and wanted to pass their time.
   (c) had to give the water to the men in the cargo vessel.
   (d) were thirsty and also wanted to save water for the future.
4. How did the turtle bump into the author's boat?
5. Why did the author feel bitter?
6. The word .... is used in the passage in place of 'unusual'.
7. What did the writer survey as the ship sailed on?
   (a) The mainsail of the ship
   (b) The smoke in the sky
   (c) The empty flare cartons
   (d) The weather
8. Complete the sentence appropriately.
   The purpose of the flares was ....
9. Complete the sentence appropriately.
   The author of the given passage seems to be ....
10. State whether the give assertion is True or False.
    The author followed survival of the fittest theory.

PASSAGE 3

1. I got posted in Srinagar in the 1980s. Its rugged mountains, gushing rivers and vast meadows reminded me of the landscapes of my native place - the Jibhi Valley in Himachal Pradesh. Unlike Srinagar that saw numerous tourists, Jibhi Valley remained clouded in anonymity. That's when the seed of starting tourism in Jibhi was planted. I decided to leave my service in the Indian Army and follow the urge to return home.
2. We had two houses - a family house and a traditional house, which we often rented out. I pleaded with my father to ask the tenant to vacate the house so that I could convert it into a guesthouse. When my family finally relented, I renovated the house keeping its originality intact, just adding windows for sunlight.
3. I still remember the summer of 1992 when I put a signboard outside my first guesthouse in Jibhi Valley! The village residents, however, were sceptical about my success. My business kept growing but it took years for tourism to take off in Jibhi Valley. Things changed significantly after 2008 when the government launched a homestay scheme. People built homestays and with rapid tourism growth, the region also changed rapidly. Villages turned into towns with many concrete buildings. Local businesses and tourists continued putting a burden on nature.
4. Then, with the 2020-21 pandemic and lockdown, tourism came to a complete standstill in Jibhi Valley. Local people, who were employed at over a hundred homestays and guesthouses, returned to their villages. Some went back to farming, some took up pottery and some got involved in government work schemes. Now, all ardently hope that normalcy and tourism will return to the valley soon. In a way, the pandemic has given us an opportunity to introspect, go back to our roots and look for sustainable solutions.
5. For me, tourism has been my greatest teacher. It brought people from many countries and all states of India to my guesthouse. It gave me exposure to different cultures and countless opportunities to learn new things. Most people who stayed at my guesthouse became my repeat clients and good friends. When I look back, I feel proud, yet humbled at the thought that I was not only able to fulfill my dream despite all the challenges, but also to play a role in establishing tourism in the beautiful valley that I call home.

Questions

1. The writer mentions looking for sustainable solutions. He refers to the need for sustainable solutions because he realises that
   (a) even though all natural ecosystems are essential pillars of resilience, we need to focus on using their resources to address the economic needs of mankind as a priority.
   (b) the exposures to pandemics are a reality and a big threat to the countries across the world.
   (c) for an economic recovery to be durable and resilient, a turn to environmentally destructive investments and activities must be avoided.
   (d) there is an increasing urgency in the climate movement and the need for collaborative action for the future.
2. Give a reason for the scepticism faced by the author from the village people. Answer in 30-40 words.
3. What was the writer reminded of in Srinagar?
   (a) Home in the Jibhi Valley
   (b) Landscape of the Jibhi Valley
   (c) Family in the Jibhi Valley
   (d) None of the above
4. What does the author feel at the end of the passage?
5. How does the scenic beauty of Srinagar make the writer feel?

6. State whether the given assertion is True or False.

The narrator left the Indian Army to convert his home town Jibhi Valley in Himachal Pradesh into a tourist destination.

Competency Based

7. Why did tourism become stagnant in the Jibhi Valley?

(a) The valley had no attractions.

(b) The 2020-21 pandemic and the eventual lockdown.

(c) The writer had no idea of what needed to be done.

(d) Everyone there wanted to go back to their day job.

8. Complete the sentence appropriately.

Jibhi Valley was different from Srinagar ....

9. Complete the sentence appropriately.

.... brought a change in Jibhi Valley.

PASSAGE 4

1. "But have you been to Nimtita? Have you been to the palace there?" asked the old man in the tea-shop, with the thatched roof. We were in the village of Lalgola, one hundred and fifty miles from Kolkata, and we had just seen our thirteenth nobleman's palace and found it unsuitable.
2. "Nimtita? Where is that?" we asked without much interest. We had never heard of the place. "It is sixty miles to the North of here. You drive up the highway. Then you come to a river which you have to cross. A ferry will take your car across. Then up the highway again for twenty miles. A sign tells you where to branch off... it's on the river Padma, on the Eastern bank. It's the palace of the Choudhary's. I've been listening to your talk, and I feel you ought to see this one before you give up."
3. We were not very hopeful. We had enough trouble taking free advice from people who had no idea of our needs. Anyway, the question was: do we or do we not undertake this last trip? If we did not like the palace, it might mean either giving up making this film altogether, or seriously changing its nature. We tossed a coin to decide whether to go or not. The coin said, 'Go!' and we set out on our sixty-mile journey.
4. It was when I was in bed with my right leg in plaster that I had decided the film on Tarasankar Banerji's famous short story, 'The Music Room' (Jalsaghar). A nasty fall on the stone steps at Banaras had brought about a serious knee injury. I lay in bed and read all the Bengali books I could lay my hands on. Just then, the film distributors were not too keen to take my film for distribution, and may be this was one of the things that made me choose 'The Music Room'.
5. Here was a dramatic story which could naturally bring in music and dancing, and distributors loved music and dancing. But here, too, was a story full of feelings. So, it would be satisfying for me as an artist. I would cast Chabi Biswas, our greatest actor, in the leading role of the zamindar-the zamindar whose love of the big musical entertainments brings about his ruin. But the most important thing was to find a palace. As we had a low budget, there was no question of having studio-built sets. I knew that, if we had the money, my art director could easily build a set which looked like our old palace with the right style. But we just did not have the money for it.
6. Nimtita turned out to be everything that the old man had claimed-and more. No one could have described in words the feeling of utter sadness that surrounded the palace. The river Padma had changed its course over the years, so that now there were endless stretches of sand where once had been villages. The palace itself- Greek pillars and all-was a perfect realisation of my dream image. It stood looking out over the stretches of sand with a sad dignity. It had somehow escaped being totally destroyed when the river changed its course. The river had reached within ten yards of the front of the palace-having swallowed the garden-and then stopped. Ganendra Narayan Choudhary, who is seventy and owns a British title and the palace, told us how it happened: "We were having breakfast one morning when we heard a low rumble. We went out to the verandah and saw a big chunk of our estate-almost a square mile of it-going under water, disappearing forever. It all happened in a few seconds. Padma's appetite is legendary."
7. "But aren't you afraid that the river might encroach further?"
8. "Oh, yes, the rains bring with them the usual fears."
9. On returning from our first trip to Nimtita, I telephoned the author, Mr. Banerji. He had been just as anxious about the location as we were.
10. "We have found our palace at last, Mr. Banerji," I said.
11. "Have you? And where is it?"
12. "At a little known place called Nimtita."
13. "Nimtita? There was a note of recognition in his voice." "You do not mean the palace of the Choudhary's, do you?"
14. "That's the one."
15. "But that is extraordinary! I have not been to Nimtita myself, but I have read about the Choudharys in a history of Bengal zamindars, and it was the music-loving Upendra Narayan Choudhary who served as the model for my rajah."

Questions

1. The writer of the passage is a ...... by profession.
   (a) painter (b) filmmaker
   (c) photographer (d) journalist
2. What suggestion did the old man at the tea-shop make to the author and his friends?
3. What helped the author and his friends decide whether or not to go to Nimtita? **Competency Based**
   (a) The suggestion made by the old man at the tea-shop
   (b) Their own intuitive feeling
   (c) Description of the palace in a travel book
   (d) Tossing of a coin
4. Why did the author not like the idea of taking free advice?
5. How did the author sustain a serious injury?
6. Find words/phrases from the passage which are similar in meaning to the word 'nobility'.
7. Why was the idea of building a set for shooting given up?
   (a) Shooting at a set would not give a real life effect.
   (b) They did not have money for a set.
   (c) Building a set is very time consuming.
   (d) Shooting at the actual palace would be more authentic.
8. Complete the sentence appropriately.
   The central character in the story, 'The Music Room' is ....
9. Complete the sentence appropriately.
   The author liked .... the most about the palace.
10. Rectify the given False statement.
    The zamindar's love of the big dance had brought about the ruin of his house.

PASSAGE 5

Dr. Wood, the capable general practitioner, has been requested to solve a case. He gathers information about the murder from the inmates of the house. The information is presented in two parts.

Part A Background story by Arthur Conan Doyle

Part B Conversation between Dr. Wood and Cecil Barker

Background Story

The village of Birlstone is a small and very ancient cluster of half-timbered cottages on the northern border of the county of Sussex. For centuries, it had remained unchanged but its picturesque appearance has attracted well-to-do residents. A number of small shops have come into being to meet the wants of the increased population.

About half a mile from the town, standing in an old park famous for its huge beech trees, was the ancient Manor House, with its many gables and its small diamond paned windows. The only approach to the house was over a drawbridge, the chains and windlass of which had been rusted and broken. The family consisted of only two individuals - John Douglas and his wife. Douglas was cheery and genial to all and had acquired great popularity among the villagers. He appeared to have plenty of money. Thus, it came about that John Douglas had, within five years, won himself quite a reputation in Birlstone. His wife was a beautiful woman, tall, dark and slender, younger than her husband; a disparity which seemed in no way to mar the contentment of their family life. It was remarked sometimes, that the confidence between the two did not appear to be complete. There were signs, sometimes, of some nerve strain upon the part of Mrs. Douglas.

Cecil Barker was a frequent and welcome visitor at Manor House. Barker was an easy going, free handed gentleman.

It was on 6th Jan at 11:45 that the alarm reached the small local police station that John Douglas had been murdered. Dr. Wood seemed to be unnerved and troubled.

Conversation between Dr. Wood and Cecil Barker

Dr. Wood: We will touch nothing until my superiors arrive. (He spoke in a hushed voice, staring at the dreadful head)

C Barker: Nothing has been touched until now.

Dr. Wood: When did this happen?

C Barker: It was just half-past eleven. I was sitting by the fire in my bedroom when I heard the gun shot. In thirty seconds, I was in the room.

Dr. Wood: Was the door open?

C. Barker: Yes, it was open. Poor Douglas was lying as you see him.

Dr. Wood: Did you see anyone?

C. Barker: No, I heard Mrs. Douglas coming down the stairs behind me, and I rushed out to prevent her from seeing this dreadful sight.

Dr. Wood: But I have heard that the drawbridge is kept up all night.

C. Barker: Yes, it was up until I lowered it.

Dr. Wood: Then, how could any murderer have got away? It is out of question! Mr. Douglas must have shot himself.

C. Barker: That was our first idea. But see! The diamond paned window is open to its full extent.

Dr. Wood: I think someone stood there while trying to get out.

C. Barker: You mean that someone waded across the moat?

Dr. Wood: Exactly!

C. Barker: I agree with you.

Dr. Wood: But what I ask you is, how did he even get into the house at all if the bridge was up?

C. Barker: Ah, that's the question.

Dr. Wood: At what time was the bridge raised?

C. Barker: It was nearly 6 o'clock.

Dr. Wood: Then it comes to this, if anyone came from outside - if they did - they must have got in across the bridge before six and had been in hiding ever since. The man was waiting. He shot him, when he got the chance.

- Adapted MCB Theme : Mystery

Questions

Answer the following questions based on the passage given above.

1. The only change in Birlstone in years has been ....

(a) the opening of a few shops
(b) the timbered cottages
(c) an improvement in its picturesque appearance
(d) a number of well-to-do residents have settled there

2. Why do you think this passage is named a 'Tragedy'?

3. The Manor House stood out because of its ....

(a) diamond-paned windows
(b) huge beech trees
(c) drawbridge and windows
(d) residents

4. Cecil Barker was a sensible person. Justify the statement giving evidence from the text.

5. Examine the importance of the time, 6 o'clock, in the given excerpt. Answer in 30-40 words.

6. Substitute the underlined word in the sentence with a word from the passage that means the same.

The <u>stress</u> on the foot has been aggravated.

7. What is the initial thought of Dr. Woods regarding John's death?

(a) Someone murdered him.
(b) He committed suicide.
(c) The murderer is someone from the family.
(d) Take legal action.

8. Complete the sentence appropriately.

John Douglas had won quite a reputation for himself in Birlstone because of his ....

9. Complete the sentence appropriately.

Cecil Barker's first reaction at the sight of the dead Douglas was to ....

PASSAGE 6

Working 12 to 18 hours a day was not uncommon for scientists at the rocket launching station, Thumba. A group of such scientists was frustrated due to the work pressure and meeting their boss' demands; however, they were loyal to him.

One day, a scientist gathered enough courage to go up to his boss and say, "Sir, I have promised my children that I will take them to the exhibition this evening. Therefore, I have to leave the office by 5.30 pm. Can I leave early today, Sir?" His boss replied, "Alright. You may leave early today." The scientist was happy for having received the permission and continued with his work. He stayed on to work after lunch, and, as always, got so engrossed in his work, that he peered at his watch only when he thought he was done. Unfortunately, it was past 08:15 pm.

With a jolt, he remembered his promise to his children. He looked for his boss who was not in his office. Having told him just that morning, he wrapped up his work and hurried home.

As he drove home, he felt very guilty for having let his children down. When he reached, the children were not at home. His wife was busy reading. He felt that initiating any conversation with her would only add fuel to the fire, so he stayed quiet.

Looking up at him, his wife asked, "Do you want something hot to drink or would you like to have dinner right away?"

The man could only ask, "Where are the children?"

His wife said, "Don't you know? Your boss came here around quarter past five and took the children to the exhibition you had promised to take them to." He was surprised, but it did not take him very long to guess what had happened.

The boss, who had granted him permission, had observed him working very seriously well past 5.00 pm. He realised that the scientist would not leave the work half done, but if he had promised his children a visit to the exhibition, then they deserved it. So, he took the lead in taking them to the exhibition himself.

The boss did not have to do it every time. But once it was done, loyalty was established.

No wonder all scientists at the Thumba continued to work under this boss, in spite of the great pressure.

This boss was none other than Dr. APJ Abdul Kalam.

MCB Theme : People

Questions

1. What quality does the passage depict in the scientists?

(a) Frustration (b) Loyalty
(c) Dedication (d) Career-centric

2. Why were the scientists frustrated?

3. For what reason did the scientist ask for an early dismissal for that day?

(a) He wanted to relax.
(b) He wanted to spend some time with his children.
(c) He wanted to take his children to an exhibition.
(d) He wanted to go to an exhibition.

4. When did the scientist finish his work?

5. How was the scientist feeling when he drove back home?

6. Substitute the underlined word in the given sentence with a word that means the same from the passage.

The <u>starting</u> point of the project was to be discussed with the boss.

7. What reaction did the scientist expect from the wife?

(a) Sad (b) Shocked (c) Anger (d) Regret

8. Complete the sentence appropriately.

The scientist's children were ....

9. Complete the sentence appropriately.

The scientist's boss took the children because ....

10. State whether the given assertion is True or False.

The passage shows that Dr. APJ Abdul Kalam was a great leader.

PASSAGE 7

Abandoned Farmhouse

He was a big man, says the size of his shoes
On a pile of broken dishes by the house;
A tall man too, says the length of the bed
In an upstairs room, and a good, God-fearing man,
Says the Bible with a broken back
On the floor below a window, bright with Sun;
But not a man for farming, say the fields
Cluttered with boulders and a leaky barn.
A woman lived with him, says the bedroom wall
Papered with lilacs and the kitchen shelves
Covered with oilcloth, and they had a child
Says the sandbox made from a tractor tyre.
Money was scarce, say the jars of plum preserves
And canned tomatoes sealed in the cellar-hole,
And the winters cold, say the rags in the window frames.
It was lonely here, says the narrow country road.

Something went wrong, says the empty house
In the weed-choked yard. Stones in the fields
Say he was not a farmer; the still-sealed jars
In the cellar say she left in a nervous haste.
And the child? Its toys are strewn in the yard
Like branches after a storm - a rubber cow,
a rusty tractor and a broken plow,
a doll in overalls. Something went wrong, they say.

–Ted Koose MCB Theme : People

Questions

1. Select the most suitable option that fill the blank.

The man can be described as ....

(a) a big footed man
(b) an obese man
(c) a tall man
(d) Both (a) and (c)

2. How does the poet's use of personification of objects bring the people of the house to life?

3. Choose the option that correctly completes the given literary devices.

Bible with a broken back: .... :: .... : Personification

(a) Alliteration : Says the length of the bed
(b) Alliteration : Good, God-fearing man
(c) Personification : God-fearing man
(d) Personification : Bright with Sun

4. Comment on the overall tone of the poem.

5. With proper reference, speculate the problems the woman must have faced in the house.

6. Substitute the underlined word in the given sentence with a word that means the same in the poem.

The room was <u>filled</u> with clothes that she never wore.

7. The usage of the words 'weed-choked farm' suggest that

(a) the house has been abandoned for some time
(b) the man has been too busy to de-weed
(c) there is a drought in the area
(d) weeds grow well on farms where there are boulders

8. The expression "the Bible with a broken back" implies that the man ....

9. Complete the sentence appropriately.

The poet has chosen specific details such as 'still-sealed jars', 'left in a nervous haste', 'toys strewn' in the last stanza. The impact of these words is that they ....

Competency Based

PASSAGE 8

Rhyme of the River Aven

By : Bhavna Ramakrishnan

1. The river flows, where it goes, nobody knows
The trees are like towers touching the stars
Down they blow their heads in a row
To the river as it flows
Down the town the river flows as swirling it goes
Meandering the playground and houses in rows
2. The rocks on the bank look still and stern
The waves, from eddies that twirl and turn
Water bubbles drench the flowers and ferns
Lovers gaze with a faraway look and yearn
Children enter into boats that cruise and return
3. Slipping and sliding through the hills and forest green
The blue waters roaring, and then placid and serene
The bard's town sliced by enigmatic stream
The waves dancing on the rainbow coloured sun beams
Through the labyrinth of branches, filtered sunlight gleams
4. The river flows, silent and deep
Life's lesson learnt as it bound and leaps
Spread the message of peace, friendship you reap
Forget all sorrows, wonderful memories you keep
Life is a playground and sometimes mountains steep
5. The river never stops till it merges with the ocean
Success and failure in life unfold in slow motion
Cut your own path and stay steadfast in this notion
Let ambition and determination be interspersed with emotion
Like the river, never stop until you reach your destination

Questions

1. Trees are compared to
(a) Towers so tall that they are reaching heads
(b) Towers so tall that they are reaching houses
(c) Towers so tall that they are reaching the sky
(d) Towers so tall that they are reaching the clouds

2. At which point does the river stop?

3. The poet calls life a
(a) Playground and enigmatic stream
(b) Playground and steep mountains
(c) Playground and coloured rainbow
(d) Playground and grasslands

4. How does the sunlight come to the river?

5. How do the rocks on the shore appear to be?

6. Find a word from the poem that means 'whirlwind'.

7. Which of the following best describes the blue ocean?
(a) Like the ocean
(b) Like raging waterfall
(c) Sometimes placid and quiet
(d) Absolutely quiet

8. Complete the sentence appropriately.

The waves of the river appear to be dancing due to the ....

9. Complete the sentence appropriately.

The flowing river flashes the message that ....

10. State whether the given assertion is True or False.

The journey of a river is symbolic of the journey of life.

PASSAGE 9

I wandered lonely as a cloud
That floats on high o'er voles and hills.
When all at once I saw a crowd.
A host, of golden daffodils;
Beside the lake, beneath the trees,
Fluttering and dancing in the breeze.
Continuous as the stars that shine
And twinkle on the milky way,
They stretched in never-ending line
Along the margin of a bay:
Ten thousand saw I at a glance,
Tossing their heads in sprightly dance.
The waves beside them danced, but they
Out-did the sparkling leaves in glee;
A poet could not be but gay,
In such a jocund company!
I gazed - and gazed - but little thought
What wealth the show to me bad brought:
For oft, when on my couch
I lie in vacant or in pensive mood,
They flash upon that inward eye
Which is the bliss of solitude;
And then my heart with pleasure fills,
And dances with the daffodils.

Questions

1. Complete the sentence appropriately.
   The sight of dancing daffodils was a ....
2. What were the daffodils doing? Which literary device is used here?
3. The expression 'a crowd' is used for
   (a) lake
   (b) trees
   (c) breeze
   (d) daffodils
4. Which wealth is referred to by the poet? Explain in 30-40 words
5. What happens to the poet when he is sometime in a pensive mood? Explain in 30-40 words.
6. Find a word from the poem that means happiness.
7. The phrase 'never-ending line' of daffodils is compared with
   (a) margin of a bay
   (b) sprightly dance
   (c) stars on the milky way
   (d) long line of honeybees
8. Complete the sentence appropriately.
   The narrator just felt .... seeing the dance of daffodils.

ANSWERS (REVIEW EXERCISE)

Factual Passages

Passage 1

1. A doll is a girl's best friend and the first toy of her life that symbolises her own demeanour.
2. (b) The special significance of a doll in a girl's life
3. 1965
4. False
5. (d) a famous political cartoonist
6. The museum is divided into two halves, one for collection of dolls from Europe, the US, Australia, New Zealand and other for dolls from Asian countries including India.
7. (c) Some dolls in the museum are a representation of various forms of Asia.
8. (d) is both a joyous and an educational experience for children
9. houses

Passage 2

1. (c) Buddhist monks in Tibet
2. The Cherry Blossom Bonsai is breathtakingly attractive.
3. (d) Japan
4. We can take care of Bonsai plants through constant pruning, watering, shaping and providing the correct environment.
5. (b) Ten years
6. There is a great demand for Bonsai in Indian hotels, homes, garden houses, farm houses, restaurants and guest houses.
7. The writer says 'a thing of beauty is a joy forever' as the Bonsai lasts in one's imagination long after the plant has lived its life span.
8. (a) liking something very much.
9. mushroomed
10. (b) Patience

Passage 3

1. (d) endangered
2. (c) Chennai
3. 'The Turtle Walk' is an initiative aimed at educating the fishing community and the general public living near the beach on the need to protect the Oliver Ridley turtle and its nests.
4. At night, the sea shore is brighter than the sea due to night time lighting which distracts the turtles and they stray towards human habitations.
5. (d) All of these
6. (c) Attack from dogs and crows
7. The lost baby turtles are carried to the sea after they are rescued and are set free in the water.
8. Mexico
9. (b) containing a lot of eggs
10. at close quarters

Passage 4

1. The Indian Rhinoceros is a large mammal with a single horn which naturally black. The horn is absent in the new born.
2. (c) Only 3

3. (d) All of these
4. The major steps taken by the government to protect the Indian Rhinoceros are to declare some of the famous national parks as biosphere reserve forests and home to Indian Rhinoceros.
5. The Indian Rhinoceros and the White Rhinoceros in Africa are the largest rhinoceros in the world.
6. relentless
7. (a) Assam
8. grasslands and riverine forests
9. Indian Rhinoceros
10. The Indian and Nepalese Governments have taken steps individually to preserve Rhinoceros.

Passage 5

1. The influx of a large number of tourists and the urgency to accommodate them puts pressure on the infrastructure of that place, leading to several illegal constructions in the area.
2. (c) Only 1
3. Consumers
4. (b) plantation of trees in a non-forest/degraded forest area equal to or twice the trees it's clearing
5. (d) Both (a) and (b)
6. (c) detrimental
7. Unlawful
8. Unsustainability prevails in the Dev Bhoomi because of
   (i) Unchecked number of tourists causing stress on infrastructure.
   (ii) Self-transportation causes pollution and raises the temperature.
9. The tourist statistics showed that in Uttarakhand domestic footfall is much greater than international footfall.

Passage 6

1. Large business interests exploit sportsmen's skills by
   (i) making large profits out of selling sports gear which is a replica of the gear used by the professionals
   (ii) selling more newspapers copies by improving their sports coverage
2. The popular image of professional sport is that it is a highly glamorous occupation. The media helps to keep up this image by exposing the smallest detail of the sportspersons' private life to public scrutiny.
3. The crowds on the terraces flatter sportsmen by chanting their names with acclaim when they are playing. However, crowds are fickle and soon forget such sportsmen when they retire.
4. The sacrifices sportsmen make in their careers include disruption of their own social lives as they have to travel worldwide.
5. (d) The media
6. (c) To maintain his physical fitness
7. (c) By practicing their game
8. stars
9. at an early age

Passage 7

1. (c) A puzzle game meant for a single player.
2. (b) Life
3. The similarities between life and Sudoku are
   (i) Both start with a given set of notions or numbers.
   (ii) Both are best played in a calm but focussed state.
4. While playing Sudoku, you never think of the end (the result), you just keep working on the numbers and the final result (fruits of action) accrues on its own.
5. Swiss
6. (d) In 1986
7. beliefs
8. 81
9. False
10. When you make a mistake in life you cannot erase and begin all over.

Discursive Passage

Passage 1

1. (a) California
2. The flight to Karachi was another first because no one had flown non-stop from the Red Sea to India before.
3. (b) Monsoon
4. In Darwin, Amelia waited for the direction finder to be repaired and the parachutes to be packed to be shipped home as they were of no use in the Pacific.
5. When Amelia was in Lae, she sent her last commissioned article to the Herald Tribune.
6. overwhelmed
7. (a) Amelia's plane
8. reported that she was on the way to Howland Island
9. was never successful
10. False

Passage 2

1. (c) Store owners wanting to know what attracts customers to their stores
2. The two most important findings that Sharma has identified about customer behaviour are
   (i) women take a lot longer to shop than men, and
   (ii) except in a few cases, brand loyalty is not always strong.
3. (d) Both (a) and (b)

4. (c) store the card details and other information of the customers.
5. The phrase 'moment of truth' refers to the moment when a shopper selects an item to purchase.
6. (d) customise
7. False
8. keeping an eye
9. trends
10. the passage talks about what attracts a customer to their store.

Passage 3

1. Shreya had an angry outburst because no one liked her.
2. (c) She was not self-aware.
3. (d) 1 and 2
4. Knowing our strengths helps us in acknowledging our success as well as appreciating our capacity to do something with or without other's support.
5. When we know our strengths, we get a sense of well-being and we are able to learn new skills and develop assets which leads to an increase in confidence.
6. stable
7. (a) accept our flaws
8. us to realise our potential
9. to face challenges
10. True

Passage 4

1. (b) her father
2. Winning the World's Grand Prix Women's Chess Championship in Istanbul is Koneru Humpy's biggest achievement because the event had three former world champions.
3. (b) suggested a move
4. Parents play an important role in the lives of chess players as they encourage them to play the game. They teach the children that they shouldn't expect easy and early results.
5. Koneru Humpy says this to indicate that physical exercise is crucial for every chess player as it helps a player cope with pressure and increase the brain's ability to handle it.
6. beating
7. (b) 2, 3 and 4
8. Women's World Chess Championship
9. the Arjuna Award in 2003, the Padmashri in 2007 and the Raja-Lakshmi Award 2008
10. False

Passage 5

1. (a) Advancement
2. If the future progeny digs up the land we inhabit 3000 years from now, they would find plastic.
3. (c) They emit bad fumes.
4. The author wants us to stop using plastics and use other cloth bags.
5. The Solar Mission is a plan initiated by the Indian Government to promote the use of solar energy through solar photovoltaic and thermal systems for power generation.
6. Mitigate
7. (a) Use of LPG
8. proper management of water resources
9. Sustaining Himalayas
10. False

Passage 6

1. (d) Both (a) and (b)
2. According to the news, the Air France Plane went missing carrying 216 passengers and 12 crew members.
3. (d) All of these
4. The Bermuda Triangle became famous due to the strange disappearance of ships as well as aircrafts in the sea.
5. The theory of death rays from Atlantis has been disapproved by underwater expeditions that state that no magic crystals that were supposed to give out death rays, have been found. Further, even, Atlantis haven't been found.
6. explanation
7. (b) Due to its lower density
8. there are two magnetic Norths
9. True

Passage 7

1. (d) the art and science of healthy living
2. As per the writer, people from all walks of life can practice yoga.
3. (d) All of these
4. Asanas in yoga create a feeling of well-being in a person. By practing asanas, one can sharpen one's mind and improve one's intelligence and concentration.
5. Yoga fulfills our psychological needs by providing us knowledge.
6. enhances
7. (d) Both (a) and (b)
8. our mental, emotional and spiritual thoughts
9. body, mind and soul of a person
10. True

Literary Passage

Passage 1

1. (b) Fear
2. In the beginning, the narrator seems to be swimming alone in the stormy night after his ship/boat sank with the people inside it. He did not know if there were any survivors and so, he swam alone to ensure his safety.
3. (d) Both (b) and (c)
4. The narrator grew alarmed because he could not see any land.
5. According to the author, the narrator's action of changing the direction and swimming in the South-West direction was an unforgivable mistake because the current was carrying him away from land.
6. enormous
7. True
8. swin towards this thunder of waves.
9. the island he had found was going further from him

Passage 2

1. (c) He was hungry and had nothing to eat
2. The author's shoulders drooped when the cargo ship reappeared because he realised that there was no chance of the cargo ship spotting them as it was very far off.
3. (d) were thirsty and also wanted to save water for the future.
4. The turtle bumped into the author's boat due to its flippers which got entangled in the ships anchor line.
5. The author felt bitter because they could not be saved and the things that would have got them noticed were not useful anymore.
6. unaccustomed
7. (c) The empty flare cartons
8. to get the attention of the ship
9. stranded
10. True

Passage 3

1. (c) for an economic recovery to be durable and resilient, a turn to environmentally destructive investments and activities must be avoided.
2. The village people were sceptical of the author's attempt at making Jibhi Valley a place for tourism because they did not hope that any person would prefer visiting their home town.
3. (b) Landscape of the Jibhi Valley
4. The author feels pride at realising that he had fulfilled his dream and made his home town a popular tourist destination.
5. The writer's initial thoughts of Srinagar and its scenic beauty fills him with nostalgia about his native place.
6. True
7. (b) The 2020-21 pandemic and the eventual lockdown
8. because the latter was a popular tourist destination while Jibhi Valley was not.
9. Homsestays

Passage 4

1. (b) filmmaker
2. The old man at the tea-shop suggested that the author and his friends should visit Nimtita and the palace on the banks of river Padma.
3. (d) Tossing of a coin
4. The author did not like the idea of taking free advice because they had enough trouble already taking free advice from people who had no idea of their needs.
5. The author had sustained a serious injury by having a nasty fall on the stone steps at Banaras.
6. Dignity
7. (b) They did not have money for a set.
8. a zamindar
9. its Greek pillars
10. The changing course of river had brought about the ruin of his house.

Passage 5

1. (d) a number of well-to-do residents have settled there
2. The passage is called 'Tragedy' because a cheery, genial and popular man, John Douglas was murdered by someone.
3. (a) diamond-paned windows
4. Cecil Barker was indeed a sensible woman as after hearing the gunshot which killed John Douglas, she stopped Mrs. Douglas from seeing her dead husband's body.
5. The time 6 o'clock is important in the context of John Douglas' murder. The bridge to reach the Manor House was raised at 6 o'clock. This indicated that the murderer came into the house before 6 and had been hiding in the manor.
6. strain
7. (b) He committed suicide.
8. wealth
9. stop his wife from seeing the dead body

Passage 6

1. (b) Loyalty
2. The scientists were frustrated because they had to work for 12 to 18 hours under immense pressure to meet their boss' demands.
3. (c) He wanted to take his children to an exhibition.
4. The scientist finished his work by 8:15 p.m.
5. The scientist felt upset when he drove back home as he had broken his promise to his children.
6. initiating
7. (c) Anger
8. taken to the exhibition by the boss
9. the former would not leave his work half done which would mean that he would not be able to take his children to the exhibition
10. True

Passage 7

1. (d) Both (a) and (c)
2. The poet has used personification of objects to bring the people of the house to life because only the objects of the house had been with the family to talk about them with some precision.
3. (a) Alliteration: Says the length of the bed
4. The overall tone of the poem is quite mysterious, sinister and objective. The poet presents that something bad happened to the family that lived in the farmhouse but the poet did not know what.
5. From the given lines, we can say that the lady faced many problems in the house. She had to care for her child all alone. She also had to make sure that they have plums and tomatoes to eat throughout the year for they could not afford anything else.
6. cluttered
7. (a) the house has been abandoned for some time
8. looked for comfort and answers to his troubles in the Bible
9. suggest the tragic outcome for the farm family

Passage 8

1. (c) Towers so tall that they are reaching the sky
2. The river stops only at the point where it meets the ocean.
3. (b) Playground and steep mountains
4. The sunlight reaches the river after being filtered by the labyrinth of tree branches.
5. Rocks on the shore appear to be still and stern.
6. Eddies
7. (c) sometimes placid and quiet
8. meandering path
9. hustle till you reach your destination
10. True

Passage 9

1. memorable experience for the narrator
2. The daffodils were dancing merrily in the breeze. The poet is using personification here when he compares the movement of the daffodils in the breeze to dancing humans.
3. (d) daffodils
4. The wealth which is referred to here by the poet means wealth of joy and happiness which actually comes from happy and fond memories when the poet saw a host of golden daffodils by the side of the lake beneath the trees.
5. Whenever the poet lived on his couch in an unoccupied and sad mood, the fond and happy memory of the daffodil flowers flushed upon his eye of imagination which is a source of joy and inspiration to the poet in such a lonely mood.
6. Glee
7. (c) stars on the milky way
8. excited and cheerful

ASSESSMENT EXERCISE

Factual Passages

Passage 1

The Walt Disney Company became the first major media company to ban advertisements for candy bars and junk food on its television channels, radio stations and websites, to stop food manufacturers from peddling nutritionally challenged fattening junk for kids. The ban covers foods with too much sugar, too much salt or a full meal more than 600 calories. Predictably, the outraged public said that banning smoking in public places and artery-blocking trans fats in food was bad enough, but stopping them from guzzling comfort drinks by the litres was almost a human rights violation.

It seems most people are not just happy choosing their own poison. They also want it in super-sized doses, guaranteed to kill sooner than later, for after tobacco use, obesity is the biggest public health bugbear that triggers more avoidable diseases and deaths than malnutrition. Overweight and obesity are the leading causes for global deaths, killing 2.8 million adults each year. Worldwide obesity has more than doubled since 1980. The reasons for poor lifestyle choices are many, with almost all driven by socio-economic causes such as low education and limited income. Like killer infections, obesity and the resultant type-2 diabetes affect the poor more than the affluent, largely because processed and fast food are cheaper and take less or no time to prepare than healthy home-cooked meals. Limiting food choices, however, is not enough.

The need is to get children off their chairs and into the playgrounds. Too much screen time, largely social - networking, followed by online and video gaming and television, are making healthy children fat and putting them at risk of type-2 diabetes in the second decade of their lives. The lifestyle disease that interferes with the way the body metabolises glucose typically affects people in their fifties and sixties and is linked with a host of complications.

The official measure of obesity in adults is Body Mass Index (BMI), which is calculated by dividing a person's weight in kilograms by the square of his height in metres (kg/m^2). The WHO definition is: a BMI greater than or equal to 25 is overweight, 30 is obese, but the cut-offs for the South Asians are 23 for overweight and 25 for obese.

Answer the following questions based on the passage given above.

1. What did the Walt Disney Company ban?
(a) Candy bars
(b) Junk food
(c) Sugary foods
(d) Advertisement for candy bars and junk food

2. What was the purpose behind the ban?
(a) The foods were unhealthy
(b) The foods were cheap
(c) The foods were healthy
(d) The foods were costly

3. Complete the sentence appropriately.
.... and .... are the leading causes for global deaths, killing .... adults each year.

Competency Based

4. How can you say that obesity affects the poor more than the affluent? Explain in 30-40 words.

5. How is the Body Mass Index (BMI) calculated?

6. Complete the sentence appropriately.
The lifestyle disease that interferes with .... affects older people and is linked with ....

Competency Based

7. What has put children to the risk of type-2 diabetes?

8. What did the outraged public say about the ban on comfort drinks?

9. Complete the sentence appropriately.
Obesity affects .... more than the affluent.
(a) the middle class
(b) the educated
(c) the poor
(d) the sick

Passage 2

Kausani is situated at a height of 6075 feet in the Central Himalayas. It is an unusually attractive little town. It covers just about 5.2 sq km. It lies North of Almora in Uttarakhand's picturesque Kumaon region. Kausani provides a 300 km wide breathtaking view of the Himalayas. It is the most striking aspect of this place. Snow-capped peaks are spread in a stately row. They stare at you in silvery white majesty. The most famous peak on view is Nanda Devi, the second highest mountain in India. It is situated at a height of 25645 feet and is only 36 miles away as the crow flies. The other famous peaks on view are Choukhamba (23420 feet) and Trishul (23360 feet).

Then there are also Nilkanth, Nandaghunti, Nandaghat and Nandakot. On a clear day, the blue of the sky makes a splendid background to these peaks. At sunrise and sunset, when the colour changes to a golden orange, the scene gets etched in your memory.

When Gandhiji visited this place in 1929, its scenic beauty held him spellbound. He named it the 'Switzerland of India'. He prolonged his two-day stay to fourteen days, making time to write a book, *'Anashakti Yoga'*. The place where he was staying was originally a guest house of a tea estate. It was renamed *'Anashakti Ashram'* after the book.

Kausani is the birthplace of Sumitranandan Pant, India's poet laureate. Its natural surroundings inspired many of his poems. Its tea gardens mingle with dense pine forests and fruit orchards. The area is also host to many fairs and religious ceremonies. If Uttarakhand is the abode of Gods, Kausani is the God's own backyard. There is no traffic; no one is in a hurry. If serenity could be put on a canvas, the picture would resemble Kausani.

Answer the following questions based on the passage given above.

1. Kausani is situated in the state of ....
   (a) Himachal Pradesh (b) Punjab
   (c) Jammu and Kashmir (d) Uttarakhand
2. What is the most striking aspect of Kausani?
   (a) It lies North of Almora
   (b) Nanda Devi
   (c) It provides a 300 km view of the Himalayas
   (d) Choukhamba
3. Substitute the underlined word in the following sentence with a word/phrase from Paragraph 1, that means the same. **Competency Based**
   This little valley is surrounded by <u>majestic</u> waterfalls.
4. How does the view of the mountains get etched in our memory when we see them at sunrise or sunset on a clear day?
5. Why did Gandhiji call Kausani the 'Switzerland of India'?
6. What all does the vegetation of Kausani include?
7. The second highest peak in India is ......
   (a) Choukhamba (b) Nilkanth
   (c) Nanda Devi (d) Trishul
8. Select the correct word/phrase to fill in the blank and complete the analogy.
   Uttarakhand : Abode of Gods : : Kausani : ......
9. Which of the following is not true as per the information given in the passage?
   (a) Nanda Devi is only 35 miles away from Kausani.
   (b) Gandhiji visited Kausani in the year 1929.
   (c) Kausani's natural surrounding inspired many of Sumitranandan Pant's poems.
   (d) The atmosphere in Kausani is very serene.
10. Rectify the given False statement.
    Kausani is human's little heaven in India.

Passage 3

Parental pressure on children to excel–especially academically, is an enduring characteristic of middle class India. Over the past two decades with the accelerated growth of the pre-school sector - there are over 300,000 private pre-primaries in the country–the pressure on children to start learning begins early. Research studies in the West have confirmed that overemphasis on formal education and abstract concepts of literacy and numeracy before age five can result in a sense of failure, long term underachievement, disaffection and even truancy. The pressure to learn too much too early kills children's innate curiosity and burns them out. Unfortunately in India, there are two extremes–on the one hand there is no teaching-learning happening in the country's 1.3 million *anganwadis*, whereas on the other hand there is too much learning going on in private schools. Parental and societal pressure to perform well academically is a global phenomenon. Even in Australia, after the introduction of National Assessment Programme for Literacy and Numeracy, parental pressure on Kindergarteners to prepare for NAPLAN has increased enormously. In countries such as Korea and Japan, it's much worse.

In Singapore, as in India, parental pressure on pre-schools to begin early reading, writing and numeracy is intense yet Singapore boasts of one of the world's best Early Childhood Care Education (ECCE) systems; that's because not only their ECCE curriculums are standardised but also have to be approved by the education ministry. The government is also making an effort to introduce holistic education at the pre-primary level. In India there is no government mandated national ECCE curriculum resulting in wide disparity in programmes followed by pre-schools. The consequences of pushing children into structured formal learning are devastating, manifesting in teenage years when children are unable to cope with stress and failure. There is an urgent need for pre-school managements to re-examine and re-shape their curriculums to ensure age appropriate learning, educate parents on the adverse effects of early learning, respect for child rights and the long term benefits of holistic curriculum.

Answer the following questions based on the passage given above.

1. Complete the sentence appropriately.
   .... parents in India pressurise their children to excel in academics.
   (a) High-class (b) Low-class
   (c) Middle-class (d) Backward-class
2. Who are pre-primaries?
3. Complete the sentence appropriately.
   The pressure to learn too much at an early age results in ....
4. Complete the sentence appropriately.
   India presents two contrasting pictures of pre-schooling, one is of .... where even essential levels are not taught and the other is of .... where too much is happening on the teaching-learning front.
5. Which programme in Australia has led to increase in parental pressure on Kindergarteners?
6. Which of the following statement is not true?
   (a) Parents should not be educated about the ill-effects of early learning.
   (b) There is no government mandated national ECCE curriculum in India.
   (c) Parental pressure on pre-schools to begin early numeracy is intense in Singapore.
   (d) There are about 13 lakh *anganwadis* in India.
   Competency Based

7. State reasons of wide disparity in programmes of pre-schools in India is. Answer in 30-40 words.
8. What needs to be done to improve the standard of pre-primary education in India?
9. Substitute the underlined word in the following sentence with a word/phrase from the last paragraph that means the same. **Competency Based**

   The results of not eating healthy food can be disastrous to one's health.

Discursive Passages

Passage 4

Disability refers to any kind of physical or mental incapacity that limits a person's ability to work. Millions of people suffer from hearing impairment, vision impairment, speech impairment, mental retardation and a range of other problems.

Have you ever wondered how fortunate you are to be what you are and to have what you have? The smallest of actions like seeing the sunrise, brushing your teeth, tying your shoelaces, using a remote control, popping a peanut into your mouth comes to you so naturally, effortlessly, and yet we are never grateful, never satisfied, always discontented. Life, we feel owes us much more.

Not so for the disabled. For them it requires immense concentration, effort, willpower, energy and so much time. Despite this, it could be a long way to perfection. It takes great courage and determination to cope with disability. We can make life easier for the disabled by becoming sensitive to their handicap, their needs and their problems. Respect them for what they are, understand that they can never be completely independent. To insist that a disabled child be independent would be a form of oppression. Feelings like pity and undue sympathy will only shake their confidence. Give them encouragement, facilities and resources, then watch them as they learn, play, work, earn and even start families.

What we need to understand is that the disabled too are human beings. They have thoughts, ideas, wishes, ambitions, hopes, emotions and feelings just like anyone else. They can be good friends. What they need are more friends, a genuine concern and spontaneous integration into the community. They should feel themselves connected with it. Very often we find that a person lacking in one faculty is gifted in some other way. That is nature's way of maintaining a balance. Some of the most beautiful greeting cards are made by disabled children, using one hand, one foot or even the mouth. Nothing stops them from using their talent, their intelligence, their knowledge. All they need is acceptance, encouragement and admiration.

Answer the following questions based on the passage given above.

1. Fill in the blank with one word only.

   The second paragraph highlights that one should be .... for what one has.
2. Why is it a long way to perfection for the disabled?
3. How can we encourage the disabled?
   (a) By donating to organisations supporting the disabled
   (b) By ignoring the disabled
   (c) By becoming sensitive to their needs, their handicaps and their problem
   (d) By giving financial help to the disabled
4. How does nature compensate for the incapability of disabled persons? Why?
5. What kind of feeling would shake a disabled child's confidence?
   (a) Pity (b) Undue sympathy
   (c) Respect (d) Both (a) and (b)
6. Which of the following statements is False as per the information given in the passage?
   (a) It takes a lot of courage to deal with disability.
   (b) A disabled person can never be a good friend.
   (c) A disabled person should be respected for what he/she is.
   (d) We must understand that a disabled person can never be independent.
7. Substitute the underlined word in the following sentence with a word/phase from Paragraph 3 that means the same.

   Did you fully complete the work that was given to you, Sakshi?
8. How does a disabled person make a greeting card? What does it show about them? Answer in 30-40 words.

Passage 5

Road rage never seems to be outside the headlines for long, particularly in Delhi. There are also enough instances in all major cities where anyone could be beaten up for arguing with a motorist or biker. There is no accurate data on the incidents of road rage but other statistics such as the number of road accidents in India are working indicators of how unsafe using roads in India can be.

The frequency of incidents implies that there may be something wrong with not just our traffic management but also with the attitude of people who live in cities. There is some basis in the argument that the police are unable to cope with rapidly increasing motorisation coupled with more and more people moving to cities, particularly as some of the new arrivals are unaware of urban niceties. But the fact remains that in most cities in India, traffic laws are not enforced and there is no accountability when someone flouts the rules. This is a major contributing factor in causing road rage.

We have abysmally failed to develop a road safety culture in this country. Road rage occurs because road users believe they can do what they want with impunity. Most people seem to think that their political or business connections make them invulnerable. Unique to Delhi though, is a lack of assistance from bystanders. When someone on a scooter drove over a man repeatedly a few days ago, people stood and watched. Significantly, nobody called the police.

Stringent enforcement of traffic laws, while necessary, can only go so far. Communities must step up and hold responsible those who resort to violence on the road. Here, the media has a role to play in discouraging road rage. Reportage of road rage cases mustn't stop with reporting the crime the next day. Newspapers and news channels must follow up the cases and find out what has happened to the perpetrators in order to ensure that due legal punishment is meted out. When the regular arms of law fail, the media has to step in with determination to arouse public consciousness.

Answer the following questions based on the passage given above.

1. What is the major factor causing road rage in Indian cities?
   (a) Traffic laws are fully enforced in cities.
   (b) There is no accountability when someone breaks the rules.
   (c) Traffic laws are not enforced in cities.
   (d) Both (b) and (c)
2. Why does the police find it difficult to control road rage?
3. What role does media play to help control road rage?
4. Give a unique feature about road rage in Delhi. What may be the probable reasons for this?
   (a) Delhi has the maximum number of vehicles.
   (b) Delhi has shortage of traffic police personnel.
   (c) Bystanders do not offer any assistance when a road rage incident happens.
   (d) All of the above
5. Given reasons for road rage.
6. State an inference that can be drawn from the given paragraph.
7. Complete the sentence appropriately.

   Based on the first sentence of the passage, we can infer that ....
8. What is an indicator of the danger of using roads in India?
9. Substitute the underlined word in the following sentence with a word/phrase from the last paragraph, that means the same. **Competency Based**

   Strict rules should be made to stop smoking in public areas.

Passage 6

Want to feel better, have more energy and perhaps even live longer? Look no further than exercise. The health benefits of regular exercise and physical activity are hard to ignore. And the benefits of exercise are yours for the taking, regardless of your age, sex or physical ability.

Regular physical activity can improve your muscle strength and boost your endurance. Exercise and physical activity deliver oxygen and nutrients to your tissues and help your cardiovascular system work more efficiently. And when your heart and lungs work more efficiently, you have more energy to go about your daily chores.

Physical health affects the mind and *vice-versa*. Let us be clear that a sound mind and a sound body are prerequisites for high efficiency and good quality work in the office, factory or field, which lead to a sense of achievement and fulfilment.

Our health is, of course, important not only to us but also to our families and even to our employers. No wonder then that companies everywhere have a stake in the health and fitness of their employees and are willing to spend considerable money towards this purpose. Japanese companies particularly excel in this and the more successful among them start off the day with a body bending and stretching session and even singing the company song designed to promote loyalty and motivation among the workforce!

It is estimated that some 20,000 American firms have established in-house health clubs. Typical of these is the soft drink manufacturer, Pepsi Cola which has spent about 2 million in setting up a health club at its head office in New York state. Such expenditure has proved to be a wise investment in achieving better efficiency and high productivity. It has indirectly also helped reduce the premium on the health insurance of staff. Hundreds of consultancies have sprung up for the management of health clubs and fitness centres.

Exercise and physical activity are a great way to feel better, gain health benefits and have fun. As a general goal, aim for at least 30 minutes of physical activity every day. If you want to lose weight or meet specific fitness goals, you may need to exercise more.

Answer the following questions based on the passage given above.

1. What do exercise and physical activity do?
2. How does regular physical activity help us?
   (a) It improves one's muscle strength.
   (b) It improves one's body image.
   (c) It boats one's endurance.
   (d) Both (a) and (c)
3. What shows that the health of the employees is important in a company?
4. Why is expenditure on health considered a wise investment?
5. The employers in which country lead in focusing on the health of their employees?
   (a) India
   (b) America
   (c) Japan
   (d) South Korea

6. The amount that a firm invests in health helps in achieving
(a) high productivity
(b) better efficiency and high productivity
(c) low efficiency and high productivity
(d) better efficiency and low productivity

7. When does a person need to exercise more?
(a) When he wants to gain weight
(b) When he wants to lose weight
(c) When he wants to achieve specific goals
(d) Both (b) and (c)

8. What leads to a sense of achievement and fulfillment?

9. Substitute the underlined word in the following sentence with a word/phrase from Paragraph 5 that means the same.
A number of beauty salons have mushroomed in my locality.

10. Complete the sentence approximately.
If the title 'The Drawbacks of Exercising' is given to this passage, it would be an inappropriate title because ....
Competency Based

Literary Passages

Passage 7

1. We sit in the last row, bumped about but free of stares. The bus rolls out of the dull crossroads of the city and we are soon in open countryside, with fields of sunflowers as far as the eye can see, their heads all facing us. Where there is no water, the land reverts to desert. While still on level ground, we see in the distance the tall range of the Mount Bogda, abrupt like a shining prism laid horizontally on the desert surface. It is over 5000 metres high and the peaks are under permanent snow, in powerful contrast to the flat desert all around. Heaven Lake lies part of the way up this range, about 2000 metres above sea-level, at the foot of one of the higher snow-peaks.

2. As the bus climbs, the sky, brilliant before, grows overcast. I have brought nothing warm to wear: it is all down at the hotel in Urumqi. Rain begins to fall. The man behind me is eating overpoweringly smelly goats' cheese. The bus window leaks inhospitably but reveals a beautiful view. We have passed quickly from desert through arable land to pasture, and the ground is now green with grass, the slopes dark with pine. A few cattle drink at a clear stream flowing past moss-covered stones; it is a Constable landscape. The stream changes into a white torrent, and as we climb higher I wish more and more that I had brought with me something warmer than the pair of shorts that have served me so well in the desert. The stream (which, we are told, rises in Heaven Lake) disappears, and we continue our slow ascent. About noon, we arrive at Heaven Lake and look for a place to stay at the foot, which is the resort area. We get a room in a small cottage and I am happy to note that there are thick quilts on the beds.

3. Standing outside the cottage we survey our surroundings. Heaven Lake is long, sardine-shaped and fed by snowmelt from a stream at its head. The lake is an intense blue, surrounded on all sides by green mountain walls dotted with distant sheep. At the head of the lake, beyond the delta of the inflowing stream, is a massive snow-capped peak which dominates the vista; it is part of a series of peaks that culminate, a little out of view, in Mount Bogda itself.

4. For those who live in the resort, there is a small mess-hall by the shore. We eat here sometimes and sometimes buy food from the vendors outside, who sell kabab and naan until the last buses leave. The kababs, cooked on skewers over charcoal braziers, are particularly good; highly spiced and well-done. Horse's milk is available too from the local Kazakh herdsmen but I decline this. I am so affected by the cold that Mr. Cao, the relaxed young man who runs the mess, lends me a spare pair of trousers, several sizes too large but more than comfortable. Once I am warm again, I feel a pre-dinner spurt of energy - dinner will be long in coming - and I ask him whether the lake is good for swimming in.

5. "Swimming?" Mr. Cao says. "You aren't thinking of swimming, are you?"

6. "I thought I might", I confess. "What's the water like?"

7. He doesn't answer me immediately, turning instead to examine some receipts with exaggerated interest. Mr. Cao, with great off-handedness addresses the air. "People have often drowned here," he says. After a pause, he continues. "When was the last one?" This question is directed at the cook, who is preparing a tray of mantou (squat, white steamed bread rolls), and who now appears, wiping his doughy hand across his forehead. "Was it the Beijing athlete?" asks Mr. Cao.

Answer the following questions based on the passage given above.

1. One benefit of sitting in the last row of the bus was that ....
(a) the narrator enjoyed the bumps
(b) no one stared at him
(c) he could see the sunflowers
(d) he avoided the dullness of the city

2. What did he regret as the bus climbed higher?

3. The narrator was travelling to ....
(a) Mount Bogda
(b) Heaven Lake
(c) a 2,000 metre high snow-peak
(d) Urumqi

4. What made the scene look like a Constable landscape?

5. Why did the narrator like to buy food from outside?

6. Find word from the passage which means the same as 'sellers'.

7. On reaching the destination the narrator felt relieved because
   (a) he had got away from the desert
   (b) a difficult journey had come to an end
   (c) he could watch the snow-peak
   (d) there were thick quilts on the beds
8. Complete the sentence appropriately.
   Mount Bogda is compared to ....
9. Why did Mr. Cao not like the fact that the narrator was going to swim in the lake ?
10. State whether the following assertion is True or False.
   The two things in the bus which made the narrator feel uncomfortable are smell of goat cheese and leaking of the bus window. **Competency Based**

Passage 8

1. Suspense was over when my high school results finally came out. But I was upset. I hadn't done as well as I had expected. My father tried to console me. "Why are you worried? You have done very well my dear." "No, I haven't Baba", I protested, controlling my tears and wondering if I had disappointed him. "It doesn't really matter", he assured me. "Do you know what I got when I finished high school?" I looked into Baba's face and waited for the answer to his own question. "You know", he told me. "I've never told you this. I got just a third division. But, look at me, I've done quite well." Baba got a third division! I was almost in shock but the thought of my having done a lot better than that made me realise that I had no reason to complain.

   I certainly felt better! "Everything is under control!" said Baba, smiling. That was his favourite phrase. Posted in Kolkata, my father was then a senior official in the Indian Railway Service and an expert in goods traffic operations. He was soon to become a director with the Railway Board. By the time he retired in 1981, he was general manager of the Central Railways. By the time Baba passed away in November 2000, his name had found place in several hearts as well.

2. In September 2000, he was in hospital for treatment of cancer and given just two months to live. When he found out, his reaction was an extremely rational one. He asked me to fetch files from his cupboard so that he could explain the details of my mother's pension. He also dictated his will from his hospital bed."Everything is under control!" After Baba's death, Satish, our old family retainer was inconsolable. We tried to cheer him up. "Your Baba had scolded me only once in all these years!" he cried. Satish pointed to the watch on his left hand. "I had been coming late for work and everyone in the family was complaining about it", said Satish. "Then, one day, your Baba gave me this watch and told me, 'now that you have a watch, you can't be late'." That was the scolding Satish received.

3. On the fourth day after Baba's death, my sister and I had to perform a ceremony. Since several relatives were expected, we decided to order lunch from a caterer in our locality, reputed for his home cooked food. But when we went to pay the owner, we got a surprise. He refused to accept any money! "When I wanted to start my catering business, it was your father who lent me money", he told us. It seems Baba never asked for it back. Now, after four or five years the caterer wanted to repay that debt. Of course, we made him accept the full payment for the fine food and service. 'It was Baba's gift and it ought to remain so,' I told him.

4. Some days later, there was yet another piece of information as we were preparing for the main ceremony. Vikram, my brother drove me to the local market. On recognising our car, the parking assistant, in his twenties, came running towards us and asked why he had not seen its owner for long. We had to break the news to him and to our utter surprise, he started crying. We were really surprised by this reaction from a stranger - until the man told us that Baba used to pay his daughter's school fees and buy her books. It seems it was on my father's advice that he'd even started sending the child to school. More than three years after Baba's death, as we were looking into Baba's personal things, we came across an old file with Baba's certificates and I found among them, his high school diploma from 1937, the one he'd told me about 30 years earlier, about the third division that had made no difference in his life or career. It had made me see beyond mere marks and first classes as the main road to success.

Answer the following questions based on the passage given above.

1. Why was the narrator in tears when her school results came out?
   (a) She did better than she expected.
   (b) She did not do as expected.
   (c) Her Baba had not done well.
   (d) Her Baba had done better than her.
2. Why did Baba buy Satish a watch?
3. On knowing the result, how did the narrator's father react?
   (a) He scolded her (b) He beat her
   (c) He consoled her (d) He made fun of her
4. Why did the caterer not want to take money from the narrator?
5. Why were the narrator and her brother surprised on meeting the parking assistant? Answer in 30-40 words.
6. Complete the sentence appropriately.
   Today years after his passing away the narrator has realised about her Baba that ....
7. Why did the narrator say that she had nothing to complain?
8. Complete the sentence appropriately.
   The narrator's sick father wanted her to fetch files from his cupboard because ....
9. State whether the given assertion is True or False.
   Baba was a senior official in the Indian Railway Service.

Passage 9

Dispute

A man and a tiger once had a dispute,
Which was reckoned greater, the man or the brute.
The tiger discoursed on his side at some length,
And greatly enlarged on his courage and strength,
Said the man, 'Don't be prating; look yonder, I pray,
At that sculpture of marble: now what will you say?
The tiger is vanquished; but as for the man,
He is striding upon him: deny if you can.'
'But pray,' said the tiger, 'Who sculptured that stone?
'One of us,' said the man. 'I must candidly own.'
'But when we are sculptors,' the other replied,
'You will then on the man see the tiger astride.'

Answer the following questions based on the passage given above.

1. What was the cause of dispute between the tiger and the man?
(a) To establish who was superior.
(b) To prove beasts were inferior.
(c) To justify that beasts should be caged.
(d) To prove that man was more intelligent.

2. Why do you think the Man wants to assert his superiority?

3. What did the man do to prove his point?
(a) He caged the tiger.
(b) He carved a statue of a man riding a tiger.
(c) He put the tiger in a cage.
(d) He enslaved the tiger.

4. How would you resolve the dispute between Man and the Brute?

5. Convey the central idea of the poem in about 30-40 words.

6. Choose the option that displays emotion that the poet is expressing with regards to the tiger.
(a) Agony, anger, excitement.
(b) Agony, frustration, hurt.
(c) Anger, hurt, frustration.
(d) Anger, hurt, anxiety.

7. Pick the option that best describes the mood of the poem.
(a) Gloomy (b) Reflective
(c) Ominous (d) Hopeful

8. Complete the sentence appropriately.
The tiger's counter-argument was that ....

9. State whether the given assertion is True or False.
It is the man who brags about his false strength.

Passage 10

Upon Westminster Bridge

Earth has not anything to show more fair:
Dull would he be of soul who could pass by
A sight so touching in its majesty:
This City now doth like a garment wear
The beauty of the morning; silent, bare,
Ships, towers, domes, theatres, and temples lie
Open unto the field, and to the sky;
All bright and glittering in the smokeless air.
Never did sun more beautifully steep
In his first splendour valley, rock, or hill;
Ne'er saw I, never felt, a calm so deep!
The river glideth at his own sweet will:
Dear God! The very houses seem asleep;
And all that mighty heart is lying still!

- William Wordsworth

Answer the following questions based on the passage given above.

1. The narrator would call a person dull if he/she ....
(a) does not talk to him openly
(b) does not know about romantic sites
(c) passes by without experiencing the beautiful sight
(d) passes over the site and shouts loudly

2. What is meant by "houses seem asleep"?

3. The city of London appears as if it is ....
(a) covered with thick layer of smoke
(b) clad in attractive colourful clothing
(c) desolate and lonely
(d) sleeping beauty

4. How does the poet feel on seeing such a sight?

5. What do you understand by the line 'The beauty of the morning: silent, bare'? Answer in 30-40 words

6. State whether the given assertion is True or False.
The poet is in the awe of the scenery he sees.

7. The morning sight of the city bears a ....
(a) peaceful and serene look
(b) noisy and crowdy look
(c) dark and dreary scene
(d) enchanting and haunting appearance

8. Complete the sentence appropriately.
'All bright and glittering', 'all' refers to ....

9. Complete the sentence appropriately.
The movement of the river is ....

ANSWERS (ASSESSMENT EXERCISE)

Passage 1

1. (d) Advertisement for candy bars and junk food
2. (a) The foods were unhealthy
3. Overweight, obesity, 2.8 million
6. The way the body metabolises glucose typically, a host of complications
9. (c) The poor

Passage 2

1. (d) Uttarakhand
2. (c) It provides a 300 km view of the Himalayas
3. Striking 7. (c) Nanda Devi 8. God's own backyard
9. (a) Nanda Devi is only 35 miles away from Kausani.

Passage 3

1. (c) Middle-class
3. the killing of curiosity in children
4. anganwadis, private schools
6. (a) Parents should not be educated about the ill-effects of early learning.
9. Consequences

Passage 4

1. grateful
3. (c) By becoming sensitive to their needs, their handicaps and their problems
5. (d) Both (a) and (b)
6. (b) A disabled person can never be a good friend.
7. Completely

Passage 5

1. (d) Both (b) and (c)
4. (c) Bystanders do not offer any assistance when a road rage incident happens.
8. road rage cases are very common, especially in Delhi
9. Stringent

Passage 6

2. (d) Both (a) and (c) 5. (c) Japan
6. (b) better efficiency and high productivity
7. (d) Both (b) and (c) 9. Sprung up
10. the passage discusses the benefits of exercising

Passage 7

1. (b) no one stared at him
3. (b) Heaven Lake
6. Vendors
7. (d) there were thick quilts on the beds
8. a shining prism
9. True

Passage 8

1. (b) She did not do as expected.
3. (c) He consoled her
8. he wanted to explain the details of her mother's pension
9. True

Passage 9

1. (a) To establish who was superior.
3. (b) He carved a statue of a man riding a tiger.
6. (a) Agony, anger, excitement.
7. (b) Reflective
8. the situation would be reversed if he was the sculptor
9. True

Passage 10

1. (c) passes by without experiencing the beautiful sight
3. (b) clad in attractive colourful clothing
6. True
7. (a) peaceful and serene look
8. sky
9. according to its sweet will

SECTION B Writing Skills

SECTION C Grammar

CHAPTER 1

Notice Writing

A notice is a very important form of written communication issued by individuals and organisations to convey information about functions, events and occasions or to make announcements about somethings that are about to happen.

Parts of a Notice

- **Format** It includes the name of the organisation, the word 'Notice', date, subject of the notice and name and the designation of the person issuing the notice at the end.
- **Content** It must answer the questions 'What?' 'When?' 'Where?' 'How?' 'Why?', etc., and present all other necessary details related to the subject of the notice.
- **Expression** It relates to the overall grammatical and spelling accuracy as well as fluency.

Types of Notice

(i) Notice for Meeting

(ii) Notice for Events like Competition/Tour/Celebration/Cultural Events, etc.

(iii) Notice for Lost or Found

(iv) Notice for Seminar/Workshop/Debate/Other Literary Events

(v) Notice for Appeal

(vi) Other Notices

Points to be Kept in Mind

- The language used must be simple and clear.
- Use third person pronouns. Personal pronouns like I, me, you, mine, etc. should not be used except in lost notices.
- Always write the content of the notice in present or future tense.
- Always put the notice in a box.
- Adhere to the word limit, if given in the question.
- A notice should/must include some value points (necessary details) in order to make it precise and effective.

Format of a Notice

You are Vandita of Class IX. As the Cultural Secretary of your school, draft a notice for an Inter School Dramatics Competition Auditions.

Name of the Organisation/ Institution issuing the notice	**XYZ Public School, Delhi**
The word NOTICE is written in Capital letters	**NOTICE**
Date Date of issuing the notice on the left side	27th January, 20XX
Subject of the Notice	**Inter School Dramatics Competition Auditions**
Content The content of the notice	This is to inform all the students that an Inter School Dramatics Competition is being organised on 12th February at Tagore Theatre. Those willing to take part in the competition as a part of the school team should come for auditions and selection on 1st February, 20XX at 12:30 pm in the Assembly Hall. Students of Classes VI to XII are eligible. For further details, contact the undersigned.
Name and Designation of the person issuing the notice	Vandita (Cultural Secretary)

Type 1 Notice For Meeting

Details Required

- Who has called the meeting
- Date and time/duration of the meeting
- Venue
- Purpose or agenda of the meeting
- People/departments who are required to attend the meeting.
- Specific instructions for the persons called for the meeting

SOLVED EXAMPLES

1. You are Nandita/Nandan of Class IX, Happy Senior School. Being an Activity Coordinator, draft a notice to request all the other Activity Council members to attend a meeting to discuss and plan the activities for 15th August (Independence Day) celebrations.

Ans.

Happy Senior School, Delhi

NOTICE

6th August, 20XX

Activities for Celebration of Christmas Day

All the Activity Council members are informed to attend a meeting on 7th August, 20XX at 10:30 am in the Biology Lab. The meeting is called to discuss the activities to be organised for Independence Day celebrations. Members are expected to come up with suggestions and ideas along with the estimated cost and other necessary requirements. For further details, please contact the undersigned.

Nandita

Class IX C

(Activity Coordinator)

2. **You are Deepak/Deepika Kapoor, Secretary, Modal School Football Association. It has been decided that a meeting of all the members of the school football team will be held to discuss plans and strategies for the coming Zonal Tournament. Write a notice in not more than 50 words informing the members of the team about the meeting and requesting them to attend it.** Competency Based

Ans.

Modal School

NOTICE

3rd March, 20XX

Football Association Meeting

All the members of the school football team are informed that a meeting has been scheduled for 7th March, 20XX at 2 pm in the Sports Room. You are requested to be there on time for the selection process and for planning the strategies for the coming Zonal Tournament. For further details, please contact the undersigned.

Deepika Kapoor
(Secretary, Cricket Association)

3. **You are Secretary of Sri Parthasarathy Sabha, Salem. Draft a notice in not more than 50 words to be sent to the members of the *Sabha* requesting them to attend an extraordinary meeting. Invent necessary details such as items on the agenda, date, time, etc. Sign as Kama/Komal.** Competency Based

Ans.

Sri Parthasarathy Sabha, Salem

NOTICE

21st January, 20XX

Extraordinary Meeting of Members

An extraordinary meeting of our members has been scheduled for the coming Sunday to hold elections for the posts of the President, the Secretary and the Treasurer. Details of venue and time are given below

Venue	Conference Hall of Society
Date	Sunday, 28th January, 20XX
Time	11 am

For further details , contact Ms. Sachini, Room 103B.

Komal
(Secretary)

4. **As the Secretary of Resident Welfare Society, draft a notice in 50 words calling for the Annual General Meeting to discuss issues of security and maintenance of public spaces. Specify the day, date, time and venue. Request the members to attend the meeting. You are Razia/Rashid.**

Ans.

Sahar Grouping Housing Society

NOTICE

5th May, 20XX

Annual General Meeting

This is to inform the residents of the society that a meeting is being held to discuss the issue of security and maintenance of public spaces. The details of the meet are as follows

Day	Sunday
Date	10th May
Time	9 am onwards
Venue	Community Hall

At least one member from each house is requested to attend the meeting.

Rashid
(Secretary, RWS)

Type 2 Notice for Events (Competition/Celebration/ Tour/Visit /Sports Meet/Cultural Event, etc.)

Details Required

- Who is organising
- Who can participate
- Occasion
- Number of days (in case of tours/visit)
- Fare cost and other costs included
- Last date for depositing the advance (tour/visit)
- Any specific instructions
- Name and designation of the Issuing Authority

SOLVED EXAMPLES

1. You are the Secretary of the Environment Club of Aradhya Public School. Write a notice to invite students of Class IX to the environmental a wareness drive organised by the club on the World Environment Day.

Ans.

Aradhya Public School

NOTICE

25th May, 20XX

Environmental Awareness Drive

All the students are hereby informed that the Environment Club of the school is organising a environmental awareness drive on the occasion of World Environment Day on 5th June, 20XX. The club needs volunteers to make the drive successful. Interested students of Class IX may register their names with the undersigned by 2nd June, 20XX. For further details, contact the undersigned.

XYZ
(Secretary, Environment Club)

2. You are Josely Mathew, the President of the School Book Club. The club is organising a drive to promote the reuse of study materials and books. Draft a notice in about 50 words for the school notice board, addressing students of classes IX-XII and informing them about this drive and urging them to contribute to the endeavour. Mention how the donated books would benefit a charitable cause. Competency Based

Ans.

XYZ International School

NOTICE

25th September, 20XX

Drive for Promoting Reuse of Study Materials and Books

This is to inform all the students of Classes IX to XII that the Book Club of our school has decided to organise a drive to promote the reuse of study materials and books. Students are urged to donate unusable study material and books for the cause to Miss Abha in Room No. 12 by 4th October. For further details, please contact the undersigned.

Josely Mathew
(President, Book Club)

3. Your school is organising a special school assembly. Write a notice to be put in your school informing the students about assembly and call for participants.

Ans.

XYZ School, Delhi

NOTICE

16th October, 20XX

A SPECIAL SCHOOL ASSEMBLY

This is to inform all the students that our school is organising a special school assembly on 24th October, 20XX to celebrate its founding day. All of the students are encouraged to attend the assembly. Further, students who are interested to participate in any of the events of the assembly can give their names to respective class teachers on or before 19th October, 20XX. For further details, contact your respective class teachers.

PQR

4. The Students' Council of Greenland School, New Delhi has organised an excursion to Kullu, Manali and Rohtang Pass for students of Classes XI and XII. As the Headgirl/Headboy of the school draft a notice for the notice board of your school to this effect inviting students who wish to join the excursion to give in their names for the same. Add relevant details like duration and cost of excursion and last date for submission of authority letter signed by parents and making the payment. Do not exceed 50 words. Put the notice in a box.

Competency Based

Ans.

Greenland School, New Delhi

NOTICE

20th March, 20XX

Excursion to Kulu, Manali and Rohtang Pass

This is to inform all the students of Class XI and XII that the school is organising a weeklong excursion to Kullu, Manali and Rohtang Pass. The details of the excursion are as follows

Date 14th to 21st May, 20XX

Expense 6000 per person

Things required for confirmation Submission of authority letter signed by parents and payment.

Last date of submission of excursion fees-4th April, 20XX.

The itinerary will be provided after the finalisation of the number of students. For further enquires, contact the undersigned.

XYZ

(Head Girl)

5. You are Savita/Sandeep, Secretary of Royal Housing Society. Your society is going to organise a Blood Donation Camp. Write a notice in not more than 50 words urging the members of your society to come in large numbers for this noble cause. Invent the necessary details.

Ans.

Royal Housing Society

NOTICE

11th March, 20XX

Blood Donation Camp

This is to inform all the residents that the Royal Society is organising a Blood Donation Camp on 15th March, 20XX in the Community Hall from 11 am. Qualified doctors will be available to carry out the procedure. Residents above the age of 18 and below 50 years with a good medical history are urged to volunteer in large numbers for this noble cause. For further details, please contact the undersigned.

Sandeep

(Secretary, Royal Housing Society)

6. **You are Health Secretary, Students' Council, Citizen Public School, Ram Bagh, Varanasi. The Council has decided to start, from the 2nd October, a week-long cleanliness drive around the school. Draft a notice in about 50 words asking the students of Class IX to enroll as volunteers for the drive.**

Ans.

Citizen Public School, Ram Bagh, Varanasi

NOTICE

30th September, 20XX

Cleanliness Drive around the School – Volunteers Required

This is to inform all the students that as part of the *SWACHH PATHSHALA* campaign, our school is holding a week-long cleanliness drive around the school premises starting on 2nd October, 20XX. Volunteers are required from Class IX for guiding students and staff during this drive. Interested volunteers should contact the undersigned during the lunchtime tomorrow for detailed instructions.

Kalawati, IX A
(Health Secretary, Students' Council)

Type 3 Notice for Lost or Found

Details Required

- Article/Object lost or found
- Where you lost or found it
- Description of the article like colour/size/model, etc.
- Date/Time/Day when you lost it/found it
- Whom to contact
- A suitable gift/reward for the person who returns that article/product
- Writer's name and designation/class

SOLVED EXAMPLES

1. **Manvi Mishra, a student of Class IX, has lost her calculator somewhere in the school premises. Write a short notice for the school notice board requesting the finder to return it to her. Manvi is a student of Jain Model School.**

Ans.

Jain Model School

NOTICE

15th October, 20XX

Lost! Lost! Lost!

This is to inform all the students that I have lost a Sharp-VM Calculator in the school premises during recess today. My intials MM are engraved on its black back. The finder is requested to return the same to the undersigned. A treat is promised.

Manvi Mishra
(Class IX B, Roll no. 67)

2. You have found a canvas bag in the park near your house. Write a notice for the same in about 50 words. Invent the necessary details.

Ans.

Central Park, Shastri Nagar

NOTICE

3rd February, 20XX

Canvas Bag Found

This is to inform all that a small canvas bag containing some papers and cash was found in the park premises on 2nd February, 20XX around 10 a.m. The genuine owner of the canvas bag is requested to collect it from the undersigned after giving proper identification.

Anuj
(The Secretary)

3. Yesterday, during lunch break, you misplaced your English All-in-One book. Write a notice in about 50 words for the school notice board. You are Sanchit/Siya, a student of Class IX A.

Ans.

Model Public School, Janakpuri

NOTICE

25th February, 20XX

Lost-Class IX English All-in-One Book

This is to inform all the students that I, Siya, have misplaced my English All-in-One (Class IX) in the school during lunchtime yesterday. The notes bear my name along with the title 'All-in-One English Class IX' on the cover. Anybody who finds them is requested to give them back to the undersigned in Class IX A or to the Administrative Officer. The person will be suitably rewarded.

Siya
(Class IX A)

4. Ira is the Head Girl of Vanasthali Public School, Ludhiana. She lost her hall ticket for the Board Examinations. She has to put up a notice on the school notice board. Draft the notice in not more than 50 words.

Ans

Vanasthali Public School, Ludhiana

NOTICE

25th February, 20XX

Lost Hall Ticket

This is to inform all that a hall ticket belonging to me, Ira Sachdeva, for Class X Board Examinations was lost in the school playground during lunchtime. It has a photograph along with the Roll no. 1234567. Anybody who finds it is requested to give it to the Administrative Officer. The person finding it and handing it over will be suitably rewarded.

Ira
(Head Girl, Class X A)

5. You are Ashish Khanna of Class XII. You have found a pouch in the school playground. Write a notice for the school notice board inviting its rightful owner to claim the pouch after furnishing necessary details about it.

Ans.

ABC School, Mysore

NOTICE

10th November, 20XX

Found! Found! Found!

This is to inform all the students that I have found a blue-coloured pouch in the school playground today *i.e.,* 10th November, 20XX at 8:30 am. The genuine owner of the pouch can claim it back from the undersigned after giving necessary details about the pouch and identification marks if any.

Ashish Khanna

(Class XII A, Roll no. 25)

6. You lost your Apple Smart Watch in your school. Draft a notice in not more than 50 words to be placed on your school notice board. You are a student of Class XII of Rani Jhansi Senior Secondary School, Gwalior. Sign as Rani/Ram.

Ans.

Rani Jhansi Senior Secondary School, Gwalior

NOTICE

20th April, 20XX

Watch Lost

This is to inform all that an Apple Smart-watch was lost near the playground yesterday. It has a black square dial and a brown strap. If anyone finds it, she/he is requested to return it to the undersigned. The person finding it will be suitably rewarded.

Rani

(Class XII C)

Type 4 Notice for Seminar/Workshop/Debate/Other Literary Events

Details Required

- Body organising it
- Who can attend
- Subject of the seminar/debate/workshop
- Duration of the programme
- Speakers/Chief Guest/Honourable Persons
- Date/Time
- Specific instructions
- Name and designation of the Issuing Authority

SOLVED EXAMPLES

1. You are Vikram, School Captain of Meerut Public School, Shastri Market, Meerut. Write a notice in not more than 50 words informing the students of Class IX about a guest lecture by Mr. Rajiv, an IT Professional, on the topic 'Future of Artificial Intelligence'.

Ans.

Meerut Public School, Shastri Market, Meerut

NOTICE

31st October, 20XX

Guest Lecture by IT Professional

All the students of Class IX are informed that a guest lecture on the topic 'Future of Artificial Intelligence' by a renowned IT professional Mr. Rajiv is being organised by the school. The lecture will be held on Saturday, i.e., 3rd November, 20XX in the school auditorium from 10:30 a.m. to 11:30 a.m. Attendance of Class IX students is compulsory. For more information, contact the undersigned.

Vikram

(School Captain)

2. You are Vijay/Veena, Head Boy/Girl of Minerva Public School, Bhopal. Your school is planning to organise a Career Counselling Workshop for the students of Classes IX to XII. Draft a notice in about 50 words informing students about the workshop mentioning day, date, time and venue.

Ans.

Minerva Public School, Bhopal

NOTICE

24th February, 20XX

Career Counselling Workshop

This is to inform all the students of Classes IX to XII that our school is organising a Career Counselling Workshop. The details of the event are

Day	Saturday
Date	5th March, 20XX
Time	10:00 a.m. to 1:00 p.m.
Venue	School Auditorium

This workshop aims to provide insights and guidance to help you choose the right career path. We encourage all students to attend this informative workshop. For further details, contact the undersigned.

Vijay/Veena

(Head Boy/Girl)

3. The Literary Society of your school is setting up an Editorial Board for the forthcoming academic session. Draft a notice in 50 words to be put up on the school notice board, inviting students from Classes IX to XI to join the board. The members would be expected to stay back after school for 2 hours once a week to work on the school magazine. You are Shiela/Sameer, Secretary of the Literary Society.

Ans.

XYZ Public School

NOTICE

25th April, 20XX

Setting up of Editorial Board

This is to inform all the students of Classes IX to XI that the Literary Society of our school is setting up an Editorial Board for the forthcoming academic session. Members of the board would be expected to stay back after school for 2 hours once a week to work on the school magazine. Interested students can give their names to Ms. Sukriti in room no. 204 by 30th April, 20XX. For further details, contact the undersigned.

Shiela

(Secretary, Literary Society)

4. **The Debating Society of your school is organising an Inter-School Debate Competition. The last date for submitting names for the audition is Friday, 17th March. There will be on-the-spot trials. Draft a notice in about 50 words informing students about the team selection time, date and venue. You are Sarita /Sarit, President, Debating Society, Flora International School.**

Ans.

Flora International School

NOTICE

24th February, 20XX

Inter-School Debate Competition

This is to inform all the students of Classes IX to XI that the Debating Society of our school is organising an Inter-School Debate Competition. The society is organising audition for the same. The details of the audition are

Day	Friday
Date	17th March, 20XX
Time	10:00 a.m. to 1:00 p.m.
Venue	School Auditorium

Interested students are requested to register their names with the undersigned by the due date. For further details, contact the undersigned.

Sarita/Sarit
(President, Debating Society)

5. **There has been an increase in the Number of cyberbullying cases in our schools. This has led to parents and students getting very anxious. As the School Counsellor, you are organising a talk during the morning assembly by Mr. Kakkar, Director, Cybercrime Department inviting both students and parents. Draft a notice in about 50 words informing students of the same mentioning day, date, time and venue.**

Ans.

ABC International School

NOTICE

10th March, 20XX

Cyber Bullying Talk

This is to inform all the students that our school is organising a Cyber Bullying Talk to address the issue of the increase in the number of cyber bullying cases in schools. The details of the event are as follows

Day	Friday
Date	17th March, 20XX
Time	10 a.m.
Venue	School Auditorium

Mr. Kakkar, the Director of Cybercrime Department, has accepted to address this issue. The talk is open to both students and parents. All students and parents are requested to attend the talk.

PQR
(School Counsellor)

Type 5 Notice for Appeal

Details Required

- Whom to appeal/warn
- Issuing authority (if different from the person signing the notice)
- A slogan or message
- Important instructions
- Courteous way to appeal
- Name and designation of the issuing authority
- Any punishment (if required, in case of warning type only)

SOLVED EXAMPLES

1. Recently, it was in the news that a hurricane hit West Bengal adversely affecting the state. Being the Head Girl of your school, draft a notice for the students and staff appealing for donations of relief products like clothes, money, books and other articles in not more than 50 words.

Ans.

Vijay Public School, Vijay Nagar

NOTICE

8th December, 20XX

Appeal for Donations

This is to inform all that the Student Council of our school has organised a rehabilitation drive for the victims of the recent hurricane in West Bengal. One can donate clothes, books and other articles like blanket, blazer, quilt, etc. to help the poor and affected. By doing this, we will show our humanitarian nature. Certificates will be given to the major contributors. For other details, contact the undersigned.

XYZ

(Head Girl)

2. As the Librarian of Crescent International School, Gwalior, draft a notice in not more than 50 words asking all students to return the library books they have borrowed before the commencement of the examination. You are Neeta Gupta, Librarian.

Ans.

Crescent International School, Gwalior

NOTICE

25th February, 20XX

Last Date for Return of Library Books

This is to remind all the students to return the books borrowed from the library latest by 1st March, 20XX. Students who do not return the books in the given time would not be allowed to sit for the final examination. Your prompt action will be appreciated.

Neeta Gupta

(Librarian)

3. Write a notice in about 50 words to advise the residents of your society to store water for a day as the water supply will be suspended for the cleaning of the water tank.

Ans.

Janata Group Housing Society

NOTICE

25th March, 20XX

Suspension of Water Supply

This is to inform all the residents that the water supply will be suspended on 27th March due to the cleaning of the water tank. All the residents are advised to store water for a day.

The inconvenience caused is deeply regretted.

XYZ

(Secretary)

Type 6 Other Notices

Details Required

- Whom to inform about the change
- Existing/Current and changed
- Reason for change
- Writer's name and designation

SOLVED EXAMPLES

1. You are the proprietor of a company which has changed its office address from 2A, Phool Bagh Colony to Mangal Pandey Nagar. Draft a notice to be inserted in the local newspaper informing about the change in not more than 50 words. You are Rajat Sharma.

Ans.

Rajat Enterprises, Meerut

NOTICE

13th October, 20XX

Change of Address

This is to inform all that Rajat Enterprises has changed their office address from 2A, Phool Bagh Colony to 334/3, Mangal Pandey Nagar. Anyone needing their services is requested to contact them at their new address. Their phone no. 0121-248276X remains unchanged.

Rajat Sharma

(Proprietor)

2. **As the House Captain of A.B.M Public School, Telangana, draft a notice in not more than 50 words for the school notice board informing house members from classes X to XII about the change in topic and submission dates for Round 1 of 'Discovery' - the upcoming Inter-House Reasearch-based Paper Presentation Competition. Do not forget to issue an apology for the same. You are Kruthika Reddy.** Competency Based

Ans.

A.B.M Public School, Telangana

NOTICE

25th September, 20XX

Change in Topic and Submission Dates For 'Discovery'

This is to inform all the house members of classes X to XII that there has been a change in the topic and submission dates for Round 1 of 'Discovery' - the upcoming Inter-House Reasearch-based Paper Presentation Competition. The details of the competition are as follows

Topic	Ancient Ruins of Hampi
Date of Submission	4th October, 20XX
Time	12 noon
Venue	Room No.14

For further details, contact the undersigned.

The inconvenience caused by the sudden change is deeply regretted.

Kruthika Reddy
(House Captain)

3. **As Principal, Kendriya Vidyalaya, Kanpur, write a notice in about 50 words informing the students of Class XII that their Biology paper in the first term examination shall take place on 5th October instead of 29th September. Give a reason for the change.**

Ans.

Kendriya Vidyalaya, Kanpur

NOTICE

22nd September, 20XX

Class XII Biology Paper Postponed

This is to inform all the students of class XII that their first term Biology paper scheduled for 29th September 20XX shall now take place on 5th October, 20XX. This is because the school will remain closed on 29th September which has been declared a gazetted holiday. Other than a change in the date of the Biology paper, the first term examination date sheet remains the same.

Principal

4. **As Principal, National Public School, Ramnagar, write a notice in about 50 words informing the students that with effect from 20th of January, the school shall start at 9 a.m. instead of 8 a.m. Give reasons for the change.**

Ans.

National Public School, Ramnagar

NOTICE

14th January, 20XX

Change in School Timings

This is to inform all the students that with effect from the 20th of January, the school shall start at 9 a.m. instead of 8 a.m. due to certain contractual issues with the private buses plying with our school. Until these issues are completely resolved, the school will start at 9 a.m.

Principal

ASSESSMENT EXERCISE

1. You are Ram/Rajani, Secretary, Social Service Club, Sun Public School, Nagpur. Your club is organising a book fair for your school students. Draft a notice for your school notice board giving all relevant information about the event in not more than 50 words.
2. RJ Public School is located in a Central Government employees' residential colony. Cultural Society of the school has decided to organise a Fancy Dress Show on 25th January in which each participant will wear the dress particular to his/ her region. The aim is to show the cultural diversity of India. As Secretary, write a notice in about 50 words inviting the names of those who want to participate.
3. An Inter-Class Drama Competition is to be held in St. Stephens School, Visakhapatnam. As Akash, Head Boy of the school, draft a notice to be put up on the notice board inviting entries. Provide all necessary information in about 50 words.
4. Your club is going to organise an Inter-Class Singing Competition. Write a notice in about 50 words inviting names of the students who want to participate in it. Give all the necessary details. You are Navtej/Navita, Secretary, Music Club, Akash Public School, Agra.
5. Every year in the central park of the city a flower show is held in the month of February. Your school has received a circular from the District Collector inviting your students to visit it. Write a notice in about 50 words informing the students about the show and advising them to go and enjoy it. You are Navtej/Navita, Head Boy/Head Girl, Sunrise Public School, Surat.
6. An Inter-School Kabaddi Competition is organised by your school. Write a notice, in not more than 50 words, requesting the students to be present at the venue to encourage the players. Invent the necessary details. You are Arjun, the Sports Captain of your school.
7. Chennai Book Society is going to organise a week-long book fair in the city. It has requested your school for volunteers to manage various counters. As Secretary, Cultural Club, Chennai Public School, write a notice in about 50 words informing all the members to join the meeting regarding the same.
8. Your school has planned an excursion to Lonavala near Mumbai during the autumn holidays. Write a notice in not more than 50 words for your school notice board, giving detailed information and inviting the names of those who are desirous to join. Sign as Naresh/Namita, Head Boy/Head Girl, DV English School, Thane, Mumbai.
9. You are Mohit/Madhuri Saw of Class VI of RPB Public School, Jaipur. You lost your geometry box in the school playground last Tuesday. Draft a notice in not more than 50 words for your school notice board informing the students about the loss of your geometry box.
10. You are Rameshwaram/Rameshwari, Secretary, Literary Club of ABC School, Vikaspuri. Your schoolmate, Gautam Adhikari, a budding writer, has won the first prize in the State Level Story Writing Competition. The club has decided to organise a function to felicitate him on his laudable achievement. Write a notice in not more than 50 words, informing all the students of your school about the function and urge them to attend it to make the occasion memorable. Invent the necessary details.
11. You are Megha Gupta/Mehul Gupta, the Head Girl/Head Boy of St Mary's School, Dehradun. Draft a notice, informing the students of Classes IX to XII about a workshop on 'Understanding What the New Education Policy Entails' to be held in the school premises. Give all the necessary details.
12. You are Neelam/Nitesh, Secretary of the School Library Club. The club is organising an inter- school 'Let's Read a Book' week to help develop and encourage the habit of reading among children. Draft a notice in about 50 words for the school notice board inviting club members from Classes X to XII to be student volunteers for the event. Mention day, date, time and venue.
13. As the Managing Head of Smilekro NGO, you have to approach some schools to bring in book grants to needy students. Write a notice in about 50 words informing the members to attend a meeting regarding the same.
14. After the rains, cases of dengue, chikungunya, etc. are on the rise in your city. As Principal, Sunshine Public School, Manu Vihar, you have decided to allow your students to wear full sleeve shirts and trousers in the school for a period of one month. Write a notice regarding the same in about 50 words.
15. Your school has decided to introduce Mass Media Studies as a subject under the vocational stream. This is going to help students who want to pursue a career in films, its production and other attached fields. Write a notice for your school notice board informing all students regarding the course.

Dialogue Writing

CHAPTER 2

Dialogues are a form of communication between two or more people. They are generally spoken but are widely used in writing fiction, poems and dramas to convey the view point of the characters/speakers.

Knowing how to write dialogues is an important skill as it helps students to develop communication skills, understand different perspectives, and express themselves better.

A dialogue or conversation may be formal or informal, depending on the following factors

1. Relationship between the speakers
2. The topic of conversation
3. The situation in which the speakers are placed

Points to be Kept in Mind

- Always use the correct punctuation marks in your dialogue.
- Separate the dialogue from the speaker using a hypen (-) or colon (:)
- Use simple and clear language in the dialogue.
- Understand the situation for which you have to write a dialogue clearly.
- Reread your conversation to make sure you have not made any grammatical of punctuation error in it.

SOLVED EXAMPLES

1. Two friends, Rehan and Kriti are trying to fix a date and time to meet each other over the telephone. Write the dialogue between them.

Ans. **Rehan :** Hello!

Kriti : Hi, Rehan! How are you?

Rehan : I am well. How are you?

Kriti : I am quite well too. I think we should schedule that meet. I haven't seen you for quite some time.

Rehan : I was thinking the same. Are you free on the thirteenth in the afternoon?

Kriti : No, I am afraid not. I have to work in the afternoon. I am available in the evening though. How about then?

Rehan : Yes, I am available in the evening. Let's meet at the Merth Plaza for coffee, and cookies, and then we can go for dinner.

Kriti : Good idea! Is 7 pm okay?

Rehan : That's fine. See you there!

2. Write a dialogue between you and your teacher about which course to study during vacations.

Ans. **Student :** Good morning, Sir. How are you?

Teacher : Good morning. I am fine. How are you?

Student : I am fine as well. I was wondering which course to learn during my vacations.

Teacher : It can be confusing with so many options online. You should make a list and narrow it down as per your interests.

Student : I have tried that but I am left with three options- Artificial Intelligence, Machine learning and Data Science.

Teacher : Well! All of them are very interesting courses but as far as I remember, you have always been interested in Artificial Intelligence.

Student : Yes, I am! I believe it is our future.

Teacher : Well then, it's no harm in pursuing it and later, if you find it less interesting, you can always switch.

Student : Yes, it sounds like a great idea. Thank you Sir.

REVIEW EXERCISE

1. Write a dialogue between Tanya, who needs to buy a birthday gift for her younger brother, and a shopkeeper at the gift shop.

Ans. **Tanya :** Hello, I am looking to buy a birthday gift for my younger brother.

Shopkeeper : Hello! What would you like to buy for him?

Tanya : He likes to play video games on the computer. Do you have something related to that?

Shopkeeper : Yes, we have a brand new car-racing computer game CD. It is the latest edition. Does he enjoy playing car-racing games?

Tanya : Yes, he is very fond of racing games. Can you please pack that for me?

Shopkeeper : Yes, of course. Would you also like to buy some chocolates for your brother along with the gift?

Tanya : Sure, that would be great. Thank you so much.

Shopkeeper : You're welcome. Please come with me so you can select the chocolates and the card you want. Afterwards, I can gift-wrap them for you.

2. Write a dialogue between two friends who have met after a long time.

Ans. **Divya :** Hi, Smitha! What a pleasant surprise! I am so glad to see you after so many years.

Smitha : Me too, Divya. It feels like ages! How are you? And what are you doing here?

Divya : I am good. I got married three years ago, and I live here with my husband and son.

Smitha : That's great news. I also moved back with my husband from Pune six months ago.

Divya : So, where do you live?

Smitha : I live in Khar.

Divya : We live very close. We should meet sometime.

Smitha : Yes, we should. How about this weekend?

Divya : Sounds great. You should bring your husband along.

Smitha : I sure will.

Divya : I'm sorry, I have to rush now. I have to pick up my son from school.

Smitha : I understand. Mother duty come first.

Divya : Well then, see you on Saturday!

Smitha : Bye.

3. Amrita and her sister Roshni are discussing how to spend their pocket money wisely. Write a dialogue between them.

Ans. **Amrita :** I always have very little money to spend near the month end.

Roshni : I have tried to tell you to be more careful with your spending. You waste too much money on things you don't need and then, suffer towards the end of each month.

Amrita : You are right but I can't stop myself from buying chocolates, candies and comic books as soon as I receive the pocket money at the start of the month.

Roshni : I agree but you need to learn to manage your spending properly.

Amrita : Yes. I see that you never face such problems. How do you do it, Roshni?

Roshni : Well, I make a list of the most important things I would need to buy each month before I start spending my pocket money. It helps me to make sure that I would have sufficient funds to last me the entire month.

Amrita : That's a great idea! Will you teach me too?

Roshni : Yes, of course.

Amrita : Thank you so much!

4. Write a dialogue between two friends who are trying to decide how to spend their holiday.

Ans. **Anil :** Hi Gautam! Do you have plans for the weekend?

Gautam : Hello Anil! No, I haven't yet decided what to do over the weekend. What about you?

Anil : I was thinking we should go to see a movie. It has been a while since we went to the cinema together.

Gautam : You are right but I am not planning to go out. I want to do something more relaxing at home.

Anil : Okay, I understand. What about playing Chess at home together?

Gautam : We always do that. Can't we do something different?

Anil : Should we play video games?

Gautam : Yes, that sounds like a great idea. I have bought a new joystick too.

Anil : Great! I will see you on Saturday then, Gautam.

Gautam : Bye Anil. See you.

5. Karan wants to get a health certificate from his doctor for his new job. Write a conversation between the doctor and Karan.

Ans. **Doctor :** Hello Karan. What brings you here today?

Karan : Hello doctor. I need a letter from you stating that I am healthy enough to work on a ship.

Doctor : We will have to do some tests for that. When do you need it?

Karan : I have to submit it tomorrow.

Doctor : Okay, let's get the tests done then.

Karan : You know I am a healthy person. What is the need for tests? Can't you just give it to me right away?

Doctor : I can't just give it to you, Karan. I should check you properly to make sure there won't be any problems for you at work. It's for your own safety.

Karan : Okay doctor. I understand.

Doctor : Now should we start the tests?

Karan : Yes doctor. Thank you so much.

6. Two friends, Anita and Saba are trying to plan a birthday surprise for their mutual friend Nupur. Write a dialogue between them.

Ans. **Anita :** Hi Saba. How are you?

Saba : Hello Anita. I am well. Good to see you. What brings you to my house today?

Anita : I wanted to discuss with you how we should celebrate Nupur's birthday. It is next week.

Saba : Oh, I nearly forgot. Maybe we should organise a party.

Anita : That's a great idea. We should gather all our friends and her parents, and also bring a cake.

Saba : Perfect! I can also cook some snacks at home and bring them.

Anita : That sounds great. But remember Saba, Nupur can't know anything about it. It has to be a surprise.

Saba : You are right Anita. I will make sure no one tells her.

Anita : See you next week.

Saba : Bye. See you Anita.

7. Gaurav has called his friend Ashish to find out why he didn't come to school. Ashish's mother, Mrs. Sharma picks up the call. Write a dialogue between them.

Ans. **Mrs. Sharma :** Hello, who is this?

Gaurav : Hello, I am Gaurav, Ashish's friend. May I speak to him?

Mrs. Sharma : Hello Gaurav. I am his mother. Unfortunately, Ashish is not well and is asleep in his room.

Gaurav : What has happened to him, Aunty?

Mrs. Sharma : He has not been feeling well since yesterday evening. He had a headache and high fever. We took him to the doctor yesterday. He thinks it is the flu.

Gaurav : Oh, I am sorry to hear that. I hope he gets better. Has he felt better today?

Mrs. Sharma : Yes, he felt much better this morning but not good enough to go to school.

Gaurav : I understand. Can you please give him a message from me? I will come to visit him tomorrow if he's not well enough to come to school.

Mrs. Sharma : That is very kind of you Gaurav. Sure, I will give him your message.

Gaurav : Thank you Aunty. Bye.

Mrs. Sharma : You are welcome. Take care Gaurav. Bye

8. Jyoti is confused about what she wants to do in her life. Write a dialogue between Jyoti and her father discussing her career.

Ans. Jyoti : Dad, I am very confused about my career.

Father : Don't worry Jyoti. Everyone goes through this difficulty at your age. Tell me, what interests you the most?

Jyoti : I like modelling and Cricket. You know I am not that good at studies which I think is really important for a good job.

Father : You have a really diverse range of hobbies Jyoti. It is really good for your overall development. Not everyone gets good grades at school. It doesn't mean you can't have a good job.

Jyoti : But how can I make a good career out of these hobbies dad?

Father : You can work hard at sports by practising daily after school and also join additional courses related to the fashion industry. If something you like becomes your profession, you will surely be successful in it.

Jyoti : I understand dad. Thank you so much for your help.

Father : You are welcome Jyoti.

9. Write a dialogue between a man in a cage and a tiger.

Ans. Man : Have mercy on me, O Tiger! You have caged me for no fault of mine. I am starving from yesterday. You have not given me any food.

Tiger : What! Haven't I given you food? What is all this in the bowl next to you?

Man : O my lord, Tiger! How can I eat raw food? The food you have given is not cooked. I can't eat this food.

Tiger : Eat what you have got and stop weeping.

Man : O Tiger! I want to meet my wife and children. They are at home. I do not know how they are. Please release me and let me go! For the sake of my children, please let me go!

Tiger : What exactly do you want? Tell me. You have not been caged for nothing. I will carry you to the jungle where you will perform in a circus in front of the animals. You are going to perform feats and the animals will clap and applaud your performance. Ha ha ha...

Man : Oh no! Please don't do that. I understand that you are taking revenge for the ill treatment we give to the tigers.

Tiger : I have put you in a cage to teach you a lesson. I hope you can now empathise with our condition when we are put in a cage. I will let you go if you pledge to protect the tigers and other animals. I will let you be free if you encourage people not to buy any product made of animals' body parts. I will let you go you if you can educate people that they should stop hunting us.

Man : I agree to your conditions. Please free me. You are very wise and generous. O Tiger, you have not eaten me.

Tiger : I am setting you free. When you go back to your society chant this slogan: Save Tiger, The King Of The Jungle.

10. Ravi has a problem so he asks his friends for advice. Write a conversation about the same.

Ans. Ravi : My neighbours play very loud music which disturbs me when I'm studying.

Mohan : Why don't you try persuading them to turn down the volume?

Shiela : If that doesn't work, you could think of changing your study time.

Rahim : Why should Ravi have to do that? He really ought to report such anti-social behaviour to the police.

Shiela : Before taking drastic action like that, I would advise you to sort it out amicably with your neighbours.

Rahim : If I were you, I would play my music even louder!

Mohan : That won't solve his problem. Ravi, I think you should ask your father to take it up with your neighbours.

ASSESSMENT EXERCISE

1. Rohan and his mother are discussing the advantages and disadvantages of social media with each other. Write a dialogue between them.
2. Ali and Rakesh are planning a hiking excursion. Write a dialogue between them.
3. Mantesha has called the dentist to fix an appointment for herself. The call is picked up by the receptionist. Write a dialogue between Mantesha and the receptionist.
4. Shubham wants to ask his mother's permission to go to the cinema with his friends. Write the dialogue between them.
5. Write a dialogue between Amina and her brother talking about the merits and demerits of online classes.
6. Shahid is performing poorly at school. Write a dialogue between him and his class teacher, Mr. Mehta discussing the reasons for his lack of concentration in class.
7. Ajit is planning an anniversary celebration party for his parents along with his sister, Sujata. Write a dialogue between them.
8. Brandon goes to the car showroom and converses with a car salesman to find a good car to buy for himself. Write the conversation between the car salesman and Brandon.
9. Rahul and Varun are conversing about their friend, David who has met with an accident recently. Write a dialogue between them.
10. Anuj asks a passerby for directions to reach the bakery. Write the dialogue between them.
11. Write a dialogue between a tiger in a cage and a man.
12. Arif has lost his wallet at the book fair and he approaches a police officer for help. Write a dialogue between the officer and Arif.

CHAPTER 3

Informal Letters

Informal letters include the letters written to family members, relatives, friends and acquaintances. Hence, there are no formal rules as such on how to write these types of letters. In fact they are written in a friendly manner as it generally includes the senders emotions, ideas or experiences. The style of writing may depend upon an individual's nature and mood as well as the recipient of the letter. If you are writing to an elderly person, you should use the language which is respectful and courteous. While writing to friends, one can use casual and friendly language.

Purpose of Writing Informal Letters

- To express feelings and emotions
- To ask their whereabouts and howabouts
- To describe an event or incident
- To stay connected with relatives and friends
- To send invitations and to express gratitude

Parts of an Informal Letter

Informal letters consist of the following parts

1. **Sender's Address** The sender's address is written at the top right corner along with the pin code. Do not write sender's name with the address.

   e.g. K-127, Ashok Nagar
   New Delhi-110092

2. **Date** It appears directly below the sender's address, after leaving a one line space. It is advisable to always write the full date in the following format.

   e.g. 25th December, 20XX

3. **Greeting/Salutation** This consists of greeting and name of the recipient or the sender's relation with the recipient, e.g. Dear Ashi.

   (a) **For Parents**
   Dear/My dear father/mother, etc.

   (b) **For Relatives**
   Dear uncle/aunty, etc.

   (c) **For Brother/Sister/Cousin, etc.**
   Dear/My dear (name), etc.

   (d) **For Acquaintances**
   Dear Mr. (last name)/Ms. (name)

4. **Body of the Letter/Message**

   (a) **Introduction/Opening**

   - This may begin with enquiring howabouts, e.g. 'How are you?', 'How are you (Akshay/Rahul)?' or 'I hope you are hale and hearty', 'I hope you are doing well', or 'It's been a long time since I have heard from you.'
   - The letter may also begin with acknowledging/thanking for the previous letter/gift received, e.g. 'Thank you for such a precious gift of yours' or by apologising if you are writing/replying after too long.

e.g. 'Hi Preeti. I received your letter but I was so busy with my new project that I could not reply earlier.'

(b) **Main Body of the Letter**

- Here, you write about the actual purpose of your letter, sharing the current events happening in your life, school, college, etc.
- Try to write your message according to the theme of the question asked.
- While you share your experiences, your feelings, ask questions in between to arouse interest of the reader. This will give your letter a touch of live conversation.
- Also, give replies to the questions of the recipient if he/she has written to you earlier.

5. **Closure/Concluding Sentence** Even if you are writing an informal letter, you cannot end it abruptly. So, give your letter a proper closure to the reader. e.g. 'Hope to see/hear from you soon'. Also, you may convey love to family members and good wishes to friends and acquaintances. E.g. 'Convey my regards to aunty and uncle', 'Love to little Chinu', etc.

6. **Subscription or Leave-Taking** As in formal letters, informal letters too need to be courteous and respectful to the person you are writing to. Below the subscription comes the signature or name of the writer as, e.g.

- **Family Members and Relatives** Your affectionate/loving son/daughter/ brother/ sister/ nephew, etc.
- **Close Friends** Yours lovingly/loving friend, etc.
- **Acquaintances** Yours faithfully/sincerely, etc.

Format of an Informal Letter

You are Rohit/Reena residing at 35, Munirka Enclave, DDA flats, New Delhi. Write a letter to your friend Rahim/Rishika, telling him/her about your new school in 120 words.

Sender's/Writer's address {

35, Munirka Enclave, DDA Flats
New Delhi – 110092

Date (Appears directly after the writer's address after leaving a line) {

13th May, 20XX

Salutation (the customary greeting with which the sender starts the letter) {

Dear Rahim/Rishika

Main Body
(It contains all the information that the sender wants to share) {

I hope that this letter finds you in good health. I am doing well. You will be glad to know that I have recently joined a new school in Vasant Vihar. The name of my school is Mother Mary Sr. Sec. School. It is located in neat and clean surroundings full of greenery. My school has a very attractive building with beautifully constructed modern classrooms. The rooms are big, airy and spacious. Even the furniture is very comfortable.

It also has a proper playground space dedicated to different sports including basketball, volleyball, badminton, cricket, etc. The studies are done using the latest of technologies and the teachers are very polite as well as friendly. Instead of the bookish language, they want us to frame our own answers. The best part is that the school offers a variety of extracurricular activities that we must participate in.

In all, my new school focuses on the overall development of a child. With such kind of education, I hope to fulfil all the goals that I have set up for myself. I hope to see you in the coming summer holidays. Give my best wishes to uncle and aunty.

Complimentery Closing (The end of the letter with either Yours lovingly, Yours affectionately or Your friend which is followed by a signature) {

Your friend

Rohit/Reena

SOLVED EXAMPLES

1. Your friend has recently passed an examination securing very high marks. Write a letter to him or her in 120 words congratulating him/her on his/her success.

Ans. 39, Raj Bhawan Road,
T. Nagar
Chennai

27th May, 20XX

Dear Rita

I have just come to know that you have passed the School Certificate Examinations with flying colours. May I offer you my heartiest congratulations! It is an achievement which you ought to be proud of since you really worked very hard and certainly deserved such high marks.

I was examining the previous year cut-offs for your desired course last night. With your brilliant results, you will surely get admission in the course and college of your choice with a merit scholarship. Nothing can stop you from pursuing the career of your dreams and becoming a lawyer who would advocate the rights of women from the backward communities. I feel so proud of you.

Mother joins me in congratulating you. She says your parents must be proud of you. You have really gained distinction and brought honour to your family.

Do write to me about how your teachers and Principal reacted when your result came.

Will catch up with you later.

Yours lovingly
Manorama

2. You are Mahesh/Mukti. You had heard that your friend had met with an accident. Write a letter to him/her in about 120 words telling them about safety and wishing him/her a speedy recovery.

Ans. ABC Apartments
Lodhi Road
New Delhi
29th September, 20XX

Dear Madhav
How are you?

I met Shiva at the coffee house yesterday and he told me about how you met with an accident last week resulting in a minor fracture in your left hand. I was really shocked to hear the news and am quite concerned about your well-being. Road accidents are really becoming a cause of concern nowadays.

The government has set such strict policies, still there has been no relief from these accidents. This incident is a lesson for all of us. Our safety is our responsibility. A small mistake can lead to a huge blunder. Now, don't get sad. You will recover soon. I hope to meet you soon. My parents and younger sister have sent you lots of love and wishes.

Wish you a speedy recovery! Take care.

Yours lovingly
Mahesh/Mukti

REVIEW EXERCISE

Including Competency Based Questions

1. You had shifted into a new hostel building of your school in Rohtak. Write a letter to your parents telling them about your life in the new hostel in about 120 words.

Ans. Alberta Hostel,
XYZ School
Rohtak

2nd May, 20XX

Dearest Mom and Dad

I received your letter this morning. I am glad that everyone is doing well and grandma is recovering. I am well here too.

Till now, my experience in the new hostel has been satisfactory. The kitchen is open for all of us but we can only cook under the hostel-in-charge's guidance. Initially, I was a little scared but soon my fear was gone as I found myself around lovely friends. Most of the hostel students are friends with each other.

In fact, the hostel-in-charge is also very friendly. Whenever we want to cook something, she is always there to help us. There is a cook but most of the times, she helps us in making what we want to eat. The hostel also has a big theatre room where we all can watch movies or series for 1 hour daily. This hostel even has a library where all of us sit together and study.

Even though all the students belong to different parts of India and have different cultures, we all live like a family. This atmosphere is very comforting and always reminds me of home. I miss all of you and hope to see you soon in the upcoming vacations.

Your loving daughter
Sharia

2. Imagine that you are Ashok, living in Pune. You have received a letter from a friend who has asked you to describe the picnic you recently enjoyed in the company of your friends. Write a letter in reply in about 120 words.

Ans. 8, Mahatma Gandhi Marg
Pune

10th April, 20XX

My dear Raman

I received your letter on 20th March and was pleased to learn that you are well and are enjoying your holidays. I have written this letter to tell you all about the picnic that I enjoyed in the company of my friends. Last Sunday, we had a picnic on the bank of the river. The day after the summer vacations started, my friends Teeny, Satish and I, along with our parents started off in our car in high spirits with our picnic baskets, fruits and sandwiches.

In about half an hour we reached the destination. We took a boat and rowed down the river. We had no idea how splendid the river looks at this time of the year. We were so engrossed in the beauty surrounding the river that we did not realise that we had approached the bridge.

Teeny gathered some dry sticks and started a fire. Satish made tea while I buttered the cakes. We all drank cups of tea and greedily ate cake, biscuits, pastries and sandwiches. These were followed by bananas and oranges carried by my mother.

Then, we lay down on the grass and played games. In the afternoon, we swam about in the safety zone of the river under our parent's guidance.

At sunset we returned home, having spent a very enjoyable day.

Your friend
Ashok

3. You are Asim/Asmita. Your school organised a visit to the Old age home. When you visited the place, the old people greeted you with smiles. But when you talked to them you realised how sad and lonely they felt. You want to share your experience with your childhood friend Randeep/Samara. Write a letter in about 120 words describing what you saw, how you felt and what you resolved to do. Competency Based

Ans. 30, Ram Vihar Road
New Delhi

13th August, 20XX

Dear Randeep/Samara

It has been a while since I have heard from you. How have you been? I hope this letter finds you in the best of your health. Last week, our school organised a trip to an old age home. My experience there was bittersweet.

Even though the old people have a home, we could see that they were not really happy. They welcomed us with a smile and even talked to us very cheerfully. However, we could all see that they all felt lonely and sad as they missed their families terribly. Just the thought of that angers me. How can you abandon the parents who not only gave birth to you, but also made sure that you would grow up feeling loved and safe? They sacrifice their entire lives for us and in return expect only love.

I was overwhelmed at seeing their happy faces when we gave them gifts. We could see that they want someone to share their feelings with. Hence, when we returned, I along with my friends decided to visit the Old age home whenever we could.

Give my respects to your parents and love to your sister.

Yours affectionately
Asim/Asmita

4. Write a letter to your uncle, describing the damage caused by the unexpected rains to your house. You are Mumtaz/Manmohan, resident of Odisha.

Ans. ABC road
Odisha

28th May, 20XX

Dear Uncle

I received your letter today. We are glad to learn that you and aunt are well. Thank you very much for enquiring about our welfare. It shows how deeply you care for us. You must have heard it on the news channels about the unexpected heavy rains in Odisha last week.

The unexpected downpour continued for 4 days causing damage to many houses of our locality. Our house, as you know, was in a very poor state and thus, in need of repairs which had not been carried out in time. As a result, the heavy rains caused great damage to our house. The roof started leaking as soon as the rain started. The wind was blowing with such force that water started coming inside the house from the windows. The garden that I had grown in the balcony of my room was completely destroyed.

By the time the rain stopped, the whole house was a pool of water. We are now getting our house repaired so that we do not face such a situation in future.

Hoping to meet you soon.

Yours lovingly
Mumtaz/Manmohan

5. Imagine you are Satya living in Chennai. You have received a birthday present from your best friend Roma who has shifted abroad recently. Write a letter in about 120 words thanking your best friend for it.

Ans. 39, Bhawan Road
Chennai

26th January, 20XX

Dear Roma

I hope that this letter finds you in great health and happiness. I received your delightful present this morning. Thank you very much for the lovely present and the best wishes that you have sent. I was thoroughly surprised when I found that you had indeed gifted me the camera that I had been wanting for months.

I don't think anything could give me more pleasure. It is just the model that I wanted and all thanks to you, now I will be able to take some fine pictures with it. And obviously the first one will be dedicated to you, my best friend. I know you will laugh after reading this but you know I would have never gotten this camera had it not been for you. So, once again thanks from the bottom of my heart.

You know, recently I was going through my drawer and found some of our old pictures. It reminded me of the old days when you were here. I miss you and wish that you were with me. I am sending you a whole lot of pictures that will remind you of me.

Your best friend
Satya

6. Imagine that you are Ashok, living in Hyderbad. You have made an appointment with your friend Mohammad Saad to meet him at 6 o'clock on 9th April, but unfortunately you could not meet him.

Write a letter of apology to him, explaining what prevented you in 100-120 words. Competency Based

Ans. 15, Nehru Street
Hyderabad

10th April, 20XX

Dear Saad

I must begin this letter with the most heartfelt apology. I hope you will excuse me for my inability to meet you last evening. I promised to meet you at the Capital Cinema at 6 o'clock and I am afraid you must have thought of me as rude when I failed to turn up at the appointment time. You may think that I am making an excuse but I hope that you understand the circumstances and will be able to set up another appointment. So, this is what happened.

I was just going to start in order to keep my appointment with you, when I received an express telegram from my elder brother informing me that father had met with a serious accident. He wrote to me that if I wished to see him alive, I must reach home by the first train. So, I hurriedly left for the station to catch the 5.30 train. I was so terribly upset by the bad news that I forget to send you a message. Reaching home, I found that though he was seriously hurt, he was out of danger.

Then, with hope in my heart that our friendship isn't ruined, I took the earliest opportunity of writing you this letter apologising for the inconvenience I caused you.

Hoping for forgiveness and a desire to plan to meet soon.

Your friend
Ashok

7. Write a letter to your friend in 120 words, whose house you went to visit, to say how much and for what reasons you enjoyed your stay with their family.

Ans. ABC colony
Nagpur

17th October, 20XX

Dear Aryan

I reached my home yesterday in the afternoon and took the first opportunity to thank you for letting me stay with you. I would also like to thank you for the kindness and the hospitality you and your family showed me. I can never forget the love and care of your parents. It almost felt like home with your family.

I would also like to take this opportunity to apologise to you for breaking the window pane on the last day of my stay. You were sleeping, so your neighbour and I started to play cricket in front of the window. During a match, the ball hit the window pane and smashed it. I am ready to bear the expenses to get the window repaired.

With this, I hope that we meet soon and enjoy some fun time together. I want to invite you to my house in the October vacations. You are welcome to break a window pane in retaliation. I hope that you will come and stay with me for at least a week. Give my respect and love to your family members and tell them that I miss them.

Yours affectionately
Sanjay

8. You have received a letter from your mother. She had written to you about your sister's bad eating habits because of which she is falling ill frequently. Write a letter to your sister in 120 words advising her to eat healthy food and to take care of her health.

Ans. 10, Palace Building
R.A.R, S/Mandi
Delhi

28th June, 20XX

Dear Drishti

How are you? I received a letter from Mom telling me about you eating junk food every day. She also told me that you have been feeling ill lately. I have written this letter to you to make you understand how important it is for us to eat healthy food.

The first thing that you should know is that your health is your real wealth. Without sound health, you won't be able to enjoy all those things that surround you. I am not telling you to stop eating tasty junk food. But you must reduce it. You may not realise that the food that you eat everyday may be the real reason for you constantly falling ill.

If you change your diet and eat healthy food, then you will see for yourself that what I am telling you is true. Eat green leafy vegetables, fruits, pulses, etc. and do not forget to exercise. With some simple habits you can be healthy and active.

I hope you will follow my advice and wish that when I come home I will find a healthy sister.

Your elder brother
Krish

9. You were a part of an organising committee for an inter-school event which was very successful. You and the other committee members were congratulated and praised at the school assembly by the Principal. Write a letter to your grandmother telling her about the event and your feelings at being recognised and praised in front of the school. The word limit is 100-120 words. Competency Based

Ans. 12/24, Karol Bagh
Delhi-6

15th May, 20XX

Dear Grandma

Hope you are doing well. I am sorry that I haven't been able to write to you for the last two months as I was busy organising an inter-school talent fair for my school. I was a part of the organising committee and was responsible for managing the hospitality for the 7 guest schools. There were 16 finalists in all, 14 of which had come from schools all over the state.

The fair was very successful and our committee was praised for our courteous behaviour with the participants. Our Principal addressed the school assembly today and read out a letter of thanks from all the guest schools and you know what they had specially mentioned all our names.

It was a proud moment for me and I was overwhelmed to have received appreciation for being a good person. Thank you for instilling these values in me. Without your pearls of wisdom, I would have never been able to take care of strangers as my own people without losing my cool under pressure.

I hope I can always remain a kind person even when I am as old as you, grandma.

Until next time, love you and miss you!

Yours lovingly
Bhumika

10. You are Ramesh/Raveena living at 131/5, Lawrence Road, Railway Colony, Patna. Write a letter in about 120 words to your father, posted in Baroda, telling him of your plan to attend a National Service Camp for three weeks during the summer vacation.

Ans. 131/5, Lawrence Road
Railway Colony
Patna

19th March, 20XX

Dear Father

Our Board Examinations are over finally. You will be pleased to know that I have done all my papers well and hope to get a distinction. In your last letter, you had desired to know how I plan to pass my summer vacations.

Well, I have decided to take part in a very important and socially useful project. Our school is organising a three-week-long National Service Camp during the summer vacations. If you permit me, I intend to join it. This will provide me with an opportunity to see common people from close quarters.

During the three-week stay, we shall take up the projects of adult literacy, health and hygiene, awareness of diseases and need of cleanliness in the rural parts of our state. We will be going to different small towns and villages to create awareness through various activities.

We propose to follow up on our work by weekend camps and get-togethers in the school. I hope you will approve of my plan and bless me.

Yours affectionately
Raveena

11. Amit from Hyderabad has got admission to a college in Bengaluru. He has to share his room with another boy. When he arrives at the hostel he learns that his roommate has gone home for a few days. Based on his observations of the room, Amit writes a letter to his friend Sumit, about his new roommate. As Amit, write the letter.

Ans. Hill Top College
Bengaluru

9th April, 20XX

Dear Sumit

How are you? I am well here and hope that you would be hale and hearty as well. I have reached Bengaluru safely. I was just settling things up in my room when I thought of writing to you. I am so dead tired. My room was a mess when I entered. I have been dreading this day for so long and here it is. I am very tensed because of my existing roommate Ritesh. He is presently on vacation at his parents' place in Mumbai. The entire room gave an impression of him as a very untidy person. His things are thrown all over the place and the floor is sticky because of spilled coke. There was a wet towel strewn over the only chair in the room. I am clueless about how to survive this chaos. You already know that I have grown up in a very disciplined, neat and tidy environment. I don't think I will be able to befriend him. Hope the future holds good things for us and we become tolerant towards each other.

You take care and do keep in touch. I miss you and all of my friends already.

Amit

12. Write a letter to your school going younger brother or sister who is sleep deprived. Advise him or her to make lifestyle changes to his/her daily schedule in order to get the desired hours of sleep daily.

Ans. B-25, Civil Lines
Bhopal

18th September, 20XX

Dear Rajeshwari

How are you? I am well here and hope that you would be hale and hearty there. Yesterday, I had a long talk with mum. After mother's phone call, I was very troubled as she had told me about your sleep deprivation. What happened to my ever so very health conscious younger sis?

I am aware that you are preparing for your twelfth standard exams this year. As you know, there is a lot of pressure associated with board exams in our country. I know that the pressure must be getting to you too. You come home very late at night and leave very early. Mother tells me that you have not been eating properly as well. If you carry on with such a lifestyle then it is going to be harmful to your health in the long run.

I have some suggestions that you could follow for your own well-being. First of all, don't get worked up about the board exams. They are simply exams and nothing more than that. Second, get organised. Make a schedule and organise the subjects that you need to study and the amount of time you can spend on each of them. Third, you must sleep at least 7 hours a day in order to remain healthy. Finally, eat very well and do not skip a single meal. I know that this is a tough time in every student's life. However, remember what George Herbert said: 'Living well is the best revenge.'

Yours truly
Durgeshwari

ASSESSMENT EXERCISE

1. Your brother has recently recovered from high fever. Write a letter to your brother in 120 words advising him on how to stay healthy during the rainy season. You are Shiv/Shivani.
2. You have come to know that your younger brother is a spendthrift. He is always shopping and does not save any money. Write a letter to him in about 120 words advising him on the importance of saving money. **Competency Based**
3. You are Krishna/Kusha, living in Jaipur. Your father is away from home on a business trip. You have received a letter from him asking you to inform him about the state of affairs at your home in his absence. Write a letter as a reply in 120 words.
4. You recently visited the International Book Fair held at Pragati Maidan, New Delhi. Throughout the fair, you missed your cousin who is a bookworm just like you. So, you decide to write a letter to her sharing your experience in this year's book fair.
5. You are Shaira/Roy. Your friend, Mohit just failed in his half-yearly English examination. Write a letter consoling him in 120 words. Also, include some tips that he/she can use to secure good marks in his/her compartment paper.
6. While you were returning from your tuition, you found that a small shop had caught fire and a few small kids were stuck inside the burning shop. You decided to take action and helped the firefighters to save the kids. Write a letter to your father telling him about this adventurous experience that will make him proud of you.
7. You have recently shifted into a new city. Write a letter in 120 words describing your new city and new house to your cousin.
8. Pratik Sinha is a student of St. Paul School, Chennai. He has just returned to his home from a trekking expedition organised by his school. His uncle paid for the trip, and now Pratik wants to give him a brief account of his trip. Write a letter on behalf of Pratik to his uncle in 120 words.
9. Your school had organised a talent hunt which was judged by your favourite artist of all time. As a part of the organising team, you personally met the artist and was shocked by his/her rudeness. Write a letter to your sister/brother describing the event and how you felt while you met your favourite artist. (120 words)
10. Manmeet was shocked when the Principal informed her that the policy regarding the scholarship has been changed from this year. She has not been informed of the change and had prepared according to what she had known. But with hard work she won it. Write a letter on behalf of Manmeet to her parents telling them about her journey to the victory. **Competency Based**
11. One of your neighbours, Mr. Manish has met with an accident and has been hospitalised for some days. Write a letter to him telling him about how his family reacted to the news. Assure him that he needs not to worry at all and that your family will always help them during such times. You are Rohan Mehta, living in Paschim Vihar, New Delhi.
12. You have just returned from a trip to Kerala. The highlight of the whole trip was the boat ride that you took in the backwaters. Write a letter to your best friend describing the wondrous experience of the boat ride.
13. A year ago you lent your favourite book to your friend who you thought would enjoy it. Unfortunately, your friend has forgotten to return it. The book has sentimental value to you as it has been presented to you by your grandmother. Write a letter to your friend in about 100-120 words reminding him/her about it.
14. You went on a holiday to Mount Abu with your family during the Winter break. Write a letter to your friend, Shweta at Jaipur, sharing with her how you enjoyed your tour. You are Umang, living at A-11, Govind Marg, Delhi. (120 words)

Paragraph Writing

CHAPTER 4

A paragraph is a short composition that revolves around a specific idea or topic. It generally comprises a group of sentences that are organised in a meaningful order and united by its central theme. Writing a paragraph is very easy. You just need to remember that it should have unity, coherence and emphasis.

- **Unity** ensures that the paragraph talks about only the central theme or topic.
- **Coherence** ensures that all of the sentences are related to each other in the paragraph.
- **Emphasis** makes sure that all details are put in the order of importance starting from the most important one.

A paragraph should always include

- **Introduction** It is an introductory line that addresses what the main idea of the paragraph is going to be. It can be a famous quote, a proverb or just a general statement about the topic.
- **Body** The paragraph should contain 8-10 sentences related to the topic in a meaningful order.
- **Conclusion** The last sentence of the paragraph should be the concluding sentence. It should tie the supporting thoughts together.

In the Class IX examination, you would be asked to write a paragraph out of two in about 150 words. You will be provided verbal or visual clues.

Points to be Kept in Mind

- Use simple and easy language to present your ideas.
- Take care of the tenses. Present tense is used when we describe something and past tense is used to talk about an event that has already taken place.
- If a word limit has been mentioned, do not exceed it.
- Remember to read your paragraph to make sure there are no grammatical or punctuation errors in it.

REVIEW EXERCISE

Including Competency Based Questions

1. Write a paragraph on 'The Benefits of Rising Early' in about 150 words. Use the following clues to frame your article.

Benefits of early rising

- Early mornings are so peaceful and quiet.
- Rise early and you actually have time for breakfast.
- Easier to exercise : Exercising right after work is liable to be cancelled because of other things that come up.

Ans. The benefits of early rising have been put into our minds from the time we are very young. As young children, we are taught by our elders that sleeping late and rising late is a bad habit. We all have heard the old proverb 'Early to bed, early to rise, makes a man healthy, wealthy and wise'. Rising early has always been associated with numerous scientifically proven benefits. When we rise early we get those extra hours during which we can work to keep our mind and body fit. This is a time when our minds are most receptive and hence, you may have heard people getting up early to study and to do all kinds of important work. During these early hours there are less distractions and hence, our productivity increases immensely. Rising early enables us to be on time. By beginning our day early, we are able to manage our work properly leading to better time management. One who rises early is able to get the most sound and peaceful sleep. Rising early gives us time to meditate which gives our body an energising and positive start to the day. And this positivity is the key to a stress free life.

2. Write a paragraph on global warming using the following clues. **MCB Theme: Environment**

Definition of global warming – causes of global warming – impact of global warming – 1.15 degree Celsius rise in past decade – can damage ecosystems – result in the disruption of the environment – taking steps to restore vegetations – using clean energy sources **Competency Based**

Ans. Global warming refers to a hike in the average global temperature on Earth. Burning of fossil fuels and the release of toxic fumes into the atmosphere are major causes of global warming. It can have disastrous effects on living organisms. The impacts of global warming are widespread and unspecific. Some areas experience a sudden rise in the temperature while others witness a sudden fall. It has been noted that the average temperature on the Earth has increased by 1.15 degree Celsius in the past decade. This is a reason for worry as it can damage ecosystems and might result in the disruption of the environment. Global warming can be checked if we take concrete steps towards restoring the lost vegetation in our forests. We can also use clean energy sources like wind energy, solar energy and tidal energy to check the rise in global temperature caused by excessive burning of fossil fuels.

3. Write a paragraph on water conservation. You can use the hints given below.

Essential common asset – water for fundamental exercises – water is wasted in drains – industrialisation renders water useless – underlying asset – save water for future generation

Ans. Water is an essential common asset. We need water every day for our body's survival, sustenance and other activities. People likewise need water for regular fundamental exercises like washing, bathing, cooking and so on. While tons of water is utilised daily, very little is reused and most is wasted in drains. Further, taps are left open at homes, leading to wastage of water. Add to this the fact that industries damage to our limited fresh water supply by dumping modern waste into water bodies and you will realise why the world is facing water shortage. At this point, it is essential for us to understand the importance and need for water conservation. Water is an underlying asset and subsequently, we should spare it for our future generations. Rainwater harvesting, for instance, is an excellent way of saving water by collecting rainwater for different households as well as farming activities. People can build tanks and filters to collect rainwater from the rooftop of the house. It will be collected in the tank from the pipe and then, the water will be filtered for future uses. It is high time that we learn from our mistakes and start conserving water.

4. Write a paragraph on the importance of newspaper. You can use the hints given below.

Mirror reflecting conditions of a country - update on the happenings of the nation and world - enhance our knowledge - educational value - inform people - provides the public with a platform to let their opinion be heard - important to a democracy - habit of reading newspaper **Competency Based**

Ans. A newspaper is the mirror which reflects the political, economical and social conditions of a country. It updates us with the happenings of the nation and the world. It enhances our knowledge and have great educational value. It serves the society in multiple ways by informing people about what's happening around them, by making the government programmes and policies public. It is also integral in letting everyone knows what the people/public thinks. If a particular policy is good, people appreciate it and if it is harmful, a cry against it can be raised through newspapers. They are an eye-opener for the government. Thus, they are very important to a democracy and we should inculcate the habit of reading newspapers.

5. Write a paragraph on the visual clue given below.

Ans. Time is like a treasure that we can't hold or see but it is very important in our lives. Every moment that goes by is a chance for something good. What we do with our time shapes how our life goes. Time lost is irretrievable. Therefore, it is crucial for us to utilise our time wisely. Being productive and reaching our goals depend on how well we manage our time. It is the backdrop of our lives where we create our stories of success and dreams. Acknowledging the preciousness of time instills a sense of urgency and purpose, thus, inspiring us to give more importance to our goals and efforts. When Frodo Baggins despaired over the impossible task given to him, the Wizard Gandalf said, "All we have to decide is what to do with the time that is given us."

6. Write a paragraph on the visual clue given below.

Ans. Good manners are not born with us. They are acquired over time. They help a person become a better human being. They make a person a useful member of the society. They are a ladder to success. If a person has good manners, they are liked by all. People praise such people and respect them. Good manners cost nothing but their effects are very valuable. We should demonstrate good manners at home, in school and everywhere else. We should respect our parents, teachers, people older and younger to us alike. We should not argue unnecessarily with anyone and always try to be polite in our endeavours. Thus, if we practice good manners, not only will our lives be happier but they will also bring us honour.

7. Write a paragraph on the verbal clue given below.
Electronic gadget used to process-grouped in three kinds-can serve few capacities an important part of every day life.

Ans. A computer is an electronic gadget used to process, store and show information. The given description is an act of excessive simplification of what a computer is as the gadget has developed to play out a few different capacities. Computers are commonly grouped into three kinds, depending on how they process data. These three kinds of computers are simple, digital and hybrid computers. This characterisation decides the speed and precision of every computer. A computer can serve a few capacities besides the remarkable capacity of storing and preparing information. Some of them are to control machine and hardware, to arrange business and adventure, to sell items and services, and to assist research for scholarly purposes. The computer is now an important part of our everyday lives. The innovation has found its way into all parts of our lives. And we can expect that, the computers will remain valuable in each field.

8. Write a paragraph on nature. You can use the hints given below.

Living and non-living components – nourishes the survival needs of plants, animals and humans – provides essential components – other products – slaughter of trees and destruction of nature – harmful gases and chemicals – reducing deforestation, reusing good and recycling

Ans. Nature includes living and non-living components that together make life on Earth possible. Some forms of nature can be seen through the lush green forests, the vast sky above us, the oceans stretching towards the horizon, the mountains raising their heads in the clouds and so on. Nature nourishes the survival needs of plants, animals and humans alike. It provides the essential components of oxygen, sunlight, soil and water. Several other products are obtained indirectly from nature which include timber, paper, medicinal herbs, fibers, cotton, silk and various kinds of food. To fulfill the demand for these products, human beings have now engaged in the slaughter of trees and the destruction of nature. Different industries also poison nature with harmful gases and chemicals in addition to using excessive natural resources. It is the need of the hour now to reduce deforestation, reuse goods and recycle used elements to form newer ones. People from all parts of the world should come together to lessen the pressure on nature and restore its balance.

9. Write a paragraph on the visual clue given below.

MCB Theme: People

Ans. Sunita Williams, is a veteran of two long-duration space flights and has spent a total of three hundred and twenty two days in space. She holds a record for total cumulative space walk time by a female astronaut which covers fifty hours and forty minutes. She has been selected by NASA for commercial flights to the International Space Station from the US soil. Sunita is a US Navy Captain who received her commission in the Navy in May 1987. Later, she became a helicopter pilot logging more than 3000 flight hours in more than thirty different aircrafts. She now ranks sixth on the all-time US endurance list and second all-time for a female astronaut. Being an Indo-American, Sunita Williams mentioned Kalpana Chawla in a talk saying "I had to continue Kalpana's dream".

10. Write a descriptive paragraph based on the visual clue given below.

MCB Theme: People

Ans. Jawaharlal Nehru was a leader of India's nationalist movement and became India's first Prime Minister after its independence. He was born on 14th November, 1889 in Allahabad, Uttar Pradesh. He was the son of Motilal Nehru, a renowned lawyer and leader of Indian independence movement. He completed his education in England and qualified as a barrister. After returning to India, he joined politics and participated in India's freedom struggle under the guidance of Mahatma Gandhi. In 1947, India became independent after the British withdrew from India. Nehru became the first Prime Minister of India and enjoyed an iconic status in India. He was also widely admired internationally for his idealism and statesmanship. His four pillars of domestic policy were democracy, socialism, unity and secularism. His birthday is celebrated as Children's Day in recognition of his lifelong passion and work on behalf of children and youth. He established many Indian institutions of higher learning, including the All India Institute of Medical Sciences, Indian Institute of Technologies (IITs) and National Institute of Technologies. He died on 27th May, 1964 in New Delhi.

11. Write a paragraph about adventure. You can use the following clues.

MCB Theme: Adventure

The feeling of adventure – reasons for seeking adventure - activities to do for adventure - challenging ourselves - benefits of adventure

Ans. An adventure is something associated with massive adrenaline rush, which is why a variety of emotions are experienced at once upon thinking of it, including thrill, fear, nervousness, excitement and danger. It is a unique and daring experience that people usually undertake during their leisure time as a means to rejuvenate themselves after an exhausting routine. It can be a form of escape from ordinary life. One can seek adventure in many ways such as mountain climbing, river rafting, trekking, skydiving, scuba diving, etc. Even exploring new cities and meeting new people can be considered an adventure. Adventures are proven to be beneficial in many ways including maintaining a positive self-image after completing a challenging task. Besides expanding our horizons by exploring nature and cultures, adventure can help us gain insight into ourselves. We can unveil our hidden strengths in an unfamiliar situation when we test ourselves. It can force us to push our limits. It is an emotional experience that is meant to be catered to our soul to keep it alive. Adventure is the solution to boring chores.

12. Write a paragraph on the adventure sport paragliding. You can use the following clues.

MCB Theme: Adventure

Adventure sport – lightweight, free-flying, foot-launched glider aircraft – pilot sitting in harness – air pressure entering vents in front of the wing – no engine used – cover many hundreds of kilometres – 1-2 hour flight is more common

Ans. Paragliding is an adventure sport comprising a lightweight, free-flying, foot-launched glider aircraft with no rigid primary structure. The pilot sits in a harness suspended below a fabric wing comprising a large number of interconnected cells. Wing shape is maintained by the suspension lines, the pressure of air entering vents in the front of the wing and the aerodynamic forces of the air flowing over the outside. Despite not using an engine, a paragliders' flight can last many hours and can cover many hundreds of kilometres, though flights of one to two hours and covering some tens of kilometres are more the norm. By skillful exploitation of sources of lift, the pilot may gain height, often climbing to altitudes of a few thousand metres. When one takes to the skies in a paraglider, one is embracing the sky in a way that only a few other activities can match. The feeling of freedom and weightlessness is truly liberating. It's a leap of faith that requires trust in oneself, the equipment and the elements.

13. Write a paragraph based on energy conservation. You can use the following clues.

MCB Theme: Environment

Energy is service that the world is using on a daily basis – misbalance between energy available and being spent – secure for the future – harmful effects of Air Conditioners and Refrigerators on the environment – installation of stabilizers

Ans. Energy conservation is a common phenomenon for the world of the growing population. In a real sense, energy is the service that the world is using on a daily basis. The growing population demands more and more energy to be consumed. This can create a misbalance between the energy available for society and the energy which is continuously exhausted. For financial security and nation wide social security, conservation of energy services is necessary. There are various methods and simple steps that we can include in our day-to-day lives to save energy. What are we using today, we have to secure for the future. By keeping this in mind, energy saving can be done on a mass level. Refrigerators and Air Conditioners are said to be the appliances that consume electricity on a large and regular basis.

The gases produced by these coolers are harmful to the environment. Thus, simple habits like the installation of stabilisers for maintaining the voltage can consume less electricity. It is through small steps that we can achieve the goal of saving energy.

14. Write a paragraph based on the visual clue given below.

MCB Theme: Environment

Ans. Deforestation is the permanent destruction of forests in order to make land available for other uses. An estimated 7.3 million hectares of forests are lost each year, according to the United Nations Food and Agriculture Organisation (FAO). The effects are far-reaching and will prove disastrous for humanity in the long run. Deforestation is considered to be one of the contributing factors to global climate change. Cutting trees impacts the global carbon cycle. This not only lessens the amount of carbon stored but also releases carbon dioxide into the air. This is because when trees die, they release the stored carbon dioxide.

Deforestation is the second largest human-caused source of carbon dioxide to the atmosphere, the first being combustion in various forms. Further, 70 per cent of the world's plants and animals live in forests and are losing their habitats to deforestation. It also has negative consequences for local populations and medicinal research which rely on the animals and plants in the forests for hunting and medicine, respectively. There are many other problems like soil erosion, interruption of the water cycle, etc. which occur due to deforestation.

15. Write a paragraph on the mysterious Bermuda Triangle. You can use the clues given below

MCB Theme: Mystery

Also called the Devil's Triangle – located near Miami, Florida, San Juan, Puerto Rico, and the Bahamas in the United States – Vincent Gaddis: first to define its boundary in 1964 – situated in the Atlantic Ocean – no one and nothing returns from there – may be scientific – 5,00,000 square

Ans. The Bermuda Triangle, also called the Devil's Triangle is located near Miami, Florida, San Juan, Puerto Rico and the Bahamas in the United States. The American author Vincent Gaddis was the first to define its boundary in 1964 in an issue of the magazine named Argosy and called the area 'The Deadly Bermuda Triangle'. It is situated in the Atlantic Ocean. It is claimed that whoever goes around this area does not come back, whether it is a plane or a ship. There are many studies which show that there may be a scientific reason behind it but there are people who claim that there are some aliens who take the people as some sort of experiment. This triangle is a mysterious area which covers about 5,00,000 square miles of ocean off the South-Eastern tip of Florida.

16. Write a paragraph on the Pyramid of Giza. You can use the following inputs

MCB Theme: Mystery

Part of a larger complex called the Giza Necropolis – two major pyramids – Great Sphinx and several cemeteries – built as a tomb for pharaoh Khufu – dimensions of the pyramid – three major rooms – limestone covering – no treasure found – how the pyramids were built – shrouded in mystery

Ans. The Great Pyramid of Giza is part of a larger complex called the Giza Necropolis. There are two other major pyramids in the complex including the Pyramid of Khafre and the Pyramid of Menkaure. It also includes the Great Sphinx and several cemeteries. The Great Pyramid was built as a tomb for the pharaoh Khufu. The pyramid once held all the treasures that Khufu would take with him to the afterlife. The pyramid is around 455 feet tall. At its base, each side is approximately 755 feet long. It took 20,000 workers around 20 years to build the Great Pyramid. Inside the Great Pyramid, there are three major rooms: the King's Chamber, the Queen's Chamber and the Grand Gallery. The pyramid was originally covered with flat polished white limestone. Over time, most of the smooth white limestone casing was removed. There was no treasure found inside the pyramid. It was likely looted by grave robbers over a thousand years ago. No one is quite sure how the pyramids were built. There are a lot of different theories as to how the Egyptians were able to lift such large stone blocks all the way up to the top of the pyramids. Till date, the Great Pyramid remains shrouded in mystery.

17. Write a paragraph based on the visual clue given below.

MCB Theme: Children

Ans. The term 'child labour' is best defined as work that deprives children of their childhood, their potential and their dignity, and that is harmful to their physical and mental development. It refers to work that is mentally, physically, socially or morally dangerous and harmful to children. This work interferes with the ability of the children to attend regular school and affects their ability to focus during school or experience a healthy childhood. According to a 2008 study by ILO, among the most important factors driving children to harmful labour is the lack of availability and quality of schooling. Many communities, particularly in rural areas, do not possess adequate school facilities. Even when schools are sometimes available, they are too far away, difficult to reach, unaffordable or the quality of education is so poor that parents wonder if going to school is really worthwhile. The Factories Act of 1948 prohibits the employment of children below the age of 14 years in any factory. The Mines Act of 1952 prohibits the employment of children below 18 years of age in a mine. The Child Labour

(Prohibition and Regulation) Act of 1986 prohibits the employment of children below the age of 14 years in hazardous occupations identified in a list by the law. Yet, child labour is a reality that continues to exist in our society.

18. Write a paragraph on the relevance of school uniforms in a student's life using the picture given below.

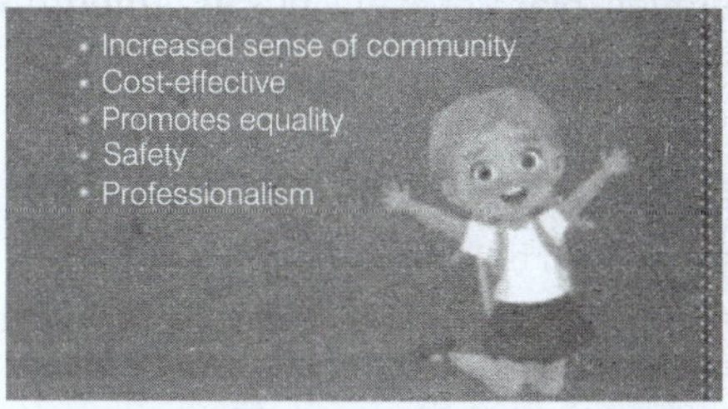

Ans. In today's educational landscape, the debate surrounding school uniforms remains a contentious issue, with differing opinions on their impact on student life and academic performance. Advocates of school uniform policies argue that they offer a multitude of benefits, ranging from promoting equality among students to enhancing discipline and focus within the school environment. One of the most significant advantages of implementing school uniforms is the promotion of equality among students. When students are required to wear uniforms, it levels the playing field, minimising the visible indicators of wealth or social status. This uniformity can help foster a sense of belonging and inclusivity within the student body, reducing peer pressure associated with fashion trends and the fear of being judged based on attire. Moreover, when students wear the same clothing, there is less emphasis on personal appearance, allowing for academic and social interactions to take precedence over superficial judgements. This shift promotes a culture of acceptance and camaraderie, as students can focus on friendships and teamwork rather than competing for attention based on their clothing choices. In addition, school uniforms contribute to a positive educational atmosphere by instilling a sense of pride and identity within the student body. Wearing a school uniform often evokes a sense of belonging and loyalty to the institution. Further, uniforms shape a students' attitudes towards discipline and responsibility. In conclusion, while the debate over school uniforms will likely continue, the benefits they provide in terms of fostering community, improving focus, and instilling a sense of pride cannot be overlooked.

19. Using the hints given below, write a paragraph about the importance of games and sports.

MCB Theme: Sports and Games

Importance of games and sports - Need of games and sports – health benefits – physical and mental advantages - careers

Ans. Games and sports keep one physically and mentally fit. They keep one away from diseases relating to the heart, obesity, mental stress and sleeplessness. They instil in the player a spirit of self-confidence, self-reliance, discipline, justice, fair play and patriotism. Games provide us with recreation and enjoyment. Physical and mental fitness is essential for every person. Students have very busy schedules and they often get tired. To perform best, it is necessary to have a sound mind in a sound body and for that, games should also be played along with studies. Games are good exercises and help to build a strong physique for all boys and girls. They make them mentally alert and physically strong. Students also learn to cope with difficult situations. By displaying their feats before many spectators, people can overcome their nervousness. It gives a necessary break from the everyday monotonous life. There are exciting career opportunities in sports these days. So, it is true that sports and games have advantages since they decrease the stress, teach us skills that we need, satisfy us, and socialise our lives.

20. Write a paragraph based on Badminton you can use the verbal clue given below. **MCB Theme: Sports and Games**

A fantastic fitness sport – a quickest racket sport – played with light weight racket and shuttlecock – Some Indian to Badminton players.

Ans. All ages can benefit from playing badminton which is a fantastic fitness sport. It is an excellent option if one wishes to try out a new racquet sport. It has been referred to as the 'quickest racket sport' in the entire world. An astonishing speed of up to 288 kph can be used by a player to hit the shuttlecock in the opponent's direction. The equipment needed to play badminton is a racquet and a shuttlecock.

This game is great for physical conditioning because it requires a lot of energy. The game is played with a lightweight racquet and a shuttlecock. There are few players necessary for this game. Each team can consist of one or two players. Saina Nehwal, P.V. Sindhu, P. Gopichand, Srikant Kadambi, and P. Kashyap are some of India's top badminton players. These athletes compete for India in international badminton competitions.

ASSESSMENT EXERCISE

1. Write a paragraph based on the International Yoga Day using the verbal clues given below.

   Celebrated on 21st June across the world – UN's promotion of good health, harmony and peace – aims to raise awareness – benefits of practising yoga

2. Write a paragraph on a place you visited recently with your family. You can use the clues given below.

   Name of place – mode of travelling – distance from home – who went – duration/place of stay – places visited – what you liked the most

3. Write a paragraph based on the verbal clues given below.

   Gateway of India – Mumbai – built in 1924 – memory of the arrival of King George V and Queen Mary

4. Write a paragraph on the harmful effects of global warming based on the hints given below.

   Rise in sea level – change in rainfall patterns – increased risks of droughts and floods – threats to biodiversity – heat waves

5. Write a paragraph based on the visual clue given below.

6. Write a paragraph on Mahatma Gandhi using the clues given below.

   Born in Gujarat – discrimination faced in South Africa – movements against the British rule – role in Indian freedom

Section C : Grammar

Tenses

CHAPTER 1

1.1 Definition of Tense

Tense is defined as the form of verb that gives the relation between Time and Action. It gives the time of when the action is done.

There are three phases of time

(i) **Present** (now) (ii) **Past** (passed)

(iii) **Future** (yet to come)

Let's consider the sentences given below

- We go to walk everyday. (Present)
- We went to walk everyday. (Past)
- We will go to walk everyday. (Future)

We can observe that each sentence given above has a different meaning. The reason is that each sentence has a different form of verb. These different forms of verbs are called tenses.

Classification of Tenses

On the basis of the phases of time, there are three tenses

(i) Present Tense (ii) Past Tense (iii) Future Tense

Each tense has four forms. Study the chart given below to understand more about all tenses and their forms.

TENSE

Present	Past	Future
Indefinite	Indefinite	Indefinite
Continuous	Continuous	Continuous
Perfect	Perfect	Perfect
Perfect Continuous	Perfect Continuous	Perfect Continuous

1.2 Present Tense

Present Indefinite Tense

(Also Called Simple Present Tense)

This tense is used in the following ways

(i) It is mainly used to express habit or unchanging situation.

e.g. • Seema gets up every morning at 5 o'clock. (habit)
• I live in India. (unchanging situation).

(ii) To talk about a universal truth.

e.g. • The Earth revolves around the Sun.
• Where there is a will, there is a way.

(iii) To indicate a future event which is part of a plan or arrangement.

e.g. • The college reopens on Tuesday.
• The programme commences next week.

(iv) To introduce quotations with the verb 'says'.

e.g. • Newton says, "Every action has an equal and an opposite reaction."
• Keats says, "A thing of beauty is a joy forever."

(v) Vivid narration, as a substitute for the simple past.

e.g. Jeeva fights bravely but he loses in the end.

(vi) Exclamatory sentences that begin with here or there.

e.g. • Here you go!
• There he goes!

(vii) Time clauses and conditional clauses in place of simple future.

e.g. • If you are not honest, you will not earn respect.
• If you do not work hard, you will fail.

Rules for Affirmative Sentences

- Singular subject + first form of verb + s/es + ...
- I/You/Plural subject + first form of verb + ...

e.g. • My father exercises in the morning.
• We study in PQR institution.

Rules for Negative Sentences

- Singular subject + does not + first form of verb + ...
- I/You/Plural subject + do not + first form of verb + ...

e.g. • Abhishek does not like Economics.
• We do not eat onions.

Rules for Interrogative Sentences

- Do/does + subject + first form of verb + ...?
- Question word + do/does + subject + first form of verb + ...?

e.g. • Do you do theatre?
• Does she dance?
• Why do you sing now?
• Which subject do you not want to study?

Present Continuous (or Progressive) Tense

This tense is used in the following ways

(i) To describe an action in progress.

e.g. • She is going to the Cinema.
• They are playing games.

(ii) An action that is not happening at the time of speaking but is in progress.

e.g. • He is attending medical school.
• She is learning Japanese language.

(iii) An action that has been pre-arranged to take place in the near future.

e.g. • The seminar is taking place tomorrow.
• She is going back home next week.

(iv) Persistent and undesirable habit, especially with adverbs like always, continually, constantly.

e.g. • You are always running around.
• He is constantly talking loud.
• He is continually nagging me.

› Rules for Affirmative Sentences

- Singular subject + is/am + first form of verb + ing +.......
- You/Plural subject + are + first form of verb + ing +.......

e.g. • I am solving a problem.
• We are taking a break.

› Rules for Negative Sentences

- Singular subject + is/am + not + first form of verb + ing +.......
- You/Plural subject + are + not + first form of verb + ing +.......

e.g. • She is not studying now.
• They are not coming today.

› Rules for Interrogative Sentences

- Is/are/am + subject + first form of verb + ing + ...?
- Question word + is/are/am + subject + first form of verb + ing + ... ?

e.g. • Is Akash attending the exhibition?
• Why are you speaking like that?

Exceptions for Continuous Tense

The following verbs are not normally used in continuous forms

- Verbs of perception or senses, e.g. see, hear, smell, notice, recognise, etc.
- Verbs of appearance, e.g. appear, look, seem, etc.
- Verbs of thinking, e.g. think, suppose, believe, agree, consider, forget, know, imagine, mean, etc.
- Verbs of emotion, e.g. want, wise, desire, feel, love, prefer, etc.
- have, own, possess, be (except when used in the passive).

Present Perfect Tense

This tense is used in the following ways

(i) To express an action that has recently been completed.

e.g. I have just completed my assignment.

(ii) To describe an action whose time is not given.

e.g. She has read Illiad.

(iii) To describe past events whose effects still exist.

e.g. She has finished cooking and now she is free.

(iv) To show how a past situation relates to the present.

e.g. He has graduated, so he can teach you now.

› Rules for Affirmative Sentences

- Singular subject + has + third form of verb + ...
- I/You/Plural subject + have + third form of verb + ...

e.g. • She has asked for a tissue paper.
• They have already showered.

› Rules for Negative Sentences

- Singular subject + has + not + third form of verb + ...
- I/You/Plural subject + have + not + third form of verb + ...

e.g. • The bus has not left yet.
• I have not eaten lunch today.

› Rules for Interrogative Sentences

- Has/have + subject + third form of verb +.....?
- Question word + has/have + subject + third form of verb + ... ?

e.g. • Have you done your homework?
• What have they done today?

Present Perfect Continuous Tense

This tense is used to describe an action that began in the past and is still continuing.

e.g. I have been watching the series since afternoon.

› Rules for Affirmative Sentences

- Singular subject + has + been + first form of verb + ing + ... + for/since +......
- I/You/Plural subject + have + been + first form of verb + ing + ... + for/since +......

e.g. • He has been working out since 6 o'clock.
• They have been planning for an hour now.

› Rules for Negative Sentences

- Singular subject + has + not + been + first form of verb + ing + ... + for/since +......
- I/You/Plural subject + have + not + been + first form of verb + ing + ... + for/since +......

e.g. • It hasn't been raining since yesterday.
• They have not been studying for two days.

› Rules for Interrogative Sentences

- has/have + subject + been + first form of verb + ing + ... + since/for +.....?
- Question word + has/have + subject + been + first form of verb + ing + since/for + ...?

e.g. • Has he been playing since noon?
• Why have they been sleeping since morning?

Note it We use Simple Present Tense to describe events that happen in succession, like cricket commentaries, demonstrations of an experiment or asking for and giving instructions. However, the Present Progressive or continuous Tense is used for changing and developing situations e.g. Rates of packaged food are going up.

1.3 Past Tense

Past Indefinite Tense

(Also Called Simple Past Tense)

This tense is used in the following ways

(i) To indicate an action that happened in the past. It is used often in recounts and narratives.

e.g. • She lived in seclusion. (narrative)
• I visited my grandmother last winter. (recount)

(ii) To indicate past habits or repeated events that are now over.

e.g. • In those days, my mother packed me lunch boxes. (repeated events)
• I always studied in the evening. (past habit)

(iii) The habitual past can also be expressed by using 'used to'.

e.g. My grandfather used to read the newspaper daily.

(iv) To indicate another action which happened in the middle of a longer action.

e.g. The light went out while I was washing my clothes.

› Rule for Affirmative Sentences

- Subject + second form of verb +......

e.g. • I played the piano.
• They used to play football in the evening.

› Rule for Negative Sentences

- Subject + did not + first form of verb +......

e.g. • I did not go to school last week.
• They did not ask for compensation.

› Rules for Interrogative Sentences

- Did + subject + first form of verb + ... ?
- Question word + did + subject + first form of verb +........?

e.g. • Did you complete your homework?
• When did she leave for the station?

Past Continuous Tense

This tense is used in the following ways

(i) To indicate an action that was happening at some time in the past. The time of action may or may not be indicated.

e.g. I was working on my painting the whole day.

(ii) Used with *always*, *continually*, etc. for persistent habits in the past.

e.g. • He was always playing video games.
• Reema was continually working.

(iii) The past continuous is also used for an action that was going on during a given period when another action was happening at the same time in the past.

e.g. While Rohan was watering the plants, his sister was taking photos.

› Rules for Affirmative Sentences

- Singular subject + was + first form of verb + ing +.....
- You/Plural subject + were + first form of verb + ing +.....

e.g. • She was writing an article.
• They were asking for directions.

› Rules for Negative Sentences

- Singular subject + was + not + first form of verb + ing +....
- You/Plural subject + were + not + first form of verb + ing +.....

e.g. • She was not eating anyting.
• I was not going to leave today.

› Rules for Interrogative Sentences

- Was/were + subject + first form of verb + ing +......?
- Question word + was/were + subject + first form of verb + ing +.....?

e.g. • Were you making coffee?
• What were you doing last weekend?

Past Perfect Tense

This tense is used in the following ways

(i) To indicate an action that was completed before a definite time or before another action that took place in the past.

e.g. She reached here after the band had finished singing.

(ii) It indicates desires in the past that have not been fulfilled.

e.g. I wish I had visited her before she died.

(iii) It expresses those conditions of the past that were impossible to fulfill.

e.g. If you had met him earlier, things would have been different.

Rule for Affirmative Sentences

- Subject + had + third form of verb + ...

e.g. • She had finished her work.
• They had seen the lion.

Rule for Negative Sentences

- Subject + had + not + third form of verb + ...

e.g. • They had not done their work.
• He had looked after the children.

Rule for Interrogative Sentences

- Had + subject + third form of verb + ... ?
- Question word + had + subject + third form of verb + ... ?

e.g. • Had he seen the itinary?
• What had you done this time?

Past Perfect Continuous Tense

This tense is used in the following way

It indicates an action which began in the past and continued up to a certain point of time in the past.

e.g. He had been teaching there for 2 years when we met him.

Rule for Affirmative Sentences

- Subject + had been + first form of verb +ing + ... + since/for +.....

e.g. • You had been studying non-stop since morning.
• I had been reading a novel for three hours.

Rule for Negative Sentences

- Subject + had + not + been + first form of verb + ing + ... + since/for + ...

e.g. • They had not been working since Monday.
• She had not been asking for money since last month.

Rules for Interrogative Sentences

- Had + subject + been + first form of verb + ing + ... + since/for + ... ?
- Question word + had + subject + been + first form of verb + ing + ... since/for + ... ?

e.g. • Had you not been exercising since morning?
• When had he ever been paying attention in class?

1.4 Future Tense

Future Indefinite Tense

(Also Called Simple Future Tense)

This tense is used in the following ways

(i) To describe an action that will happen in future.

e.g. I shall get the first position.

(ii) Things which we cannot control and are factual.

e.g. The Sun will set at 7 O'clock.

(iii) To indicate an instant decision.

e.g. I shall go to the station right away.

Rules for Affirmative Sentences

- You/He/She/It/They (Second and Third Person Pronouns) + will + first form of verb + ...
- I/We (First Person Pronouns) + shall + first form of verb + ...

e.g. • He will reach tomorrow morning.
• I shall work hard for the coming exam.

Rules for Negative Sentences

- You/He/She/It/They (Second and Third Person Pronouns) + will + not + first form of verb + ...
- I/We (First Person Pronouns) + shall + not + first form of verb + ...

e.g. • We shall not buy the house.
• They will not leave today.

Rules for Interrogative Sentences

- Will/Shall+ subject + first form of verb + ... ?
- Question word + will/shall + subject + first form of verb + ... ?

e.g. • Will you come on time?
• Why shall I help you?

Future Continuous Tense

This tense is used in the following ways

(i) To indicate an action that will occur in the normal course.

e.g. • She will be running the marathon next week.
• I will be coming home tomorrow.

(ii) To indicate an action that will be in progress at a given point of time in the future.

e.g. • At this time tomorrow, we shall be leaving for Varanasi.
• We shall be attending a function at this time tomorrow.

Rules for Affirmative Sentences

- You/He/She/It/They (Second and Third Person Pronouns) + will + be + first form of verb + ing + ...
- I/We (First Person Pronouns) + shall + be + first form of verb + ing + ...

e.g. • Next year, my teacher will be retiring.
• I shall be collecting the assignments in a while.

Rules for Negative Sentences

- You/He/She/It/They (Second and Third Person Pronouns) + will + not + be + first form of verb + ing + ...
- I/We (First Person Pronouns) + shall + not + be + first form of verb + ing + ...

e.g. • They will not be playing for the school.
• I shall not be cooking this morning.

Rules for Interrogative Sentences

- Will/shall + subject + be + first form of verb + ing + ...?
- Question word + will/shall + subject + be + first form of verb + ing +.....?

e.g.
- Shall I be waiting for long?
- What will you be watching tonight?

Future Perfect Tense

This tense is used to describe an action which will be completed at some point of time in the future.

e.g.
- I shall have reached the venue by then.
- They will have left by now.

Rules for Affirmative Sentences

- You/He/She/It/They (Second and Third Person Pronouns) + will + have + third form of verb + ...
- I/We (First Person Pronouns) + shall + have + third form of verb + ...

e.g.
- Your test result will have come by today.
- We shall have made the presentation by evening.

Rules for Negative Sentences

- You/He/She/It/They (Second and Third Person Pronouns) + will + not + have + third form of verb + ...
- I/We (First Person Pronouns) + shall + not + have + third form of verb + ...

e.g.
- I shall not have played this piano before the teacher comes.
- They will not have left the station.

Rules for Interrogative Sentences

- Will/shall + subject + have + third form of verb +......?
- Question word + will/shall + subject + have + third form of verb ......?

e.g.
- Will he not have left before I come back home?
- Why will they have destroyed the evidence?

Future Perfect Continuous Tense

This tense is used in the following way

It describes an action that will be in progress over a period of time that will end in the future.

e.g.
- She will have been playing basketball for an hour at 2'0 clock.
- I will have been working as a writer for two years next month.

Rules for Affirmative Sentences

- You/He/She/It/They (Second and Third Person Pronouns) + will + have + been + first form of verb + ing + ... + since/for + ...
- I/We (First Person Pronouns) + shall + have + been + first form of verb + ing + ... + since/for + ...

e.g.
- By next April, we shall have been preparing for the wedding.
- You will have been working here for a year.

Rules for Negative Sentences

- You/He/She/It/They (Second and Third Person Pronouns) + will + not + have + been + first form of verb + ing + ... + since/for + ...
- I/We (First Person Pronouns) + shall + not + have + been + first form of verb + ing + ... + since/for + ...

e.g.
- Shanti will not have been staying here for long.
- We shall not have been waiting for more than twenty minutes.

Rules for Interrogative Sentences

- Will/shall + subject + have + been + first form of verb + ing + ... + since/for + ... ?
- Question word + will/ shall + subject + have + been + first form of verb + ing + ... + since/for + ... ?

e.g.
- Shall I have been cooking for two hours?
- What will you have been doing since the morning?

REVIEW EXERCISE

1. Fill in the blanks with the correct forms of the words given in brackets.

I *(a)* ……….. (learn) English for seven years now. However, last year I *(b)* ……….. (not work) hard enough for English, that's why my marks *(c)* ……….. (not be) really that good then. As I want to *(d)* ……….. (pass) my English exam successfully next year, I *(e)* ……….. (study) harder this term.

2. Fill in the blanks with the correct forms of the words given in brackets.

During my last summer holidays, my parents *(a)* ……….. (send) me on a language course to London. It *(b)* ……….. (be) great and I *(c)* ……….. (think) I *(d)* ……….. (learn) a lot. Before I *(e)* ……….. (go) to London, I *(f)* ……….. (not enjoy) learning English. But while I *(g)* ……….. (do) the language course, I *(h)* ……….. (meet) lots of young people from all over the world. There, I *(i)* ……….. (notice) how important it *(j)* ……….. (be) to speak foreign languages nowadays. Now I *(k)* ……….. (have) much more fun learning English than I *(l)* ……….. (have) before the course.

3. Fill in the blanks with the correct forms of the words given in brackets.

At the moment, I *(a)* ……….. (revise) English grammar. And I *(b)* ……….. (begin already) to read the texts in my English textbooks again. I *(c)* ……….. (think) I *(d)* ……….. (do) one unit every week. My exam *(e)* ……….. (be) on 15th May, so there *(f)* ……….. (not be) any time to be lost. If I *(g)* ……….. (pass) my exams successfully, I *(h)* ……….. (start) an apprenticeship in September. And after my apprenticeship, maybe I *(i)* ……….. (go) back to London to work there for a while.

4. Fill in the blanks with the correct forms of the words given in the brackets.

The Supreme Court on 10th December ……….. *(a)*………….. (direct) educational institutions to adopt a zero tolerance policy to ragging and ……….. *(b)*………….. (expel) students who are *(c)* ……….. (find) guilty of maltreating freshers. The apex court …………… *(d)* ……….. (say) expulsion of offenders should be the minimum punishment as it ……… *(e)* …….. (be) necessary to end the menace that could lead to extreme torture and harassment, and sometimes even loss of life.

5. Fill in the blanks with the correct forms of the words given in the brackets.

NASA says its robot rover Spirit ……….. *(a)* ………….. (discover) a patch of ground that ……….. *(b)* ………….. (show) evidence of a past environment that would ……….. *(c)* ………….. (has) perfect for microbial life. The deposits were probably ……….. *(d)* ………….. (produce) when hot spring water or steam came into contact with volcanic rocks. On earth, these are the locations that ……….. *(e)* ………….. (tend) to teem with bacteria, said Nasa scientists.

6. Fill in the blanks with the correct forms of the words given in the brackets.

The students ……….. *(a)* ………….. (talk) just as Miss Sarkar ……….. *(b)* ………….. (enter) the classroom. Then, in a loud voice she ……… *(c)* ………, (say) 'Good Morning' and ……….. *(d)* ………….. (glance) quickly around the room. All the children ……….. *(e)* ………….. (watch) her intently to find out what sort of a person she *(f)* ………….. (be). "I suppose you ……….. *(g)* ………….. (want) to know my name," she said. But before she could tell them, someone in the class yelled out, "You are Miss Sarkar."

7. Chilli's friend Della was on holiday in Jamaica. Read her letter to Chilli and complete it with the correct verbs given in the box below.

Dear Chilli

I had a fantastic holiday in Jamaica. It was hot and the sea was blue and lovely. I ***(a)*** .... (travel) by plane from London to Kingston. I really ***(b)*** .... (enjoy) the flight. It was eight hours long but I ***(c)*** .... (not sleep) at all because I ***(d)*** .... (be) so excited. During the flight, I ***(e)*** .... (listen) to music, ***(f)*** .... (watch) a film and ***(g)*** .... (talk) to the girl in the seat next to me.

I ***(h)*** .... (stay) with my aunt and uncle in Kingston. They ***(i)*** .... (invite) me on a trip to Montego Bay. We ***(j)*** .... (stop) at an Orchid Farm. It was brilliant. On my last night there, I ***(k)*** .... (not go) to bed until 3 o'clock in the morning!

See you soon!
Love
Della

8. Fill in the blanks with the correct forms of the words given in brackets.

Last September, Tamsin ***(a)*** .... (go) to Bali. She ***(b)*** .... (go) by plane and ***(c)*** .... (stay) in a big hotel. It ***(d)*** .... (is) very hot, so she ***(e)*** .... (swim) every day. In the evenings she ***(f)*** .... (go) to different restaurants; the food ***(g)*** .... ***(is)*** very good. She ***(h)*** .... (meet) some nice people and every night she ***(i)*** .... (dance) with them at the disco. She ***(j)*** .... (happy) because she ***(k)*** .... (not alone).

9. Fill in the blanks with the correct forms of the words given in brackets.

Ram and Shyam are from Delhi, but they ***(a)*** .... (live) in Madrid. They .... ***(b)*** (work) for Opel, the car factory. Ram and Shyam ***(c)*** .... (like) swimming and cooking. They ***(d)*** .... (not have) a car. They ***(e)*** .... (not like) driving.

10. In the following paragraph, one word has been omitted in each line. In your answer sheets, remember to unite the missing word along with the word that comes before and after it, as shown below.

	Before	Omission	After
(a) There a case of a couple	....	....	....
(b) who were through a thick forest for a pilgrimage to a shrine.	....	....	....
(c) Suddenly, the husband a precious stone on the path.	....	....	....
(d) It shining brilliantly as the sun's rays fell upon it.	....	....	....
(e) He hastily some sand over it with so that his wife was not tempted.	....	....	....

11. In the following paragraph, one word has been omitted in each line. In your answer sheets, remember to unite the missing word along with the word that comes before and after it, as shown below.

	Before	Omission	After
(a) The animals said, "He cruel, greedy, immoral, insatiable	....	....	....
(b) and unashamed. He a bad example to the animal world"	....	....	....
(c) The tiger said, "We not know from where we will get our next meal.	....	....	....
(d) We no fixed a place to rest. We have nothing	....	....	....
(e) to round ourselves except our skin"	....	....	....

12. In the following paragraph, one word has been omitted in each line. In your answer sheets, remember to unite the missing word along with the word that comes before and after it, as shown below.

One day, Krishna approached the guru and said, "Oh wise	Before	Omission	After
(a) one! We often your eyes filled with tears.	....	....	....
(b) There must be a strong reason for this. Please us.	....	....	....
(c) No act or service can be so holy as joy in our guru's	....	....	....
(d) heart. The guru said, "I reminded of the son whom I have lost.	....	....	....
(e) Krishna at his feet, saying, "Tell us what happened to him and where he is."	....	....	....

13. In the following paragraph, one word has been omitted in each line. In your answer sheets, remember to unite the missing word along with the word that comes before and after it, as shown below.

There was a great sage called Gautama in ancient India.	Before	Omission	After
(a) He a number of disciples. One day, he called all of them	....	....	....
(b) and said, "I worried about our cattle in our hermitage.	....	....	....
(c) I am unable to the suffering of these creatures. These	....	....	....
(d) cows have to be to a distant place where	....	....	....
(e) there sufficient pasture and plenty of water.	....	....	....

14. In the following paragraph, one word has been omitted in each line. In your answer sheets, remember to unite the missing word along with the word that comes before and after it, as shown below.

Rukmini was the daughter of the	Before	Omission	After
(a) King of Vidharba. She five brothers.	....	....	....
(b) She determined to marry none other than Lord Krishna. One would expect that	....	....	....
(c) her five brothers would be advantageous to her when it came to celebrating her			
(d) marriage. But though she herself had such an excellent suitor, her brothers were bent on presenting her marriage to Krishna.	....	....	....

15. The following passage has not been edited. There is an error in each line against which a blank has been given. Write the error and correction in your answer sheet against the correct blank number. Remember to underline the word/phrase that you have supplied.

	Error	Correction
(a) Wrote effective letters is an art that everyone	....	....
(b) mastered with practice. Nowadays although telephone, fax and	....	....
(c) e-mail replacing personal (informal) letters, formal letters	....	....
(d) will still in vogue. Commerce, trade, official correspondence, public representation, complaints, transactions and communication	....	....
(e) with people is still conducting through letters. Therefore, one	....	....
(f) must cultivating the art and skill of letter writing. Different kinds	....	....
(g) of letters following different conventions. Every letter	....	....
(h) was wrote according to a plan which	....	....
(i) are also calling the layout of the letter. In this, the sender's	....	....
(j) address writing at the top left hand corner.	....	....

ANSWERS

1. (a) have been learning (b) did not work
(c) were not (d) pass
(e) shall study

2. (a) sent (b) was
(c) think (d) have learned
(e) went (f) had not enjoyed
(g) was doing (h) met
(i) noticed (j) was
(k) have (l) had

3. (a) am revising (b) have already begun
(c) think (d) will do
(e) is (f) won't be
(g) pass (h) will start
(i) will go

4. (a) directed (b) expel
(c) found (d) said
(e) was

5. (a) discovered (b) shows
(c) have been (d) produced
(e) tend

6. (a) were talking (b) entered
(c) said (d) glanced
(e) were watching (f) was
(g) want

7. (a) travelled (b) enjoyed
(c) didn't sleep (d) was
(e) listened (f) watched
(g) talked (h) stayed
(i) invited (j) stopped
(k) didn't go

8. (a) went (b) went
(c) stayed (d) was
(e) swam (f) went
(g) was (h) met
(i) danced (j) was happy
(k) was not alone

9. (a) live (b) work
(c) like (d) don't have
(e) don't like

10.

	Before	Omission	After
(a)	There	Was/is	A
(b)	Were	Passing	Through
(c)	Husband	Saw	On
(d)	It	Was	Shining
(e)	Hastily	Threw	Some

11.

	Before	Omission	After
(a)	He	Is	Cruel
(b)	He	Sets	A
(c)	We	Do	Not
(d)	We	Have	No
(e)	To	Wrap	Round

12.

	Before	Omission	After
(a)	Often	Find	Your
(b)	Please	Tell	Us
(c)	As	Restoring	Joy
(d)	I	Am	Reminded
(e)	Krishna	Fell	At

13.

	Before	Omission	After
(a)	He	Had	A
(b)	I	Am	Worried
(c)	To	See	The
(d)	Be	Sent	To
(e)	There	Is	Sufficient

14.

	Before	Omission	After
(a)	She	had	five
(b)	She	was	determined
(c)	her	having	five
(d)	had	found	such

15.

	Error	Correction
(a)	Wrote	Writing
(b)	mastered	can master
(c)	replacing	have replaced
(d)	will	are
(e)	is still conducting	are still conducted
(f)	cultivating	cultivate
(g)	following	follow
(h)	was wrote	is written
(i)	are also calling	is also called
(j)	writing	is written

Modals

CHAPTER 2

Modal Auxiliary Verbs or Modals are verbs that are used to express the mood or attitude of the speaker. They do not appear alone in the sentence and always have a main verb with them. Further, they are non-finite verbs meaning they do not change forms in any case.

For example

- You should go for a morning jog every day.
- They must attend tomorrow's party.
- May I use your phone please?
- You can park the car in front of the pole.

There are primarily 9 Modals- Can, Could, Shall, Should, Will, Would, May, Might and Must

2.1 Functions of Modals

Will

(i) To show promise, willingness and determination with the first person (I, we)

e.g.
- I **will** buy you a mobile phone. (promise)
- We **will** accompany you to the seminar. (willingness)
- We **will** bring a change to the society. (determination)

(ii) To express request, insistence, assumption, characteristic or habit

e.g.
- **Will** you please open the window? (request)
- He **will** be taking his music class now. (assumption)
- I **will** go shopping with you. (insistence)
- Animals **will** hibernate during winter. (characteristic or habit)

- **Negative Form of will** : Will not/Won't

  e.g. I **will not** waste my time.

Would (Past Form of 'Will')

(i) To express past habit

e.g. I **would** drink milk every day.

(ii) For request

e.g. **Would** you please lend me your car?

(iii) To express wish

e.g. I wish you **would** be happy.

(iv) To express an imaginary condition

e.g. I **would** have a big car if I earned more.

- **Negative Form of Would** : Would not/Wouldn't

  e.g. She **would not** eat anything after 8 o'clock at night.

Shall

(i) To ask for suggestion or request with the first person (I, We) in the interrogative

e.g.
- **Shall** I have a glass of water? (request)
- **Shall** we write a book? (suggestion)

(ii) With the second and third person to indicate threat, warning, command, promise and advice.

e.g.
- If you neglect your duties, you **shall** be punished. (threat/warning)
- You **shall** leave right away. (command)
- She **shall** get a new laptop. (promise)
- You **shall** only take liquid food for some days. (advice)

- **Negative Form of Shall** : Shall not/Shan't

  e.g. He **shall not** exercise today.

Should (Past Form of 'Shall')

(i) To express duty or obligation

e.g.
- You **should** study well. (duty)
- We **should** protect our loved ones. (obligation)

(ii) To express opinion

e.g. They **should** be feeling better now.

(iii) To give or take advice or suggestion

e.g.
- We **should** leave early. (suggestion)
- You **should** eat on time. (Advice)

(iv) After 'lest' when someone expresses fear, possibility or warning.

e.g. Eat on time lest you **should** fall sick.

- **Negative Form of Should** : Should not/Shouldn't

  e.g. You **shouldn't** talk loudly here.

Can

(i) To express an ability, capability, capacity or power

e.g.
- She **can** run 10 kms in a day. (ability)
- He **can** pass the examination. (capacity)
- **Can** you understand Sanskrit? (capability)
- She **can** give me a promotion. (power)

(ii) To show possibility

e.g.
- He **can** slip down the stairs.
- My father **can** visit here this year.

(iii) To take or give permission

e.g. • **Can** I use your pen?
• You **can** use my pen.

• **Negative Form of Can** : Cannot/Can't

e.g. I **cannot** run faster than this.

Could (Past Form of 'Can')

(i) To express ability/talent in the past

e.g. I **could** type really fast.

(ii) To express polite request

e.g. **Could** you please move aside?

• **Negative Form of Could** Could not/Couldn't

e.g. I **couldn't** reach there on time.

May

(i) To show possibility or probability

e.g. • She **may** come tonight. (possibility)
• It **may** rain tomorrow. (probability)

(ii) To give or take permission

e.g. • **May** I take this plate?
• Yes, you **may** take it.

(iii) To wish or pray

e.g. • **May** you become healthy! (wish)
• **May** God bless us abundantly! (pray)

(iv) To show a purpose

e.g. My friend is working hard, so that he **may** achieve his wishes.

• **Negative Form of May** : May not/Mayn't

e.g. It **may not** be his fault.

Might (Past Form of 'May')

(i) To express less possibility

e.g. The programme **might** start late.

(ii) For permission

e.g. **Might** I turn on the speaker?

(iii) To express a guess

e.g. That **might** be the cause of the fire.

• **Negative Form of Might** : Might not/Mightn't

e.g. She **might not** reach today.

Note It 'May' and 'Might' can be used interchangeably to express possibility. However, we usually use 'Might' when something is less likely and 'May' when it is more likely.

Must

(i) To express necessity or obligation

e.g. • You **must** finish this project this week. (necessity)
• We **must** serve our nation. (obligation)

(ii) To indicate assumption or conclusion

e.g. • She **must** be here for the dress. (assumption)
• Mr Gupta **must** be a good speaker. (conclusion)

(iii) In case of prohibition

e.g. You **must** not cheat during examinations.

• **Negative Form of Must** : Must not/Mustn't

e.g. You **must not** get up late.

2.2 Semi Modals

Need, used to, ought to and dare are considered semi-modals because they can be used either as modal auxiliaries or as main verbs.

Need/Need to

As a modal auxiliary verb in negative terms, it expresses the speaker's authority or advice and is used for the present and the future.

e.g. You **needn't** type this letter.

(i) The interrogative is formed by inversion.

e.g. **Need** I go now?

(ii) Its past is needed to in the affirmative sentence, need not have in the negative and need have in the interrogative.

e.g. • **Need** I have asked for her advice? (Interrogative in the past)
• I **needed** to study hard. (Affirmative in the past)
• You **needn't** have eaten spicy food. (Negative in the past)
• You **need to** go to for swimming class–it is helpful. (Affirmative in the future)

Dare

As a modal auxiliary, dare refers to being bold and courageous. The negative is formed by dare not and the interrogative by inversion.

e.g. • **Dare** we ask him?
• I **dare** not skip classes.

Used to

As a modal auxiliary, it presents a discontinued habit or a past situation which is no more applicable in the present.

e.g. He **used to** get up early in the morning.

Ought to

(i) To express moral obligation or duty

e.g. • You **ought to** respect your teachers. (moral obligation)
• We **ought to** help the needy. (duty)

(ii) To give advice

e.g. You **ought to** work hard to achieve success.

• **Negative Form of Ought to** Ought not to/Oughtn't to

e.g. You **ought not to** treat animals badly.

REVIEW EXERCISE

1. Complete the passage by filling the blanks with appropriate modals.
Mr. Kapoor *(a)* .... to pay Rajender back; otherwise, Rajender has said that he *(b)* .... inform the police. Everyone feels that Mr. Kapoor *(c)* .... return the money. Rather, he *(d)* .... not have taken the money in the first place, especially because he is from a well-to-do family.

2. Complete the passage by filling the blanks with appropriate modals.
I was delighted to know that you are building a new house. As a friend, I *(a)* .... like to offer a word of advice that *(b)* .... largely solve your water problems in future years. You *(c)* .... build in a water harvesting system in your house. This *(d)* .... be done by digging a percolation tank near your house. Drains from the roof *(e)* .... carry the rainwater to the tank. This *(f)* .... help to recharge groundwater.

3. Complete the passage by filling the blanks with appropriate modals.
If we sit in an incorrect posture, we *(a)* .... strain our back. As far as possible, this *(b)* .... be avoided. If the posture becomes a part of habit, a low back pain invariably develops. It *(c)* .... be cured if we become conscious of our posture. We can also take time to perform a few exercises. If the exercises are done regularly, the back ache *(d)* .... certainly be cured. It *(e)* .... also improve the blood circulation within the spine.

4. Complete the passage by filling in the blanks with appropriate modals.
God is great and we *(a)* .... be grateful to him. We *(b)* .... do our duty and leave the reward in the hands of God. Ultimately, God *(c)* .... help us. We *(d)* .... leave everything to God.

5. Complete the passage by filling in the blanks with appropriate modals.
If you *(a)* .... some assistance organising your desk, your cupboard and your room, Tidy Teens *(b)* .... help. This student-run group raises money for charity by cleaning up. "We didn't realise it when we started, but we *(c)* .... thought of a better way to raise money", says 17-years-old Brian Mason, who helped establish the group. We *(d)* .... support such groups.

6. Complete the passage by filling in the blanks with appropriate modals.
Anubha *(a)* .... thought she was dreaming when she heard that she'd won the National Secondary School Essay Contest. "I didn't believe it", she explains. "I just laughed at first, which I probably *(b)* .... done." The prize, a cheque for ₹ 10000 will be awarded to Anubha at a ceremony in March. "I *(c)* .... guessed that there would be a price to pay for the award and there is. I *(d)* .... write a speech to give at the ceremony", Anubha says. "I'm pretty nervous but I hope I *(e)* .... able to do a good job."

7. In the following paragraph, one word has been omitted in each line. In your answer sheets, remember to unite the missing word along with the word that comes before and after it, as shown below.

Let's go shopping. I have to buy many things.	**Before**	**Omission**	**After**
(a) I believe I get them all in this shop. You	....	....	....
(b) see, I buy a present for my friend. Gloves, I think would be	....	....	....
(c) a great idea. I think they be on this floor.	....	....	....
(d) I see just the kind we want.	....	....	....
(e) You try these on.	....	....	....

8. In the following paragraph, one word has been omitted in each line. In your answer sheets, remember to unite the missing word along with the word that comes before and after it, as shown below.

	Before	**Omission**	**After**
(a) People not ask a writer why he writes his	....	....	....
(b) biography. They know that every	....	....	....

(c) life be interesting if properly presented.	…………	…………	…………
(d) Moreover, we learn many things if	…………	…………	…………
(e) we want to, from a great life. It not	…………	…………	…………
(f) necessarily be the life of a great leader that inspires us.	…………	…………	…………

9. In the following paragraph, one word has been omitted in each line. In your answer sheets, remember to unite the missing word along with the word that comes before and after it, as shown below.

	Before	Omission	After
(a) She thought she do something	…………	…………	…………
(b) for the lake. It cost Rs. 42 crore	…………	…………	…………
(c) to clean the lake. "Still", I thought, "I do	…………	…………	…………
(d) something. I reach out to the people.	…………	…………	…………
(e) I decided that I talk to the people.	…………	…………	…………

10. There is an error in each line. Write the incorrect word and the correction in the answer sheet as given below.

	Incorrect	Correct
(a) Plastic **are** not be used because	…………	…………
(b) they **should** cause much pollution.	…………	…………
(c) They **need** never disintegrate with	…………	…………
(d) time. They **should** block the sewerage.	…………	…………
(e) Even if buried they **can** never be destroyed.	…………	…………

ANSWERS

1. (a) ought to (b) will
(c) should (d) should

2. (a) would (b) will
(c) should (d) can
(e) will (f) will

3. (a) might (b) should
(c) can (d) will
(e) will

4. (a) should (b) must
(c) will (d) should

5. (a) need (b) might
(c) could not have (d) must/should

6. (a) must have (b) should not have
(c) should have (d) have to
(e) would be

7.

	Before	Omission	After
(a)	I	Can	Get
(b)	I	Have to	Buy
(c)	They	Might	Be
(d)	I	Can	See
(e)	You	Should	Try

8.

	Before	Omission	After
(a)	People	need	not
(b)	They	should	know
(c)	life	can	be
(d)	we	may	learn
(e)	It	need	not
(f)	that	can	inspire

9.

	Before	Omission	After
(a)	She	Could	Do
(b)	It	Would	Cost
(c)	I	Must	Do
(d)	I	Could	Reach
(e)	I	Would	Talk

10.

	Incorrect	Correct
(a)	are	should
(b)	should	can
(c)	need	might
(d)	should	could
(e)	can	might

CHAPTER 3

Determiners

Determiners are the words that modify the meanings of nouns. They function like adjectives and are also called 'fixing words'.

3.1 Classification of Determiners

Determiners can be classified into

1. **Articles** a, an, the.
2. **Demonstrative Adjectives** this, that, these, those.
3. **Quantifiers** A quantifier is a word or phrase which is used before a noun to indicate the amount or quantity.

   Types of quantifiers are as follows

   (i) **Definite** one, two, hundred, ..., first, second, both, etc.

   (ii) **Indefinite** some, many, much, enough, few, a few, the few, all, little, a little, the little, several, most, etc.

   (iii) **Distributive** each, every, either, neither.

   (iv) **Difference** another, other.

   (v) **Comparative** more, less, fewer.
4. **Possessives** my, your, his, her, its, our, their, mine, hers, yours, ours, theirs, etc.

Articles – A, An, The

An article is used before a noun. It is used to point out the noun that is being referred to in a sentence. It also tells us whether it is referring to a noun in general or to a specific noun.

e.g.
- I'll write a letter today.
- Can you accompany to **an** exhibition?
- I don't know where **the** station is.

Types of Articles

There are only three articles- A, An and The. These three articles can be categorised into two types- Definite and Indefinite articles.

Indefinite Articles

The words 'A' and 'An' are Indefinite articles. They do not refer to any specific or unique noun. They make the noun general and are used only with singular nouns.

e.g.
- She needs to buy **a** car.
- I want to eat **an** apple.

Use of Article 'A'

The article 'a' is used before singular countable noun that start with a consonant sound.

e.g.
- She should have got a dog by now.
- I am a woman.

In some cases, the article a is used before words that start with a vowel letter. This is so because the words begin with a consonant sound.

e.g.
- He is a **European**. (European starts with the sound of 'y')
- This is **a one-time** chance. (One- time starts with the sound of 'w')
- She doesn't have **a unicorn.** (Unicorn starts with the sound of 'y')
- The employees have decided to form **a union**. (Union starts with the sound of 'y')

Uses of Article 'An'

The article 'an' is used before singular countable noun that start with a vowel sound.

e.g.
- I want to have **an** omelette for breakfast.
- What **an** excellent performance!

In some cases, the article 'An' is used before words that start with a consonant letter. This is so because the consonant letter is silent and the word starts with a vowel sound.

e.g.
- He is **an heir** to the throne. (Heiress starts with the sound of 'e')
- Mr. Kumar is **an honest** man. (Honest starts with the sound of 'o')
- He has **an MA degree** in English honours. (MA starts with the sound of 'a')

In these sentences, the sound of 'h' and 'm' are silent. The words start with the sound of 'e', 'o' and 'a'.

Definite Article (The)

The word 'The' is the only Definite article. It is used to refer to particular nouns and is used with both countable and uncountable nouns.

Uncountable nouns do not have plural forms, e.g. we cannot say 'soils', we will say 'the soil'.

e.g.
- Doctor said that I should take **the** medicine on time.
- I have **the** novel written by Khaled Housseini.

Use of Definite Article 'The'

'The' is used

I. While talking about a particular person or thing or one already referred to (that is, when it is clear from the context which one we mean).

e.g. **The** person you are asking for is not here today.

II. When a singular noun represents the whole class.

e.g. **The** pigeon is a domestic bird.

III. Before some proper names that denote physical features.

(i) Oceans and Seas e.g. **the** Pacific, **the** Greenland Sea

(ii) Rivers e.g. **the** Ganges, **the** Nile

(iii) Canals e.g. **the** Panama Canal

(iv) Deserts e.g. **the** Thar, **the** Sahara

(v) Group of islands e.g. **the** West Indies, **the** Netherlands

(vi) Mountain ranges e.g. **the** Himalayas, **the** Satpura

(vii) A few names of countries, which include words like states, Republic or Kingdom e.g. **The** People's Republic of China, **the** United Kingdom, **the** USA, **the** Republic of Korea, **the** Hague, etc.

IV. Before the names of religious, mythological books.

e.g. **The** Vedas, **the** Puranas, **the** Mahabharata (but we say Homer's Iliad, Valmiki's Ramayana).

V. Before the names of things which are unique or one of their kind.

e.g. **the** Sun, **the** Moon, **the** Pacific Ocean

VI. Before a proper noun, when it is qualified by an adjective or a defining adjectival clause.

e.g.
- **The** King of Rome, Ashoka **the** Great
- **The** Mr. Singh that you met last time is my maternal uncle.

VII. With superlative degrees.

e.g.
- This is **the** best dessert I have ever eaten.

VIII. With ordinals.

e.g.
- He was **the** first man to build the telescope.

IX. Before musical instruments.

e.g.
- He can play **the** cello really well.

X. Before an adjective when the noun is understood.

e.g.
- **The** needy are to be helped.
- Here the word 'people' is understood.

XI. As an adverb with comparatives.

e.g. **The** more wealth one has, **the** greedier one becomes.

Omission of Article 'The'

- Before material, abstract and proper nouns used in a general sense.

  e.g.
  - This table is made of wood.
  - Freedom is every man's right.
  - Goa is a famous tourist spot.
- Before plural countable nouns used in a general sense.

  e.g. My teeth are aching.
- Before names of people

  e.g. Narendra, Mark
- Before names of continents, countries, cities, etc.

  e.g. Asia, India, Shillong
- Before names of individual mountains.

  e.g. Mount K2.
- Before names of meals used in a general sense.

  e.g. Breakfast is all set.
- Before languages and words like school, college, university, church, hospital.

  e.g.
  - I can speak Assamese well.
  - My uncle is a priest in church.
- Before names of relations, like father, mother, etc.

  e.g. Mother is feeling unwell.
- In certain phrases consisting of preposition followed by its object.

  e.g. At home, in hand, by night, in case, on foot, by train, on demand, etc.

3.2 Demonstrative Adjectives

(This, That, These, Those)

I. **This** (in case of plural these) It refers to person(s) or thing(s) near the speaker.

e.g. • This flower is very beautiful.
• These shoes are quite expensive.

II. **That** (in case of plural those) It refers to person(s) or thing(s) far from the speaker.

e.g. • Bring **that** file here.
• **Those** people are foreigners.

3.3 Quantifiers

Quantifiers are words or phrases that are used before nouns to indicate their amount or quantity. Quantifiers can be used in affirmative sentences, questions, requests or commands with both countable and uncountable nouns.

e.g. • I haven't got much money.
• She has a few books with her.

Some quantifiers can go only with countable nouns (e.g. friends, people, cups), some can go only with uncountable nouns (e.g. sugar, tea, money, advice), while some can be used with both countable and uncountable nouns.

Examples of quantifiers are given below

Only with Uncountable Nouns	With both Countable and Uncountable Nouns	Only with Countable Nouns
a little	no, none, not any	a few
a bit of	some, all	a number of
—	any	several
a great deal of	a lot of, lots of	a great number of
a large amount of	plenty of	a large number of

Usage of quantifiers are as follows

I. **Use of few/a few/the few and little/a little/the little**

(a) **Few/a few/The few.**

Few emphasises the lack of something.

e.g. She has **few** chances left for the final round.

A few emphasises that something still remains.

e.g. I have got a **few** days left to finish this work.

The few signifies not many but all there is.

e.g. He has given away the few rupees that he had.

(b) **Little/a little/the little**

Little emphasises the lack of something.

e.g. We have little rice left for dinner.

A little emphasises that something still remains.

e.g. There's a little milk in the fridge.

The little signifies not much, but all there is

e.g. She gave away the little sugar that she had to her neighbour.

Note It Few, a few, and little, a little and the little have similar usage. However, few, a few and the few are used with countable nouns. While little, a little and the little are used with uncountable nouns.

II. **Use of much and many**

(a) We use much with singular uncountable nouns and many with plural countable nouns.

e.g. • She hasn't got **much** time left till the exams begin.
• I have **many** novels on my bookshelf.

III. **Use of more, less and fewer** (comparative determiners)

(a) We use more or less before singular uncountable nouns by adding than after it, or for an additional or lesser quantity of something.

e.g. • I want **more** sugar in my tea.
• She does **less** work than her sister.

(b) We use **fewer** before plural countable nouns to refer to a group of things smaller than another.

e.g. We have **fewer** books left to sell than last week.

IV. **Use of each and every** (distributive determiners)

We use each when the number in the group is limited or definite, but every is used when the number is indefinite or unknown. Both of these are followed by singular countable nouns and singular verbs.

e.g. • **Each** person was given a certificate of participation.
• **Every** person has their own potential.

V. **Use of either and neither**

(a) We use either to refer to two things, people, situations, etc. It may mean one or the other of two or each of the two.

e.g. I want to have **either** rice or pasta.

(b) We use neither with only singular countable nouns and a singular verb. Neither is the negative of either.

e.g. **Neither** of the children learns the lesson.

VI. **Use of most, several and all**

(a) We usually use most with plural uncountable nouns.

e.g. **Most** of the employees are busy today.

(b) We usually use several with plural nouns, but it refers to a number which is not very large. (i.e. less than **most**)

e.g. I have asked **several** people to write feedbacks on our new product.

(c) All requires a plural verb when used with a countable noun, but requires a singular verb with an uncountable noun.

e.g. • **All** of them have already left
• **All** that glitters is not gold.

VII. **Use of another and other**

We use another only with singular countable nouns, whereas other can be used with singular countable, plural countable or uncountable nouns.

e.g. • Can you give me **another** pen?
• I have **other** options if this one doesn't work out.

3.4 Possessives

(My, Your, His, Her, Its, Our and Their)

Possessive determiners or possessive adjectives tell us who owns something. We use a possessive determiner before a noun to show who owns the noun we are talking about. They come in front of any other adjectives.

e.g. • She is my niece. • That is your house.

Subject	Possessive Determiner	Used with Type of Noun
I	my	first person singular
We	our	first person plural
You	your	second person singular/plural
They	their	third person plural
He	his	third person singular masculine
She	her	third person singular feminine
It	its	third person singular neuter

Determiners and Kinds of Nouns with which they are Used

- **A, an, each, everyone, another** and **either** are used with singular countable nouns.
- **This** and **that** are used with uncountable nouns/singular countable nouns.
- **These** and **those** are used with uncountable nouns/plural countable nouns.
- **A little, a lot of, a great deal of, much** are used with uncountable nouns.
- **More, most, a lot of, enough, adequate, some** are used with uncountable nouns/plural countable nouns.
- **A few, several, many, both** are used with plural nouns.
- **The, some, any, my, her, your, our, their, its, which, whose, what** are used with any type of noun.

REVIEW EXERCISE

1. Fill in the blanks with appropriate determiners.

A cup of tea may seem like ....*(a)*........... ordinary thing to ....*(b)*........... of us in India. However, drinking tea is ....*(c)*........... ritual which is taken very seriously in ....*(d)*........... Japanese homes.

2. Fill in the blanks with appropriate determiners.

It was ....*(a)*........... grand occasion for ....*(b)*........... children. ....*(c)*........... of them had won prizes and ....*(d)*........... parents felt proud. ....*(e)*........... of them introduced their parents to their teachers.

3. Fill in the blanks with appropriate determiners.

Gravitation is *(a)* .... force that holds us all down to *(b)* .... surface of the Earth. Anything thrown *(c)* .... upwards falls back to the Earth. It is not only the Earth that has the pull of gravity, but also everything else in *(d)* .... universe. Everything in this universe attracts *(e)* .... other body to *(f)* .... itself.

4. Fill in the Blanks with appropriate determiners.

Mark Twain was *(a)* .... pen name of Samuel Langhorne Clemens, who was one of *(b)* .... greatest fiction writers of America. He grew up in *(c)* .... small town on the banks of the Mississippi River. As *(d)* .... small boy, he moved to Hannibal, on the banks of this river *(e)* .... he experienced *(f)* .... excitement of travelling on a river.

5. Fill in the Blanks with appropriate determiners.

Lecture as a method of teaching is as old as civilisation. It is *(a)* .... commonly practiced and very widely used. In *(b)* .... countries, *(c)* .... traditional and almost the only technique employed was *(d)* .... formal lecture. The effective use of lecture requires skilful preparation, *(e)* .... is incomplete until followed by *(f)* .... questions and answers.

6. Fill in the blanks with appropriate determiners.

Once, there was a very rich man. He was neither handsome nor clever but he worked hard and saved .... *(a)* .... of money. There was a beautiful lady who lived just two doors away from his house. She was a widow with few children. .... *(b)* .... morning, the rich man would steal a few glances at the widow when she came out to do her chores in the garden. One evening, the man decided to pay her a visit. He brought with him .... *(c)* .... presents, one for .... *(d)* .... child. .... *(e)* ....the children liked him and so every time he visited her, he brought presents for the children. This went on for several months. Just when the man thought that he could propose to the widow, something happened. A handsome strange man came to the town. He was not as rich as the man. But somehow, ... *(f)* .... eligible lady of the town fell in love with him.

7. Fill in the blanks with appropriate determiners.

Traditionally, Ilkal saris were made using natural indigo dyes. Then, in the 1970s, ... *(a)* .... synthetic German indigo replaced .... *(b)* .... vat dyeing process. Today, this has given way to naphtha based dyes. The famed and centuries old indigo dyeing is now on the verge of extinction. As the new generation steps into more profitable avenues, the skyline of Ilkal is fast changing too. "The .... *(c)* .... profitable business in the area now is granite", states .... *(d)* .... weaver. With .... *(e)* .... stone being available in plenty here, ... *(f)* .... number of granite selling agencies and chimneys of granite posses units are spreading all over.

8. In the following paragraph, one word has been omitted in each line. In your answer sheets, remember to unite the missing word along with the word that comes before and after it, as shown below.

	Before	Omission	After
(a) The old man remained dreaming in the sun. kite-shop	…………	…………	…………
(b) had gone, the premises had been sold years	…………	…………	…………
(c) ago to junkdealer. Though he still made kites for his	…………	…………	…………
(d) own amusement and playthings for his grandson, Ali.	…………	…………	…………
(e) Then, of his kites were sold for so much as three or four annas.	…………	…………	…………

9. In the following paragraph, one word has been omitted in each line. In your answer sheets, remember to unite the missing word along with the word that comes before and after it, as shown below.

	Before	Omission	After
(a) There are so ways of entertainment in	…………	…………	…………
(b) life. The circus is one of the entertaining media.	…………	…………	…………
(c) Last Sunday, of our friends went to	…………	…………	…………
(d) see Diamond Circus. My uncle took us	…………	…………	…………
(e) there. one paid for their ticket.	…………	…………	…………

10. There is an error in each line. Write the incorrect word and the correction in the answer sheets as given below.

	Incorrect	Correct
(a) I have met some people in my life	…………	…………
(b) but a person who has influenced me	…………	…………
(c) the most is Mother Teresa. Fewer people	…………	…………
(d) can do what she has done. if we adopt hers	…………	…………
(e) ideology, the world would become the better place to live in.	…………	…………

ANSWERS

1. (a) an (b) some (c) a (d) many

2. (a) a (b) many (c) some (d) their (e) some

3. (a) the (b) the (c) No determiner required (d) the (e) every (f) No determiner required

4. (a) the (b) the (c) a (d) a (e) where (f) the

5. (a) most (b) many (c) the (d) the (e) which (f) No determiner required

6. (a) a lot (b) every (c) many/several (d) each (e) all (f) every

7. (a) the (b) this (c) most (d) a (e) this (f) a

8.

	Before	Omission	After
(a)	Sun	His	Kite-shop
(b)	Sold	Many	Years
(c)	To	A	Junkdealer
(d)	And	A few	Playthings
(e)	Then	Some	Of

9.

	Before	Omission	After
(a)	So	Many	Ways
(b)	The	Most	Entertaining
(c)	Sunday	Some	Of
(d)	See	The	Diamond
(e)	There	Every	One

10.

	Incorrect	Correct
(a)	some	many
(b)	a	the
(c)	fewer	Few
(d)	hers	her
(e)	the	a

CHAPTER 4

Subject-Verb Concord

Subject Verb concord refers to a set of rules that suggests that the subject and verb present in the sentence should agree with each other for the sentence to be grammatically correct and meaningful.

It suggests that the verb present in the sentence should agree with the subject in number and person.

Rules Involved in Subject-Verb Agreement

(i) Singular Subject → Singular Verb

e.g. **She is** wearing a dress.

(ii) Plural Subject → Plural Verb

e.g. **They are** playing basketball.

(iii) When two or more singular subjects are joined together by 'and', plural verb is used.

e.g. My brother and sister **are** studying abroad.

(iv) When two subjects together express one idea, singular verb is used.

e.g. Bread and butter **is** my least favourite breakfast.

(v) If the given nouns look like plurals (i.e. they end with 's') but they are, in fact, singular nouns, then we use a singular verb.

These nouns include news, physics, politics, measles, aerobics, diabetes, etc.

e.g. Physics **is** an interesting subject.

(vi) A collective noun takes a singular verb, when the collection is thought of as one whole. It takes a plural verb when the stress is on the individuals.

e.g.
- The team **has** been selected for the national game.
- The team **have** received their recommendation letters from the Sports' University.

(vii) Everybody, somebody, nobody, anybody and anyone take a singular verb.

e.g. **Has** anyone seen my phone?

(viii) If subjects are joined by 'or', 'nor', 'either', 'neither', etc. The verb agrees with the subject nearest to it.

e.g.
- Either my friends or I **am** getting blamed for it.
- Neither she nor her sisters **are** living a comfortable life.

(ix) The title of a book, play, story or a musical composition, even though plural, takes a singular verb.

e.g. 'War and Peace' is a classic book.

(x) If words are joined by 'with', 'together with', 'along with', or 'as well as', then the verb must agree with the first subject, irrespective of whether it is singular or plural.

e.g. My siblings as well as my father **are** going to Shimla next month.

(xi) Two nouns qualified by each or every, even though connected by 'and', require a singular verb.

e.g. Each student and each parent **was** asked to attend the meeting.

(xii) None is singular subject but takes a plural/singular verb according to the sense involved in the sentence.

e.g.
- None of them **were** selected for the final round.
- I'm in need of some inspiration, but none **comes** to mind.

(xiii) When the plural noun is a proper name for some single object or some collective unit, it must be followed by a singular verb.

e.g. The United Nations **has** become an ineffective body for ensuring world peace.

(xiv) Uncountable nouns like advice, news, media, stationery, weather, progress are singular and take a singular verb.

e.g. Media, nowadays, **is** not a reliable source.

(xv) A singular verb is used when a plural noun denotes some specific quantity or amount.

e.g.
- One thousand rupees **is** a small amount for the rich.
- Three kilometres **is** a very short distance.

Exceptions Remember that a few nouns are always plural, even though they don't end in 's' and they always take a plural verb.

e.g.
- **People** have expressed their resistance against it.
- The **police** are on duty.

Quite a few common plurals don't end in 's'.

e.g.
- The **children** are reading story-books.
- My feet **are** too large.

REVIEW EXERCISE

1. Fill in the blanks with the correct forms of the words given in the brackets.

I ...... *(a)* ...... (feel) that I am the ideal candidate for the receptionist position in your company. I ...... *(b)* ...... (has) five years of experience as a receptionist in a company in New Delhi. My telephonic skills and written communication ...... *(c)* ...... (be) excellent. The skills that I have learned from the job, ... *(d)* ...... (help) me understand that every person in a company helps make the business a success. ...... *(e)* ...... (be) there any other details about me that you would like to know?

2. Fill in the blanks with the correct forms of the words given in the brackets.

"The most important things are the hardest to say. They are the things you get ashamed of, because words .... *(a)* .... (diminish) them-words shrink things that seemed limitless when they ...... *(b)* ...... (be) in your head to no more than living size when they're brought out. But it's more than that, isn't it? The most important things ...... *(c)* ...... (lie) too close to wherever your secret heart is buried, like landmarks to a treasure that your enemies would love to steal away. And you may make revelations that cost you dearly only to have people look at you in a funny way, not understanding what you ...... *(d)* ...... (say) at all, or why you thought it was so important that you almost cried while you were saying it. That's the worst, I think. When the secret ...... *(e)* ...... (stay) locked within not for want of a teller but for want of an understanding ear."

3. Fill in the blanks with the correct forms of the words given in the brackets.

Mohan and Shyam ...... *(a)* ...... (be) my best friends. They always ...... *(b)* ...... (help) me in my work. None of them ...... *(c)* ...... (play) football. I ...... *(d)* ...... (has) never seen them wasting their time. Neither Mohan nor Shyam ...... *(e)* ...... (be) lazy. Each of them ...... *(f)* ...... (be) very active. All the students of my class ...... *(g)* ...... (like) them.

4. Fill in the blanks with the correct forms of the words given in the brackets.

Vivek had gone to the bank. He ......*(a)*...... (want) to take out some money. First he ......*(b)*...... (have) to fill in a form for a new cheque book, since all the cheques in the old book ......*(c)*...... (has) already been used. He, then ......*(d)*...... (make) out a cheque for the amount he ......*(e)*...... (want) to withdraw. The manager ......*(f)*...... (inform) him about the ATM card and e-banking which ......*(g)*...... (be) introduced shortly. The manager as well as the counter-clerks ......*(h)*...... (try) to persuade him to go for an ATM card.

5. Fill in the blanks with the correct forms of the words given in the brackets.

Do you know how to play bocce? The game ......*(a)*...... (do) not require any special athletic abilities. There is a new bocce league at the recreational centre. There ......*(b)*...... (be) several teams in the league. I have a new set of bocce balls. My friend ......*(c)*......(have) a new pallino ball. Bocce is a game for people of all ages. I ......*(d)*...... (be) going to show you how to play. The players take turns rolling a ball down the court. Each of the players ......*(e)*...... (take) one ball and aims for the pallino. We try to get our balls as close to the pallino as possible. Rick often ......*(f)*......(try) to bounce his ball off the side of the court. Everybody who ......*(g)*...... (play) Bocce ......*(h)*...... (enjoy) the game.

6. Fill in the blanks with the correct forms of the words given in the brackets.

There .... *(a)* .... (be) a story from the Buddha's childhood. Prince Siddhartha, with his cousin, ... *(b)* .... (be) out in the jungle. The brother .... *(c)* .... (shoot) down a swan with his arrow. Both the princes .... *(d)* .... (run) to the spot where the bird .... *(e)* .... (has) fallen. Siddhartha .... *(f)* .... (reach) first and bandages the bird's wound. The cousin .... *(g)* .... (arrive) later and .... *(h)* .... (lay) claim on the bird since he .... *(i)* .... (be) the one who shot it down. The dispute .... *(j)* .... (reach) the king's court. Who is right?

7. Fill in the blanks with the correct forms of the words given in the brackets.

Besides encountering the strange aborigines, the first English settlers ....*(a)*............ (find) themselves in the presence of new and wide variations of climate. In their old home, they ....*(b)*............... (accustom) to a moderate temperature. Now, they .... *(c)* .... (has) before them a great range of climate from the cold coasts of Maine to the hot savannahs of Georgia, with all the gradations from the far North to the deep South. To the exigencies of these variations, all the immigrants, from the British Isles as well as the Continent, ... *(d)* .... (has) to adapt themselves. Wherever the colonists set to work, they .... *(e)* .... (be) braving hostile weather conditions.

8. Fill in the blanks with the correct forms of the words given in the brackets.

I sit by Kemmerich's side. He ....*(a)*............ (sink) rapidly. Around us ....*(b)*............ (be) great commotion. A hospital train ....*(c)*............ (has) arrived and the wounded who ....*(d)*............ (be) fit to be moved are being selected. The doctor ....*(e)*............ (pass) by Kemmerich's bed without once looking at him. Kemmerich ....*(f)*............ (raise) himself on the pillows with his elbows.

9. Fill in the blanks with the correct forms of the words given in the brackets.

In November 2009, sales of cars .... *(a)* .... (go) up. This .... *(b)* .... (be) the largest car boom the country .... *(c)* .... (has) seen in years. Today, the largest growth .... *(d)* .... (be) seen for small cars. There .... *(e)* .... (be) currently 1.7 million new cars .... *(f)* .... (buy) every year but Maruti Suzuki .... *(g)* .... (be) not profiting from this development.

10. There is an error in each line. Write the incorrect word and the correction in the answer sheet as given below.

		Incorrect	Correct
(a)	There are too much oil and gas being used	....	....
(b)	around the world. There is many solutions	....	....
(c)	to this problem. Using public transport lead to	....	....
(d)	saving oil and gas. This will also improves our carbon footprint.	....	....

ANSWERS

1. (a) feel (b) have (c) are (d) help (e) are

2. (a) diminish (b) were (c) lie (d) have said (e) stays

3. (a) are (b) help (c) play (d) have (e) is (f) is (g) like

4. (a) wanted (b) had (c) had (d) makes (e) wanted (f) informed (g) were being (h) tried

5. (a) does (b) are (c) has (d) am (e) takes (f) tries (g) plays (h) enjoys

6. (a) is (b) is (c) shoots (d) run (e) has (f) reaches (g) arrives (h) lays (i) is (j) reaches

7. (a) found (b) had been accustomed (c) had (d) had (e) were

8. (a) is sinking (b) is (c) has (d) are (e) passes (f) raises

9. (a) went (b) is (c) has (d) is (e) are (f) bought (g) is

10.

Incorrect	Correct
(a) are	is
(b) is	are
(c) lead	leads
(d) improves	improve

CHAPTER 5

Clauses

A clause is a group of related words containing a subject and a finite verb. A clause is a larger word group than a phrase and includes a little more information.

5.1 Types of Clauses

There are two types of clauses

1. Independent Clause (Main/Principal Clause)

Independent clause refers to a group of words that gives a complete meaning and proper sense. It can stand alone and can be called a sentence.

e.g.
- Let's go play now.
- The movie has started.
- He will tell us about the plan.

2. Dependent Clause (Subordinate Clause)

A dependent clause or a subordinate clause, refers to a group of words that doesn't express a complete thought or meaning. It cannot stand alone as a sentence and is labelled according to its function in the sentence.

Dependent clauses are further divided into three kinds

Kinds of Dependent Clause

- (i) Noun clause
- (ii) Relative clause
- (iii) Adverb clause
  - (a) Adverb clause of time
  - (b) Adverb clause of condition

(i) Noun Clause

A noun clause is a dependent clause that acts as a noun. Noun clauses begin with words such as how, that, what, whatever, when, where, whether, which, whichever, who, whoever, whom, whomever and why.

These words generally come before the subject and the verb of the noun clause.

e.g.
- You can call **whoever you want.**
  (Whoever you want is a noun clause and it contains the subject 'you' and the verb 'want'. The clause acts as an object in the sentence.)
- She can take **whatever she wants** from here.
  (Whatever she wants is a noun clause and it contains the subject 'she' and the verb 'wants'. The clause acts as a direct object in the sentence.)
- He's asking us **how long we should wait here.**
  (How long we should wait here is a noun clause and it contains the subject 'we' and the verb phrase 'should wait'. The clause acts as a direct object in the sentence.)

(ii) Relative Clause (Or Adjective Clause)

A relative clause is a dependent clause introduced by a relative pronoun (that, which, whichever, who, whoever, whom, whomever, whose and of which). Relative clauses add extra information to a sentence by defining a noun and are also called adjective clauses. The introductory words used for various categories of nouns are

For people	who, whose or what
For things	which or that
For places	where
For times	when
For possession	whose

e.g.
- He went to the building **where his mother works.**
  (where his mother works is a relative clause. It contains the relative adverb 'where', the subject 'mother', and the verb 'works'. The clause modifies the noun building.)
- We're going to a concert of a band **whose lead singer is a friend of ours.**
  (whose lead singer is a friend of ours is a relative clause. It contains the relative pronoun 'whose', the subject 'singer', and the verb 'is'. The clause modifies the noun 'band'.)
- The place **where my brother goes to school** is in a metropolitan city.
  (where my brother goes to school is a relative clause. It contains the relative adverb 'where', the subject 'brother', and the verb 'goes'. The clause modifies the noun 'place'.)

(iii) Adverb Clause

An adverb clause (also called adverbial clause) is a dependent clause or expression in a sentence that functions as an adverb. It tells you something about how the action in the verb is done. It adds extra information about the time, place, manner, etc. to a sentence and modifies the verb.

The adverbial clause may come before or after the main clause. When it comes before the main clause, a **comma is used** to separate the two clauses. When it comes after the main clause, no comma is necessary.

e.g.
- You will be successful in life **if you work hard.** (Tells us under what condition you will be successful)
- **Although we ran really fast,** we could not reach on time. (Tells us under what condition we couldn't reach on time.)
- I had to go back **while she was still sleeping.** (Tells us under what condition I had to go back)

Types of Adverb Clause

Although these are many kinds of clauses, the two most commonly used adverb clauses are.

(a) **Adverb Clause of Time** Adverb clause of time modifies a verb in the main clause and tells the time when the action takes place.

Subordinating Conjunctions used are: when, whenever, anytime, before, after, till, until, while, since, just as, as soon as, as often as, now that, as long as, etc.

e.g.
- He was working on his assignment **when she arrived.**
- He waited for him **until he was ready.**
- It doesn't matter **as long as you are here.**

(b) **Adverb Clause of Condition** Adverb clause of condition modifies a verb in the main clause and tells the condition under which an action takes place.

Subordinating Conjunctions used are if, even if, whether, if.....not, unless, supposing that, provided that, in the condition that, etc.

e.g.
- **Supposing that he doesn't come on time,** what should we do?
- I'll cancel the appointment **if you are tired.**
- She'll get a promotion **provided that she excels the project.**

Clauses at a Glance

Clauses	Definition	Begins with	Examples
Noun Clause	• Any clause that functions as a noun. • Ask the question 'what' to the main verb and the answer is always the noun clause.	**Connectives** like who, whose, whom, when, where, which, what, why, how, that, if and whether	• Nisha told me that **she was going back home.** • Your success depends on **whether you give your best or not.**
Relative Clause/Adjective Clause	• It describes or modifies a noun or pronoun. • It adds extra information to a sentence by defining a noun.	**Relative Pronouns** like who, whose, whom, that, which, whichever, whoever, of which	• He is asking for the person **whom he had met during an exhibition.** • The child likes the chocolate **that his mother bought.**
Adverb Clause	It functions as an adverb; it tells you something about how the action in the verb is done. **Adverb Clause of Time** It modifies a verb in the main clause to tell the time when the action takes place.	**Subordinating Conjunctions** like when, whenever, anytime, before, after, till, until, while, since, just as, as soon as, as often as, now that, as long as	• You can call me **whenever you have time.** • **Just as I was about to leave,** I saw my father coming towards me.
	Adverb Clause of Condition It modifies a verb in the main clause to tell the condition under which the action takes place or someone does something.	**Subordinating Conjunctions** like if, whether, as long as, unless, provided that, supposing that, in that condition	• She will have to go there **whether she likes it or not.** • I'll go there **as long as there is decent food available.**

REVIEW EXERCISE

1. Complete the following sentences keeping in mind the uses of clauses.

(a) Alexander Fleming was the man .... discovered penicillin.

(b) I like meeting people .... have travelled widely.

(c) The school .... I was educated has been demolished.

(d) The man .... I was talking to last week gave me another version of the events.

(e) I am working for a construction company .... head office is in London.

2. Join the following sentences paying particular attention to word order.

(a) Look at the teacher. He is talking to his pupil.

(b) Ireland exports computer components. They are mostly made in Dublin.

(c) John looked anxiously at his watch. He wished he hadn't come to the party.

(d) There were a lot of people here earlier. They wanted to talk to you.

(e) There was an actor there. His work took him all over the world.

3. There is an error in the following sentences. Find the error and rewrite the sentences correctly.

(a) The man which lives next door is very friendly.

(b) Everything what he said was correct.

(c) The person which I wanted to see was not available until Monday.

(d) Yesterday I met Mario whom told me he was getting married.

(e) Mr. Smith is going to Moscow when his daughter has been living for some time now.

4. Join the two sentences into one keeping in mind the uses of clauses.

(a) A plane crashed into the ocean yesterday. It was carrying 345 passengers.

(b) The paintings have now been recovered. They were stolen from a mansion in London.

(c) At the end of the street is a path. The path leads to a lake.

(d) I live in a very nice flat. It overlooks some beautiful gardens.

(e) Somebody phoned while you were in town. He was called Jack.

5. Complete the following dialogue. There may be more than one possible answer.

Swati	Please tell me (a) ....
Sumedha	Can't you see (b) ....?
Swati	I can also see (c) ....

6. Complete the following sentences keeping in mind the uses of clauses.

(a) My grandfather, ... was an extraordinary pianist, lived till the age of 78.

(b) The book .... we read in the course was written by Roald Dahl.

(c) For years, he lived a life .... was very pleasurable.

(d) My car, ... I bought in Germany, needs repairing.

(e) Jeremy, ... is a famous author, is coming to see me today.

7. Join the following sentences paying particular attention to word order.

(a) I was talking to a woman. Her husband was killed in the war.

(b) The man got on the bus. He was carrying a cat in a box.

(c) Somebody called while you were out. I can't remember his name.

(d) I work mainly in the Marketing Department. It is the smallest department in the company.

(e) My boss decided to employ me as his assistant. His work takes him all over the world.

8. There is an error in the following sentences. Find the error and rewrite the sentences correctly.

(a) Mr Carlisle, whom I spoke last night, is very interested in our new project.

(b) She couldn't come to the conference that was a pity.

(c) Suzanna has many friends, most of which she went to school with.

(d) She tried on several jackets, none of whom fit her.
(e) Melanie, that has just bought a house near Gatwick, is getting married.

9. Complete the following dialogue. There may be more than one possible answer.

Chaitanya	Could you tell me *(a)* ....?
Garima	From the shop (b) ....
Chaitanya	I will go there and see (c) ....

10. Complete the following dialogue. There may be more than one possible answer.

Astha	Could you do me a favour (a) ....?
Tanmay	First tell me (b) ....
Astha	Please go to Jyoti's place and bring my book (c) ....

11. Join the following sentences paying particular attention to word order.

(a) The shoes are too big. My grandma bought them for me.
(b) The boy is very nice. I know him from school.
(c) We ate chicken at the restaurant. It was delicious.
(d) I have to learn new words. They are very difficult.
(e) The photographer could not develop the pictures. I had taken them in Australia.
(f) A girl is talking to Tom. Do you know the girl?
(g) The bananas are on the table. George bought them.
(h) Kamal helps a man. The man is my teacher.
(i) I watched a film last night. The film was interesting.
(j) You are sitting on a bench. The paint on the bench is still wet.

12. There is an error in the following sentences. Rewrite them correctly.

(a) She told me which she would be delighted to come.
(b) Pay attention to whom I am going to say.
(c) I went to see which had happened.
(d) Which you should cheat me, hurts me.
(e) I don't know which I can get out of this mess.
(f) don't know whose he wants.
(g) I thought whom she would arrive tomorrow.
(h) He asked me unless I knew his name.
(i) I want to know whom she is angry with me.
(j) I often wonder whose he is getting on.

ANSWERS

1. (a) who (b) who (c) where
(d) whom (e) whose

2. (a) Look at the teacher who is talking to his pupil.
(b) Ireland exports computer components which are mostly made in Dublin.
(c) John, who wished he hadn't come to the party, looked anxiously at his watch.
(d) There were a lot of people here earlier who wanted to talk to you.
(e) There was an actor there whose work took him all over the world.

3. (a) The man who lives next door is very friendly.
(b) Everything that he said was correct.
(c) The person whom I wanted to see was not available until Monday.
(d) Yesterday I met Mario, who told me he was getting married.
(e) Mr. Smith is going to Moscow where his daughter has been living for some time now.

4. (a) A plane, which was carrying 345 passengers, crashed into the ocean yesterday.
(b) The paintings, which were stolen from a mansion in London, have now been recovered.
(c) At the end of the street is a path which leads to the lake.
(d) I live in a very nice flat which overlooks some beautiful gardens.
(e) Somebody called Jack phoned while you were in town.

5. (a) what you are doing
(b) that I am doing my homework
(c) that you have made many mistakes

6. (a) who (b) which
(c) which (d) which
(e) who

7. (a) I was talking to a woman whose husband was killed during the war.
(b) A man, who was carrying a cat in a box, got on the bus.
(c) Somebody, whose name I can't remember, called while you were out.
(d) I work mainly in the Marketing Department which is the smallest department in the company.
(e) My boss, whose work takes him all over the world, decided to employ me as his assistant.

8. (a) Mr. Carlisle, to whom I spoke last night, is very interested in our new project.
(b) She couldn't come to the conference, which was a pity.
(c) Suzanna has many friends, most of whom she went to school with.
(d) She tried on several jackets, none of which fit her.
(e) Melanie, who has just bought a house near Gatwick, is getting married.

9. (a) where you bought these trousers from
(b) that is in the main market
(c) if I can find a similar pair for myself

10. (a) if you have some free time
(b) what you want me to do
(c) which I have forgotten there

11. (a) The shoes that my grandma bought for me, are too big.
(b) The boy whom I know from school is very nice.
(c) The chicken which we ate at the restaurant was delicious.
(d) The new words which I have to learn are very difficult.
(e) The photographer could not develop the pictures that I had taken in Australia.
(f) Do you know the girl who is talking to Tom?
(g) The bananas which George bought are on the table.
(h) The man whom Kamal helps is my teacher.
(i) The film that I watched last night, was interesting.
(j) The paint on the bench which you are sitting on, is still wet.

12. (a) She told me that she would be delighted to come.
(b) Pay attention to what I am going to say.
(c) I went to see what had happened.
(d) That you should cheat me, hurts me.
(e) I don't know how I can get out of this mess.
(f) I don't know what he wants.
(g) I thought that she would arrive tomorrow.
(h) He asked me if I knew his name.
(i) I want to know why she is angry with me.
(j) I often wonder how he is getting on.

CHAPTER 6

Reported Speech

The act of reporting the words of a speaker is called **narration**. There are basically two ways in which a speaker can convey the intended message/idea to the listener.

(a) **Direct Speech** (Direct Narration) The reporting of the exact words of the speaker is known as Direct Speech.

(b) **Indirect Speech** (Indirect Narration) The act of reporting the words of a speaker by making necessary changes to it is called Indirect Speech. In indirect speech, while narrating something, changes are made in the original words of the person. For example, tenses and pronouns are changed according to the reporting verb.

e.g. (i) Sneha said, "Mother is out of town."

(ii) Sneha said that mother was out of town.

In sentence (i) we can notice that this is the speaker's direct words are shown inside double quotation marks. However, in sentence (ii) the tense and pronouns are changed, and quotation marks are removed.

Reporting Verb and Reported Speech

The verb that is not part of the speech inside the quotation marks is called the **Reporting verb**. It is placed before the statement in the sentence.

The words spoken by the speaker and placed inside inverted commas or quotation marks ("......") are collectively the Reported Speech.

e.g. Reported Verb — Reported Speech

He says, "I shall leave tomorrow morning."

Rules	Direct Speech	Indirect Speech
Remove separating comma, inverted commas and use the connector 'that' when there is no object in the sentence.	• He said "I work in a shipyard." • Sheena said, "My teacher is highly educated."	• He said that he worked in a shipyard. • Sheena said that her teacher was highly educated.

Rules	Direct Speech	Indirect Speech
The reporting verb 'said' becomes 'told' along with the subject and the connector 'that' when it is followed by an object.	• Kamya said to me, "You have been a great help." • He said to me, "I shall go to the party."	• Kamya told me that I had been a great help. • He told me that he would go to the party.

Changes into Reported Speech With Respect to the Tense

When we convert a sentence from direct to indirect speech, the tense of the speech may or may not change depending on the reporting verb.

If the reporting verb is in the present tense, the tense of the verbs in the introductory phrase and exact words of the speaker does not change.

e.g. • My mother **says**, "You **are going** to the concert." (Direct Speech)
• My mother **says** that **I am going** to the concert. (Indirect Speech)

If the reporting verb is in Past Tense, the tense of the speech in double quotation marks undergoes a change as given in the table

Present Tense

Rules of Conversion	Direct Speech	Indirect Speech
Simple present changes into past simple	• He said, "I do not like computers." • They said, "We love our country."	• He said that he did not like computers. • They said that they loved their country.
Present continuous changes into past continuous	• I said, "It is raining." • She said, "I am not laughing."	• I said that it was raining. • She said that she was not laughing.
Present perfect changes into past perfect	• She said, "He has finished his work." • They said, "We have not gone to New York."	• She said that he had finished his work. • They said that they had not gone to New York.
Present perfect continuous changes into past perfect continuous	• He said, "I have been studying since 3 o' clock." • Radha said, "It has been raining for three days."	• He said that he had been studying since 3 o' clock. • Radha said that it had been raining for three days.

Past Tense

Rules of Conversion	Direct Speech	Indirect Speech
Simple past changes into past perfect	• My teacher said to me, "You answered correctly." • He said, "I didn't buy a car."	• My teacher told me that I had answered correctly. • He said that he had not bought a car.
Past continuous changes into past perfect continuous	• They said, "We were enjoying the weather." • He said, "Mohit was listening to music."	• They said that they had been enjoying the weather. • He said that Mohit had been listening to music.

Note It Past perfect remains past perfect and past perfect continuous tense also remains the same. (tense does not change)

Future Tense

Rules of Conversion	Direct Speech	Indirect Speech
Simple future: will changes into would	• He said, "I will study the book." • They said to me, "We will send you gifts."	• He said that he would study the book. • They told me that they would send me gifts.
Future continuous: will be changes into would be	• Shreya told him, "I will be waiting for you." • He said, "He will not be flying kites."	• Shreya told him that she would be waiting for him. • He said that he would not be flying kites.
Future perfect: will have changes into would have	• He said, "I will have finished the work." • Narayan said, "I will have gone."	• He said that he would have finished the work. • Narayan said that he would have gone.

EXCEPTIONS

The tense of the reported speech may not change if the narration is about a universal truth, habitual fact or past historical fact.

e.g. (i) My father said, "I am slow to start." (Direct)
My father said that he is slow to start. (Indirect)

(ii) She said, "Two and two makes four." (Direct)
She said that two and two makes four. (Indirect)

(iii) The teacher said, "Ashoka left war after the conquest of Kalinga." (Direct)
The teacher said that Ashoka left war after the conquest of Kalinga. (Indirect)

Changes in Pronoun

The pronoun in the indirect speech remains unchanged if the speaker is in first person.

e.g. • I said, "I have eaten my lunch." (Direct speech)
• I said that I had eaten my lunch. (Indirect speech)

The pronoun in the indirect speech is changed to second person if the speaker is in second person.

e.g. • You said, "I am going on a walk." (Direct speech)
• You said that you were going on a walk. (Indirect speech)

The pronoun in the indirect speech is changed to third person in accordance with the gender of the speaker, if the speaker is in third person.

e.g. • She said, "I shall study now." (Direct speech)
• She said that she should study then. (Indirect speech)

Change in Modals

Modal verbs are changed in the following manner

- May - might
- Can - could
- Must - had to
- Ought to - ought to

Change in Time and Place Expressions

The words that indicate time or position also undergo changes when we convert a direct speech into indirect speech.

Time Indicators

Direct Speech	Indirect Speech
Now	Then
Ago	Before
Today	That day
Tonight	That night
Yesterday	The previous day/the day before
Tomorrow	The next day/ the following day
In an hour	An hour later

Place Indicators

Direct Speech	Indirect Speech
Here	There
This	That
These	Those

Rules for Changing Interrogative Sentences into Indirect Speech

(The reporting verb 'said' becomes 'asked' and 'to' is removed)

Rules	Direct Speech & Indirect Speech
Use 'if' or 'whether' in place of 'that' as a connector.	• She said to me, "Do you like tea or coffee?" (Direct) She asked me whether I liked tea or coffee. (Indirect)
Remove the question mark while forming an assertive sentence.	• She said to Shyam, "Do you have an extra copy?" (Direct) She asked Shyam if he had an extra copy. (Indirect)
For questions starting with question words like 'when', 'why', 'where', do not use 'if' or 'whether'. The question words are retained to introduce the reported question.	• He said, "What is your problem?"(Direct) He asked me what my problem was. (Indirect) • She said, "Why are you not coming?" (Direct) She asked me why I was not coming. (Indirect)

Rules for Changing Imperative Sentences into Indirect Speech (Commands, Requests and Suggestions)

Rules	Direct and Indirect Speech
Use conjunction 'to' instead of 'that'.	• I said to Hari, "Do not pluck the flowers." (Direct) I ordered Hari not to pluck the flowers. (Indirect) • The Principal said to the students, "Get out of the office." (Direct) The Principal ordered the students to get out of the office. (Indirect)
In sentences beginning with 'Let', the reporting verb is changed to 'proposed' or 'suggested'/ 'propose' or 'suggest'.	• He said, "Let us keep quiet in this matter." (Direct) He suggested that we should keep quiet in that matter. (Indirect)

Rules for Changing Exclamatory Sentences into Indirect Speech

Rules	Direct and Indirect Speech
Words such as Alas, Bravo, Oh, Wow, etc. should be left out in indirect speech and replaced with 'exclaimed with joy/sorrow/excitement, etc.'	• Ram said, "Alas! I have been ruined." (Direct) Ram exclaimed with sorrow that he had been ruined. (Indirect)
Forms of the verb 'wish' is used in places of 'If/I were'.	• She said, "If I were a bird." (Direct) She wished to be a bird./She wished that she were a bird. (Indirect)

REVIEW EXERCISE

1. **Directions (Ques. Nos. 1 to 10) Report the dialogues to complete the paragraph that follows.**

Maya When are you going to do your homework?

Twinkle I will do it at 4'o clock.

Maya You said the same thing yesterday too.

Twinkle Yesterday, I had something else to do. I'll surely do it today.

Maya asked Twinkle (a) .... Twinkle replied that she would do it at 4 o'clock. Maya told her that (b) .... Twinkle responded that (c) .... but she would surely do it that day.

2. **Subash** I am really excited about this excursion.

Ramesh I have been to that place and I really enjoyed it.

Subash Really? When did you go there?

Ramesh Yes, last year with my classmates.

Subash told Ramesh that (a) .... Ramesh replied by saying that he had been to that place and he (b) .... Subash was surprised and asked him (c) .... Ramesh replied in affirmative and said that he went to that place the previous year with his classmates.

3. **Mother** What a lovely day today is! The weather has never been this pleasant.

Son Yes, mother. Can we go on a picnic today?

Mother Sure, let's pack up first and tell your father and siblings to get ready.

Son Hurrah! We're going on a picnic today.

Mother (a) .... and that the weather had never been that pleasant. Son replied to his mother in affirmative and asked her (b) .... Mother responded that they totally could and (c) .... and to tell his father and siblings to get ready. Son was excited and happily announced that they were going on a picnic that day.

4. **Mansi** Do you know who will be presiding over our annual function?

Priya I was told an eminent poet has been invited.

Mansi Are you talking about the Indian poet, Ramdhari Singh Dinkar?

Priya Yes, he has composed a number of patriotic songs.

The curiosity about the Chief Guest was uncertain among the students on the annual day function. Mansi asked Priya if she knew *(a)* .... over their annual day function. Priya replied that *(b)* .... that an eminent poet had been invited. Mansi enquired *(c)* .... about the Indian poet, Ramdhari Singh Dinkar. Priya replied in the affirmative and said that he had composed a number of patriotic songs.

5. **Ankit** Where are you going?
   Atul To the airport.
   Ankit May I drop you there in my car?
   Atul Thanks a lot. It will be a great help to me.

   Ankit asked Atul where *(a)* .... Atul replied *(b)* .... airport. Ankit further asked him *(c)* .... there in his car. Atul thanked him, adding that it would be a great help to him.

6. **Sneha** Do you know that the school trip to the Andaman has been postponed?
   Deepti No, I didn't know that. Why has the trip been postponed?
   Sneha I heard that it is due to bad weather conditions.

   Sneha asked Deepti *(a)* .... postponed. Deepti replied that she didn't know that. She asked Sneha *(b)* .... Sneha told her that *(c)* ....

7. **Tanmay** How did you spend your vacation?
   Astha I visited Kashmir with my parents.
   Tanmay Have you been there earlier too?
   Astha No, it was my first trip.

   Tanmay asked Astha *(a)* .... vacation. Astha replied that *(b)* .... with her parents. Tanmay further asked her if she had been there earlier too. Astha replied in *(c)* ....

8. **Teacher** Why are you late?
   Sumit I missed my school bus.
   Teacher Why didn't you leave on time?
   Sumit Sorry, I will do so from tomorrow.

   The teacher asked Sumit *(a)* .... late. Sumit replied that *(b)* .... When the teacher asked him *(c)* ...., Sumit apologetically replied that he would do so from the next day.

9. **Sonu** What makes you weep?
   Rohan Someone has stolen my wallet.
   Sonu Where did you keep it?
   Rohan In the back pocket of my trousers.

   Sonu asked Rohan *(a)* .... He replied that someone *(b)* .... Next, Sonu enquired *(c)* .... Rohan said that he had kept it in the back pocket of his trousers.

10. **Servant** Please give me leave for a week.
    Master Why do you need such a long leave?
    Servant I have to visit my village.
    Master OK, but don't overstay on your leave.

    The servant requested his master *(a)* .... for a week. The master asked him why *(b)* .... At this, the servant said *(c)* .... The master acceded to his request, but asked him not to overstay on his leave.

ANSWERS

1. (a) when she was going to do her homework
   (b) she had said the same thing the previous day too
   (c) she had something else to do the previous day
2. (a) he was really excited about that excursion
   (b) had really enjoyed it
   (c) when he had gone there
3. (a) exclaimed with joy that it was a lovely day
   (b) if they could go on a picnic that day
   (c) suggested that they should pack up first
4. (a) who would be presiding
   (b) she had been told
   (c) if she was talking
5. (a) he was going
   (b) that he was going to the
   (c) if he might drop him
6. (a) if she knew that the school trip to the Andaman had been
   (b) why the trip had been postponed
   (c) she had heard that it was due to bad weather conditions
7. (a) how she had spent her
   (b) she had visited Kashmir
   (c) the negative, saying that it had been her first trip
8. (a) why he was
   (b) he had missed his school bus
   (c) why he had not left on time
9. (a) what made him weep
   (b) had stolen his wallet
   (c) where he had kept it
10. (a) to give him leave
    (b) he needed such a long leave
    (c) that he had to visit his village

Integrated Exercise

Type I : Gap Filling

1. **Complete the following passage by choosing the most appropriate option from the ones given below. Write your answers in the answer sheet against the correct blank number. Do not copy the entire passage.**

Kabir, ***(a)*** .... (a/an/the) famous saint, was neither a Muslim nor a Hindu. He ***(b)*** .... (is/was/were) a *Fakir* who ***(c)*** .... (preach/preaches/preached) love, peace and unity to humanity.

2. **Complete the following passage by choosing the most appropriate option from the ones given below. Write your answers in the answer sheet against the correct blank number. Do not copy the entire passage.**

Seema bought a new bedsheet but ***(a)*** .... (nobody/somebody/everybody) liked it at her home. She ***(b)*** .... (feel/feels/felt) very bad and decided to give it to ***(c)*** .... (her/his/my) maid.

3. **Complete the following paragraph by choosing the appropriate options from the ones given below. Write your answers in the answer sheets against the correct blank number. Do not copy the entire paragraph.**

The history of man is ***(a)*** .... (replete/repletes/repleted) with crime and folly. Wars between nations, religious persecution, ethnic cleansing and other forms of genocide ***(b)*** ....(take) a heavy toll on human lives. The Spanish conquest of South America was ***(c)*** .... (accompany) by the extinction of millions of 'natives' through killings and disease.

4. **Complete the passage with the correct words.**

You ***(a)*** .... come to school in proper dress. You ***(b)*** .... make it a habit to visit the library in your vacant periods. You ***(c)*** .... borrow the books you like for your studies. But spoiling the books ***(d)*** .... be avoided at any cost. Tearing off pages or underlining the passages ***(e)*** .... be seriously dealt with. Remember, you ***(f)*** .... behave like gentlemen to be worthy students of this school.

5. **Complete the passage with the correct words.**

Chennai was ***(a)*** .... first Indian city to have suburban rail established in 1930. Chennai is well-connected by ***(b)*** .... train network. In spite of this history, Chennai does not boast of ***(c)*** .... strong train culture. The problem lies not in ***(d)*** .... infrastructure but in access to ***(e)*** .... stations. Effective transportation is ***(f)*** .... basis of a successful city.

6. **Complete the following passage by choosing the most appropriate option from the ones given below. Write your answers in the answer sheet against the correct blank number. Do not copy the entire passage.**

The human body is like a machine containing ***(a)*** .... systems ***(b)*** .... out the processes of life. Each system is ***(c)*** .... up of organs ***(d)*** .... consist of specialised cells and tissues.

(a) (i) little	(ii) several	(iii) much	(iv) more
(b) (i) to carry	(ii) carry	(iii) carries	(iv) carried
(c) (i) makes	(ii) making	(iii) make	(iv) made
(d) (i) that	(ii) who	(iii) whose	(iv) those

7. Complete the following passage by choosing the most appropriate options from the ones given below. Write your answers in the answer sheet against the correct blank number. Do not copy the entire passage.

While planning your career, it *(a)* .... very important that you understand yourself. You need to evaluate and *(b)* .... your abilities. You *(c)* .... make sure that your interest and aptitude are suitable for the career you wish to pursue.

(a) (i) is (ii) are (iii) was (iv) were
(b) (i) recognise (ii) recognised (iii) will recognise (iv) recognising
(c) (i) could (ii) will (iii) must (iv) shall

8. Complete the following paragraph by choosing the most appropriate options from the ones given below. Write your answers in the answer sheets against the correct blank number. Do not copy the entire paragraph.

Volleyball is a popular recreation sport which is *(a)* .... all over India. The Indian senior men's team *(b)* .... ranked forty sixth in the world. The major problem that confronts is *(c)* .... lack of sponsors.

(a) (i) playing (ii) played (iii) plays (iv) is played
(b) (i) was (ii) has been (iii) is (iv) had been
(c) (i) a (ii) the (iii) some (iv) few

9. Complete the following passage by choosing the most appropriate options from the ones given below. Write your answers in the answer sheet against the correct blank number. Do not copy the entire paragraph.

Sandalwood is the name of a class of fragrant woods from trees in *(a)* .... genus Santalum. Unlike many other aromatic woods, they retain *(b)* .... fragrance for decades. Essential oils *(c)* .... also extracted from these woods.

(a) (i) the (ii) an (iii) a (iv) are
(b) (i) its (ii) there (iii) their (iv) those
(c) (i) can (ii) are (iii) could (iv) will

10. Complete the following passage given below by choosing the most appropriate options from the ones that follow. Write your answers in the answer sheet against the correct blank numbers. Do not copy the entire passage.

In Uganda, smallpox was a fatal disease. Once it struck a village, it *(a)* .... through it like a plague, destroying hundreds, blinding and disfiguring the rest. There *(b)* .... no known remedy. It was the custom to put the sick into little huts outside the village and abandon them to *(c)* ....

(a) (i) spreads (ii) spread (iii) had spread (iv) has spread
(b) (i) was (ii) had been (iii) has been (iv) have been
(c) (i) death (ii) dying (iii) die (iv) dies

11. Choose the most appropriate option from the ones given below to complete the following passage.

Today, Monet's work sells for millions of dollars and hangs in *(a)* .... of the most prestigious institutions in the world. Yet, during *(b)* .... own time, it was mocked and rejected by the artistic elite, the Paris Salon. Monet kept at his impressionist style, which caught on and in many ways was a starting point for some major changes to art *(c)* .... ushered in the modern era.

(a) (i) few (ii) some (iii) all (iv) majority
(b) (i) her (ii) him (iii) his (iv) their
(c) (i) been (ii) be (iii) being (iv) that

12. Choose the most appropriate option from the ones given below to complete the following paragraph.

Orville and Wilbur Wright battled depression and family illness before *(a)* .... the bicycle shop that would lead them to experimenting with flight. After numerous attempts at creating flying machines, *(b)* .... years of hard work, and tons of failed prototypes, the brothers finally created a plane (c) .... could get airborne and stay there.

(a) (i) start	(ii) started	(iii) starts	(iv) starting
(b) (i) little	(ii) much	(iii) no	(iv) several
(c) (i) which	(ii) one	(iii) who	(iv) that

13. Choose the most appropriate option from the ones given below to complete the following paragraph.

In the ancient days, the Gods of Egypt *(a)* .... on Earth along with man. Of the Gods, Osiris was the Lord of water and vegetation. He made rivers *(b)* .... and trees *(c)* .... fruit; he gave the jasmine its fragrance and the marigold its colours.

(a) (i) lives	(ii) live	(iii) lived	(iv) living
(b) (i) flow	(ii) flew	(iii) flowed	(iv) flowing
(c) (i) birth	(ii) bear	(iii) borne	(iv) bearing

14. Choose the most appropriate option from the ones given below to complete the following paragraph.

(a) .... (Much/No/Most) people are familiar with Louisa May Alcott's most famous work, 'Little Women'. Yet, Alcott faced a bit of a battle to get her work out there and was *(b)* .... (encourage/encourages/encouraged) to find work as a servant by her family to make ends meet. It was *(c)* .... (hers/her/she) letters back home that narrated her experience as a nurse in the Civil War that gave her the first big break she needed.

Type II Sentence Reordering

Look at the words and phrases given below. Rearrange them to form meaningful sentences. The first one has been done for you as an example in each question.

1. e.g. are located/the Arctic and Antarctica/the South/around the North/of the Earth/poles/and

Ans. The Arctic and Antarctica are located around the North and the South poles of the Earth.

(a) the/at both/atmosphere/is/cold/these places/very
(b) experience/they/extreme/ solar/periods/exposure
(c) several/therefore/similarities/weather patterns/in the/there/are

2. e.g. Institute/AIDS/Research/National/Pune/located/is/in

Ans. National AIDS Research Institute is located in Pune.

(a) one/oldest/research/bodies/in the/it/is/of the/and/largest/medical/world
(b) Research/Medical/Council/of/under/Indian/it/functions
(c) point/of/starting/achievement/all/purpose/of/definiteness/is the

3. e.g. many Indians/sandalwood/to be/is considered/sacred by

Ans. Sandalwood is considered to be sacred by many Indians.

(a) medicinal properties/it/fragrance/for its/and/ highly/valued/is
(b) in ancient times /sandal and turmeric/blemish free skin/ for a/was used/a paste of/ by women
(c) sandalwood trees/the purest/comes from/ renowned sandal oil/ of Mysore

4. e.g. important/it/to/is/rules/observe/traffic

Ans. It is important to observe traffic rules.

(a) not/children/below/of/age/the/must/drive/eighteen/ years
(b) protection/our/we/must/helmets/own/wear/for
(c) must/used/phones/not/mobile/driving/while/be

5. e.g. by/childhood/are/memories/everyone/cherished

Ans. Childhood memories are cherished by everyone.

(a) childhood/generally/I/as being/remember/my/happy
(b) carefree/some of/recall/my/I/can/times
(c) frightening/remember/I/can/moments/also/my

6. **e.g. streets/during/can see/slogans/elections/supporters/political parties/the/shouting/of/ in/we.**

Ans. During elections, we can see supporters of political parties shouting slogans in the streets.

(a) on foot/the/to greet/candidates/walk/the/even/people

(b) opportunity/they/the/of/catch/shaking hands/anyone/meet/they/with

(c) their problems/people/their/assure/that/they/will/supporters/solve

7. **e.g. old people/we/a feeling/should/acceptability/give/of**

Ans. We should give old people a feeling of acceptability.

(a) are not/citizens/respected/senior/or cared for

(b) ill-equipped/are not only/insufficient/old age homes/also/but

(c) must/anyone else's/place them/the society/before/interest

8. **e.g. is heard/is dialled/when/the/dial tone/required number/the**

Ans. When the dial tone is heard the required number is dialled.

(a) go/the/can/on/conversation/three minutes/for

(b) disconnected/gets/after/soon/the/line

(c) near and dear/it is/good/way/ones/with/in/touch/a/your/to get

9. **e.g. feared by/snakes are/in our/worshipped/and/many/country**

Ans. Snakes are worshipped and feared by many in our country.

(a) of the/are venomous/only/300 out/species/2700 known

(b) which is/yellow liquid/water/snake venom/90%/is a

(c) expelled/poison gland/that is/it is/from the/a substance

10. **e.g. is the/consume/carbon dioxide/that plants/food**

Ans. Carbon dioxide is the food that plants consume.

(a) absorb this/leaves of/the green/and plants/carbon dioxide/trees

(b) carbon/into/it is/and/broken down/oxygen

(c) is/ make starch/and oxygen/the carbon/is released/used to/air/into

Rearrange the following jumbled words/phrases in the given dialogue to create a meaningful sentence.

11. **Reena :** Where are you going?
Teena : I am going to the bank to withdraw money.
Reena : is/today/the bank/as/it is/closed/ the second Saturday/the month/of

12. **Tushar :** Did you watch today's IPL match?
Rishabh : No. I did not watch it.
Tushar : Why?
Rishabh : not/I/well/so I/whole day/was/feeling/slept the

13. **Sadaf :** Ma'am, I will be unable to attend school tomorrow.
Teacher : Why? What happaned?
Sudaf : to take/my mother/I have/hospital/as she is/ to the/ keeping well/ not

14. **Father :** Do you know what you can do to help the environment?
Shamshu : I don't have any idea about it.
Father: five minutes/to find/watch the/out/video/the world/ your day!/change/how to/in/just/of.

15. **Rohan :** Why do we need to save water?
Teacher : We need it to drink, wash, cook and flush down the toilet.
Rohan : That's OK there's a lot of water on our planet.
Teacher : know/most of/ did you/can't use/that we/it?/but

Type III Sentence Transformation

Read the conversations and complete the passage given below the conversations in each question.

1. **Ranbir** Where is my car? I remember parking it here.
Policeman The car has been towed away as you parked it in the 'No Parking Area'.
Ranbir Sir, can I be excused this time?
Policeman I hope you'll remember the lesson you learnt today.

Ranbir asked the policeman standing there where his car was for he remembered parking it there. The policeman replied ***(a)*** .... it in the 'No Parking Area'. Ranbir requested the policeman ***(b)*** .... The policeman then reminded him that ***(c)*** ....

2. **Detective** What were you doing yesterday between 10:00–10:30 pm?
Bharat I was walking my dog in the park.
Detective Did you meet anyone in the park?
Bharat I saw two men sitting on a bench.

The detective asked Bharat ***(a)*** .... between 10:00-10:30 pm. Bharat replied that ***(b)*** .... The detective then asked Bharat ***(c)*** ...., to which Bharat replied that he had seen two men sitting on a bench.

3. **Teacher** Can you read what is written on this page?
Student I can't read all the words.
Teacher Would you like to read them?

The teacher asked the student ***(a)*** .... The student regretfully replied that ***(b)*** .... The teacher then asked him ***(c)*** ....

4. **Wife** Our servant has run away.
Husband Is anything missing?
Wife Yes, my gold watch.
Husband Where did you keep it?
Wife On the dressing table as usual.

A wife told her husband that their servant had run away. The husband asked the wife ***(a)*** .... The wife replied in the affirmative and said that her gold watch was missing. The husband then asked her ***(b)*** .... The wife replied that she ***(c)*** .... as usual.

5. **Santa** How did your hen die?
Banta I poured hot water into its mouth.
Santa But why did you do it?
Banta Actually I thought it would give me boiled eggs.

Santa asked Banta ***(a)*** .... Banta replied that ***(b)*** .... Now Santa wanted to know why he had done it. To which Banta replied that ***(c)*** ....

6. **Customer** Can I have a small bottle of tomato sauce?
Shopkeeper Sorry, I have only big bottles.
Customer When will it be available?
Shopkeeper I can give it to you tomorrow.
Customer Thank you, then I will take it tomorrow.

The customer asked the shopkeeper ***(a)*** .... The shopkeeper said that he only had big bottles of tomato sauce. The customer wanted to know ***(b)*** .... The shopkeeper said that he could give it to him the next day. The customer thanked him and said that ***(c)*** ....

7. **Rohan** Let's go out for dinner today.
Riya Which restaurant would you like to go to?
Rohan I would like to go to Rama's because I like the Chinese food there.
Riya I am not in a mood for eating Chinese. Today let's go out to some South Indian restaurant.

Rohan suggested to Riya that they should go out for dinner that day. Riya asked Rohan ***(a)*** .... Rohan replied ***(b)*** .... the Chinese food there. To this, Riya said that she was not in a mood for eating Chinese food and further suggested ***(c)*** ....

8. **Patient** Can I have an appointment with the doctor this evening? I am very sick.
Receptionist I'm sorry. There's a long waiting list. You will have to wait for at least two weeks.
Patient But by then I could be dead.
Receptionist No problem. If your wife informs me, I can cancel the appointment.

A patient went to his doctor's clinic and asked the receptionist ***(a)*** .... as he was very sick. The receptionist apologised, saying that there was a long waiting list. She further added that ***(b)*** .... When the patient said that he would be dead by then, the receptionist calmly replied that ***(c)*** .... the appointment.

9. **Beggar** Please give me some money.
Lady Why don't you do some work?
Beggar Madam, begging is also work.

A beggar requested a lady ***(a)*** .... The lady asked him why ***(b)*** .... some work. At this the beggar replied ***(c)*** ....

10. **John** Do you know swimming ?
David No, can you teach me how to swim ?
John Of course I can. Come to my place tomorrow at 5:00 pm.

John asked David ***(a)*** .... David replied in the negative and asked him ***(b)*** .... how to swim. John replied in affirmation and asked him ***(c)*** .... at 5:00 pm.

11. **Malika** Will you come to my birthday party on Wednesday ?
Manjula Are you celebrating it at your home ?
Malika No, I have booked a few tables at McDonalds.

Malika asked Manjula ***(a)*** .... on Wednesday. Manjula wanted to know ***(b)*** .... Malika informed her ***(c)*** .... McDonalds.

12. **Tom** What are you doing there, Jerry?
Jerry I'm writing a letter to my friend.
Tom How long will it take you to finish it?
Jerry I may finish it in ten minutes.

Tom asked Jerry what ***(a)*** .... Jerry answered that he was writing a letter to his friend. Tom wanted to know how long ***(b)*** .... to finish it. Jerry said that ...... ***(c)*** .... it in ten minutes.

13. **Teacher** What happened, Ramesh?
Student Madam, I lost my book.
Teacher Don't worry, it can be in your bag.
Student Madam, I can't find my bag.

(a) The teacher asked Ramesh ....
(b) Ramesh told his teacher that ....
(c) The teacher told him not to worry as ....
(d) The student replied that he couldn't find his bag.

14. **Radha** I went to see an English play last night.
Pixie Was it good?
Radha It was marvellous.

Radha told Pixie *(a)*...... an English play the previous night. Pixie asked her *(b)* .... Radha replied *(c)* .... .

15. Read the conversation given below and complete the paragraph that follows. Write the answers against the correct blank numbers in your answer sheet. Do not copy the whole sentences.

On the way from the market a mother and son see beggars on the sidewalk.

Son Why are they asking for money, Mummy?
Mother It is because they are poor, darling.
Son Can't we give them the fruits we have bought?
Mother We will give them money to buy whatever they choose.

On seeing the beggars the son *(a)* .... When the mother replied that it was because they were poor, the boy wondered *(b)* .... The mother replied that *(c)* ....

16. Read the conversation given below and complete the paragraph that follows. Write the answers against the correct blank numbers in your answer sheet. Do not copy the whole sentences.

Asha Who is the person leaning on the iron pole?
Lan He is a beggar. He is a trouble to the passengers.
Asha He seems to be blind.

Asha asked Lan *(a)* ...... Lan told her *(b)* ...... and was a trouble to the passengers. Asha commented *(c)* ....

Type IV Editing and Omission

1. The following passage has not been edited. One word is missing from each line. Identify the missing word and write it in your answer sheet along with the word that comes before and after it. Remember to underline the missing word. The first one has been done as an example for you.

	Before	Missing	After
e.g. Two hundred seamstresses employed to make my shirts. They	seamstresses	were	employed
(a) took measurement	....	....	....
(b) as lay on the ground.	....	....	....
(c) Then measured my right	....	....	....
(d) thumb desired no more.	....	....	....

2. The following passage has not been edited. One word is missing from each line. Identify the missing word and write it in your answer sheet along with the word that comes before and after it. Remember to underline the missing word. The first one has been done as an example for you.

	Before	Missing	After
e.g. The initial step making popcorn balls	step	in	making
(a) is popping the popcorn. Cover bottom	....	....	....
(b) of the pan cooking oil. Put the burner on high, or, on a gas stove,	....	....	....
(c) turn flame high. Gas stoves	....	....	....
(d) seem heat much more quickly and evenly.	....	....	....

3. The following passage has not been edited. One word is missing from each line. Identify the missing word and write it in your answer sheet along with the word that comes before and after it. Remember to underline the missing word.

	Before	Missing	After
(a) A man getting very impatient. Again and again	....	....	....
(b) he would peep the doctor's room to see how	....	....	....
(c) many patients were left. After a long time his turn	....	....	....
(d) came, he got up said, "Sorry doctor I don't have a headache now."	....	....	....

4. The following passage has not been edited. One word is missing from each line. Identify the missing word and write it in your answer sheet along with the word that comes before and after it. Remember to underline the missing word.

	Before	Missing	After
(a) Fresh vegetables be cooked to perfection in the	....	....	....
(b) microwave. They retain their full flavour, nutrients and colour. Vegetables can be cooked in casserole	....	....	....
(c) dishes lids, stirring once during the cooking period.	....	....	....
(d) Roasting boiling bags can also be used for some vegetables with the ends loosely closed.	....	....	....

5. The following passage has not been edited. One word is missing from each line. Identify the missing word and write it in your answer sheet along with the word that comes before and after it. Remember to underline the missing word.

	Before	Missing	After
(a) Nowadays, most the children get an opportunity	....	....	....
(b) to go on school trips. They jump the chance to be	....	....	....
(c) away home for a week or two. Some children,	....	....	....
(d) especially those leaving home for first time, very much miss their parents.	....	....	....

6. There is an error in each line. Write the incorrect word and the correction in the answer sheet as given below.

	Incorrect	Correct
(a) The global obesity crisis or rising levels of	....	....
(b) chronic disease such as diabetes and strokes	....	....
(c) has put pressure on fast food chains to cut	....	....
(d) the salt, fat and sugar content in what they sell.	....	....

7. There is an error in each line. Write the incorrect word and the correction in the answer sheet as given below.

	Incorrect	Correct
(a) Summer always spells magic. That is the time	....	....
(b) when schools closed their gates and loved	....	....
(c) ones—cousins, uncles or aunts descend	....	....
(d) in the spacious family home.	....	....

8. There is an error in each line. Write the incorrect word and the correction in the answer sheet as given below.

Tens of thousands of bats emerged from under

	Incorrect	Correct
(a) the bridge. It was a amazing sight.	....	....
(b) I learnt a few fact about these creatures.	....	....
(c) The baby bats is known as pups.	....	....
(d) Each mother bat delivers only one pups.	....	....

9. There is an error in each line. Write the incorrect word and the correction in the answer sheet as given below.

	Incorrect	Correct
(a) A one-eyed man was travelling through a bus	....	....
(b) one day. He was carrying a huge bag on him	....	....
(c) shoulder. Anyone sitting next to him said,	....	....
(d) "Why didn't you keep your bag under the seat?" The man smiled and said, "It is too big."	....	....

10. **There is an error in each line. Write the incorrect word and the correction in the answer sheet as given below.**

		Incorrect	Correct
(a)	In the process to learning, self-help is the	....	....
(b)	better help. Depending always on others,	....	....
(c)	even on teachers or parents, is a sign of	....	....
(d)	weakness. In the Mahabharata, their is a	....	....
	wonderful character of Eklavya who is an ideal for modern students.		

11. **There is an error in each line. Write the incorrect word and the correction in the answer sheet as given below.**

		Incorrect	Correct
(a)	Satyajit Ray, which conceived	....	....
(b)	and directed a long number	....	....
(c)	of films, were one of India's	....	....
(d)	most talented film maker.	....	....

12. **There is an error in each line. Write the incorrect word and the correction in the answer sheet as given below.**

Neem is used by Ayurvedic practioners in India

		Incorrect	Correct
(a)	for years at a wide range of ailments.	....	....
(b)	In many tropical countries, Neem as referred to	....	....
(c)	for 'the village pharmacy'. In India	....	....
(d)	villagers chewed the Neem twig to brush his teeth.	....	....

13. **There is an error in each line. Write the incorrect word and the correction in the answer sheet as given below.**

		Incorrect	Correct
(a)	During the water cycle some of a water in	....	....
(b)	the oceans and freshwater bodies are warmed	....	....
(c)	on the Sun and it evaporates. During the process	....	....
(d)	of evaporation, impurities in the water is left behind.	....	....

14. **The following passage has not been edited. One word is missing from each line. Identify the missing word and write it in your answer sheet along with the word that comes before and after it. Remember to underline the missing word. The first one has been done as an example for you.**

		Before	Omission	After
e.g.	Mark Twain, had earned a reputation	Twain	who	had
(a)	as a humour writer, got invitation to	....	....	....
(b)	address public meeting. He reached the city	....	....	....
(c)	on the day the meeting. When he reached	....	....	....
(d)	there, he did not find single person. He realised	....	....	....
	that the joke was on him.			

15. **The following paragraph has not been edited. One word is missing from each line. Identify the missing word and write it along with the word that comes before and after it in your answer sheet.**

		Before	Omission	After
e.g.	Proteins are hard digest.	hard	to	digest
(a)	Coupled heat and dehydration	....	....	....
(b)	they bring discomfort you. Your	....	....	....
(c)	protein intake not exceed 57gm	....	....	....
(d)	if your body weight 57 kg.	....	....	....

ANSWERS

Type I : Gap Filling

1. (a) the (b) was (c) preached
2. (a) nobody (b) felt (c) her
3. (a) replete (b) have taken (c) accompanied
4. (a) must (b) should (c) may (d) should (e) will (f) must
5. (a) the (b) a (c) a (d) the (e) these (f) the
6. (a) (ii) several (b) (i) to carry (c) (iv) made (d) (i) that
7. (a) (i) is (b) (i) recognise (c) (iii) must
8. (a) (ii) played (b) (iii) is (c) (ii) the
9. (a) (i) the (b) (iii) their (c) (ii) are
10. (a) (ii) spread (b) (i) was (c) (iii) die
11. (a) (ii) some (b) (iii) his (c) (iv) that
12. (a) (iv) starting (b) (iv) several (c) (iv) that
13. (a) (iii) lived (b) (i) flow (c) (ii) bear
14. (a) Most (b) encouraged (c) her

Type II : Sentence Reordering

1. (a) The atmosphere is very cold at both these places.
   (b) They experience extreme solar exposure periods.
   (c) Therefore, there are several similarities in the weather patterns.
2. (a) It is one of the oldest and largest medical research bodies in the world.
   (b) It functions under Indian Council of Medical Research.
   (c) Purpose of definiteness is the starting point of achievement.
3. (a) It is highly valued for its medicinal properties and fragrance.
   (b) In ancient times, a paste of sandal and turmeric was used by women for a blemish free skin.
   (c) The purest renowned sandal oil of Mysore comes from sandalwood trees.
4. (a) Children below the age of eighteen years must not drive.
   (b) We must wear helmets for our own protection.
   (c) Mobile phones must not be used while driving.
5. (a) I remember my childhood as being generally happy.
   (b) I can recall some of my carefree times.
   (c) I can also remember my frightening moments.
6. (a) The candidates even walk on foot to greet people.
   (b) They catch the opportunity of shaking hands with anyone they meet.
   (c) Their supporters assure people that they will solve their problems.
7. (a) Senior citizens are not respected or cared for.
   (b) Old age homes are not only ill-equipped but also insufficient.
   (c) The society must place them before anyone else's interest.
8. (a) The conversation can go on for three minutes.
   (b) The line gets disconnected soon after.
   (c) It is a good way to get in touch with your near and dear ones.
9. (a) Only 300 out of the 2700 known species are venomous.
   (b) Snake venom is a yellow liquid which is 90% water.
   (c) It is a substance that is expelled from the poison gland.
10. (a) The green leaves of trees and plants absorb this carbon dioxide.
    (b) It is broken down into carbon and oxygen.
    (c) The carbon is used to make starch and oxygen is released into air.
11. The bank is closed today as it is the second Saturday of the month.
12. I was not feeling well so I slept the whole day.
13. I have to take my mother to the hospital as she is not keeping well.
14. Watch the video to find out how to change the world in just five minutes of your day!
15. But did you know that we can't use most of it?

Type III : Sentence Transformation

1. (a) that the car had been towed away as he had parked
   (b) if he could be excused that time
   (c) he hoped he would remember the lesson he had learnt that day
2. (a) what he had been doing the day before
   (b) he had been walking his dog in the park
   (c) if he had met anyone in the park
3. (a) if he could read what was written on that page
   (b) he couldn't read all the words
   (c) if he would like to read them
4. (a) if anything was missing
   (b) where she had kept it
   (c) had kept it on the dressing table
5. (a) how his hen had died
   (b) he had poured hot water into its mouth
   (c) actually he had thought it would give him boiled eggs
6. (a) if he could have a small bottle of tomato sauce
   (b) when it would be available
   (c) he would take it the next day

7. (a) which restaurant he would like to go to
(b) that he would like to go to Rama's because he liked
(c) that that day they should go out to some South Indian restaurant

8. (a) if he could have an appointment with the doctor that evening
(b) he would have to wait for at least two weeks
(c) it was no problem, and if his wife informed her, she would cancel

9. (a) to give him some money
(b) he didn't do
(c) that begging was also work

10. (a) if he knew swimming
(b) if he could teach him
(c) to come to his place the next day

11. (a) if she would come to her birthday party
(b) whether she was celebrating it at her home
(c) that she had booked a few tables at

12. (a) he was doing there
(b) it would take him
(c) he might finish

13. (a) what had happened
(b) he had lost his book
(c) it could be in his bag

14. (a) that she had gone to see/watch
(b) whether it had been good
(c) that it was marvellous

15. (a) inquired why they were asking for money
(b) if they couldn't give them the fruits they had bought
(c) they would give them money to buy whatever they choose.

16. (a) who the person leaning on the iron pole was
(b) that he was a begger
(c) that he seemed to be blind.

Type IV : Editing and Omission

	Before	Missing	After
1.	(a) took	my	measurement
	(b) as	I	lay
	(c) Then	they	measured
	(d) thumb	and	desired
2.	(a) Cover	the	bottom
	(b) pan	with	cooking
	(c) flame	to	high
	(d) seem	to	heat
3.	(a) man	was	getting
	(b) peep	into	the
	(c) time	when	his
	(d) up	and	said
4.	(a) vegetables	can	be
	(b) They	can	retain
	(c) dishes	with	lids
	(d) Roasting	or	boiling
5.	(a) most	of	the
	(b) jump	at	the
	(c) away	from	home
	(d) for	the	first

	Incorrect	Correct
6.	(a) or	and
	(b) disease	diseases
	(c) has	have
	(d) in	of
7.	(a) That	It
	(b) closed	close
	(c) or	and
	(d) in	into
8.	(a) a	an
	(b) fact	facts
	(c) is	are
	(d) pups	pup
9.	(a) through	in
	(b) him	his
	(c) Anyone	Someone
	(d) didn't	don't
10.	(a) to	of
	(b) better	best
	(c) or	and
	(d) their	there
11.	(a) which	who
	(b) long	large
	(c) were	was
	(d) maker	makers
12.	(a) at	for
	(b) as	is
	(c) for	as
	(d) his	their
13.	(a) a	the
	(b) are	is
	(c) on	by
	(d) is	are

	Before	Missing	After
14.	(a) got	an	invitation
	(b) address	a	public
	(c) day	of	the
	(d) find	a	single
15.	(a) Coupled	with	heat
	(b) discomfort	to	you
	(c) intake	should	not
	(d) weight	is	57 kg

SECTION D LITERATURE TEXTBOOK

How I Taught My Grandmother to Read

by Sudha Murty

CHAPTER 1

CHAPTER SUMMARY The chapter 'How I Taught My Grandmother to Read' has been written by Sudha Murty. It presents the story of how with the help of her granddaughter, an old lady learned to read. The story portrays how with keen interest and strong determination, we can do anything irrespective of our age.

Kashi Yatre—A Famous Novel

The narrator remembers the times when she was twelve years old. She resided in a village in North Karnataka with her grandparents. In those days, due to an inefficient transport system, the bus carrying magazines and newspapers arrived a day late in the village. The villagers got the morning paper in the afternoon.

During that time, a novel titled *Kashi Yatre*, authored by Triveni, was being published serially in the Kannada weekly magazine named *Karmaveera*. Triveni was a famous author as her novels dealt with complex psychological problems in the lives of ordinary people. Further, her writing style was easy, interesting and convincing. The protagonist of *Kashi Yatre* was an old woman, who had a dream of going to Kashi. However, she donated all of her savings to assist an orphan girl to get married as according to her, the girl's happiness was more important than going to Kashi.

Krishtakka's Passion for Literature

Krishtakka, the narrator's 62-year-old grandmother, loved to hear the episodes of *Kashi Yatre* from her granddaughter. The grandmother had never gone to school so she could not read. On the arrival of the magazine, the grandmother left all her work and sat near her granddaughter to hear the episode. She identified herself with the main character of *Kashi Yatre* as both of them had never been to Kashi. The narrator's grandmother heard the story with the greatest concentration.

Later, she could repeat the entire text by heart. Having heard the episode, she even discussed it with her friends in the temple. Once, the narrator was not in the village as she had gone to attend a relative's marriage. She enjoyed herself thoroughly and stayed there for a week. So, Krishtakka could not hear the next episode of her favourite novel. When the narrator finally returned, she found her grandmother crying. When the narrator asked her grandmother if everything was alright, her grandmother just nodded indicating that everything was fine.

Krishtakka's Childhood

It was at night that the narrator's grandmother told the narrator the reason for her sorrow. She explained why she could not study. Grandmother had lost her mother when she was very young. Her father had remarried. At that time, education was not considered important for girls.

So, the grandmother was not sent to school. She was married at a young age and she got busy with household duties for the rest of her life. She often regretted the fact that she couldn't attend school. The narrator could not understand the reason the grandmother was telling her the story of her life.

Then, the grandmother told her how helpless she felt during the narrator's absence, as she did not get to know how the story of *Kashi Yatre* progressed. She kept on rubbing her hands on the pictures wishing that she could somehow understand the story. However, nothing happened. She felt embarrassed to ask anyone in the village to narrate the episode to her.

Krishtakka's Decision to Learn to Read and Write

The grandmother further said that though they were wealthy, all their wealth was useless when she could not be independent. So, she decided to learn the Kannada alphabet. When she announced her decision, the narrator tried to stop her grandmother from her decision stating her old age. However, the old lady was firm in her desire to learn to read and write.

The narrator made fun of her grandmother but the grandmother smiled and explained that age was no bar for learning. Krishtakka fixed the Saraswati Pooja during Dassara as a deadline to complete her studies.

Sudha Started Tutoring her Grandmother

The narrator started tutoring her grandmother the very next day. Her grandmother proved to be a hardworking student who practised her lessons well. Soon, she could read, write, learn and recite (narrate). The narrator remembers that her grandmother was her first student. Later, she became a teacher in computer science.

Soon, the Dassara festival came and the narrator secretly bought the novel *Kashi Yatre*. On the day, her grandmother called her and she gifted the narrator a frock on the occasion of the Dassara festival.

She also expressed her regard for her granddaughter by touching her feet. This gesture disturbed the narrator as according to her, youngsters touch the feet of God, elders and teachers. The grandmother explained that she touched her feet because it was written in the scriptures that teachers must be respected, irrespective of their gender and age.

Grandmother Passed with Flying Colours

The narrator touched her grandmother's feet as well, and gifted a copy of *Kashi Yatre* to her. The grandmother read the title and the publisher's name on her own. Finally, she had achieved her goal and learnt the Kannada alphabet.

Word Meaning

Word	Meaning
convincing	forceful, capable of causing someone to believe that something is true or real
psychological	related to the mental and emotional state of a person
ardent	very enthusiastic or passionate
punya	reward (in hindi)
concentration	attention
identified	associated, regarded as having strong links with
protagonist	the leading character in a play, film, novel etc

Word	Meaning
debate	discussion
savouring	enjoying slowly to the full
embarrassed	uncomfortable, self-conscious
determination	resolve, self-confidence
reverse	opposite
scriptures	sacred or religious texts
irrespective	without taking into consideration

Textbook FOLDER

Here, we have covered questions given in the CBSE Textbook along with their answers.

ON PAGE 6-7

Q.4A Now that you have enjoyed reading the story, answer the following questions by choosing the correct option.

(i) The grandmother could relate to the central character of the story *'Kashi Yatre'* as ....

(a) both were old and uneducated.

(b) both had granddaughters who read to them.

(c) both had a strong desire to visit Kashi.

(d) both were determined to learn to read.

Ans. (c) both had a strong desire to visit Kashi.

(ii) Why did the women at the temple discuss the latest episode of *Kashi Yatre*?

(a) To pass their time.

(b) The writer, Triveni was very popular.

(c) They could relate with the protagonist of the serial.

(d) Women have a habit of discussing serials.

Ans. (c) They could relate with the protagonist of the serial.

(iii) The granddaughter found her grandmother in tears on her return as

(a) the grandmother had been unable to read the story *Kashi Yatre* on her own.

(b) the grandmother had felt lonely.

(c) the grandmother wanted to accompany her granddaughter.

(d) she was sad that she could not visit Kashi.

Ans. (a) the grandmother had been unable to read the story *Kashi Yatre* on her own.

(iv) Why did the grandmother touch her granddaughter's feet?

(a) She did it as a mark of respect to her teacher.

(b) It was a custom in their family.

(c) Girls should be respected.

(d) She had read the story of '*Kashi*' *Yatre* to her.

Ans. (a) She did it as a mark of respect to her teacher.

(v) "Childishly I made fun of the old lady. But she just smiled." The smile of the grandmother explains that she understood that her granddaughter

(a) was determined to teach her

(b) might be too immature to understand her pain.

(c) would ridicule her later

(d) could be contemplating

Ans. (b) might be too immature to understand her pain

(vi) "Those days, the transport system was not very good, so we used to get the morning papers only in the afternoon." What can you infer from this?

(a) The transport system especially the bus service, was running at loss.

(b) The transport system especially the bus service, was not fully functional in rural areas.

(c) The transport system had stopped services in villages.

(d) The transport system failed to introduce the bus service in rural areas.

Ans. (b) The transport system, especially the bus service, was not fully functional in rural areas.

ON PAGE 8

Q.4B Answer the questions based on the extracts by selecting the correct options.

I. Many times, I rubbed my hands over the pages wishing to understand what was written. But I knew it was not possible. If only I was educated enough .... I waited eagerly for you to return. I felt you would come early and read for me. I could have asked somebody in this village but I was too embarrassed to do so. I felt so very dependent and helpless. We are well-off, but what use is money when I cannot be independent?

1. What made the grandmother feel inadequate?

(a) She was unable to read the story.

(b) She was unable to stay attentive.

(c) She was unable to buy the magazine.

(d) She was unable to understand the story.

Ans. (a) She was unable to read the story.

2. Select the relevant option that best supports the context of the given extract.

1. Grandmother was elated to get the magazine

2. Grandmother was embarrassed to ask for help

3. Grandmother eagerly waited for her granddaughter's arrival

4. Grandmother loved gazing at the pictures from the story

(a) 1 and 2 (b) 2 and 3

(c) 3 and 4 (d) 1 and 4

Ans. (b) 2 and 3

3. Select the option that tracks the progression of emotions experienced by the grandmother in the given extract.

(a) reassured – inquisitive – thankful - uncertain
(b) surprised – grateful – perplexed - excited
(c) yearning - uncertain - dejected - helpless
(d) perplexed – uncertain - panic-stricken – appreciative

Ans. (c) Yearning - uncertain - dejected - helpless

II. She said, "I am touching the feet of a teacher, not my granddaughter; a teacher who taught me so well, with so much of affection that I can read any novel confidently in such a short period. Now I am independent. It is my duty to respect a teacher. Is it not written in our scriptures that a teacher should be respected, irrespective of the gender and age"? I did return namaskara to her by touching her feet and gave my gift to my first student. She opened it and read the title Kashi Yatre by Triveni and the publisher's name immediately. I knew, then, that my student had passed with flying colours.

1. Choose the option that lists the most likely response to ".... I am touching the feet of a teacher".

(a) feel shy (b) get anxious
(c) feel overwhelmed (d) get upset

Ans. (a) feel shy

2. "A teacher should be respected irrespective of gender and age." Select the quote that suggests a reason for this sentiment.

(a) Educating the mind without educating the heart is no education.
(b) A teacher aims to give equal attention to all the students.
(c) A teacher elevates the mind and gives energy to the character.
(d) Teaching is a profession that teaches all other professions.

Ans. (d) Teaching is a profession that teaches all other professions.

3. Select the sentence that best brings out the meaning of 'confidently' as used in the extract.

(a) Some of the information was confidently misleading.
(b) The report asserts confidently that the world economy will boost from the market collapse.
(c) The present memoir is confidently a tribute to his ability and character.
(d) The pandemic has confidently brought down the market.

Ans. (b) The report asserts confidently that the world economy will boost from the market collapse.

4. Which of the given option stands closest in meaning to 'flying colours'?

(a) Risky (b) Courageous
(c) Profitable (d) Successful

Ans. (d) Successful

ON PAGE 9-10

Q.5 Answer the following questions briefly.

(a) Why did the grandmother depend on her granddaughter to know the story?

Ans. The grandmother depended on her granddaughter to know the story because she could not read. The grandmother was illiterate and she had never been to school. So, she had to wait for her granddaughter to read the story to her.

(b) Pick out two sentences which state that the grandmother was desperate to know what happened in the story.

Ans. The two sentences that state that the grandmother was desperate to know what happened in the story are

(i) "During that time, she would forget all her work and listen with the greatest concentration."
(ii) "So more than anybody else she was the one most interested in knowing what happened next in the story and used to insist that I read the serial out to her."

(c) Could the grandmother succeed in accomplishing her desire to read? How?

Ans. Yes, the grandmother succeeded in accomplishing her desire to read by Dassara festival. She did so with the help of her granddaughter and her will as well as sheer determination. She would practice what was taught to her with sincerity and thus, finally learned to read.

(d) Which of the following traits would be relevant to the character of the narrator's grandmother?

(i) Determined (ii) Selfish (iii) Emotional (iv) Mean

Give reasons for your choice.

Ans. The traits that were relevant to the character of the narrator's grandmother were

(i) **Determined** Though the grandmother was quite old, she took the decision to learn how to read Kannada alphabet and she worked hard. This shows her determination towards learning.
(ii) **Emotional** When the narrator's granddaughter went to a wedding event, she felt helpless and cried as she could not read her favourite novel. She also became emotional while telling about her past life.

(e) "Good fiction's job is to comfort the disturbed and disturb the comfortable." How does this apply to the grandmother after she had finished reading Kashi Yatre? Explain with a reason. Competency Based

Ans. It is true to say that a good fiction comforts the disturbed and disturbs the comfortable. We can say so for the grandmother who lived a very comfortable life. However, her calm nature was disturbed due to the fiction Kashi Yatre. Not only did the grandmother relate to the old lady of the story, but the novel also made her realise how the lack of education was impacting her. She was highly disturbed when she was unable to read Kashi Yatre and decided to learn the Kannada alphabet.

(f) 'Kashi Yatre' was the catalyst in the transformation of the grandmother. Support with an example.

Ans. 'Kashi Yatre' was the catalyst in the transformation of the grandmother as it was due to her interest in its story that she understood the importance of reading on her own.

(g) What message does the story "How I Taught My Grandmother" hold for the present generation and the elders?

Ans. The story "How I taught My Grandmother" teaches the present generation and elders that there is no age-limit to learn things if one is determined and works hard. Anything can be achieved with diligence and willingness.

(h) Grandmother comes across a post online: 'Don't let age be a concern. Live your dream!' As grandmother, write a short paragraph expressing your heartfelt emotion on your achievement.

Ans. Recently, I came across a post online. 'Don't let age be a concern. Live your dream!' It reminded me of my recent achievement-learning to read at on old age. I felt really grateful towards my granddaughter who taught me. If feels great to be self-sufficient and be able to read whatever I like by myself. I no longer have to be dependent on anyone to read anything for me. I thanked my granddaughter by touching her feet and gifting her a frock.

ON PAGE 10

Q.6 Here are some direct quotations from the story. Identify the speaker and write what each quotation suggests about the speaker. You can use the adjectives given in the box and may also add your own.

amiable, tender, gentle, sympathetic, understanding, determined, diligent, kind, concerned, systematic, wise, helpful, enthusiastic, selfish, cruel, humble, religious, prudent, grateful, respectful

Speaker	Quotation	Quality Highlighted
(a)	'Avva, is everything all right? Are you O.K.?'	
(b)	'At times, I used to regret not going to school, so I made sure that my children and grandchildren studied well.'	
(c)	'Avva, don't cry. What is the matter? Can I help you in anyway?'	
(d)	'We are well-off, but what use is money when I cannot be independent.'	
(e)	'I will keep Saraswati Pooja day during Dassara as the deadline.'	
(f)	'For a good cause if you are determined you can overcome any obstacle.'	
(g)	I am touching the feet of a teacher not my granddaughter.'	

Ans.

	Speaker	Quotation	Quality Highlighted
(a)	Writer/granddaughter	'Avva, is everything all right? Are you O.K.?'	Concerned /gentle
(b)	The grandmother	'At times, I used to regret not going to school, so I made sure that my children and grandchildren studied well.'	Determined
(c)	The writer/grand daughter	'Avva, don't cry. What is the matter? Can I help you in anyway?'	Helpful understanding
(d)	The grandmother	'We are well-off, but what use is money when I cannot be independent.'	Wise
(e)	The grandmother	'I will keep Saraswati Pooja day during Dassara as the deadline.'	Determined
(f)	The grandmother	'For a good cause if you are determined you can overcome any obstacle.'	Diligent
(g)	The grandmother	I am touching the feet of a teacher not my granddaughter.'	Religious

WRITING TASK ON PAGE 11

Q.8 Imagine you are the grandmother. How would you feel if your granddaughter gave you the novel 'Kashi Yatre'? Write your feelings in your diary.

To make your diary entry interesting, read the following information about what is a diary entry.

A diary entry is a purely personal piece of writing. The writer expresses his/her thoughts and feelings. Reactions to incidents are generally poured out in a diary. Hence expressions that are emotionally charged are used.

For example - When you are happy about something, you could start like this -

> 8th July 20xx, Wednesday 8 pm
> Today I am very happy as.
> ....

Ans. Thursday, 8th July, 20XX 8 pm

Dear Diary

Today, I am very happy as my granddaughter had gifted me the novel Kashi Yatre. Yes, it is the same novel whose story comes in that magazine that I have to wait for every week. Now, I can read it in one go. Yes, I myself can read it, all thanks to my Sudha.

I had never being educated due to the circumstances of my childhood. Hence, I felt dependent and so sad because I couldn't read my favourite novel while my granddaughter was not here. So, I decided to learn how to read. It took a lot of hard work and dedication but finally, I was able to do it.

My teacher, my dear Sudha gifted me the entire novel which I plan to read in one go.

Krishtakka

ON PAGE 12

Q.9 While the country has made significant progress in improving adult literacy over the years, it continues to be home to 313 million illiterate people; 59 percent of them are women.

The story 'How I Taught My Grandmother to Read' showcases a young girl helping her unlettered grandmother grow self-sufficient. The story is also a subtle eye-opener for the youth that if they realise their moral obligation, they can take the country to greater heights. Pen down your thoughts in a blog on how the youth brigade of the nation can help alleviate Adult Illiteracy.

You may begin your blogpost like this:

India is considered one of the potential superpowers of the world but.

To create a blog, read the given information about what is a blog

> Blog is a short form for the word weblog and the two words are used interchangeably.
>
> A blog is a regularly updated online personal journal or diary. It is a platform to express yourself to the world.

Ans.

How the Youth Brigade can Alleviate Adult Literacy?

India is considered one of the potential superpowers of the world but it is still a home to 313 million illiterate people and 59% of them are women. In the times when education is an important criterion for everyone, it is cruical for all of us as Indians to ensure that everybody learns how to read and write. Some people might think that they are too old for this. However, I disagree. Everybody can learn anything irrespective of their age. The story 'How I taught my grandmother to read' can tell us exactly how. It is the story of Sudha Murthy's grandmother who decided to learn the Kannada language at 62 and was successful in it.
Thus, learning has no age. The story encourages the youth of the country to fulfil their moral obligation and teach their elders to read and write. This would make them self-sufficient and educated as they would be able to learn by reading more. Since the elders didn't get many opportunities to learn, this will be really helpful for them and benefit the entire society.This would also reduce the stigma around learning and education, promoting its value in our society.

REVIEW EXERCISE

Including Exam Pattern Practice Questions

Extract Based Questions

Read the following extracts carefully and answer the questions that follow.

1. At that time, Triveni was a very popular writer in the Kannada language. She was a wonderful writer. Her style was easy to read and very convincing. Her stories usually dealt with complex psychological problems in the lives of ordinary people and were always very interesting. Unfortunately for Kannada literature, she died very young. Even now, after forty years, people continue to appreciate her novels.

(a) **Why does the narrator call Triveni a wonderful writer ?**

Ans. The narrator calls Triveni a wonderful writer because, her style was quite simple and easy to read.

(b) **What were the two special characteristics of her stories?**

Ans. Two special characteristics of her stories are

- Her stories dealt with complex psychological problems in the lives of ordinary people.
- Her stories were quite interesting.

(c) **Who is appreciated even after 40 years of death and how?**

Ans. Triveni is appreciated even after 40 years of death as people continue to read and appreciate her novels.

(d) **Why has the author used the word 'unfortunately'?**

Ans. The author has used the word unfortunately to mention the untimely death of Triveni, a young author.

2. Most Hindus believe that going to Kashi and worshipping Lord Vishweshwara is the ultimate punya. This old lady also believed in this, and her struggle to go was described in that novel. In the story, there was a young orphan girl who falls in love but there was no money for the wedding. In the end, the old lady gives away all her savings without going to Kashi.

(a) **Who is the orphan young girl mentioned in the extract?**

Ans. The orphan young girl mentioned in the extract is one of the characters in *Kashi Yatre,* a novel by Triveni, a very popular writer in the Kannada language.

(b) **Why does the old lady give away all her savings without going to Kashi?**

Ans. The old lady was saving money to go to Kashi and worship Lord Vishweshwara there. However, she believed that helping a young orphan girl in getting married, and thus making her happy was more important than visiting Kashi.

(c) **What does the old lady in the story show?**

Ans. The old lady in the story shows her religious and selfless nature.

(d) **Select the phrase in the extract which means to donate.**

Ans. Give away

3. I could have asked somebody in this village but I was too embarrassed to do so. I felt so very dependent and helpless. We are well-off, but what use is money when I cannot be independent?

(a) **Whom is the speaker talking to?**

Ans. The speaker Krishtakka is talking to her granddaughter, the narrator.

(b) **What could the speaker have asked somebody for?**

Ans. The speaker could have asked somebody in the village to read the story of *Kashi Yatre* to her, as her granddaughter was not in the village.

(c) **Antonym of 'helpless' is ....**

Ans. 'capable'

(d) **By 'independent' the speaker here means ....**

Ans. to be able to read and write on her own

4. But I knew it was not possible. If only I was educated enough ......I waited eagerly for you to return. I felt you would come early and read for me. I even thought to going to the village and asking you to read for me. I could have asked somebody in this village but I was too embarrassed to do so. I felt so very dependent and helpless. "We are well-off, but what use is money when I cannot be independent?"

(a) **Who is the speaker?**

Ans. The grandmother 'Krishtakka', is the speaker.

(b) **Why is the speaker not independent?**

Ans. The speaker is not independent because she is illiterate and has to depend on her granddaughter for reading her favourite novel.

(c) **What does the word 'well-off' mean?**

Ans. The phrase 'well off' means 'wealthy'.

(d) **What is the speaker feeling in the given extract?**

Ans. The speaker is feeling helpless in the extract.

5. I will work very hard. I will keep *Saraswati Pooja* day during *Dassara* as the deadline.

(a) **What is the task for which the deadline is fixed?**

Ans. The grandmother fixes a deadline for the day she will be able to read and write on her own.

(b) **Why will the speaker work hard?**

Ans. The speaker will work hard to become a literate person.

(c) **What do you mean by 'deadline'?**

Ans. The word 'deadline' means 'target date'.

(d) **Is the speaker successful in meeting the deadline?**

Ans. Yes, the speaker is successful in meeting the deadline.

6. We have always touched the feet of God, elders and teachers. We consider that as a mark of respect. It is a great tradition, but today the reverse had happened. It was not correct.

(a) **What was the reverse that had happened?**

Ans. It was unusual for the narrator when her grandmother touched her feet because elders never touch the feet of youngsters.

(b) **Why did the grandmother touch the feet of the narrator?**

Ans. She touched the feet of the narrator as a mark of respect to her, because the narrator was also the grandmother's teacher.

(c) **Why was it 'not correct'?**

Ans. It wasn't correct because according to tradition, youngsters touch the feet of elders. However, here the narrator's grandmother touched her feet.

(d) **A word from the extract which can replace 'sign' is ....**

Ans. mark

7. "I am touching the feet of a teacher, not my granddaughter."

A teacher who taught me so well, with so much of affection that I can read any novel confidently in such a short period. Now I am independent. It is my duty to respect a teacher. Is it not written in our scriptures that a teacher should be respected, irrespective of the gender and age?

(a) **Name the speaker.**

Ans. The speaker's name is Krishtakka.

(b) **Why does the speaker say this?**

Ans. The speaker says this because, when she touched the feet of her granddaughter, the latter was quite shocked and surprised.

(c) **Which quality of the speaker is highlighted here?**

Ans. These lines show that the speaker is very humble and full of gratitude towards her granddaughter, who taught her to read and write.

(d) **Who is the teacher here?**

Ans. The young Sudha Murthy is the teacher here.

8. I did return *namaskara* to her by touching her feet and gave my gift to my first student. She opened it and read the title *Kashi Yatre* by Triveni and the publisher's name immediately. I knew then that my student had passed with flying colours.

(a) **Whom does 'I' here refer to?**

Ans. 'I' here refers to Sudha Murty, the narrator of the story.

(b) **What is the relationship between the student and the teacher?**

Ans. The student refers to the narrator's grandmother and the teacher refers to her granddaughter, Sudha.

(c) **The phrase 'to pass with flying colours' means ....**

Ans. 'to pass successfully'.

(d) **What quality of the student is revealed in the above lines?**

Ans. These lines show that the student is diligent, determined and dedicated.

Short Answer Type Questions

Answer the following questions in 30-40 words.

1. Write a note on the transport system in the narrator's childhood days.

Ans. In the narrator's childhood days, the transport system was not efficient. The bus carrying magazines and newspapers arrived very late in the village. The villagers got the morning paper only in the afternoon and the weekly magazine after one day.

2. Discuss the theme of *Kashi Yatre*.

Or What is described in the novel, *Kashi Yatre*?

Ans. The theme of the novel *Kashi Yatre* is selflessness. The old lady, who is the protagonist (main character) of the novel, saves up money to visit Kashi. However, when she learned about an orphan girl who needed money for her marriage, she gave all her savings to the orphan girl and decided not to visit Kashi.

3. Krishtakka was illiterate but a very intelligent learner. Explain.

Ans. Even though Krishtakka, the narrator's grandmother was illiterate, she was a very intelligent learner. She could reproduce the entire story of *Kashi Yatre* after it was read to her by her granddaughter. Further, at the age of 62, with her strong willpower, she successfully learned to read and write Kannada.

4. *Kashi Yatre* was grandmother's favourite novel. Why?

Ans. *Kashi Yatre* was grandmother's favourite novel because there was one similarity between the novel's protagonist and the grandmother; both wanted to visit Kashi but never went there. The grandmother also discussed the latest episode of the novel with her friends in the temple.

5. How did the grandmother identify herself with the protagonist of *Kashi Yatre*?

Or How could the grandmother relate herself to the central character of the story *Kashi Yatre*?

Ans. The novel's protagonist was an old woman who had a great desire to go to Kashi, but could not. Similarly, the grandmother too had never been to Kashi and was very eager to go there. This was the reason that the grandmother identified herself with the novel's protagonist.

6. The novel's protagonist longed to go to Kashi. Yet she donated all her savings for the marriage of an orphan girl. Why?

Ans. The novel's protagonist longed to go to Kashi. However, when she learnt that an orphan girl was unable to get married as she had no money, she donated all her savings for the orphan's marriage. This was so because she believed that the happiness of the orphan girl was more important than worshipping Lord Vishweshwara at Kashi.

7. Why was the grandmother in tears?

Or Which incident made the grandmother realise the importance of education? Competency Based

Or Why did the grandmother feel so helpless when her granddaughter went to attend a marriage?

Ans. Once, when her granddaughter was not in the village, the grandmother could not hear the story of her favourite novel. She couldn't read it either, as she was illiterate. She also could not dare ask anyone to narrate the story to her. She got so frustrated at her helplessness that she cried.

8. What provoked the grandmother to decide to learn the Kannada alphabet?

Ans. When her granddaughter had gone to attend a marriage, no one was available to read the story of her favourite novel to the grandmother. She realised that it was a serious drawback that she was illiterate.

Upset over her inability to read on her own, the grandmother decided to learn the Kannada alphabet.

9. Why did the grandmother remain illiterate?

Or What reason did the grandmother give for women not being educated?

Or Why did the grandmother never go to school?

Ans. When the grandmother was a young girl, she lost her mother. There was no one to look after and guide her. Her father was a busy man and had remarried.

As education for girls was not considered essential in those days, the grandmother never went to school. Besides, she got married very young and got busy with household responsibilities.

10. Why did the narrator grow sarcastic after learning that her grandmother wanted to learn the Kannada alphabet?

Or How did the narrator tease her grandmother when she expressed her desire to read?

Ans. When the grandmother announced her decision to learn the Kannada alphabet or expressed her desire to read, the narrator could not believe her ears and laughed at her. She never imagined such a situation that at the age of 62, her grandmother wanted to learn how to read and write. So she made fun of her grandmother.

11. How did the grandmother react to her granddaughter's sarcasm?

Ans. The grandmother did not lose her temper nor did she feel hurt. Rather, she smiled. She said that if one was determined for a good cause, one could overcome any obstacle.

12. How did Sudha Murty help her distressed grandmother?

Ans. Sudha Murty helped her distressed grandmother by accepting her request to teach her. She was aware that at the age of 62, it would be difficult to learn the alphabet. However, with her patient efforts, and her grandmother's hard work and determination, Sudha succeeded in teaching her how to read and write.

13. Why did the grandmother touch the narrator's feet?

Or **The grandmother touched the feet of her granddaughter. How did she justify this gesture of hers?**

Ans. The grandmother touched the narrator's feet as a mark of respect and gratitude. She justified her gesture by saying that it was written in the scriptures that a teacher should be respected, irrespective of gender and age.

14. How had the narrator planned to surprise her grandmother? How was she herself surprised?

Or **Why was Sudha Murty surprised when her grandmother touched her feet?**

Ans. The narrator, Sudha Murty had planned to surprise her grandmother by gifting her a copy of the novel *Kashi Yatre* on the day of *Saraswati Pooja.*

However, on that day she herself was surprised when her grandmother touched her feet because according to traditions, elders never touched the feet of youngers. Instead, it is the youngsters who show respect to elders by touching their feet.

15. Describe the relationship between Avva and the narrator in the lesson 'How I Taught My Grandmother to Read'.

Ans. Krishtakka was Sudha Murty's grandmother, but she was called Avva, meaning mother, out of affection. They shared a very good relationship. They were more like friends and both understood each other very well. Sudha taught Krishtakka how to read and write, finally making her literate.

16. Justify the title of the story.

Ans. The title, 'How I Taught My Grandmother to Read' is very appropriate as it indicates how the narrator taught her grandmother who had remained illiterate till she was 62 years old.

It also reflects on the narrator's ability to teach her old grandmother, which becomes important in the light of the fact that the narrator took up teaching as a profession when she grew up.

Long Answer Type Questions

Answer the following questions in 120 words.

1. 'I want to be independent.' What does it tell you about the theme of 'How I Taught My Grandmother to Read'?

Ans. It is very difficult to cope up with the present world and its challenges without the tool of education. Only educated people are independent. One realises one's true self only with education. The best example is of the grandmother who at the age of 62 realises the importance of education. She used to listen to the story of *Kashi Yatre* from her granddaughter. She identified herself with the protagonist as both of them were old and illiterate, and had a desire to go to Kashi. However, it was during the absence of her granddaughter that she realised her mental handicap. She cried at her helplessness. She, then, decided to learn the Kannada alphabet. She was determined to get educated and become independent. With the help of her granddaughter along with her dedication and hard work, she did achieve her goal.

Thus, she proved that for learning, age is no bar. One can learn to read and write at any age, at any time.

2. 'I am independent.' Based on this statement of the grandmother, write a paragraph on the topic 'Education Can Make One Independent' in about 120 words. Highlight the important values that we learn through education. Competency Based

Ans. Education Can Make One Independent

Education is an important human activity which develops an individual's innate powers and potentialities and makes him/her self-dependent. A person who is not educated cannot be independent as he has to depend on others for a number of things. Such a person has no idea of his own rights. He/she finds difficulties in doing simple things such as filling forms, reading notices/ newspapers, opening a bank account etc. Such a person cannot do things independently.

The grandmother in this story, who could read the episodes of the novel after being made literate by her granddaughter, exemplifies what an educated person can do.

3. Krishtakka is firm to learn the Kannada alphabet though her granddaughter teases her. Krishtakka just smiles and says, "For a good cause if you are determined, you can overcome any obstacle. I will work harder than anybody, but I will do it. For learning there is no age bar." Her weak faculties do not disturb her at all and she is overpowered by her determination and self-motivation. Motivated by her story, you decide to write a letter to your younger brother, who has indulged in disreputable activities at the cost of his studies, telling him about the value of determination and self-motivation.

Ans. 16, ABC Street
Agra

12th December, 20XX

Dear Piyush

How are you? Yesterday mother told me that you have been ignoring your studies, although you had been sent to the hostel for concentrating on them. If you are self-motivated and determined to reach the top, nothing can deter you.

Recently, I read a story called 'How I Taught My Grandmother to Read'. Although the protagonist of the story is a 62 years old illiterate lady, she decides to learn the alphabet. She works hard and passes with flying colours. When she can succeed at such an old age, can't you succeed being so young, energetic and enthusiastic? So, fix your goal, leave your time-wasting activities and you'll surely perform very well.

Awaiting a positive reply.

Yours affectionately
Rajeev

4. Your grandparents want to study despite their weak faculties and they have chosen you as their teacher. You are happy as well as confused. Write a diary entry expressing your feelings and the values that are required to study and learn the alphabet.

Ans. Friday, 18th March, 20XX 10 pm

Dear Diary

I have a surprising news for you. My grandparents want to study at this age. It came as a shock to me, but I am happy as they want to study, irrespective of their age and are aware of the fact that they have to work hard.

At the same time, I am also confused. They have weak faculties. One needs constant attention and strong faculties to pursue studies, which they have lost. I wonder how I will teach them. Will I be able to teach them? Where do I start from? Nevertheless, I have decided to teach them. I will do my duty honestly. They have placed all their trust in me and I will remain faithful to them. I wish them success.

May God bless my old but lovable and caring students!

Sudha

5. Write a character sketch of Krishtakka, the grandmother.

Or **Give the character sketch of the grandmother as depicted in the story 'How I Taught My Grandmother to Read'. Mention the values that you learn from her character.** **Competency Based**

Ans. The grandmother is the central character, around whom the entire story revolves. She is 62 years old and all her life has been devoted to the kitchen-chores and well-being of her family. Though she had not been educated herself, she knew the value of education and made sure that all her children and grandchildren were well-educated. She was however, a determined and independent women.

The novel *Kashi Yatre* stirs in her a yearning (longing) for a visit to Kashi. This shows that the grandmother is quite religious.

She is a lady of great commitment, courage and indomitable spirit, which is evident in her desire to master the Kannada alphabet, even at the age of 62. The grandmother proves to be an ideal and diligent student who achieves her desired goal. Moreover, she is quite humble and grateful. She is not even a bit hesitant in touching her granddaughter's feet as a mark of respect and gratitude towards her young teacher.

ASSESSMENT EXERCISE

Extract Based Questions

Read the following extracts carefully and answer the questions that follow.

1. The weekly magazine used to come one day late. All of us would wait eagerly for the bus, which used to come with the papers, weekly magazines and the post.
   (a) Why did the weekly magazine come late?
   (b) Why did the speaker's family wait eagerly for the weekly magazine?
   (c) Name the weekly magazine.
   (d) The opposite of 'late' is ....
2. The amount of homework she did was amazing. She would read, repeat, write and recite.
   (a) Who is she in the above lines? What 'homework' is being talked about here?
   (b) Why was she so keen on doing the homework?
   (c) What does the given line tell us about 'she'?
   (d) How is the speaker/author feeling about 'she'?

Short Answer Type Questions

Answer the following questions in 30-40 words.

1. Everyone in the village would eagerly wait for the bus which brought papers, weekly magazines and the post. What does this tell us about the villagers?
2. Why was Triveni immensely popular among the people?
3. Do you think the protagonist of *Kashi Yatre* completed her pilgrimage, even though she could never visit Kashi? How?
4. Why was the narrator's grandmother so eager to know what happened in the story *Kashi Yatre*?
5. What kind of relationship did Sudha Murty and her grandmother share?
6. Why did the grandmother think of learning to read and write at the age of sixty-two?
7. Do you think Krishtakka was a good student? Support your answer with examples from the story.
8. How did the grandmother show respect for her 'teacher'? How did the 'teacher' react?

Long Answer Type Questions

Answer the following questions in 120 words.

1. Does Sudha Murty's story 'How I Taught My Grandmother to Read' sensitise its readers to family bonding especially to the needs of elders? Explain with suitable examples from the story.
2. Krishtakka, the narrator's grandmother, says, 'For learning there is no age bar.' She then herself goes on to prove her statement. How? Is she successful?
3. Though the narrator's grandmother was illiterate, yet she was quite well-versed in the teachings of the scriptures. Do you agree with this statement? What values taught in the scriptures are reflected in the grandmother's character? Explain.

CHAPTER 2

A Dog Named Duke

by William D Ellis

CHAPTER SUMMARY

The story, 'A Dog Named Duke' authored by William D Ellis, describes a dog's amazing loyalty towards his paralysed master, Charles Hooper (Chuck), as well as the bond of love between the two. The story conveys that love knows no species or language and can do wonders.

Duke and Charles Hooper

Duke was a four year old Doberman Pinscher. He weighed 23 kilos, and had red as well as fawn coloured fur. Charles Hooper got him even though his wife, Marcy, wanted a Pomeranian. Chuck visited Duke at the kennel several times before he made up his mind. However, it took a long time before Marcy was more than polite to the dog.

Charles Hooper (Chuck) was a tall and smart young man. He was cheerful, physically fit and a professionally-settled man, who worked as a Zone Sales Manager for a chemical company. Charles Hooper was quite ambitious and highly competitive.

Charles Hooper's Paralysing Accident

One day while driving home, Charles Hooper met with a car accident. He was taken to the hospital with a subdural haemorrhage (bleeding of the brain) which completely paralysed the left side of his body.

While in recovery, Charles couldn't talk. He was alive but couldn't see properly. Charles stayed in the critical condition for a month and after five weeks, he was asked to take a one year leave. He was also told that he would get a desk job at the headquarters of his company after the year.

When Charles was in the hospital, Duke, his dog, was sent to a kennel while his wife, Marcy came to the hospital.

Charles Hooper's Recovery

About six weeks after the accident, Charles Hooper was put on a wheelchair and someone was working on his paralysed arm and leg daily but charles' recovery was very slow. In March, he was discharged from the hospital. After the initial excitement of homecoming, Charles began to get bored at home. Life became lonely for him as his wife used to go to her job and he was left alone for the whole day.

Duke Returns Home

Finally, Duke was brought home from the dog shelter. Charles insisted on standing when Duke came in. As soon as Duke saw Charles, he jumped on him due to which Charles could hardly keep his balance. From then onwards, Duke took up his position near Charles Hooper's bed and never jumped on him, as if he understood everything.

Charles is Changed

The accident had a huge impact on Charles. He lost his smile and used to stare at the ceiling, out the window and Duke all day. This change affected Marcy who used to cry upon seeing her husband in such a state.

Duke Helps Charles Hooper to Start Walking

Right from day one, Duke seemed to understand his master's needs and did not leave his bedside even for a moment. Soon, Duke lost patience and began pushing and teasing his master, persuading him to respond. The dog guided his master and was apparently (probably) bent upon making him walk again.

One day, Charles took hold of the leash of Duke's collar. With the help of Duke and Marcy, Charles stood up and took one step. However, he collapsed on the wheelchair after this. Next day, again due to Duke's constant pushing Charles took four steps. The progress was slow but gradually, Charles learned to balance his body without Marcy. Slowly, Charles started walking and in two weeks, he walked till the front porch.

The neighbours saw Duke struggling with Charles everyday. They would notice how Duke would wait for Charles to reach him and then, move forward. Gradually, Duke and Charles set targets- on Monday they would reach the sixth fence post and on Tuesday, the seventh post. When Marcy told the doctor about Charles's progress and he prescribed a course of physiotherapy for him along with walking everyday with Duke.

Charles' Progress

On 1st June, Charles and Duke reached an intersection located far away. Then, Duke started pushing Charles for two trips a day and they increased the targets. Duke no longer waited at each step. On 4th January, Charles walked the 200 metres from the clinic to the local branch office of his company without Duke. This had been one of the district offices under his jurisdiction as Zone Manager.

At the office, Charles told Gordon Doule, the manager, to get him up to date on what's happened so that he could get to work. He told Doule that he would work for an hour on the empty desk in the warehouse each day. He also requested a dictating machine. However, his decision presented problems because he couldn't move effectively.

Charles Hooper Starts Working Again

After March, Charles did not need the physiotherapy and went to office. With the help of Duke, Charles was improving his stability and endurance (strength). After 13 months in the job, Charles started working well and he was promoted to the position of Regional Manager.

In March 1956, Charles, Marcy and Duke moved to a new house where people did not know what Duke had done for his master. All they knew was that Charles walked like a mechanical giant and the dog pulled him as if he owned him.

Duke Dies in an Accident

On 12th October, 1957, Duke met with an accident when Charles had guests. Suddenly, Charles heard the screech of brakes outside. Duke was hit by a car. Marcy insisted on carrying Duke himself and she took him to an animal hospital but the doctors could not save him. Later, Charles received a letter from his company for promotion as Assistant National Sales Manager. Charles felt that this promotion was a tribute to Duke.

Word Meaning

Word	Meaning
fawn	a light brown colour
rambunctiousness	wild or uncontrollable boisterousness, rough
grin	a broad smile
hard-charging	aggressively determined or ambitious
pulled out	moved out from the side of the road, or from its normal position
subdural	occurring between the dura mater and the arachnoid membrane of the brain and spinal cord
haemorrhage	heavy bleeding from a ruptured blood vessel
headway	progress
spied	observed carefully
quivering	trembling or shaking with a slight rapid motion
bellow	a deep roaring shout or sound
slacked	fit or hung loosely
rangy	tall and slim with long, slender limbs
reproachful	expressing disapproval or disappointment
yap	give a sharp, shrill bark
leash	rope, chain
shimmied	moving in a way that involves shaking your hips and shoulders

Word	Meaning
pranced	moved with high springy steps
snapped	quickly moved
tugged	pulled hard or suddenly
porch	a veranda or a covered shelter projecting in front of the entrance of a building
physiotherapy	the treatment of disease, injury, or deformity by physical methods such as massage, heat treatment and exercise rather than by drugs or surgery
whirlpool baths	a therapeutic bath in which all or part of the body is exposed to forceful whirling currents of hot water
intersection	a road junction, where two or more roads intersect
campaigning	striving towards a goal
jurisdiction	authority, control
gaped	stared with one's mouth opened wide in amazement or wonder
warehouse	storeroom
rampageous	boisterously or violently uncontrollable
screech	a loud, harsh, piercing sound
instinctively	spontaneously, naturally
stubbornness	determination, adamancy

Textbook FOLDER

Here, we have covered questions given in the CBSE Textbook along with their answers.

ON PAGE 18

Q.4 Based on your reading of the story, answer the following questions by choosing the correct option.

(a) With reference to Hooper, the author says, "Everything was going for him." What does it imply?

(i) He had everything that a man aspires for.
(ii) People admired him.
(iii) He did what he wanted.
(iv) He was capable of playing games.

Ans. (i) He had everything that a man aspires for.

(b) Duke never jumped on Chuck again because ....

(i) Duke was paralysed and unable to jump.
(ii) Chuck was angry with Duke for jumping at him.
(iii) Duke realised that Chuck was not well and could not balance himself.
(iv) Marcy did not allow Duke to come near Chuck.

Ans. (iii) Duke realised that Chuck was not well and could not balance himself.

(c) The author says that Duke 'knew his job'. The job was ....

(i) to look after Chuck.
(ii) to get Chuck on his feet.
(iii) to humour Chuck.
(iv) to guard the house.

Ans. (ii) to get Chuck on his feet.

(d) "......even Duke's presence didn't reach Chuck". Why?

(i) Duke was locked in his kennel and Chuck couldn't see him.

(ii) Duke hid himself behind the bed post.

(iii) Duke had come to know that Hooper was not well.

(iv) Hooper was lost in his own grief and pain.

Ans. (iv) Hooper was lost in his own grief and pain.

ON PAGE 19

Q.5 Answer the following questions briefly.

(a) In 1953, Hooper was a favoured young man. Explain.

***Or* What made Hooper a favoured man in the year 1953?**

***Or* In what sense was Hooper a favoured young man? Discuss.**

Ans. Hooper was a favoured young man because he was blessed with many positive things in life. He was a tall and handsome young man who worked as a Zone Sales Manager for a chemical company. He had a blissful (happy) married life. He was always wearing a big, genuine smile on his face. He possessed a competitive nature and was an energetic sportsman. He had everything he aspired for in his life.

(b) They said that they would create a desk job for Hooper at headquarters.

(i) Who are 'they'?

(ii) Why did they decide to do this?

Ans. (i) 'They' here refers to the representatives of the chemical company for which Charles Hooper worked.

(ii) They approached Hooper after the fifth week of his accident and decided to create a desk job for him, as he was paralysed and could not do field work.

(c) Duke was an extraordinary dog. What special qualities did he exhibit to justify this? Discuss.

***Or* What special qualities made Duke an extraordinary dog?**

Ans. Duke was an intelligent and extraordinary dog. He jumped on Hooper when he returned from the kennel, but when he saw his master fight for balance, he realised his pain and helplessness and never repeated this act.

He knew his job was to help his master recover soon. It was only because of his help that Hooper could walk on his feet again.

(d) What problems did Chuck present when he returned to the company headquarters?

***Or* How did the members of the staff react when Chuck visited his district office without Duke?**

Ans. When Chuck went to his office (company head quarters) and informed his manager that he would work for an hour daily, the authorities did not seem to welcome his comeback. However, they could not tell him that he was not fit to handle his job because of his determined spirit. Nor did they want to take back a salesman who was unable to move around and could work only an hour a day.

(e) Why do you think Charles Hooper's appointment as Assistant National Sales Manager is considered to be a tribute to Duke?

Ans. Charles Hooper appointment as Assistant National Sales Manager was a tribute to Duke because Hooper's promotion was due to Duke's constant support and inspiration. Had duke not been persistent in his efforts to get his master to walk, charle's recovery would not have been possible.

(f) What thoughts do you think might have crossed Chuck's mind when Marcy quietly went to work and Chuck was alone with his thoughts'?

Ans. When Chuck was alone with his thoughts after Marcy quietly went to work, Chuck's mind might have been filled with thoughts of loneliness and despair. He used to be a favoured young man who excelled at work. He was physically well too. Now, suddenly after his accident, all of that had changed. He could no longer go to work or even walk. He was confined to his wheelchair or bed, alone at home. It would have been really difficult and he would be hoping for quick recovery, some company as well as wishing the accident had never occurred.

(g) 'Small wins help achieve big goals.' Support, with evidence from the text, to show how this applies to Chuck.

Ans. It is true to say that small wins help achieve big goals, especially for Charles. Charles had been in a major accident which left him paralysed. Everyone including him thought that his comeback might be impossible. Things changed as Duke helps him stand up, a small victory for him which made him realise that there was still hope. Afterwards, he tried to focus on small targets as his objectives. Soon, he managed to walk outside his house as well as from one fence post to another. These small victories helped him achieve the big goal in the end as he got appointed as the Assistant National Sales Manager in his company.

Q.6 Following dates were important in Charles Hooper's life in some way. Complete the table by relating the description with the correct dates.

January 4, March 1, June 1, October 12

Date	Description
(a)	News spread that Hooper and Duke had made it to an intersection.
(b)	Hooper walked independently from the clinic to the branch office.
(c)	Hooper planned to start a full day's work at office.
(d)	Duke met with a fatal accident.

Ans. (a) June 1 (b) January 4

(c) March 1 (d) October 12

Writing Task

ON PAGE 21

Q.9 Read the diary entry written by Charles Hooper on the day he received the order, "......Charles Hooper is appointed Assistant National Sales Manager."

Ans. March 1, 19 .... Thursday 10 p.m.

Dear Diary

Last four years have been rather eventful. The day I brought Duke home.... (Marcy was almost impolite to him because she would have preferred a Pomeranian to a Doberman) .... to a stage on 12th October, 1957 (when she would not allow anyone else to carry the injured Duke to the vet)... much water has flowed under the bridge.

From being a very fit, high-charging Zone Sales Manager, I was reduced to a paralysed cripple forced to lie on a bed alone with my thoughts due to a small error by a car driver. Despair had led me on to helplessness... Was I to be a vegetable for the rest of my life? I never wanted to be a burden on Marcy.

Duke's re-entry into my life lifted my numbed spirits. The day he made me take my first step, there was a rekindling of hope. Duke assumed all the responsibility to lead me back to my office desk ... Life had taken a full circle. From shock to denial and helplessness to anger, Duke taught me to cope with the challenges and led me to accept the changed mode of my life. Today, I am happy to be living as well as working successfully.

The order that I have just received is my tribute to Duke who would always be alive with me and be a part of everything else I achieve in my life.

Charles

Q.10 When a person loses something, he is shocked and gets into a state of denial leading to anger. In such a situation coping well leads to acceptance and a changed way of living in view of the loss. Taking cues from what happened or might have happened with Hooper, write your views in the form of an article about 'Coping With Loss' in 80-100 words.

Ans.

Coping With Loss

by Anita Majumdar

Loss is as much a part of human existence as breathing. It is an everyday event. During our lifetime, we experience a variety of losses like death of a loved one, loss of job, financial security etc. With loss comes grief. Some losses can't just be shrugged off; they are voids that trigger a powerful kind of emotional response. It is a very stressful experience that can very quickly weaken your energy and emotional reserves. Chances are you've felt like this too; just like Chuck Hooper did after Duke died. A few ways in which people overcome their sadness are by crying, sharing their feelings, hitting some inanimate (lifeless) objects or similar other things. But the best way is to just shift your focus and move on from there. You should not let your grief control your life. We should thus, take inspiration from his life and should remain firm and strong in challenging times.

REVIEW EXERCISE

Including Exam Pattern Practice Questions

Extract Based Questions

Read the following extracts carefully and answer the questions that follow.

1. In 1953, Hooper was a favoured young man. A big genuine grin civilised his highly competitive nature. Standing six-foot-one, he'd played on the university football team. He was already a hard-charging Zone Sales Manager for a chemical company.

(a) Who was Hooper?

Ans. Hooper was a tall and smart young man with a cheerful and competitive disposition. He worked as a Zone Sales Manager for a chemical company.

(b) What do you mean by a 'favoured young man'?

Ans. The word 'favoured' means blessed. Charles Hooper was living his life to the fullest, and there were no obstacles in his life.

(c) Write three adjectives used for Charles Hooper.

Ans. 'Favoured', 'competitive' and 'hard-charging' are the three adjectives that have been used to describe Hooper.

(d) What is the opposite of 'genuine'?

Ans. The opposite of genuine is fake.

2. One of Chuck's district managers drove Marcy to the hospital. Her husband couldn't talk; he could only breathe and see and his vision was double. Marcy phoned a neighbour, asking him to put Duke in a kennel.

(a) Who was Marcy?

Ans. Marcy was Charles Hooper's wife.

(b) Why was Chuck's condition deteriorating?

Ans. Chuck didn't make much progress at the hospital, probably because he was feeling homesick. The thought that he was crippled (paralysed) for life also depressed him.

(c) What does the text mean by, 'his vision was double?'

Ans. The text 'his vision was double' means that Chuck was seeing two images of everything, probably due to the damage to his brain.

(d) What is a 'Kennel'?

Ans. 'Kennel' is a small shelter for dogs.

3. Finally they decided to bring Duke home. Chuck said he wanted to be standing when Duke came in, so they stood him up.

(a) Who was Duke?

Ans. Duke was a four year old Doberman Pinscher.

(b) Where was Duke?

Ans. Duke was in the kennel.

(c) "....they stood him up". Why could Chuck not stand himself?

Ans. Chuck could not stand by himself as the left side of his body was paralysed due to a serious injury.

(d) What do you mean by 'stood him up'?

Ans. The phrase 'stood him up' means to help someone stand up by supporting him.

4. Finally, they decided to bring Duke home. Chuck said he wanted to be standing when Duke came in, so they stood him up. Duke's nails were long from four months confinement and when he spied Chuck he stood quivering like 5000 volts, then he let out a bellow, spun his long-nailed wheels and launched himself across three metres of air.

(a) Who has been called a 'missile of joy'? Where had Duke been earlier?

Ans. Chuck's dog, Duke, has been called a 'Missile of Joy'. Earlier, Duke had been sent to a kennel by Marcy.

(b) How did he hit Chuck? Why?

Ans. Duke jumped with great excitement to express his joy at meeting his master.

(c) What was 'he' doing?

Ans. 'He' was excited at being reunited with his master.Therefore, he was jumping with excitement.

(d) What does the extract reflect about the dog's attitude towards Hooper?

Ans. Duke was overjoyed and excited when he saw Hooper. This shows the dog's fondness for his master.

5. The once-iron muscles slacked on the rangy frame. Secretly, Marcy cried as she watched the big man's grin fade away. Severe face lines set in like cement, as Chuck stared at the ceiling for hours, then out of the window, then at Duke.

(a) Identify 'the big man' in the current extract.

Ans. 'The big man' refers to the paralysed Charles Hooper.

(b) Why did the big man's grin fade away?

Ans. The big man's grin faded away because the left side of his body was completely paralysed. He was confined to bed and could not move around, and this made him feel really low.

(c) The word .... in the extract is a synonym of "a broad smile."

Ans. 'grin'

(d) What is the opposite of 'security'?

Ans. The opposite of 'secretly' is openly.

6. When two fellows stare at each other day in, day out, and one can't move and the other can't talk, boredom sets in. Duke finally couldn't take it. From a motionless coil on the floor he'd spring to his feet, quivering with impatience.

(a) What does the narrator mean by this?

Ans. The narrator means that Duke, the dog was no longer able to bear the long hours of silence from his master, and thus left his relaxed position on the floor and got into action.

(b) What change did Duke bring about?

Ans. Duke succeeded in coaxing Chuck to stand up on his feet and try to walk, to the effect that Chuck did take a few steps and began to walk again.

(c) Write down the antonym for the word 'motionless'.

Ans. The antonym for the word 'motionless' is 'mobile' or 'moving'.

(d) Why can't one talk and other move?

Ans. One, Duke, can't talk because he is an animal and the other Charley, can't move because he is paralysed.

7. But Duke wouldn't. He'd lie down with a reproachful eye on Hooper. An hour later, he would come over to the bed again and yap and poke. He wouldn't leave but just sit there.

(a) Explain—"But Duke wouldn't."

Ans. Hooper instructed Duke to go and run around the house, which he wouldn't do.

(b) Why would Duke cast a 'reproachful eye' on Hooper?

Ans. Duke wanted to show that he was critical of Hooper because the latter wanted him to run around the house, while he himself remained fixed to the bed.

(c) The word .... in the extract means "to express disapproval."

Ans. reproachful

(d) What does 'yap' mean?

Ans. A sharp and shrill bark is called a 'yap'.

8. By mid-April neighbours saw a daily struggle in front of Marcy's house. Out on the sidewalk they saw the dog pull his leash taut then stand and wait. The man would drag himself abreast of the dog, then the dog would surge out to the end of the leash and wait again. The pair set daily goals; Monday, the sixth fence post, Tuesday, the seventh fence post, Wednesday ...... When Marcy saw what Duke could do for her husband, she told the doctor, who prescribed a course of physiotherapy with weights, pulleys and whirlpool baths and above all walking every day with Duke, on a limited, gradual scale.

(a) What was the struggle the neighbours witnessed?

Ans. The neighbours witnessed Duke's struggle to lead his handicapped master on the sidewalk. Hooper also struggled to drag his feet and try to walk next to Duke.

(b) Why did the dog stand and wait?

Ans. The dog stood and waited for his master Charles Hooper to reach his side. Hooper had been paralysed and thus, had a great difficulty in walking.

(c) What were their daily goals?

Ans. Their daily goals were the distance Hooper would walk or cover with each passing day. Everyday they used to set their target destination and accomplished it.

(d) What does 'taut' mean?

Ans. The word 'taut' means 'tight'.

9. 'No, please.' She said. And she picked up the big Duke, carried him gently to the car and drove him to the animal hospital.

(a) What happened with Duke?

Ans. Duke was run over by a car.

(b) What does Marcy's reaction reflect?

Ans. Marcy's reaction reflects that she had developed a great liking for Duke.

(c) Which word in the extract means the same as, "lifted in the hands and transported"?

Ans. The word 'carried' means 'lifted in the hands and transported'.

(d) The word .... in the extract is a synonym of 'kindly'.

Ans. 'gently'

Short Answer Type Questions

Answer the following questions in 30-40 words.

1. Why was Hooper taken to the hospital? What was the diagnosis?

Or What happened to Hooper?

Or What was the incident that left Hooper with subdural haemorrhage?

Or How did Charles Hooper get confined to his bed?

Ans. Chuck Hooper met with an unfortunate accident when a car pulled out in front of him all of a sudden leading to an accident. The accident resulted in subdural haemorrhage in the brain that resulted in the left side of his body being completely paralysed. This made him confined to his bed.

2. Describe subsequent developments which took place in the hospital after Hooper met with an accident.

Ans. After the accident, Hooper remained critical for a month. After the fifth week some of his colleagues approached him and asked him to take a year off. They wanted to create a desk job for him. About six weeks after the accident, Hooper was put on a wheelchair. He underwent physiotherapy but did not make much progress.

3. How did Hooper feel when he returned to his home?

Ans. When Hooper returned home, he was very excited to be back after a long span of four months. However, this excitement did not last for long. He was bed-ridden (unable to move) and felt lonely and depressed when Marcy went out for work. He kept staring at the ceiling thinking about the whole situation. He felt very miserable.

4. How did Duke react when he saw Hooper after his discharge from the hospital?

Ans. Duke was very happy and excited when he saw his master. He barked and took a three metre jump towards Chuck, causing him to almost fall down.

5. "It was like lighting a fuse. Duke shimmied himself U-shaped in anticipation." Explain.

Ans. Chuck had not taken Duke out for a walk since he had been paralysed in the accident. However, when Chuck good handedly hooked the leash onto Duke's collar to hold him still, Duke anticipated (presumed) that Chuck would stand up and take him for a walk. This energised him into action.

6. How did the journey to recovery begin?

Ans. The recovery began after a constant poking and encouragement from Duke. His reproachful eyes had an effect on Hooper. He hooked the leash onto Duke's collar and, with Marcy's assistance, tried to walk. This was his first step to recovery.

7. Why was 4th January a significant day for Hooper?

Ans. 4th January was a significant day for Hooper because on this day Hooper walked the 200 metre distance from the clinic to the local branch office of his company independently without the help of Duke. This was a big move for him.

8. Differentiate between Marcy's attitude towards Duke before and after the accident.

Or Why did Marcy's attitude towards Duke change? How did she react after Duke met with a fatal accident? Competency Based

Or How did Marcy react after Duke met with a fatal accident?

Ans. Initially, Marcy did not like Duke as she wanted to have a pomeranian as a pet. However, when Hooper began to recover, aided by Duke's miraculous (magical) help and support, she developed a liking for him. She had grown so fond of him that at the time of his accident, she did not let anyone else touch him and carried him to the hospital herself.

In the dog's moment of crisis, she wanted to take care of him herself out of her love and gratitude for him.

9. What significant role had been played by Duke in Chuck Hooper's life?

Ans. Duke played a significant role in Chuck Hooper's life. It was Duke who encouraged his master to stand on his feet again and take a few initial steps. He helped tremendously in Hooper's progress and Hooper was finally able to leave his wheelchair and start walking. He revived a hope in Hooper and taught him how to cope with challenges successfully.

10. Who is the real protagonist (main character) of the story and why?

Ans. The real protagonist (main character) of the story is Duke. Not only is the story titled after him, but the entire plot also revolves around Duke. He was not only loyal but also deeply attached to his master. His love did wonders that science and medicine were not able to do.

11. What does the story teach us?

Ans. The story teaches us that, every problem can be solved through perseverance and courage. It also shows us how, love succeeds where human science fails. We should never give up hope. We cannot let adversities hamper our progress.

12. Do you think that Duke fulfils the meaning of 'Dogs are the most faithful friends of Man'? How?

Ans. Yes, Duke fulfils the meaning of 'Dogs are the most faithful friends of Man'. When Charles Hooper was paralysed on the left side of his body, he gave up all hope of ever being able to stand on his feet and walk again.

It was only because of the faithful services of Duke that Chuck could regain his strength and confidence, and could stand up and walk again. Even Hooper's wife Marcy had given up and would cry when alone. But, Duke remained loyal to his master and, like a true friend, did not lose confidence in his abilities.

Long Answer Type Questions

Answer the following questions in 120 words.

1. Duke's re-entry into Hooper's life brought a metamorphosis. As Hooper, write a diary entry recording the efforts made by Duke to revitalise you and help you walk step by step.

Ans. Wednesday, 4th January, 20XX 11 p.m.

Dear Diary

I am very happy today because I was able to walk on my own to the local branch office of my company. Very soon, I'll be joining my office and work for an hour daily. All thanks to Duke, my saviour, my best buddy. He taught me how to face the adversities of life without indulging in any self-pity. With his consistent efforts and constant poking, I took my first step and other steps followed. It was he who coaxed and encouraged me to stand on my own feet and lifted my numb spirits. His patience, perseverance and determination inspired me and filled me with an inner strength. Through his efforts I learned to focus on the solution rather than the problem.

I love you Duke. Thanks for being there, buddy.

Chuck

2. "Being deeply loved by someone gives you strength, while loving someone deeply gives you courage." Elucidate this quote with reference to the current story, explaining the value of love, which provides strength and courage? Competency Based

Ans. It is certainly true that if someone loves you deeply, you achieve strength and if you love someone, you get courage.

In the story 'A Dog Named Duke', the dog is an epitome (symbol) of love. He loves his master immensely. The sight of Charles Hooper excites the dog to such an extent that we find him quivering. He cannot talk to him nor can he take his silence and misery.

The dog manages to enable his master to take steps towards recovery. Hooper is so fond of Duke that he gathers all his courage and decides to try to walk on his feet again. In return, he derives his strength from Duke's love for him. Finally, he recovers and resumes his work. However, the dog passes away, leaving Hooper alone forever.

Had Duke not been there, Hooper's recovery was impossible. This miracle could have happened only through true love.

3. Marcy goes through a complete change of character as far as Duke is concerned in the chapter 'A Dog Named Duke', after she sees Duke's efforts to get Chuck back on his feet. What values does Marcy learn? Competency Based

Ans. Marcy Hooper was Charles Hooper's wife. Marcy loved her husband and took a good care of him when he suffered after the accident. Though, she appeared quite strong in his presence, she cried secretly as she saw his smile gradually fading away.

Initially, Marcy was not in favour of having Duke at home, as he was quite big and had a violent and agile (energetic) behaviour. Infact, it took her a long time to get used to the dog.

However, when Marcy saw Duke helping her husband recover, her initial dislike of the dog began to change to an attitude of love and gratitude (thankfulness).

When Duke had an accident, she did not let anybody else touch him, and managed to carry the dog to the hospital herself. Her attempts to save Duke show that she had learnt the values of gratitude and love for him.

4. "Nothing is impossible if one is determined and diligent enough to achieve the same". Discuss this statement with reference to the story 'A Dog Named Duke'. Competency Based

Ans. Determination and diligence are unique characteristics that make a person stand out from the crowd. If a person is determined and diligent, nothing can stop them from achieving success.

In the story 'A Dog Named Duke', Duke's determination, coupled with Hooper's diligence, makes the two achieve their goal of making Hooper walk again. The dog cannot see his master remain paralysed and confined (bound) to bed. It begins to poke and prod Hooper, finally making him try to stand on his feet. Hooper does witness a few failures and setbacks (difficulties) but the two never give up trying. It is due to their determination that they are soon able to walk long distances and Hooper is even able to resume work at his office.

5. From time immemorial, dog and man have been inseparable. How has this belief proved to be true in the story, 'A Dog Named Duke'? Describe the values that have helped them share a bond.

Ans. It is true that from ancient times, dog and man have been inseparable. In the story, 'A Dog Named Duke,' we see how the mute animal ends up performing a miracle that human science could not. With sheer determination, Duke helped his master get back on his feet after an accident that completely paralysed the left side of his body. It was Duke who taught Hooper to face the adversities of life without indulging in any self-pity. He never left his master's side and coaxed Chuck to get out of the bed and forced him to go out for a walk. Slowly and gradually, they developed a bond. Duke infused in Chuck a sense of immense self-confidence.

It was the special bond that they shared that helped Chuck recover from his severe injury and regain his position in the company. Moreover, it was because of Duke that he also gained a promotion and was able to lead a normal life all over again.

6. After Duke's death, Marcy was asked to write an article for the local newspaper. She decides to write on the topic, 'A dog is man's best friend'. Write it for her in 120 words.

Ans.

A Dog is Man's Best Friend

by Marcy Hooper

Man and dog share a very close bond. Friendship between man and dog goes back thousands of years. Dogs are affectionate creatures by nature. They want to love and be loved. Besides, they are the most loyal friends and constant companions.

Duke too was the most faithful friend to Chuck Hooper. He was not a normal pet dog but an extraordinary one who played a significant role in his master's life. During Chuck's happy times, Duke was always by his side. And, he did not leave his master alone even during his tough times.

When Chuck was paralysed, crippled and confined to bed, he had lost all his hope and confidence. But the patience, persistence, love and loyalty of Duke revived his master's self-confidence, and Chuck stepped up on his feet and began to walk again. It is only because of Duke that Chuck is leading a normal life today. A faithful and devoted friend, Duke proved to be more important than a human companion. His death has left a void in Hooper's life. He was indeed, Hooper's best friend.

ASSESSMENT EXERCISE

Extract Based Questions

Read the following extracts carefully and answer the questions that follow.

1. In March, they let him out of the hospital. After the excitement of the homecoming wore off, Chuck hit a new low.
   (a) Why was Chuck at the hospital?
   (b) Explain the phrase, "Chuck hit a new low".
   (c) What was the reason for this low feeling?
   (d) What does the phrase 'wore off' mean?
2. Duke was drugged and he made it until 11 o' clock the next morning, but his injures were too severe.
   (a) What had happened to Duke?
   (b) What does "he made it till 11 o' clock the next morning" mean?
   (c) The word .... in the extract is a synonym of 'anaesthetise'.
   (d) What does 'severe' mean?

Short Answer Type Questions

Answer the following questions in 30-40 words.

1. Chuck Hopper's wife Marcy disliked big dogs. He still chose Duke for a pet. Why?
2. Who was Charles Hooper? Describe his life before he met with a tragic accident.
3. Hooper has been described as 'a favoured young man'.What was the turning point that changed his life?
4. Why did Marcy ask her neighbour to put Duke in a kennel?
5. Why was Duke brought home from the kennel?
6. How did Duke coax his master to make an effort to walk?
7. How did Marcy contribute towards her husband's recovery?
8. Do you think Chuck was a duty-conscious man? How can you tell?

Long Answer Type Questions

Answer the following questions in 120 words.

1. In today's world where all values seem to be lost and all one can see is violence, treachery and terror, how do you feel when you read about the unconditional love and devotion of the dog named 'Duke'? What do you learn from the dog?
2. Duke's making his paralysed master step on his feet and walk again is nothing short of a miracle, he did what medical science could not do. Comment.
3. If we simply choose to sit and brood over our adversities in life, we shall never be able to overcome them. We need to look for solutions to our problems and act accordingly. How does the story 'A Dog Named Duke' reflect this important fact of life?

The Man Who Knew Too Much

by Alexander Baron

CHAPTER 3

CHAPTER SUMMARY

The story 'The Man Who Knew Too Much' written by Alexander Baron deals with the story of a soldier at an army training camp. Private Quelch is the name of the trainee who had great knowledge about army affairs but could not win the admiration of his superior officers. His fellow trainees called him the 'Professor' because of his excellent knowledge. However, his love of showing off his knowledge cost him dearly. His career was ruined yet he was not able to get rid of his habit of showing off his knowledge to prove his intellectual superiority.

Private Quelch

The narrator met Private Quelch for the first time at the training depot. In the very first week there, he was nicknamed the Professor. This was so because he was a very thin and tall man who wore horn-rimmed spectacles. Further, he had great knowledge about many things and was happy to lecture his fellow soldiers which made the title fitting.

The Lesson in Musketry

The narrator remembers their first lesson in musketry. They were standing around the Sergeant who was wearing North-West Frontier ribbons. He was describing the mechanism of a service rifle and told them about the speed at which the bullet leaves the rifle. Suddenly, the Professor gave the exact speed which was two thousand, four hundred and forty feet per second.

This interruption irritated the Sergeant who went on lecturing. When he had finished, he asked the Professor many questions. The Sergeant may have wanted revenge but it also enhanced the Professor's glory as he knew all the technical definitions, the parts of the rifle along with its use and care.

The Professor's Aim

When the Sergeant asked if he had any training, the Professor answered that it was a matter of intelligent reading. The Professor made sure that people knew him. He wanted to get a commission before everyone else and he wanted to get a stripe.

In pursuit of his ambition, the Professor worked hard. He borrowed training manuals and stayed up late at nights reading them. He irritated the instructors with questions and drilled (walked) with enthusiasm. He also lectured all other men on every aspect of human knowledge.

Everyone Disliked Professor

At first, everyone at the training depot had a certain respect for him. However, they soon began to hate talking to him. This was so because the Professor would insult them and when the others tried to insult him back, he would not pay any attention to them. The Professor would also publicly correct other's mistakes and take a superior role.

The narrator remembers that they used to take pride in aircraft recognition. Once, when they were out on a walk, they heard the drone of a plane flying. No one could see the drone but the Professor told them that it was a North American Harvard Trainer which could be unmistakably identified by the harsh engine note, due to the high tip speed of the airscrew.

The Turning Point in the Professor's Life

The narrator states that he could not forget the day which brought a turning point in his career. Corporal Turnbull, a young man who had come back from Dunkirk with all his equipment, was giving a lesson on the hand grenade. As he was giving the lesson, the Professor interrupted him and questioned his teaching methods. As a result, Corporal Turnbull asked the professor to give the lecture himself. The professor delivered the lecture without shame.

After the lecture, Corporal Turnbull decided to teach him a lesson. So, he declared that Private Quelch had been selected for permanent cookhouse duties.

The 'Professor' in the Cookhouse

Everyone was amused at his new duties and enjoyed the joke for days together. They felt that the incident would have silenced Private Quelch. However, soon they were proved wrong. One day, while passing by the cookhouse, the narrator and his friend heard Quelch lecturing three cooks in his usual knowledgeable style on the art of peeling potatoes without losing vitamin values.

The two of them ran away from there, absolutely convinced that nothing could change the 'Professor's' habit of showing off his intellectual superiority over others.

Word Meaning

Word	*Meaning*
Private	an ordinary soldier without rank
horn-rimmed spectacles	spectacles with frame made of horn or similar material
musketry	the art of using the infantry soldier's handgun
North-West frontier ribbons	decorations showing service in the North-West province of British India, presently a part of Pakistan
to get on	to get promoted
commission	become an army officer
stripe	a V-shaped band to indicate the rank of a soldier
badgered	troubled
route marches	training marches of battalions
heartiness	enjoyment and enthusiasm
pay table	table at which the salary is paid
droning	continuous, without any change in tone

Word	*Meaning*
sarcasm	use of words opposite in meaning to what is actually meant
orderly officer	officer of the day
condescending	to look down on
old man	a casual way of addressing a colleague
louts	persons behaving rudely or aggressively
sprawling	lying with arms and legs outstretched
trifled with	to play or fool around with; talk or act frivolously with
unabashed	unashamed
cowed	subdued
lingeringly	longer than expected
cookhouse duties	work in the camp kitchen
at bay	being hunted like animals
monotonous beat	voice without any change in tone
abominably	disgustingly/terribly

Textbook FOLDER

Here, we have covered questions given in the CBSE Textbook along with their answers.

ON PAGE 25-26

Q.3 The 'Professor' knew too much. How did he prove himself? Fill up the space with suitable examples from the story, using the given clues.

(a) about muzzle velocity ....

Ans. or the speed at which the bullet leaves the rifle, was "well over two thousand feet per second", the 'Professor' corrected him by giving the exact value (as given in military manuals) as "two thousand, four hundred and forty feet per second".

(b) after a thirty mile walk ....

Ans. he was not at all tired and also displayed his heartiness by saying, "What about a song, chaps?"

(c) his salute on payday ....

Ans. was a model to behold. When officers were nearby, he would swing his skinny arms and march to the canteen like a Guardsman.

(d) the loud sound of a high flying invisible aeroplane ....

Ans. The 'Professor' could unmistakably identify the airplane by the harsh engine note due to the high tip speed of the airscrew.

(e) about hand grenades ....

Ans. The 'Professor' gave very specific information (forty-four) about the number of segments of the outside of a grenade.

(f) during cookhouse duties ....

Ans. he protested against the unscientific and unhygienic method of peeling potatoes resulting in a sheer waste of vitamin values.

ON PAGE 26

Q.4A Based on your reading of the story, answer the following questions by choosing the correct options.

(i) Private Quelch was nick-named 'Professor' because of ....

(a) his appearance
(b) his knowledge
(c) his habit of reading
(d) his habit of sermonising

Ans. (d) his habit of sermonising

(ii) One could hammer nails into Corporal Turnbull without his noticing it because ....

(a) he was a strong and sturdy (well-built) man
(b) he was oblivious (ignorant) to his surroundings
(c) he was a brave Corporal
(d) he was used to it

Ans. (a) he was a strong and sturdy (well-built) man

(iii) The author and his friend Trower fled from the scene as ....

(a) they had to catch a train
(b) they could not stand Private Quelch exhibiting his knowledge
(c) they felt they would have to lend a helping hand
(d) they did not want to meet the cooks

Ans. (b) they could not stand Private Quelch exhibiting his knowledge

(iv) The main reason that the Professor remain unflinched despite the retaliation of his batch-mates was due to the fact that

(a) his desire to impress people overruled the humiliation he experienced each time.
(b) his miraculously tireless personality couldn't stop him from working extra hard.
(c) he was so involved in excelling that he barely noticed sarcastic comments.
(d) he knew that the only way to earn respect is through hard work.

Ans. (c) he was so involved in excelling that he barely noticed sarcastic comments.

(v) Choose the expression that uses the same literary device as used in the line "he was so tough that you could hammer nails into him without his noticing it."

(a) My mom made enough food to feed an army last night.
(b) My alarm clock yells at me to get out of bed every morning.
(c) The car complained as the key was roughly turned in its ignition.
(d) Lightning danced across the sky like a fairy beating against the clouds.

Ans. (a) My mom made enough food to feed an army last night.

ON PAGE 27-28

Q.4B Read the given extracts and answer the questions that follow.

1. Without even a glance upward the Professor announced, "That, of course, is a North American Harvard Trainer. It can be unmistakably identified by the harsh engine note, due to the high tip speed of the airscrew." What could a gang of louts like us do with a man like that?

(i) Choose the option that best describes the traits of the Professor in the given extract.

1. patience
2. awareness
3. knowledge
4. flamboyance
5. kindness

(a) 1, 2, 3 (b) 2, 3, 4
(c) 2, 3, 5 (d) 3, 4, 5

Ans. (b) 2, 3, 4

(ii) The author refers to himself and his peers as 'louts' to

(a) bring out the contrast with the Professor.
(b) comment on the expertise in other fields.
(c) draw attention to lack of teamwork in all.
(d) accept the display of undisciplined behaviour.

Ans. (a) bring out the contrast with the Professor.

2. In the silence that followed a dark flush stained the tan of the Corporal's face. "Here," he said at last, "you give this lecture". As if afraid to say any more, he tossed the grenade to the Professor. Quite unabashed, Private Quelch climbed to his feet and with the attitude of a man coming into his birth-right gave us an unexceptionable lecture on the grenade.

(i) Choose the statement that is not true about the depiction of the scene described in the above lines.

(a) Private Quelch knew more about hand grenades than Turnbull.
(b) Turnbull was not someone who would let things go easily.
(c) The entire batch was stunned at Quelch's audacity.
(d) Quelch was able to impress Turnbull with his vast knowledge.

Ans. (d) Quelch was able to impress Turnbull with his vast knowledge.

(ii) The silence that follows Quelch's remarks shows that the entire batch did not

(a) wish to see Turnbull humiliated.
(b) want Quelch embarrassed.
(c) know how to react.
(d) care for the conversation.

Ans. (c) know how to react

(iii) The fact that Quelch delivered the lecture when asked to do so shows that he

(a) wanted to teach Turnbull a valuable lesson.
(b) failed to take the hint that Turnbull felt insulted.
(c) knew when to flaunt his knowledge for his own benefit.
(d) established himself as a man superior to Turnbull

Ans. (b) failed to take the hint that Turnbull felt insulted.

ON PAGE 28

Q.5 Answer the following questions briefly.

(a) What is a 'nickname'? Can you suggest another one for Private Quelch?

Ans. Nickname is the alternative name or the informal name given to a person depending upon his most prominent character traits. The nickname is generally given by friends and colleagues. Private Quelch was nicknamed as 'Professor'. The other nicknames for him can be 'Mr. Intelligent' or 'Mr. Pet Parker'.

(b) Private Quelch looked like a 'Professor' when the author first met him at the training depot. Why?

Ans. Private Quelch looked like a Professor when the author first met him at the training depot as he had a tall and thin body and he wore horn-rimmed spectacles. Moreover, his habit of lecturing on any topic was a trait found in university professors.

(c) What does the dark, sun-dried appearance of the Sergeant suggest about him?

Ans. The Sergeant was a man with great confidence and knowledge of the military. His sun-dried skin expressed that he had spent most of his time outdoors and was very experienced. His knowledge was acquired through his practical and personal experience in the field.

(d) How was Private Quelch's knowledge exposed even further as the Sergeant's classes went on?

Ans. Private Quelch's knowledge was exposed even further because he corrected the instructor and told the exact muzzle velocity of the rifle bullet to the Sergeant. Later on, the Sergeant put a series of questions to him which were all answered by the Professor correctly. He answered the questions with perfect technical definitions, details about the parts of rifles, its uses and the ways to care for a rifle.

(e) What did the Professor mean by 'intelligent reading'?

Ans. By 'intelligent reading', the Professor meant reading thoroughly and not only for the sake of reading. When one reads thoroughly and not only with full concentration, one is able to understand each and every detail of the topic one has read.

(f) What were the Professor's ambitions in the army?

Ans. The Professor's ambition in the army was to get a commission and as a first step, he meant to get a stripe.

(g) Did Private Quelch's day-to-day practices take him closer towards his goal? How can you make out?

Ans. Quelch's goal was to become an officer in the army, which was very ambitious. However, his day-to-day practices did not take him closer to this goal.

The reason was that he displayed his vast knowledge by rudely interrupting his seniors when they were instructing the soldiers. In fact, he tried to ridicule the instructors, thus irritating them. We can make this out by the fact that he was transferred to the camp kitchen, which took him farther from his goal.

(h) How did Private Quelch manage to anger the Corporal?

Ans. During the Corporal's lecture, Private Quelch interrupted him by telling the correct number of fragments of a grenade. Later on, when the Corporal resumed his lecture, Private Quelch interrupted again and asked him to start off with the characteristics of grenades. As a result, the Corporal got angry.

(i) Do you think Private Quelch learnt a lesson when he was chosen for cookhouse duties? Give reasons for your answer.

Ans. No, Private Quelch did not learn a lesson when he was chosen for cookhouse duties. There also he didn't stop exhibiting his knowledge and intelligence. He lectured the cooks on the loss of vitamin values in peeling potatoes.

(j) Elaborate on any one character trait of Corporal Turnbull with evidence from the text.

Ans. Corporal Turnbull was a physically, mentally and emotionally tough man. He was not be fooled around with and got irritated easily. He also took action on the cause of irritation quickly. This behaviour can be seen when the professor interrupts him twice during the lecture. He asks the professor to give the lecture and later, assigns him permanent cookhouse duties to teach him a lesson.

(k) Infer the reason that left the squad horrified when Turnbull asked Quelch to deliver the lesson.

Ans. The squad was left horrified when Turnbull asked Quelch to deliver the lesson because they could see that Corporal was angry. To them, the Corporal was a hero who was not to be messed with. The Professor not only angered the Corporal but also insulted him by actually giving the lecture.

ON PAGE 20-29

Q.6 (a) Quelch's character teaches us that with hard work one also needs to have social and emotional intelligence. Justify.

Ans. It is true to say that Quelch's character teaches us that with hard work one needs to have social and emotional intelligence. Quelch was called the Professor because of his extensive knowledge. He had an ambition and could have successfully achieved it had he been socially and emotionally intelligent. But in his quest, he does not pay any regard to the feelings of his fellow soldiers. He belittles and corrects them publicly. He even interrupts his teachers and irritates them. As a result, he is not liked by anyone. His desire to show off makes him so socially and emotionally stupid that he is given permanent cookhouse duties. Thus, had he been aware that he was insulting his teachers and irritating them by understanding social and emotional cues, he would have been on the path of achieving his dream.

(b) Seeking and sharing knowledge about things is perceived as a quality and not a trait that needs to be curbed. Analyse why the Professor's knowledge made this quality turn sour.

Competency Based

Ans. Seeking and sharing knowledge about things is perceived as a quality. We can observe this from the story as the Professor is initially highly respected among his colleagues. He would help them learn and was very intelligent and aware of army affairs.

However, his knowledge turned this quality sour because he would always show off his knowledge and create chaos in the lectures. He also corrected the mistakes of his colleagues publically which embarrassed them. He never missed any opportunity to show his intelligence to evoke admiration or envy.

As a result, no one liked him. The teachers were irritated by him and consequently he was given the duty of a cook which took him away from his ambition.

(c) Private Quelch knew 'too much'. Give reasons to prove that he was unable to win the admiration of his superior officers or his colleagues.

Ans. Private Quelch knew 'too much' and was respected by everyone. However, soon he lost all their respect. His habit of showing off his knowledge and intelligence annoyed not only his colleagues, but also his superior officers. Each time one of his colleagues made a mistake, Private Quelch would publicly correct him. He even embarrassed his superiors by interrupting their lectures. Once he corrected a Sergeant over the bullet speed of the rifle. The Sergeant, in the hope of revenge, turned all questions to him to answer. In another instance, he interrupted Corporal Turnbull twice during his lecture.

ON PAGE 29

Q.7 **(a) Write down the positive and negative traits of Private Quelch's character by citing instances from the story.**

Positive traits	Instances from the story
(i)	
(ii)	
(iii)	
(iv)	
(v)	

Negative traits	Instances from the story
(i)	
(ii)	
(iii)	
(iv)	

(b) Now, share your notes with the class. Add details if you need to.

(c) Attempt a character sketch of Private Quelch using your notes in about 100 words.

Ans. (a)

Positive traits	Instances from the story
(i) Vast knowledge	Correct muzzle velocity, identifying an aircraft from the sound of its engine, number of parts of the outside of a grenade
(ii) Stamina and enthusiasm	Tireless even after a thirty mile drill, always doing all duties smartly
(iii) Hardworking	Reading manuals and books till late night
(iv) Striving for perfection	Excellent knowledge of everything, correct method of retaining vitamin values in potatoes
(v) Excellent memory	Remembered technical definitions and other information with accuracy

Negative traits	Instances from the story
(i) Immature in talking	Lecturing colleagues at all times, correcting his seniors
(ii) Condescending manner	He pretended to help and showed off his knowledge in the bargain
(iii) Thoughtless and ill- mannered	Rudely interrupted his instructors by displaying his superior knowledge
(iv) Undisciplined	Interrupted the Sergeant and Corporal Turnbull during their lectures and offered them advice on how to conduct their lectures

(b) Do it yourself.

(c) Private Quelch was just an ordinary soldier but had the high ambition of becoming an officer. Private Quelch's lanky body, horn-rimmed spectacles and his love for showing off his knowledge earned him the nickname the 'Professor'. He also took great pride in 'educating' and 'correcting' people in a snobbish manner. Although he meant well, his colleagues and superiors did not appreciate the manner in which he presented his intelligence. However, he was unaffected by all the criticism that he received.

Professor Quelch desired to rise through the ranks in the army, for which he worked very hard by studying manuals till late at night. Unfortunately, he brought about his own downfall through his snobbish behaviour. Despite being taught a lesson by being transferred to the camp kitchen, his attitude did not change.

Writing Task

Q.8 **You are the 'Professor'. Write a diary entry after your first day at the cookhouse, describing the events that led to this assignment; also express your thoughts and feelings about the events of the day in about 150 words.**

Ans. Wednesday, 28th July, 20XX 10:00 p.m.

Dear Diary

Today was my first day at the cookhouse. I was not used to the atmosphere of the confined place. I missed the route marches, lessons on rifles and other technical and operational training that I used to enjoy. I was not happy with my nomination for permanent cookhouse duties. To add to my woes, my colleagues mocked me and treated the entire episode as a joke. It was quite disheartening for me. Even though I am well-informed and knowledgeable, I was assigned this job. My dream of getting a commission was totally broken by Corporal Turnbull. Moreover, the staff in the cookhouse was not at all efficient. I protested against their unscientific and unhygienic method of peeling potatoes. I had to explain to them that by doing so, they were wasting the valuable vitamins present in potatoes. All in all, it was a very unpleasant and disappointing day for me.

Quelch

REVIEW EXERCISE

Including Exam Pattern Practice Questions

Extract Based Questions

Read the following extracts carefully and answer the questions that follow.

1. A man is liable to acquire in his first week of Army life-together with his uniform, rifle and equipment-a nickname. Anyone who saw Private Quelch, lanky, stooping, frowning through horn-rimmed spectacles, understood why he was known as the Professor.

   (a) What nickname had been given to Private Quelch?

   Ans. The nickname 'Professor' had been given to Private Quelch.

   (b) Why was he given that nickname?

   Ans. He was given that nickname because he was a tall and thin person who had a frowning expressing visible through his horn-rimmed spectacles.

   (c) What does the word 'frowning' here mean?

   Ans. The word frowning means furrowing the brow to show concentration.

   (d) What is the tone of the given lines?

   Ans. The tone of the given lines is factual and to some extent mocking.

2. In pursuit of his ambition he worked hard. We had to give him credit for that. He borrowed training manuals and stayed up late at nights reading them. He badgered the instructors with questions.

   (a) What was the Professor's ambition?

   Ans. The Professor's ambition was to become an army officer and as a first step, he meant to get a stripe.

   (b) How did he want to achieve his ambition?

   Ans. He wanted to achieve his ambition by working hard by reading training manuals in spare time, asking more questions, drilling with enthusiasm and behaving like a model soldier.

   (c) What is meant by the word 'badgered'?

   Ans. The word 'badgered' means 'pestered'

   (d) What is the opposite of 'credit'?

   Ans. The antonym of 'credit' is 'disapproval'.

3. "And day in and day out, he lectured to us in his droning, remorseless voice on every aspect of human knowledge. At first we had a certain respect for him, but soon we lived in terror of his approach. We tried to hit back at him with clumsy sarcasms and practical jokes."

   (a) "At first we had a certain respect for him, but soon we lived in terror of his approach." What does this tell us about the narrator and his friends?

   Ans. This tells us that the narrator and his friends started to dislike Private Quelch.

   (b) What made the narrator and his friends live in terror of Private Quelch's approach?

   Ans. Private Quelch's habit of showing off his knowledge and correcting publicly the mistakes of his colleagues, so that they were embarrassed made them live in terror of Private Quelch's approach.

   (c) What is meant by the word 'remorseless'?

   Ans. The word 'remorseless' means 'without guilt'.

   (d) Which quality of Quelch is highlighted in the extract?

   Ans. The characteristic of being superior and show off is highlighted in the extract.

4. He was not a man to be trifled with.
   He was our hero and we used to tell each other that he was so tough that you could hammer nails into him without his noticing it.

   (a) Who is 'he' in the above statement?

   Ans. 'He' here refers to Corporal Turnbull, a young officer who had come back without any injuries from Dunkirk.

   (b) What does 'trifled with' mean?

   Ans. The word 'trifled' means to treat without genuine respect.

   (c) What does this statement describe about him?

   Ans. The statement clearly describes Corporal Turnbull as a very tough man, who knows how to handle stubborn and over-smart people.

   (d) What does the given description imply?

   Ans. The given statements/description implies that the person was very strong and brave.

5. 'Forty-four segments.' The Professor beamed at him. The Corparal said nothing, but his brow tightened. He opened his mouth to resume 'And by the way' Corporal. We were all thunder struck.

(a) 'Beamed' in the above line means ....

Ans. to smile very happily.

(b) What is the topic of discussion?

Ans. The Corporal was lecturing on a grenade and informed the trainee soldiers that it was divided into a large number of segments to help in fragmentation.

(c) What does the above remark reveal about the Professor?

Ans. It shows that he is neither ashamed nor embarrassed in whatever he does or says, not even in front of the toughest of officers like Corporal Turnbull.

(d) How does the Corporal react?

Ans. The Corporal was angry and irritated at the Professor.

6. In the silence that followed, a dark flush stained the tan of Corporal's face. "Here", he said at last, "you give this lecture". As if afraid to say any more, he tossed the grenade to the Professor. Quite unabashed, Private Quelch climbed to his feet and with the air of a man coming into his birth-right gave us an unexceptionable lecture on the grenade.

(a) Why did the Corporal ask Private Quelch to give the lecture?

Ans. Private Quelch interrupted the Corporal twice in between his lecture on grenades. To embarrass the Professor, the Corporal asked him to give the lecture.

(b) Why was there a silence?

Ans. There was complete silence because the lecture had been interrupted for the second time by the Professor and so the soldiers were scared of the reaction of the Corporal.

(c) What does the word 'stained' mean? What does it show?

Ans. 'Stained' means to change the colour or discolour something. It generally shows embarassment.

(d) What is the opposite of 'unabashed'?

Ans. The opposite of 'unabashed' is 'shame'.

7. Of course it was a joke for days afterwards, a joke and joy to all of us.
I remember, though ....
My friend tower and I were talking about it a few day later. We were returning from the canteen to our own hut.

(a) What does 'it' stand for?

Ans. 'It' stands for the order by which Private Quelch was assigned to permanent cookhouse duties.

(b) Why was it a joke?

Ans. It was a joke because the Professor's intelligent reading and showing off his knowledge landed him cookhouse duties instead of a commission.

(c) Why was it given to Private Quelch

Ans. Private Quelch had disturbed the Corporal's lecture by showing off his knowledge of grenades and was thus given this duty as punishment.

(d) How did the joke impact Private Quetch?

Ans. The joke did not have any impact on Private Quetch. He was still a show off.

Short Answer Type Questions

Answer the following questions in 30-40 words.

1. Why did the Sergeant turn his questions to the 'Professor' repeatedly? What was the result of this action?

Ans. The Professor interrupted the Sergeant's lecture and corrected him by saying that the muzzle velocity of the rifle was two thousand, four hundred and forty feet per second.
This was not appreciated by the Sergeant and perhaps in the hope of revenge, he turned all his questions to the Professor. However, the only result of this action was an enhancement of the Professor's glory and confidence.

2. There was a change in the attitude of the other privates towards the Professor. Elaborate.

Ans. Earlier, the other privates had a certain respect for the Professor. However, gradually, there was a change in their attitude because the Professor publicly corrected their mistakes, which embarrassed them. He was, thus, disliked by others and they started avoiding him. They even tried to hit back at him with sarcastic comments and practical jokes.

3. Private Quelch is equally unpopular among his friends as well as superiors. Comment.

Or **How did the image of Private Quelch as a 'hero' gradually change into a 'villain' in the eyes of other trainees?**

Or **Why did certain respect towards the Professor gradually change/develop into terror among his colleagues and what kind of treatment did Private Quelch get?** Competency Based

Ans. Private Quelch was unpopular among friends and superiors alike because he believed that he was superior to others. If someone made a mistake, he would publicly correct him. He lectured to them relentlessly in his monotonous voice. They got sick of him and hit back at him with sarcastic comments and practical jokes.

4. Why were the writer and his batchmates 'thunder-struck' when Quelch tried to correct Corporal Turnbull?

Ans. Corporal Turnbull had the reputation of being a tough man. His tough demeanour (behaviour) and courage drew admiration from all. He was not a man to be trifled with. So, when Quelch tried to correct him, everyone was 'thunder-struck'.

5. What was the announcement made by Corporal Turnbull in 'The Man Who Knew Too Much'? Why did he make the announcement?

Or **What was Turnbull's reaction to Private Quelch's answer?**

Ans. Corporal Turnbull announced that the platoon officer had asked him to nominate any one of the privates for permanent cookhouse duties and he had decided that Private Quelch was the right man for the job. He made such an announcement in order to teach Private Quelch a lesson as he had interrupted him twice in the middle of his lecture.

6. Do you think the punishment given to the Professor is justified?

Ans. Yes, I believe that the punishment given to Private Quelch was justified. Although it is important to have a strong command over the theory of the weapons, it is even more important to have practical knowledge and experience. By interrupting Corporal Turnbull's lecture, Private Quelch insulted the experience gained by the Corporal from actual combat situations.

7. Why was everybody happy when he was shifted to the cookhouse?

Ans. Everybody was happy when Private Quelch was shifted to the cookhouse as they no longer had to listen to his lectures. Moreover, they were saved from the embarrassment that they faced when he used to publicly correct them.

8. What is the central idea of the chapter, 'The Man Who Knew Too Much'?

Ans. The whole story revolves around Private Quelch, who exhibits his knowledge in front of everyone. The story teaches us that there is nothing wrong in having a vast pool of knowledge but what is wrong is to make a display of it to impress others and to insult others because of their lack of knowledge.

Long Answer Type Questions

Answer the following questions in 120 words.

1. Corporal Turnbull tried to teach the Professor a lesson by assigning him permanent cookhouse duties. Did he succeed? Comment on the Professor's attitude in the cookhouse in the chapter, 'The Man Who Knew Too Much' reflecting on the values he should have possessed to avoid such duties.

Ans. No, Corporal Turnbull did not succeed because Private Quelch did not learn a lesson and was heard lecturing the cooks on the loss of vitamin values in peeling potatoes. The Professor continued showing off his knowledge and feeling of superiority. The values he should have possessed to avoid such duties include humility, maturity in speaking, respect for his seniors and a friendly attitude towards his fellow soldiers. He should never insult anybody or speak snobbishly to them due to his vast knowledge.

2. Can you guess the thoughts that were raging in the Sergeant and Corporal Turnbull's minds when Quelch happened to annoy them? Competency Based

Ans. When Quelch interrupted the Sergeant, initially he did not react much and went on lecturing. However, that interruption had angered him terribly in the mind and so when his lecture was over, perhaps in the hope of revenge, he asked questions after questions from Quelch. The sergeant must have felt terribly miserable and helpless after this as Quelch gave all the answers, and it only resulted in his glory.

In the case of Corporal, the interruption by Quelch had a stronger impact. Although initially he also did not react, his brow tightened, indicating that he completely resented Quelch's interruption. Further, when he decided to teach Quelch by asking him to teach, Quelch's unabashed decision to do so, angered him more. As a result, he was more revengeful than the sergeant and to pull Quelch down, he assigned him the job of permanent cookhouse duties.

3. None had ever dared to outsmart and rub the Corporal in the wrong way. No wonder Turnbull's ego was hurt, he felt outraged. He writes an informal letter to his friend, Peter Smith in Dunkirk, expressing his surprise at the unexpected behaviour of a new undertrainee and how he set him right.

Ans. Dear Peter

Now when I've settled down at this place, I thought of penning down a few lines to you. There is something very strange that I have come across here. Yesterday, while I was taking a lesson on hand grenade, I had an encounter with a very strange under-trainee, called Quelch. Would you believe that he had the audacity and grit to interrupt me in my lecture by giving additional information on the subject just to prove his superiority over others? Not only that, his condescending and rude manner of speaking to me almost brought my blood to a boil. I thought I must set him right and so, I assigned him the job of cookhouse duties to deflate his bloated ego.

I could see that all the other members of the squad were very happy and relieved to get rid of this constant nonsense of Private Quelch. It seems he has just one aim in life-to pull down everybody else around him, so I think the job assigned to him should be able to set him right. Sometimes, this kind of discipline is also required. How about you and your new batch there?

Rest on meeting.

Yours friendly
Turnbull

4. What were the factors that led to the decline of Private Quelch? Do you think his fall from grace was justified? Why/Why not?

Ans. Private Quelch was a conceited young man who could not handle his own knowledge. He was brainy, diligent, enthusiastic, gifted with excellent memory but his social etiquettes were wrong. Knowledge, if it is flaunted, used to overshadow and belittle others, can never bring significant gains. Knowledge is humility, its aim is to enlighten others.

In his pursuit of glory, Private Quelch disregards this basic fact. He is very self-centred, egoistic and in his desperation to earn a stripe, he happily tries to trample others in the race. His knowledge does not bring glory, it results in condemnation. Sergeant and Corporal Turnbull hate him, they want him out of their way. They sense that he was a nuisance to the squad, so he is relegated to the cookhouse. Quelch's greatest flaw is that he is not genuine, every gesture, every action is 'put on', artificially planned to impress others. No wonder the squad is fed up of his sermonising through his endless lectures on human behaviour. So, his fall from grace was expected and well deserved.

5. You expected appreciation for the Professor from Corporal Turnbull. But it was a shock of your life when the corporal assigned him permanent duty in the cookhouse. Write a diary entry expressing your feelings for him. (about 125 words)

Ans. 7th March, Tuesday 10 p.m.

Dear Diary

Today was the most shocking day of my life. In the morning when Corporal Turnbull was giving us a lecture on hand grenande, Quelch, as usual, interfered by giving the detailed knowledge he had on the subject. Corporal did not react and I was feeling very happy inside to see such a knowledgeable person amongst us. And when, after the lecture, corporal showered him with questions, he answered them with ease. I admired him for his diverse knowledge and expected an applaud from the corporal for him.

At the end of the session when the corporal said, "The platoon officer has asked me to nominate someone for .....," I thought that some important work was going to be handed down to Quelch but I got the shock of my life when he was assigned the cookhouse duties. His knowledge did not bring him glory but resulted in condemnation. I am really feeling sorry for him.

ASSESSMENT EXERCISE

Extract Based Questions

Read the following extracts carefully and answer the questions that follow.

1. "That's right," the Sergeant said without enthusiasm, and went on lecturing. When he had finished, he put questions to us; and, perhaps in the hope of revenge, he turned with his questions again and again to the Professor. The only result was to enhance the Professor's glory.
   (a) On which subject was the Sergeant giving the lecture?
   (b) How was the Professor's glory enhanced?
   (c) Which word in the extract is a synonym of 'eagerness'?
   (d) Find a word from the extract that is a synonym of 'retribution'.
2. ".............. for permanent cookhouse duties, I've decided that Private Quelch is just the man for the job." Of course, it was a joke for days afterwards; a joke and joy to all of us.
   (a) Who sent Quelch for cookhouse duties?
   (b) It was a 'joke and joy' to all. Why?
   (c) Which word in the extract is an antonym of 'temporary'?
   (d) A word from the extract which is a synonym of 'subsequently' is ....

Short Answer Type Questions

Answer the following questions in 30-40 words each.

1. Why was Private Quelch nicknamed 'the Professor'? Give two reasons.
2. What was the Professor's main ambition in life and how was he preparing himself for that aim?
3. How did Quelch's air of superiority and condescending nature make him an unpleasant man among his colleagues and senior officers?
4. What qualities about Corporal Turnbull are mentioned to show that he was a hero?
5. How did Corporal Turnbull show the Professor his place?
6. What type of man was Corporal Turnbull?
7. How did Private Quelch offend the Sergeant?
8. Was Private Quelch incorrigible? Give textual evidence supporting your answer.
9. What is the element of sarcasm in the title 'The Man Who Knew Too Much'?
10. Was Private Quelch a misfit in the army? Give reasons to support your answer.

Long Answer Type Questions

Answer the following questions in 120 words each.

1. Write the positive values displayed by Private Quelch by citing the instances where these are displayed in the chapter.
2. What values are shown by Corporal Turnbull in the action he took on Private Quelch?
3. Do you think hard work and intelligence alone are enough for success in life? What other qualities or values are required?

Keeping it From Harold

by PG Wodehouse

CHAPTER 4

CHAPTER SUMMARY

PG Wodehoue's story 'Keeping It From Harold' is based on the Bramble family. Harold was the son of a professional boxer, Bill Bramble. Bill and his wife hid the truth of his father's profession from him. Somehow, Harold came to know about his father's profession. He felt hurt and cheated not because his parents had lied to him but because he could not take due pride in his father being a well-known boxer. Ironically, what his parents were hiding from their child turned out to be the greatest thing for Harold.

The Bramble Family

The story begins with Harold asking his mother to listen to what he had learnt. His mother, Mrs. Bramble was a housewife who cared for her husband Bill and her son. At the moment, Harold was sitting on the other side of the table learning something with focus. Mrs. Bramble agreed to hear what Harold had learnt. However, as soon as he had started reciting the poem, she asked Harold to take a break and walk by the river for half an hour. So, Harold arranged his books and went out.

Harold Bramble and the Lie

Harold was a ten year old exceptional boy. He loved studying, displayed good behaviour and was admired by all. The only drawback was that because of his almost perfect behaviour, his parents had to lie to him. Both Mr. and Mrs. Bramble hated lying but they had lied to Harold about Mr. Bramble's profession. This was so because Harold had displayed a model of goodness and intelligence which was opposite of his father's job as a professional boxer.

Initially, it was only Mrs. Bramble who wanted to hide the truth from Harold. However, soon everyone including Mrs. Bramble's brother, Major Percy Stokes had told Bill Bramble to hide the truth because they insisted that his profession would be shameful for Harold. So, he agreed.

Bill Bramble's Nature

Bill Bramble was a kind and friendly man. He was mild in nature. He agreed with other and sacrificed many things to make others happy. When he got to know that he was going to become a father, he wanted to name his son John, after Mr. John L. Sullivan, or Marie after Miss Marie Lloyd if he had a daughter. However, Mrs. Bramble loved the name Harold. So, he sacrificed his desire.

Mr. Bramble's Real Profession

Bill Bramble was a great professional boxer known as Young Porky. He could win any challenge and had a great left punch. As a result, he was loved by the people and the media. However, as Harold was born, he had to be away from the media because he feared that his son would get to know about his real identity. While he was proud of his son, he and his wife were scared of him too. This was so because Harold seemed superior to them.

Harold and his achievements

Harold was opposite of his father. He had learned to read and write with amazing quickness. He sang in the choir and had already won a prize for spelling and dictation. He believed that his father was a commercial traveller and moved ahead in his life with his studies.

Bills' Last Match

Now, as Harold had left for a walk, Mrs. Bramble resumed working on the sock which she was weaving. For the first time, she was relaxed about the future as after a week, Bill would fight his last match. It was the twenty-round contest with that American Murphy at the National Sporting Club for which Bill was training at the White Hart.

Bill felt that he was growing old and it was time for him to retire from boxing. He now wanted to work as an instructor at a big school or college. He knew that he had all the qualities which headmasters demanded in those who taught boxing.

Bill Refuses to Fight

Mrs. Bramble's thoughts were interrupted by a knock and some whispers near the door. Major Percy Stokes and a hurt Bill entered the house. When Mrs. Bramble asked her husband why he wasn't training, he told her that he would not box anymore. All the while Percy was very happy as he hated Bill's profession and wanted him to leave it.

Bill's decision angered Mrs. Bramble. This was so because they were going to get good money (500 pounds) that would go into Harold's education in the private school. Now as Bill was not going to fight, they could not provide Harold with a good education. Then, Mrs. Bramble started crying.

Jerry Fischer

Bill tried to justify his decision to his wife and stated that if he won the match, he would be a part of many newspapers. He knew Harold read newspapers and so, took the decision to not fight. Just then, a man wearing a woollen sweater and cycling shorts entered the room. He saw Percy and tried to hurt him. This man was Bill's trainer Jerry Fischer.

As others tried to calm him, the man told Mrs. Bramble that Percy was responsible for Bill leaving the training. Then, he asked Bill to come to White Hart to practice when he was informed that Bill would not fight the match on Monday.

Mr. Fischer is Angry

Hearing that Bill would not fight, Jerry got angry. Bill explained to him how he had to do it for Harold. However, Jerry asked Bill to think about the money and of the training he had been receiving. He added that the audience would dislike him and he would become a target for the media. As they were talking, Harold entered the house. He greeted everyone and asked what they were talking about.

Jerry Fischer was very angry over Bill's decision and in order to take revenge, he revealed to Harold that his father was Young Porky, the professional boxer. When Bill told Jerry that he was disappointed, Jerry shared that he was also disappointed as he had never thought that Bill would leave training a week before the National Match.

Harold's Reaction

After Jerry revealed the truth about Bill's work to Harold, Bill reassured Harold that he had left boxing and he would not fight the American named Murphy at the National. Just then, Harold began to talk about the money he had bet to Dicky Saunders that Jimmy Murphy will be out of the match after ten rounds. He told his parents that he felt bad that they had hidden the fact that his father was Young Porky. He also told them that there was a boy at his school who had Phil Scott's autograph. Students in his school admired that boy and now, they will admire him too.

Harold added that the students in his school called him 'Goggles' but they would stop bullying him if they knew that Harold was Young Porky's son. His words acted as a source of encouragement for Bill.

Harold is Happy

After telling them about how the fact will affect him, Harold asked Bill for his photograph in which he was boxing. He knew that after everyone saw the photo, he would not be teased as 'Googles'. Harold was proud that his father was the famous boxer 'Young Porky'.

Jerry was happy to hear Harold's reaction. He told Bill to come back to White Hart to practice. Harold's positive reaction encouraged Bill who felt very happy and content so he got ready to continue his career as a boxer and went back to practice for his match. After Bill and Jerry had left, Harold excitedly talked about other boxers. Then, he asked his mother to listen to the poetry that he had learned. As Mrs. Bramble agreed, Harold began reciting his poetry.

Word Meaning

Word	Meaning
fat-headedness	foolishness
domestic creature	housewife
wrapped up	busy
precious	used as a term of affection
on his head	won in his name
cut-glass	glass with patterns cut in it
chandelier	a large round glass frame to hold candles or lights
decorous	polite, calm and sensible behaviour
prodigy	genius; unusually intelligent person
brought ... into the world	given birth to
evasions	avoiding telling the truth many times
Curate	a priest in charge of a church
wrath	intense anger
fallen in	agreed to
demur	reluctance or objection
Mr John L Sullivan Miss Marie Lloyd	famous people of that time
walk in life	profession
paste	hit
philanthropists	people who give donations or care about others
the species	humans
teeming millions	large population
left hook	a punch hit with the left hand in boxing
furtive	cautious or secretive
quailed	was frightened
imbued	filled with strong feeling
class	quality of elegance
formed a corner	attained mastery; gained a monopoly
being of a superior order	being a more intelligent person
run to intellect	good brains
run to muscle	good strength
wore mortar boards	were well educated
comported	conducted; behaved
young dons	young teachers at universities
commercial traveller	firm's representative who visits shops etc to get orders
no two ways	only one way
moment	importance
slipped by	passed
reached years of intelligence	started showing his extraordinary intelligence
getting on	getting old
chucking	retiring from
sobriety	being serious and sensible
the general	all-purpose servant;maid

Word	Meaning
insinuated	thrust
cocked	raised
in a sideways fashion	hesitantly sideways
propitiatory	appeasing; conciliatory
as if propelled by powerful machinery	very quickly
scales have fallen from his eyes	he has understood that his profession is not good
literal-minded	person who takes words literally
vouchsafed	guaranteed
gents	reporters
tracts	short pieces of writing to influence people's ideas
primrose path	pursuit of pleasure
head or tail	any meaning
in your time	earlier, in the past
wounded silence	silence due to his feelings being hurt
hopped it	ran away; escaped
piece	article
the fat would be in the fire	there would be trouble
ferret-faced	having a small face like a ferret
knickerbockers	loose-fitting trousers or knickers gathered at the knee or calf
became a battlefield	showed many emotions struggling against each other
turned from his wicked ways	changed his mind
guttural	sound made from the back of the throat
purse	prize money
swells	important or fashionable persons
chronic	very bad
condition	proper fitness
goggled	stared
consternation	anxiety or dismay
un-mixedly	clearly
dot	hit
crooning winningness	pleading tone
heads	public
raw	badly
come on their bended knees	ask very politely or with a lot of. emotion
bob	Shilling (a unit of English currency)
swanking	showing off
chuck it	stop calling me this name
swank	boast;show off
abstracted gravity	seriousness
convulsively	uncontrollably

Textbook FOLDER

Here, we have covered questions given in the CBSE Textbook along with their answers.

ON PAGE 41

Q.3 The sequence of events has been jumbled up. Rearrange them and complete the given flowchart.

(1) Major Percy and Bill come to the house.

(2) Harold comes to know that his father is a boxer.

(3) Bill tells his wife that he is doing it for Harold.

(4) Jerry Fisher tries to convince Bill to reconsider.

(5) Mrs. Bramble is amazed to think that she has brought such a prodigy as Harold into the world.

(6) Harold wants to know what will happen to the money he had bet on Murphy losing.

(7) Mrs. Bramble is informed that Bill had decided not to fight.

(8) Mrs. Bramble resumes work of darning the sock.

(9) Harold is alone with his mother in their home.

Mrs. Bramble is amazed to think that she has brought such a prodigy as Harold into the world.

Ans.

9. Harold is alone with his mother in their home.
5. Mrs. Bramble is amazed to think that she has brought such a prodigy as Harold into the world.
8. Mrs. Bramble resumes work of darning the sock.
1. Major Percy and Bill come to the house.
7. Mrs. Bramble is informed that Bill had decided not to fight.
3. Bill tells his wife that he is doing it for Harold.
4. Jerry Fisher tries to convince Bill to reconsider.
2. Harold comes to know that his father is a boxer.
6. Harold wants to know what will happen to the money he had bet on Murphy losing.

ON PAGE 42-43

Q.4A Based on your reading of the story, answer the following questions by choosing the correct option.

(i) Mrs. Bramble was a proud woman because ....

(a) she was the wife of a famous boxer

(b) she had motivated her husband

(c) she was a good housewife

(d) she was the mother of a child prodigy

Ans. (d) she was the mother of a child prodigy

(ii) "The very naming of Harold had caused a sacrifice on his part." The writer's tone here is ....

(a) admiring (b) assertive

(c) satirical (d) gentle

Ans. (a) admiring

(c) Harold had defied the laws of heredity by ....

(a) becoming a sportsperson

(b) being good at academics

(c) being well-built and muscular

(d) respecting his parents

Ans. (b) being good at academics

(d) Harold felt that he was deprived of the respect that his classmates would give him as ....

(a) they did not know his father was the famous boxer, 'Young Porky'

(b) his hero, Jimmy Murphy had not won the wrestling match

(c) he had not got Phil Scott's autograph

(d) Sid Simpson had lost the Lonsdale belt

Ans. (a) they did not know his father was the famous boxer, 'Young Porky'

(e) 'It's hard,' he said at length in a choked voice. What was hard according to Mr. Fisher?

(a) To accept the truth
(b) To fight with American Murphy
(c) To control his anger
(d) To give up boxing

Ans. (c) To control his anger

(f) What do you gauge about Major Percy Stokes' character from the story? Select the most appropriate option from the following.

1. man of wrath **2. persuasive**
3. argumentative **4. interfering**
5. self-important

(a) 1, 3 and 5
(b) 1, 2 and 4
(c) 2, 4 and 5
(d) 3, 4 and 5

Ans. (d) 3, 4 and 5

ON PAGE 43-44

Q.4B Read the given extracts and answer the questions by selecting the correct options.

1. The only drawback was that his very 'perfection had made necessary a series of evasions and even deliberate falsehoods on the part of herself and her husband, highly distasteful to both. They were lovers of truth, but they had realised that there are times when truth must be sacrificed. At any cost, the facts concerning Mr. Bramble's profession must be kept from Harold.

(i) His very 'perfection' refers to Harold's

1. gentlemanly manners.
2. aspiration to be the best.
3. exceptional intelligence.
4. obsession with cleanliness.

(a) 1 and 3 (b) 2 and 3
(c) 1 and 4 (d) 2 and 4

Ans. (a) 1 and 3

(ii) What was highly distasteful to both Mrs. and Mr. Bramble?

(a) Consciously choosing to lie.
(b) Harold's perfection.
(c) Mr. Bramble's profession.
(d) Their relationship with each other.

Ans. (a) Consciously choosing to lie.

(iii) The facts concerning Mr. Bramble's profession 'must be kept' from Harold because it would make him feel

(a) afraid (b) ashamed
(c) weird (d) angry

Ans. (b) ashamed

2. On the faces of three of them consternation was written. In the eyes of the fourth, Mr. Fisher, there glittered that nasty, steely expression of the man, who sees his way to getting a bit of his own back, Mr. Fisher's was not an un-mixedly chivalrous nature. He considered that he had been treated badly...

(i) Three of them felt anxious because

(a) Mr. Fisher was about to hit Major Percy.
(b) they suspected Mr. Fisher would take revenge.
(c) Harold had heard a part of their conversation.
(d) Harold did not like arguments at home.

Ans. (c) Harold had heard a part of their conversation.

(ii) Get a bit of his own back implies ....

(a) feeling offended (b) getting his way
(c) being forceful (d) taking revenge

Ans. (d) taking revenge

(iii) How was Mr. Fisher planning to get his own back?

(a) By telling Harold the truth about his father.
(b) By persuading Mr. Bramble to change his mind.
(c) By hitting Major Percy and Mr. Bramble.
(d) By kidnapping Harold and blackmailing Brambles.

Ans. (a) By telling Harold the truth about his father.

(iv) Mr. Fisher felt he had been treated badly because Mr. Bramble had

(a) cheated him and lied.
(b) called off his fight with Murphy.
(c) been spending time with Percy.
(d) been insensitive and aggressive.

Ans. (b) called off his fight with Murphy.

ON PAGE 45

Q.5A Answer the following questions.

(a) Why was it necessary to keep Harold's father's profession a secret from him?

Ans. Harold's father was a professional boxer while Harold was an intellectual genius. At that time, boxing was not considered a respectable profession and his parents thought that it may be difficult for Harold to accept that his father was such a person. Hence, they felt that it was necessary to his father's profession a secret from Harold.

(b) Describe Mr. Bramble as he has been described in the story.

Ans. Mr. Bramble was a professional boxer popularly known as 'Young Porky'. He was very talented and had won many boxing matches. However, he was gentle, mild and submissive at home. Though he looked like a tough boxer with his square jaw and irregularly shaped nose, he was a very sensitive man. He was easily persuaded and influenced. He was so selfless and sacrificing that he even decided to give up his profession for his son's sake.

(c) Who was Jerry Fisher? What did he say to try and convince Bill to change his mind?

Ans. Jerry Fisher was Bill's trainer. He tried in all possible ways to convince Bill to fight. Jerry told Bill that he would lose a lot of money, the spectators would be disappointed and the media would not be kind to him. However, if he fought and won the match, he would win a large sum of money besides gaining popularity.

(d) Why was Harold upset that his father had not told him about his true identity? Give two reasons.

Ans. Harold was upset because he regretted that he had been deprived of the pleasure of calling himself Young Porky's son. His schoolmates teased him by calling him 'Goggles' due to the spectacles that he wore. Had they known who his father really was, they would have never dared to make fun of him. He also felt bad about being denied the opportunity of showing off that he was the son of a famous boxer.

(e) Do you agree with Harold's parents decision of hiding from him the fact that his father was a boxer? Why/Why not?

Ans. I agree with Harold's parents decision of hiding from him the real nature of his father's profession. They felt that society at that time considered a professional boxer to be as a cheap entertainer. They wanted Harold to be saved from the agony of being called the son of a boxer. However, they did not realise that times had changed and boxers were heroes of the younger generation.

(f) Why did Mr. Bramble decide at the last minute not to fight with American Murphy at the National Sporting Club?

Ans. Mr. Bramble decided at the last minute to not fight with American Murphy at the National Sporting Club because he received many letters from Percy stating that the national coverage of the match would ensure that Harold will learn about his father's 'shameless' profession. He got influenced by what Percy had written and decided to quit boxing to become an instructor.

(g) 'There are times when truth must be sacrificed.' Do you agree? Why/why not?

Ans. No, I don't agree with the given statement. Many people think it is fine to lie to others, especially children, because they could develop negative feelings like anxiety and shame if they know the truth. However, lying can make things more complicated as one has to constantly lie and hide the truth. Truth would eventually come out so it is better to tell the truth now.

(h) "Don't judge a book by its cover." Discuss with reference to Mr. Bramble's personality.

Ans. It is true to say that we should not judge a book by its cover. Mr. Bramble's profession is in contrast with his personality. Although he has a big and strong body, he has a genial smile and is one of the mildest and most obliging men. He could be easily persuaded and wasn't a violent man in his private life.

Q.5B Answer in detail.

(a) Did Harold react the way his parents expected him to on finding out about his father's true profession? Give reasons for your answer.

Ans. No, Harold didn't react the way his parents expected him to react on finding out about his father's true profession.

Bill, Jane and Percy had thought that Harold would feel ashamed if he got to know the truth. Harold was considered to be a gentleman, someone who was in total contrast with Bill and Jerry. Thus, they felt that Harold would be disgraced by his father's true profession and would hate him. However, when Harold found out the truth, he was angry at his father, not because he was ashamed of his profession, but because his father had never told him that he was the popular boxer, Young Porky. He revealed that he liked boxing and wanted his father to fight because he could get rid of bullies and win the bet.

(b) Assuming you are Harold, write a letter to your father expressing how you have always admired Young Pokey, little realizing it was his Pa.

Ans. 34, Park Avenue
Yorkshire-264821

24th September, 20XX

Dear father

Recently, when I realised that the boxer that I admired was none other than my father, I was really surprised. 'Young Porky' has always been my favourite boxer and I really like his technique. It never occurred to me that it was you. I always thought you were a commercial traveller.

Initially, I was very hurt that you had not told me the truth because I like boxing and I had bet my pocket money on the defeat of Murphy. However, was also very proud to learn that I am the son of a famous boxer. I even wanted to show your photo to my friends and get treated with respect.

Wishing you good luck for your fight.
Yours lovingly.

Harold

(c) We often go with preconceived notions which are usually baseless. Do you think this was the case with Mrs. and Mr. Bramble? Give reasons for your answer.

Ans. Yes, I think Mr. and Mrs. Bramble had a preconceived notion which was baseless. They thought that since Harold was unlike his father due to his intelligence and mannerisms, he was superior. Harold was ten years old and had won prizes in spelling and dictation and was a gentleman.

When the Brambles saw his development, they thought that he would not like the fact that his father was a professional boxer. Hence, they decided to hide this fact from him. They were also encouraged to do so by the Parish priest and Major Percy Stokes. They didn't realise that they shouldn't lie to their son about such an important thing and that the truth would eventually come out. They felt that Harold would be ashamed but Harold wanted his father to fight. He was proud to know that he was the son of a famous boxer.

(d) Imagine you are Bill Bramble, write a diary entry expressing how life changed after your son's birth and how you feel currently after the truth about your profession has been revealed to your son.

Ans. Wednesday, 19th January, 20XX 9:00 p.m.

Dear Diary

My life changed completely after the birth of my son, Harold. Prior to his birth, I didn't have to worry about being a boxer or hiding it from anyone. However, when Harold was born and showed that he was no ordinary child everything changed. My dearest son is a prodigy who has won many prices at a young age and is very-well mannered. It was due to his intelligence and good behaviour that me and my wife decided to not tell him about my profession. Although I and my wife hated to lie, we had to tell Harold that I work as a commercial traveller. We didn't wish to lie but we didn't wish to upset Harold too. It was for this reason that I decided to give up boxing and not fight Murphy. Due to a series of events, Harold did eventually find out about me being a boxer. Harold was not ashamed but he was angry that we had not told him earlier about my profession. He even bet his pocket money on me winning the fight. I felt really proud to be acknowledged and appreciated by my son. It is like a big burden has been lifted off my shoulders. Harold encouraged me to fight and I am relieved that my profession won't affect my son. I have decided to not quit boxing and make my son proud by winning future bouts.

Bill

Q.6 Choose extracts from the story that illustrate the characters of these people in it.

Persons	Extracts from the story	What this tells us about their characters
Mrs Bramble	(para 12) "Bill we must keep it from Harold."	She was not honest and open with her son; concerned mother
Mr Bramble	(para 33)	
Percy	(para 109)	
Jerry Fisher	(para 110)	

Ans.

Persons	Extracts from the story	What this tells us about their characters
Mrs Bramble	(para 12) "Bill we must keep it from Harold."	She was not honest and open with her son, but she was a concerned mother.
Mr Bramble	(para 33) "The scales have fallen from his eyes."	As he was a caring father, he decided to sacrifice his profession for his son's benefit.
Percy	(para 109) "My dear sir." There was a crooning winningness in Percy's voice.	He understood well a father's feelings for his son. He showed his humility in requesting Jerry not to tell Harold about his father being a professional boxer.
Jerry Fisher	(para 110) "Tommy", said Mr .... as 'Young Porky'.	revengeful; he wanted to get his way even at the cost of hurting the young boy and causing conflict in the family.

ON PAGE 46

Q.7 Many people are of the opinion that violent, physical sports such as boxing, kick boxing and wrestling, to name a few should be banned while others think otherwise. Express your opinion on the topic by either writing in favour of banning these sports or against banning them. While writing, you should also include the rebuttal to your questions. Try not to go beyond 200 words.

Ans. I believe violent sports like boxing and wrestling should be banned. These sports often lead to serious injuries and the risk is too high. Athletes can suffer long-term damage, especially to their brains, which isn't worth the entertainment. Additionally, these sports might make people think violence is okay, which isn't good for our society.

Some say these sports teach discipline and skill but there are safer activities that offer the same benefits. We need to prioritise people's safety over entertainment. If we encourage other sports that are less harmful, we can still promote fitness and skill development without the same risks.

In summary, banning violent sports is necessary for the well-being of athletes and for sending the right message about violence in our society. We should focus on activities that keep people safe and healthy.

REVIEW EXERCISE

Including Exam Pattern Practice Questions

Extract Based Questions

Read the following extracts carefully and answer the questions that follow.

1. He sat on the other side of the table, his lips gravely pursed and his eyes a trifle cloudy behind their spectacles. Before him on the red table cloth lay an open book.
His powerful brain was plainly busy.

(a) **'Who is 'he' ....**

Ans. 'He' is Harold Bramble.

(b) **Explain '... his lips gravely pursed'.**

Ans. 'His lips gravely pursed' describes that Harold pressed together his lips seriously while trying to recall the poem he had learnt.

(c) **What are the features which describe Harold as an intelligent boy?**

Ans. The features which describe Harold as an intelligent boy are that he has a powerful brain and he always remains busy in his studies.

(d) **What is the opposite of 'huge' from the extract?**

Ans. The opposite of 'huge' is 'trifle'.

2. It jarred upon him, this habit of his mother's of referring to herself in the third person, as if she were addressing a baby, instead of a young man of ten who had taken the spelling and dictation prize last term on his head.

(a) **'It' here refers to what?**

Ans. It' here refers to Mrs. Bramble's habit of referring to herself in the third person.

(b) **How old is the person mentioned in the extract?**

Ans. The person mentioned in the extract is ten years old.

(c) **What does 'jarred upon' mean?**

Ans. 'Jarred upon' means to have an unpleasant and disturbing effect.

(d) **What quality of the young man is highlighted in the extract?**

Ans. Intelligence possessed by the young man is highlighted in the extract.

3. The only drawback was, that his very 'perfection' had made necessary a series of evasions and even deliberate falsehoods, on the part of herself and her husband, highly distasteful to both.
They were lovers of truth, but they had realised that there are times when truth must be sacrificed.

(a) **Who does 'they' refer to?**

Ans. 'They' refers to Mr. and Mrs. Bramble.

(b) **What was the truth that they had hidden?**

Ans. The truth that they had hidden from Harold was that Harold's father was a professional boxer.

(c) **Find the word in the extract which means 'gave up'.**

Ans. The word 'sacrificed' means 'to give up'.

(d) **The 'truth' must be sacrificed ....**

Ans. to make sure that Harold does not hate his father

4. Yet Harold, defying the laws of heredity, had run to intellect as his father had run to muscle.

He had learned to read and write with amazing quickness. He sang in the Choir.

(a) **What can we say about Harold on the basis of the given extract?**

Ans. We can say that Harold was an all rounded and intelligent child.

(b) **Harold's intellect is shown by ....**

Ans. his ability to learn, to read and write with amazing quickness, as well as his singing in the Choir.

(c) **The difference between Harold and his father was ....**

Ans. that Harold loved studies and his father loved boxing.

(d) **Which word in the extract is an antonym of 'obeying'?**

Ans. The word 'defying' is the antonym of obeying.

5. So, Harold grew in stature and intelligence, without a suspicion of the real identity of the square-jawed man with the irregularly-shaped nose who came and went mysteriously in their semi-detached, red-brick home.

He was a self-centred child and, accepting the commercial traveller fiction, dismissed the subject from his mind and busied himself with things of more moment.

(a) 'More moment' here means ....

Ans. more importance.

(b) Explain the sentence 'accepting the commercial traveller fiction'.

Ans. 'Accepting the commercial traveller fiction' means that Harold believed the story of Bill being a commercial traveller.

(c) Which subject is regarded as trivial?

Ans. The subject which is regarded as trivial by Harold is his father's profession.

(d) Who is the 'square jawed man'

Ans. Mr. Bill Bramble is the square jawed man.

6. "Goodness knows I've never liked your profession, Bill, but there is this to be said for it, that it's earned you good money and made it possible for us to give Harold as good an education as any duke ever had, I'm sure."

(a) Who states the given words?

Ans. Jane Bramble is the speaker of the given words.

(b) Which word in the extract is a synonym of 'vocation'?

Ans. The word 'profession' is a synonym of vocation.

(c) What does this statement indicate?

Ans. This statement indicates that Mrs. Bramble is very much concerned about her son's education and for this reason, she doesn't want her husband to quit boxing.

(d) Why does the speaker refer to Harold as a 'Duke'?

Ans. The speaker refers to Harold as a Duke to indicate that Harold's education is as important as that of a Duke.

7. "Talking of Harold," said Mr. Bramble at last, That's , really what I'm driving at.

It was him only whom I was thinking of when I hopped it from the White Hart.

It would be written up in all the papers, instead of only in the sporting ones. As likely as not, there would be a piece about it in the Mail, with a photograph of me.

(a) Who is the speaker?

Ans. Mr. Bill Bramble is the speaker.

(b) What would be written in the papers?

Ans. The boxing match that was supposed to take place between Bill Bramble and Jimmy Murphy would be written about in the papers.

(c) What does 'the sporting ones' mean?

Ans. 'The sporting ones' means the newspapers that specifically have a 'sports' section.

(d) What is the word 'Mail indicates'?

Ans. The word 'mail indicates' newspapers.

8. The little man's face became a battlefield on which rage, misery and a respect for the decencies of social life struggled for mastery. "It's hard," he said at length, in a choked voice. "I just wanted to break his neck.

for him, but I suppose it's not to be. I know it's him that's at the bottom of it."

(a) Who is the little man referred to?

Ans. The little man referred to is 'Jerry Fisher'.

(b) What does the expression "face became a battlefield" mean?

Ans. The phrase "face became a battlefield" means that there were different emotions seen on his face. His face showed signs of conflict between the emotion of anger, suffering and respect.

(c) What did the decencies of social life demand from 'the little man'?

Ans. The decencies of social life demanded that he behave like a gentleman in a lady's presence.

(d) What is the opposite of 'misery'?

Ans. The opposite of 'misery' is pleasure.

9. "Bill", he cried, "you're off your head. Think of the purse!"

"Ah" said Mrs. Bramble.

"Think of all the swell's that'll be coming to see you."

(a) What had 'Bill' done that makes the speaker say these words?

Ans. Bill had announced his decision to not fight on Monday against Jimmy Murphy.

(b) Why had Bill made such a decision?

Ans. Bill made this decision because the fight would be national news and would be reported in the newspapers with his photograph. Harold would see it and would feel ashamed of his father's actual profession.

(c) What does the speaker ask Bill to think about?

Ans. The speaker asks Bill to think about the money and praise that he would recieve of he won the match.

(d) State the meaning of 'off your head'.

Ans. The expression means crazy.

10. "My dear sir, do nothing hasty. Think before you speak. Don't go and be so silly as to act like a mutton-head. I'd be ashamed to be so spiteful. Respect a father's feelings."

(a) Why would Bill be ashamed of being spiteful?

Ans. Bill would be ashamed of being spiteful because he was a simple man who would not like to take revenge on anybody for any action hurting his interests.

(b) What do you come to know about Bill's character is the extract?

Ans. The extract shows that he is not a revengeful or unforgiving person.

(c) What does the phrase 'to act like a mutton-head' mean?

Ans. The phrase means 'behaving stupidly'.

(d) What does 'spiteful' mean?

Ans. The word 'spiteful' means malicious.

11. "One chap's got a snapshot of Jimmy Wilde. At least he says it's Jimmy Wilde, but I believe it's just, some ordinary fellow. Anyhow, its jolly blurred, so it might be anyone. Pa, can't you give me a picture of yourself boxing? I could swank like anything. And you don't know how sick a chap gets of having chaps call him, 'Goggles'."

(a) Who is Jimmy Wilde in the extract?

Ans. Jimmy Wilde is a famous boxer.

(b) Which word in the extract is a synonym of 'unclear'?

Ans. The word 'blurred' is a synonym of 'unclear'.

(c) Why does Harold want Bill's snap?

Ans. Harold wanted Bill's snap because he wanted to show off about being the son of a boxing champion and he did not want to be called 'Goggles'.

(d) The opposite of 'ordinary' is ....

Ans. 'unusual'

Short Answer Type Questions

Answer the following questions in 30-40 words.

1. Why did Mrs. Bramble address her son as 'dearie'?

Ans. Mrs. Bramble was a proud mother and used to call Harold as 'dearie' out of love. She addressed him in the third person the way one addresses a baby because to a mother her child will always be as dear as a baby.

2. What was a constant source of amazement to Mrs. Bramble?

Ans. A constant source of amazement to Mrs. Bramble was the unusually intelligent boy Harold who had grown up to be so different from his father. While his father was a professional boxer, Harold excelled in academics.

3. Why was Harold called a 'prodigy'?

Ans. Harold, a ten year old boy, is rightly termed as a 'prodigy'. He was an extraordinary child at a very young age. He won many prizes in school competitions and also had an interest in singing. He sang in the Choir. He was a multi-faceted child who excelled in academics in the same way as his father excelled in boxing.

4. What did Mrs. Bramble mean when she said to her husband, "Bill, we must keep it from Harold"?

Ans. Mrs. Bramble meant that the actual profession of his father, a professional boxer, should not be known by Harold. This is so because they felt that boxing was not considered to be a respectable profession and that Harold would become ashamed of his father.

5. Bill Bramble was a professional boxer. Why was this a trouble for both Jane Bramble and Bill Bramble?

Ans. Mr. Bramble was a very famous professional boxer and he was very proud of his name and fame. However, when Harold was born and started growing up, both his parents were amazed to see his extraordinary academic skills and his overall development.

This became a trouble for both of them because they wanted to hide his father's profession from their son Harold.

6. How has Harold defied the laws of heredity?

Ans. Harold was an extraordinary child. He was just ten years old but possessed great talent. Unlike his father, he excelled in academics and showed interest in it. Apart from this, he also sang in the Choir. On the other hand, his father was inclined towards boxing and was very proud of being a professional boxer. It can be concluded that Harold, defying the laws of heredity, had run to intellect as his father had run to muscle.

7. What is meant by "The scales have fallen from his eyes"? **Competency Based**

Ans. This means that Bill Bramble has now understood that his son is more important to him than his boxing career. As a result he will retire from boxing so that his son Harold does not come to know that his father was a professional boxer.

8. Why was Mrs. Bramble not happy to see her husband's retirement from boxing?

Ans. Though she did not like her husband's profession, this match would have given a large amount of money even if he would have lost the match. From this money, they could give Harold a better education. So when her husband decided to retire from boxing, Mrs. Bramble became extermely unhappy.

9. Why did Fisher tell Harold the truth about his father's boxing profession?

Ans. Fisher was angry with Bill Bramble at backing out from the professional fight scheduled to be held on Monday. He felt that he had been treated badly and was desperate to take revenge. So, he told Harold the truth knowing that the Brambles had not wanted this.

10. What did Harold's classmates call him? What made him so sick?

Ans. Harold's classmates used to call him 'Goggles'. There was a boy in his school who always showed off in the most unpleasant way because he had once gotten the famous boxer Phil Scott's autograph, which irritated Harold a lot and made him feel sick.

11. How did Harold take his parents by surprise at the end of the lesson, 'Keeping It From Harold'?

Ans. Harold surprised his parents when he told them that he used his pocket money to bet on the defeat of Jimmy Murphy. He was upset that he had been denied the chance to show off before his friends that his father was the famous boxing champion 'Young Porky'.

12. Describe Harold in your own words.

Ans. Harold was an extraordinarily intelligent boy with deep interest in academics. To his parents he was a genius and a model of good behaviour. In fact, his parents were in awe of him and wondered how such a child had been born to them. Later on we find that he has an interest in boxing and has in-depth knowledge about it as well.

13. Explain the irony in the story 'Keeping It From Harold'. Competency Based

Ans. Harold's parents feared that after knowing the truth, Harold would be hurt and would not like it that his father was a professional boxer. However, ironically when Harold came to know about the secret, he surprised everybody by saying that he always admired 'Young Porky'.

Long Answer Type Questions

Answer the following questions in 120 words.

1. Mr. Bramble wanted to hide the truth about his profession because he did not consider it a dignified one. Do you think it was the right attitude? Justify. Competency Based

Ans. Although parents would want their child to be truthful, they do not mind telling lies themselves to closely guard certain 'secrets' they think their child must not know. In doing so, they often end up teaching their child wrong values or depriving him/her of something he/she might have reasons to be proud of.

In short, children must be allowed to grow up as naturally as possible and should be told that there is nothing undignified about their parent's profession or economic status. Thus, Mr. Bramble's attitude towards his own profession is immature. He should realise that he earned fame, glory, recognition and money as 'Young Porky'. There was nothing undignified about his profession.

2. Jerry Fischer, by revealing the secret that the Brambles had hidden so long from Harold, actually helped the Bramble family. Comment.

Ans. It is true to say that Jerry Fischer, by revealing the secret that the Brambles had hidden so long from Harold, had actually helped the Bramble family. The Bramble family had kept a huge secret from Harold to avoid any feeling of shame and stress for the young boy. They hid the fact that Bill Bramble was a professional boxer named Young Porky. As a result, they had to make sure that Harold does not get to know the truth from anywere.

Although Bill loved his profession, he had decided to leave it behind for his son. He was dissappointed as he had to leave the sport that he loved to do. Further, with retirement from boxing , the steady flow of income that supported Harold's expensive education would be lost. Hence, in such a situation by telling Harold the truth, Jerry Fischer solved all problems. Now, Bill would not need to leave his profession, Harold could continue his education and the Bramble family became closer.

3. Harold's joy knew no bounds when he came to know that he was the son of Young Porky–a professional boxer of international repute. But the parents had robbed him of this knowledge for long. What moral value do you infer from the above context?

Ans. The Brambles left no stone unturned to raise Harold respectably. They feared that Harold would be hurt if he was told that his father's profession was boxing, which was considered violent and socially unacceptable. Ironically, he was not at all upset to learn that his father was a professional boxer, but felt bad that he was denied the chance to show off before his friends.

The story shows that parents should be broad-minded and should introduce young minds to complete truths and train them to face them boldly. They should understand the mental makeup of a child and allow him to grow in a natural environment. Knowing that every profession has a dignity of its own will boost the morale of a child and make him/her confident enough to pursue a career in the field that they love.

ASSESSMENT EXERCISE

Extract Based Questions

Read the following extracts carefully and answer the questions that follow.

1. 'Bill sank into a chair. He could see Harold's round eyes staring at him'.
   (a) Why did Bill sink into a chair?
   (b) Why was Bill observing Harold's eyes?
   (c) Which word in the extract means the same as 'looking attentively'?
   (d) The present tense of 'sank' is ....
2. "There's a fellow at our school who goes about swanking in the most rotten way because he once got Phil Scott's autograph."
   (a) Who is the speaker of the above lines?
   (b) Why does he go 'about swanking'?
   (c) Which word in the extract is a synonym of 'boasting'?
   (d) What is the synonym of 'fellow'?

Short Answer Type Questions

Answer the following questions in 30-40 words each.

1. Why did the senior Curate advise the Brambles to hide Bill's actual profession from Harold?
2. Why did Bill Bramble quail at the sight of his name in print?
3. How would life in school have been different for Harold had he known that his father was 'Young Porky'?
4. Explain the title 'Keeping It From Harold'.
5. Although Mrs Bramble did not like her husband's profession, why did she still want him to fight the last bout?
6. How was Harold different from his father?
7. How did Percy dissuade Bill from fighting the last bout?
8. Why did Harold fix his eyes upon the cut-glass chandelier at the beginning of the story when he was studying?
9. How did Harold feel about his classmates' behaviour towards him?
10. What did Percy want to convey when he said, "The scales have fallen from his eyes."?

Long Answer Type Questions

Answer the following questions in 120 words each.

1. Write a character sketch of Bill Bramble, bringing out his values of self-sacrifice, meekness and obedience.
2. Bring out the typical practical and motherly values in Mrs Bramble by mentioning instances where these are observed.
3. What values does Jerry Fisher hold important in his profession as a trainer? Do you think they are important both for a boxer and a coach? Why/why not?

Best Seller

by O Henry

CHAPTER 5

CHAPTER SUMMARY The story revolves around the life of John A Pescud, a plate-glass seller, who believes that fictions are unrealistic. According to him, a man always marries a girl of the same background. Although he hates false stories of the best-selling novels, he still reads them. Moreover, John's own love story was nothing less than the story of a best seller.

Narrator's Meeting with John

One day, the narrator was on his way to Pittsburgh for business by the chair car. He was sitting on chair no. 7 and was surrounded by many businessmen and ladies belonging from rich families. As he was looking at his surrounding, the narrator noticed someone on chair no 9.

The man threw a book to the floor between his chair and the window. As the narrator looked , it was "The Rose Lady and Trevelyan," one of the best-selling novels of the time. Then, as the man moved his chair toward the window, the narrator recognised him. He was John A. Pescud of Pittsburgh, a travelling salesman for a plate-glass company. He was an old acquaintance who the narrator had not met in two years.

Within 2 minutes, the narrator had greeted the man and discussed topics such as rain, prosperity, health, residence and destination.

John A Pescud

John A. Pescud was a simple and small man with a wide smile. He believed that the plate-glass is the most important commodity in the world and his company, the Cambria Steel Works, was the best company. He also believed that when a man is in his home town, he must be decent and lawful. When the narrator had met the man earlier, he knew nothing about John's views on life, romance, literature and ethics. However, now he was to learn about them. The narrator also got to know that their business had become successful since the party conventions and that he was going to get off at Coketown.

John's Views on the Best Seller 'The Rose Lady and Trevelyan'

John started discussing the romace best sellers with the narrator. He told the narrator about 'The Rose lady and Trevelyan' and called it unrealistic. The story dealt with the life of Trevelyan, who was an ordinary person and the princess Alwyna, who belonged to a royal family. Although, Trevelyan did not belong to a royal family, he fights the royal bodyguards and is a great fencer.

This story seemed unrealistic to John and he was of the view that in real life a man should marry a girl of the same background. John, then reads some lines from the story while the narrator agrees with them.

Conversation between the Men

As John was talking about how stupid the romance bestsellers are, the narrator shifted the conversation. He asked John about his life. John told him that his life had been good. He had his salary raised twice and got a commission too. He had bought some property and will buy some parts of his company too.

John's Personal Life

After exchanging views on various topics, the narrator asked John about his personal life. As if he was waiting for an opportunity, Pescud started a detailed story of his love which had a happy ending in marriage.

John Reached Virginia

John told the narrator that about eighteen months ago, when he was going to Cincinnati, he saw a beautiful girl. He got attracted towards her and followed her everywhere.

He followed her from Cincinnati and went to Louisville. From there, he followed her through Shelbyville, Frankford, and Lexington. It was difficult for him to follow her without being noticed. However, he never lost track of her and reached Virginia.

In Virginia, he saw her meeting a tall old man with a smooth face and white hair. John kept following them, acting like he was hunting a garnet ring in the sand that his sister had lost.

The Big House

The man and the girl entered a big house on top of the hill. It was a huge house with round white pillars and a yard full of rose-bushes, box-bushes and lilacs. John realised that the house must be Governor's mansion or the Agricultural Building of a new World's Fair. Then, he decided to go back to the village and get some information from the postmaster.

In the village, he stayed at the Bay View House stating that he was taking orders for plate-glass. Soon, he started asking questions and found that the big house belonged to Colonel Allyn, the biggest man in Virginia. He also got to know that the girl was his daughter, who had gone to Illinois to visit her sick aunt.

Meeting the Girl

On his third day in Virginia, John saw the girl walking in the front yard, next to the paling fence. So, he asked her the way to Mr. Hinkle's house. The girl told him that no one with that name lives in the village.

During the conversation, he came to know that the girl knew that he was following her from Cincinnati. She blushed while explaining this. In the course of their conversation, John told her all about himself and his purpose. He also learnt from her that her father was very status conscious and he might not like a commoner trying to woo his daughter.

John Decides to Meet the Girl's Father

The girl told John that her father would not allow him to talk to her and tried to make him go away. However, John remained firm. He told her that he would come to meet her father to which the girl replied that her father would kill him. After some fun conversation with the girl, John gets to know that her name is Jessie.

John went to meet Jessie's father the next day. An old man allowed him to enter the house which did not have much furniture. When Colonel Allyn came to meet him, John grew nervous but quickly covered it up. John, then, told the man everything including how he followed his daughter from Cincinnati and what he did it for. He also told the man about his salary and prospects.

Jessie's Father and John's Conversation

John felt that Jessie's father would get angry but he asked John many questions. The man then told John of a Sir Courtenay Pescud in the time of Charles I. However, John told him that no such relation was possible. Then, Jessie's father told him a story about fox-hunting. Hence, both of the men talked for two days. John could only meet Jessie after two days when she told him the story her father is going to tell John. Then, John had to leave.

John told the narrator that he married Jessie a year ago. He added that he built a house in the East end where he lives with his wife and the Colonel.

The Narrator's Views About John

When John prepared to get off the train at 'Coketown', the narrator remarked that John wouldn't be able to sell a lot of plate-glass there. John replied that his wife Jessie had admired some petunias she had seen in one of the windows while returning from their trip to Philadelphia. That is why he planned to take some cuttings or blossoms of the flower back for Jessie.

At the end, he referred to John as 'Trevelyan' the unlikely hero of the best-seller he had criticised earlier because John's story was very similar to the plot of that novel.

Word Meaning

Word	Meaning
profitably well-filled	occupied by many passengers
yokes	part of dresses fitting around the shoulders
tepidest	least interested
veered	turned
hurled	threw
plate-glass	high quality clear glass used for shop windows and doors
ethics	morality
browsed	talked
swell	a fashionably dressed wealthy upper class person
alias	also known by another name, false name
principality	territory ruled by a prince
royal chair-warmer	the lady was a princess who had a position in the royal court
stations	social status
he slaps	he successfully defeats any
in his way	adversaries
rank on-the-level	at equal social positions
freeing anything ...	something as easy as opening a tin of
canned sardines	canned food
Turkish pashas	high officials of the Ottoman empire
Vermont	a state in North USA
clamdiggers	people who hunt for clams (edible shell fish)
aristocracy	class of people of high social rank
jibe	match
capers	adventures
bully	yes
neat slice	good plot

Word	Meaning
shares of stock	shares of the company
general prosperity	doing well
for keeps	forever, permanently
proposition	lady
go to smash	forgotten
sleeper	a train which has sleeping berths in it
speckled hounds	dogs covered with small spots
frazzled	worn out
satchel	bag with long straps
garnet	red, semi-precious gemstone
paling fence	a fence made of wooden posts pointed at the top
weeding	removing the weeds
What I was making	how much I was earning
lineal descendant	direct descendant
belted	invested by the king with a sword worn at the waist
Earl	a British nobleman between a Viscount and a Marquess
drummer	ordinary man
belted earl	until the 17th century, an earl was invested by the king with a sword he wore at his waist
wormy English	hollow from inside with hardly anything
walnut	in it
eight-dollar	cheap
horsehair lounges	sofas filled with hair of horses
quadrille	a dance for four couples in a square
rattled	confused and nervous
ragged	having a rough or uneven surface or edge
rills	small channels made by flowing water

Textbook FOLDER

Here, we have covered questions given in the CBSE Textbook along with their answers.

ON PAGE 55

Q.3A Based on your reading of the story, answer the following questions by choosing the correct option.

(i) "Bully", said Pescud brightening at once. He means to say that he was

(a) being intimidated by his boss.
(b) harassing his subordinates.
(c) doing very well at his job.
(d) meeting all the sales targets.

Ans. (c) doing very well at his job.

(ii) The narrator says that life has no geographical boundaries implying that

(a) human beings are essentially the same everywhere.
(b) one can travel freely to other countries.
(c) boundaries exist only on maps.
(d) one should work towards the good of mankind.

Ans. (a) human beings are essentially the same everywhere.

(iii) Classify (1) to (4) as fact (F) or opinion (O), based on your reading of the story.

1. **Pescud had hurled the bestseller to the floor.**
2. **People in real life marry somebody in their own station.**
3. **Pescud got an opportunity to meet Jessie all alone two evenings after he met her father.**
4. **Pescud believed that plate-glass was the most important commodity.**

(a) F-1, 3, 4; O-2 (b) F-1, 3; O-2, 4
(c) F-1, 2, 4; O-3 (d) F-2; O-1, 3, 4

Ans. (b) F-1, 3; O-2, 4

(iv) Select the suitable option for the given statements, based on your understanding of the story.

1. The author's description of Coketown brings out the ugly face of industries that operated there.
2. Pescud got off at Coketown as it had good business prospects for a plate-glass salesman.

(a) 1 is false but 2 is true.
(b) 1 is true but 2 is false.
(c) 1 is the cause for 2
(d) 2 is a fact but unrelated to 1

Ans. (b) (1) is true but (2) is false.

ON PAGE 56

Q.3B Read the extracts and answer the questions by selecting the correct options.

1. I contrived to keep out of her sight as much as I could, but I never lost track of her. The last station she got off at was away down in Virginia, about six in the evening. There were about fifty houses.
The rest was mud, mules, and speckled hounds.
A tall old man, with a smooth face and white hair, looking as proud as Julius Caesar was there to meet her. His clothes were frazzled but I didn't notice that till later. He took her little satchel, and they started over the plank walks and went up a road along the hill. I kept along a piece behind 'em, trying to look like I was hunting a garnet ring in the sand that my sister had lost at a picnic the previous Saturday.

(i) The extract tells us that Virginia was a .... populated town.

(a) densely
(b) highly
(c) sparsely
(d) hardly

Ans. (c) sparsely

(ii) Choose the option that uses the word 'frazzled' in the same way as the extract.

(a) I feel pretty frazzled most weeks these days.
(b) The cuffs of his brown shirt looked frazzled.
(c) Father finally arrived home, tired and frazzled.
(d) Mother was frazzled looking after all the guests had left.

Ans. (b) The cuffs of his brown shirt looked frazzled.

(iii) Read the statements (1) and (2) given below, and choose the option that correctly evaluates the statements.

1. **The speaker pretended that he was searching for a lost ring.**
2. **The speaker wanted to hide the fact that he had been following her.**

(a) 1 is true but 2 is false. (b) 2 is contradictory to 1.
(c) 1 is the reason for 2. (d) 2 is the result of 1.

Ans. (d) 2 is the result of 1.

(iv) **Select the option that displays the characteristics of the speaker.**

1. discreet **2. vain**
3. ambitious **4. observant**
5. finicky **6. cautious**

(a) 1, 4 and 6 (b) 2, 3 and 5
(c) 1, 3 and 6 (d) 2, 4 and 5

Ans. (a) 1, 4 and 6

2. For about nine seconds he had me rattled, and I came mighty near getting cold feet and trying to sell him some plate-glass. But I got my nerve back pretty quick. He asked me to sit down, and I told him everything. I told him how I followed his daughter from Cincinnati, and what I did it for, and all about my salary and prospects, and explained to him my little code of living -to be always decent and right in your home town. At first, I thought he was going to throw me out of the window, but I kept on talking.

Well, that got him to laughing and I'll bet that was the first laugh those ancestors and horsehair sofa had heard in many a day.

(i) **Select the option that matches the expression with the meaning correctly.**

	Column A		Column B
I.	getting cold feet	(a)	to be exhausted
II.	dead on my feet	(b)	to become used to a new situation
III.	get your feet wet	(c)	carried away by someone on an emotional level
		(d)	feeling nervous about something

(a) I-c, II-b, III-a
(b) I-d, II-a, III-b
(c) I-a, II-c, III-d
(d) I-b, II-d, III-c

Ans. (b) I-d, II-a, III-b

(ii) **Select the option that lists the statements which can be a part of one's 'code of living'.**

1. Keep your word.
2. Never quit on yourself or your family.
3. Think about the future and ignore the present.
4. Focus on materialistic possessions.
5. Stay true to yourself.
6. Look back and wonder about your decisions.

(a) 1, 3 and 6 (b) 2, 4 and 5
(c) 2, 5 and 6 (d) 1, 2 and 5

Ans. (d) 1, 2 and 5

(iii) **"I'll bet that was the first laugh those ancestors and horsehair sofa had heard in many a day." The tone of the speaker is**

(a) satirical (b) ironical
(c) humorous (d) sarcastic

Ans. (c) humorous

(iv) **Which option best describes the sequence of the speaker's emotions in the given extract.**

(a) nostalgia-friendliness-jitters-disappointment
(b) curiosity-nostalgia-fear-mild sadness
(c) jitters-confidence-apprehension-delight
(d) shyness—friendliness-excitement-nostalgia

Ans. (c) jitters- confidence - apprehension - delight

ON PAGE 58

Q.4 Answer the following questions briefly.

(a) **One day, last summer the author was travelling to Pittsburgh by chair car. What does he say about his co-passengers?**

Ans. The author says that most of his co-passengers were either well-dressed ladies who refused to open the windows or men who wore similar looking business suits and had the same expressionless faces.

(b) **What was John A Pescud's opinion about best sellers? Why?**

Ans. John was of the opinion that all best sellers were of the kind where the hero was a wealthy American man who loves a royal princess from Europe. He strongly felt that these novels were far away from reality and purely fictional because in actual life, men marry women from a similar background as theirs.

(c) **What does John say about himself since his last meeting with the author?**

Ans. John told the author that his salary had been raised twice since he met the author last and he also gets a commission now. He had bought some property. Moreover, he would also get some shares of his company next year. On the personal front, he had gotten married and built a house at the East End.

(d) **How did John's first meeting with Jessie's father go? What did the author tell him?**

Ans. John's first meeting with Jessie's father went off very well. John honestly told him how he followed his daughter and wanted to marry her. He felt that the Colonel would disapprove of his action but soon they became friendly with each other and kept on talking for two hours. Thus, his meeting with Jessie's father was successful.

(e) Why did John get off at Coketown?

Ans. John got off at Coketown because he wanted some cuttings and blossoms of Petunia flowers for his wife. She wanted them because she liked them a lot and wanted to grow them in her garden.

(f) John is a hypocrite. Do you agree with this statement? Substantiate your answer.

Ans. John is indeed a hypocrite. He criticises the plot of a 'best Seller' romance by calling it unrealistic and fictional. However, he has demonstrated the same events in his own life by pursuing and marrying a girl of high social status.

(g) Do you think Colonel Allyn enjoyed Pescud's company? Why/ Why not?

Ans. Yes, Colonel Allyn enjoyed Pescud's company. He was amused by John's code of living. He appreciated his honesty and story-telling skills. The colonel told Pescud that he believed exchanging stories to be the perfect method of building relationship between people. Pescud agreed with him and they continued exchanging stories for a few more days.

(h) Describe John A. Pescud with reference to the following points

(i) Physical appearance
(ii) His philosophy on behaviour
(iii) His profession
(iv) His first impression of his wife
(v) His success

Ans. (i) **Physical appearence** John A Pescud was a small man with a wide smile. He had an eye which seemed to be fixed upon the little red spot on the end of your nose.

(ii) **His philosophy on behaviour** He felt that when a man is in his hometown, he ought to be decent and law-abiding.

(iii) **His profession** He was a travelling salesman. At present, he was working with a plate-glass company named Cambria Steel Works.

(iv) **His first impression of his wife** He found her to be the most beautiful and the finest looking lady in the world. She was not very spectacular but had all the qualities of an ideal wife.

(v) **His success** A Pescud had good success in his life. In two years, he twice got a raise in salary and also got a commission. He had bought a house for himself and would be buying the company's shares next year. He had married the woman whom he loved.

ON PAGE 59

Q.5 Irony refers to the use of words to convey a meaning that is the opposite of their literal meaning. Working in pairs, bring out the irony in the following

(a) The title of the story, 'The Best Seller'.

Ans. The title of the story, 'Best Seller' is quite ironical. The main protagonist of the story, John A Pescud, criticises and denounces best- selling novels throughout the story. Ironically, his own love story is very similar to the story lines of best-selling novels.

(b) Pescud's claim, "When people in real life marry, they generally hunt up somebody in their own station. A fellow usually picks out a girl who went to the same high school and belonged to the same singing society that he did."

Ans. Pescud's claim here is ironical. According to him, people generally marry within the same social circle and with a person from the same background. Ironically, he himself belongs to a middle class family yet marries a woman belonging to an aristocratic family.

(c) The name Trevelyan

Ans. Trevelyan is the name of the hero of the best-selling novel that Pescud was reading. It is ironical that Pescud criticises the romantic 'Trevelyan'. However, he is not at all different from 'Trevelyan'. He is a romantic hero who falls in love with a lady from an aristocratic background, follows her, woos her and finally marries her.

Q.5 Answer in detail

(a) Pescud had the qualities of a good salesman. Justify this statement by citing examples from the text.

Ans. A good salesman is a person with great determination and perseverance. He or she knows how to persuade someone to buy their product. One can see these qualities in John A Pescud in the story. He followed Jessie for a long time to know about her. This shows his perseverance. He didn't lose to track of her. This shows his determination. He was also willing to speak to her father even though she was not very confident about it. He wasn't afraid of talking to the Colonel about following his daughter. His communication skills were very good as he was able to make the Colonel laugh, even though he was nervous. He was also persuasive because he managed to speak to Jessie and find out about her.

(b) Imagine you are Andrew Smith, the author of the bestseller, 'The Rose Lady and Trevelyan'. You happen to meet Pescud during one of your train journeys and realise he is one of your biggest critics. Write down the possible conversation.

You may begin like this

Pescud: Hello sir! It's a pleasure to have this chance meeting with you. I have read your book, 'The Rose Lady and Trevelyan' but I must say that I beg to differ with your idea of romance. I feel it is far from reality.

Andrew: Hello Mr. Pescud! I am glad that you are candid in your opinion about my book. So, tell me what's your notion of an ideal romance?

Ans. **Pescud** Hello sir! It's a pleasure to have this chance meeting with you. I have read your book, 'The Rose Lady and Trevelyan' but I must say that I beg to differ with your idea of romance. I feel it is far from reality.

Andrew Hello Mr. Pescud! I am glad that you are candid in your opinion about my book. So, tell me what's your notion of an ideal romance?

Pescud I think that in real life, a man should marry a girl of the same background.

Andrew That's interesting Mr. Pescud. I am intrigued to know if you are married? If so, did you also marry someone from a similar background?

Pescud Yes, I am married, Mr. Andrew. However, my wife and I aren't from the same background. I work as a Salesman for a plate-glass company whereas my wife is from a family of the Belted Earls.

Andrew Wasn't it difficult for you to marry her?

Pescud Not really. I thought it would be difficult because she is from a noble family but once I spoke to her father, he seemed to like me and I got married within 6 months.

Andrew Your story is really interesting, Mr. Pescud. Like Trevelyan from my book, you also married someone from a different background. May be it would change your opinion about my bestseller.

Andrew Yes, Mr. Andrew, you really make a valid point. Perhaps. I shouldn't be as critical of these bestsellers anymore.

Andrew I am happy to hear that.

Q.7 Working in groups of four, write an article on the following:

The elderly seek attention and company from younger members of their family. They are eager to listen and long to share their life experiences. John A Pescud is not only respectful but also very patient with Colonel Allyn, Jessie's father.

As a reporter, write an article for a newspaper, on the importance of the elderly in our lives.

Ans. **The Importance of Elderly in Our Lives**

by Staff Reporter

The elderly are a very important part of any family. They have the experience and wisdom of the world to help any members of the family who are in need of guidance. They need the attention and company of the younger members of their family and are eager to listen and share their life experiences. In the story 'Best seller', John is very respectful and patient towards Jessie's father. It was his honesty that impressed the Colonel.

He told him exactly how he had followed her daughter home and his interest in her. Also, they spoke about his salary, his job, future plans and his way of life. Even though Jessie thought that her father would not approve of a commoner, Pescud's conversation with the Colonel was quite the opposite.

They shared stories and laughed together. John felt that it was after a while that the Colonel had been able to laugh like he did with John. With his true intentions and clear heart, John impressed the Colonel. He had to be very patient to develop the relationship as well as very respectful. John showed both these qualities.

REVIEW EXERCISE

Including Exam Pattern Practice Questions

Extract Based Questions

Read the following extracts carefully and answer the questions that follow.

1. "Say", said Pescud, stirring his discarded book with the hand, "did you ever read one of these best-sellers?" I mean the kind where the hero is an American swell-sometimes even from Chicago - who falls in love with a royal princess from Europe who is travelling under an alias and follows her to her father's kingdom or principality? I guess you have. They're all alike.

(a) What is the best-seller about?

Ans. The best-seller is about a rich American named Trevelyan, who romances and ultimately marries a royal princess from Europe.

(b) What do you understand about Pescud's character from the above lines?

Ans. We can understand that Pescud likes to read romantic novels.

(c) What is name of the discarded book?

Ans. The name of the discarded book is 'The Rose Lady and Trevelyam'.

(d) Find a word that means the same as 'best-seller'.

Ans. The word chart-buster is same as 'best seller'.

2. "Yet I am a man and I have a heart to do and dare. I have no title save that of an uncrowned sovereign; but I have an arm and a sword that yet might free Schutzenfestenstein from the plots of traitors."

(a) Who is 'I' here?

Ans. 'I' here refers to 'Trevelyan' who is the hero of the 'best seller' named 'The Rose lady and Trevelyan'.

(b) What can he do for his beloved?

Ans. Trevelyan tells his beloved, Princess Alwyna, that he has a sword that can save Schutzenfestenstein (an imaginary character) from traitors. He wants to impress her by saying that he is brave and can save her from any dangers.

(c) Which word in the extract means the same as 'conspiracies'?

Ans. The word 'plots' means the same as 'conspiracies'.

(d) What does a 'sovereign' mean?

Ans. The word 'sovereign' means 'a ruler'.

3. "Or plain business men with aristocracy high above em." added Pescud. "It doesn't jibe. I dont see why people go to work and buy hundreds of thousands of books which are best sillers.

"You don't see or hear of any such capers in real life."

(a) Who is the speaker and what is he talking about?

Ans. The speaker is John A Pescud and he is talking about the romance described in the best-selling novel.

(b) What is ironical about his statement?

Ans. His statement is ironical because in his own case, he romanced his wife in the same manner as given in the novel.

(c) What is meant by the word 'capers'?

Ans. The word capers means 'playful activities'.

(d) The word 'plain business men' in the extract means ....

Ans. common

4. "I contrived to keep out of her sight as much as I could, but I never lost track of her. The last station she got off at was away down in Virginia, about six in the evening."

(a) Who is the speaker here?

Ans. John A Pescud is the speaker of the above lines.

(b) Which word in the extract is a synonym of 'managed'?

Ans. The word 'contrived' is a synonym of managed.

(c) Why was he following her?

Ans. He was following her because he was attracted to her good looks from the moment when he first saw her.

(d) What is the girl's name?

Ans. The girl's name is Jessie.

5. 'Excuse me', says I, 'Can you tell me where Mr. Hinkle lives?'

She looks at me as cool as if I was the man come to see about the weeding of the garden, but I thought I saw just a slight twinkle of fun in her eyes."

(a) Who is Mr. Hinkle and why is the speaker looking for him?

Ans. There is no Mr. Hinkle. The speaker invented this name to start a conversation with the lady.

(b) Why does 'she' look at him as if he was the man who had come to see the weeding of the garden?

Ans. She wants to give the impression that it is below her dignity to talk to a stranger.

(c) What is the meaning of 'twinkle of fun in her eyes'?

Ans. The phrase means that she is either happy or amused about something.

(d) What does 'weeding' mean here?

Ans. The word weeding means removing weeds or unwanted plants.

6. "Men are very clumsy", said she. "I know you were on every train. I thought you were going to speak to me and I am glad you didn't."

"Then we had more talk; and at last a kind of proud, serious look came on her face, and she turned and pointed a finger at the big house.

(a) Who is 'she' in the above lines?

Ans. 'She' in the above lines is Jessie.

(b) Why was she glad?

Ans. She was noticing John following her on every train and was expecting that he might talk to her. However, she would not have liked to talk to a stranger. That's why she was glad that he did not speak to her.

(c) Why does she say "Men are very clumsy"?

Ans. She said this because John had been following her wherever she went and he did not manage to hide this fact because she had easily noticed him.

(d) What does 'clumsy' mean?

Ans. The word clumsy means 'awkward in movement' or 'manner'.

7. "We are a proud family. Look at that mansion. It has fifty rooms. See the pillars and porches and balconies. The ceilings in the reception-rooms and the ball-room are twenty-eight feet high."

(a) Who is the speaker here?

Ans. Jessie is the speaker of these lines.

(b) Which word in the extract is an antonym of 'humble'?

Ans. The words 'proud' is an antonym of humble.

(c) What does the above description of the house show about the speaker?

Ans. The above description of the house shows that she is proud to belong to such a rich family.

(d) Why does the speaker say these lines?

Ans. The speaker says these line to scare John into going away and not try woo her.

8. But I got my nerve back pretty quick. He asked me to sit down, and I told him everything. I told him how I had followed his daughter from Cincinnati, and what I did it for, and all about my salary and prospects, and explained to him my little code of living - to be always decent and right in your home town.

"At first, I thought he was going to throw me out of the window, but I kept on talking."

(a) Who is 'he'?

Ans. He refers to Colonel Allyn.

(b) What does the statement 'but I kept on talking' tell us about the speaker?

Ans. This shows that he is a persistent person, who is not afraid.

(c) Why did the speaker expect 'him' to throw him out of the window?

Ans. The speaker expected 'him' to throw him out of the window because he had taken the liberty of following his daughter (of a marriageable age) over such a long distance and expressing his feelings about her to 'him', her father.

(d) State the word/phrase that indicates 'future'

Ans. Prospects

9. I glanced downward and saw the best seller.

I picked it up and set it carefully farther along on the floor of the car, where the raindrops would not fall upon it. And then, suddenly, I smiled and seemed to see that life has no geographical bounds.

"Good-luck to you, Trevelyan", I said. "And may you get the petunias for your princess!"

(a) Why did the narrator pick up the best seller and set it carefully on the floor of the car?

Ans. The narrator did so as it was raining outside and he did not want the raindrops to spoil the book by falling upon it.

(b) The narrator says, "Life has no geographical bounds." What does the narrator mean here?

Ans. Through the given statement the narrator means human beings are essentially the same everywhere.

(c) **Why does the narrator call the listener Trevelyan?**

Ans. The narrator felt that the travelling salesman was as romantic as the hero Trevelyan in the best-selling novel.

(d) **Why does the narrator refer to Petunias?**

Ans. He refers to Petunias because John was getting off in Coketown to collect some Petunias for Jessie.

Short Answer Type Questions

Answer the following questions in 30-40 words.

1. **Where was the narrator going and whom did he meet in the chair car?**

Ans. The narrator was going to Pittsburgh for business by the chair car. He was sitting on chair no 7. He saw that the person on chair no 9 was an old acquaintance, John A Pescud, whom he had last seen two years ago.

2. **Who was sitting on chair no 9 and what was he reading? What sort of views were exchanged between him and the narrator?**

Ans. John A Pescud was sitting on chair no 9. He was reading 'The Rose Lady and Trevelyan', one of the best selling novels of that time.

John was the narrator's old acquaintance. They exchanged views on topics like rain, prosperity, health, residence and destination.

3. **What does the narrator describe about John's looks and his views on the plate-glass company?**

Ans. The narrator describes John as a small man with a wide smile and an eye that seems to be fixed upon a little red spot on the end of your nose. Moreover, he believed that his company's plate-glass was the most important commodity in the world and the Cambria Steel Works was the best company.

4. **According to Pescud, "when a man is in his hometown he ought to be decent and law-abiding." What light does the statement reflect on Pescud?**

Ans. The statement brings out Pescud's hypocrisy. This double-faced man is decent and law-abiding in his hometown but he is capable of losing all his decency when he happens to be among strangers where nobody recognises him. Apart from it, he is so brave that he goes about openly declaring this way of living without any sense of shame.

5. **What did John say when the narrator asked him about his company and his work?**

Or **What was John A Pescud's opinion about his own business?**

Ans. John felt very proud when he explained to the narrator about his work. He told him that he was doing very well in his company and had his salary raised twice since the narrator last saw him and got a commission too. He added that maybe next year, the firm was going to sell him some shares of stock. He considered himself on the way to becoming prosperous.

6. **What was Pescud's first impression of his wife?**

Ans. Pescud happened to come across Jessie, his wife-to-be, in a train while going to Cincinnati. He found her to be so good looking that he wished she would come into his life permanently. He felt that her very presence was making the world a prettier and a better place to live in.

7. **Describe Miss Allyn's house.**

Ans. John describes Miss Allyn's house as a huge house as big as the Capitol at Washington. Although, it may have had many rooms, there was hardly any furniture inside except some old horsehair lounges and some broken chairs, with a few framed pictures of ancestors on the walls.

8. **What impression did Jessie give John about her father, Colonel Allyn?**

Ans. Jessie told John that her father was the lineal descendant of 'belted earls'. Very status-conscious and proud of his lineage, the Colonel would never tolerate a commoner wooing his daughter. She also warned him that the old man would treat him sternly if he tried to make any further advances.

9. **How did John A Pescud succeed in impressing Jessie's father in the lesson 'Best Seller'?**

Or **How did Colonel Allyn react when he met Pescud?**

Ans. Colonel Allyn reacted favourably to Pescud when he met him. Pescud used his convincing skills and honesty to win Colonel Allyn's heart. At first, Pescud was nervous but then he told Colonel Allyn everything truthfully. It made him laugh. Then, they shared some anecdotes for two hours. The meeting cleared the way for Pescud's marriage to Jessie.

10. **Why did Colonel Allyn mention Sir Courtenay Pescud in his conversation with Pescud?**

Ans. Colonel Allyn would have liked his daughter to marry a man of royal descent, as he himself was a direct descendant of the 'belted earls', He felt that if John was also of royal descent he could agree to the marriage immediately. So, he mentioned the name of Sir Courtenay Pescud, a man of a royal family, to find out if John was related to him in any manner.

11. What according to Colonel Allyn was important for promoting family ties among the people?

Ans. The Colonel thought that telling humorous occurrences and anecdotes brings people together. He thought it to be a delightful way of promoting long-lasting friendship. Thus, he was ever ready to narrate and hear them with pleasure.

12. Why do you think the Colonel allowed the salesman to marry his daughter even though he came from a lineage of Earls?

Ans. The Colonel's family was no longer rich and all the glory they once had was a thing of the past. He was probably impressed by the honesty of the salesman and the fact that he was quite rich and successful in his own way. He may also have felt that John genuinely loved his daughter and would keep her happy. Moreover, John made him laugh with his humorous stories.

13. Why does the narrator in the story 'Best Seller' say that 'life has no geographical bounds'? **Competency Based**

Ans. The author makes the comment to emphasise that not only the heroes in romantic stories are alike but men in real life, are the same. He suggests that fiction gets inspiration from reality. We can find evidence of this in the story itself.

14. Why does the narrator call Pescud 'Trevelyan'?

Ans. Trevelyan, the hero of the best seller 'The Rose Lady and Trevelyan' chases a royal lady to her home. He gets introduced to her, woos her and eventually marries her despite a huge difference in their social positions. Pescud's romance also runs on the same lines. Hence, the narrator calls him 'Trevelyan'.

15. In what way does John's life resemble the story lines of best sellers?

Ans. John's life depicted quite a few features of best sellers. He belonged to a middle class family and fell in love with Jessie who came from descendants of a noble family. Just like it happens in novels, he fell in love with her at first sight and followed her to her home. He wooed her and ended up marrying her after convincing her father.

Long Answer Type Questions

Answer the following questions in 120 words.

1. Colonel Allyn belonged to a refined and rich stratum of society. How did John A Pescud impress him very easily? **Competency Based**

Ans. Colonel Allyn was a retired Colonel from the army. He belonged to a refined and rich stratum of society. He was a dignified looking man. However, the Colonel's family was no longer rich and all the glory they once had was a thing of the past. He had now fallen upon hard times which could be seen in his shabby manner of dress.

John A Pescud was, thus, able to impress him very easily. The Colonel was probably impressed by the honesty of the salesman and the fact that he was quite prosperous in his own way. He may have also felt that he genuinely loved his daughter and would keep her happy. Moreover, John made him laugh with his humorous stories.

2. It was love at first sight for John Pescud. It was his honesty and dedication that made it possible for Pescud to win the hearts of the Colonel and his daughter. Write your views on the above statement. **Competency Based**

Ans. It was indeed love at first sight for John Pescud. He saw Jessie reading a book in the train in which he was travelling. He got instantly attracted to her and followed her till she finally reached her home. Like any romantic hero, he followed her, met her father, wooed her and married her. It was his dedication and determination that made him go to great lengths to achieve his goal.

With his honesty, he won the hearts of both the Colonel and his daughter. He honestly informed Jessie's father in the very first meeting of his intention to marry her. He impressed him with his honesty. He truthfully told him everything about himself, his family and about his earnings. The Colonel, thus, gave his consent for their marriage.

3. What trait of John's character attracts you the most? Give instances from the story 'Best Seller'. Why do you think honesty is the best policy?

Ans. The honesty in John's character attracts me the most. John A Pescud was an honest man. Despite the warning by Jessie, John went to see the Colonel. He honestly told him that he had followed his daughter from Cincinnati and wanted to be introduced to her. As a result, John could marry the woman he liked.

In everyday life, being truthful means listening to and obeying the voice of our conscience. Honesty reveals our character, it gives us freedom from being false. Also, it gives us reliability of character. The majority of people will appreciate an honest person each and every time.

ASSESSMENT EXERCISE

Extract Based Questions

Read the following extracts carefully and answer the questions that follow.

1. "I'm coming to see the belted earl tomorrow", I says.
" He'll feed you to his fox-hounds", says she, laughing.

(a) Who does 'he' refer to?

(b) Why would he be fed to the fox-hounds?

(c) Which word in the extract means 'a British nobleman'?

(d) Explain "I'm coming to see the belted earl tomorrow".

2. "Here's where I have to trail", say I to myself. I thought before that she seemed to be in moderate circumstances, at least.

(a) Who is the speaker?

(b) Why is he trailing the woman?

(c) Which word in the extract is a synonym of 'appeared'?

(d) Who is the woman?

Short Answer Type Questions

Answer the following questions in 30-40 words each.

1. What does John Pescud want fiction-writers to be like?

2. Describe the man who came to receive the woman at the railway station in Virginia.

3. What impression did Jessie give John about her father?

4. Jessie was proud of her family. Comment.

5. In what ways is John Pescud like the hero of a romantic novel?

6. How do the characters in 'Best Seller' differ from characters in real life?

7. Was Pescud reading 'The Rose Lady and Trevelyan' with great interest? How can you tell?

Long Answer Type Questions

Answer the following questions in 120 words each.

1. Imagine you are John Pescud. You have just returned to your hotel from Elmcroft after meeting Colonel Allyn. Write a diary entry about the values that the Colonel possesses which impressed you most.

2. What traits of Colonel Allyn's character attract us? Explain by giving instances from the story 'Best Seller'.

3. Do you agree that John's sales skills helped him to win his lady love? Give textual evidence supporting your answer.

4. Imagine you are Jessie, who is of a royal background. Yet an ordinary salesman like John Pescud could impress you. What qualities of John did you admire from the time when you first met him till the time you married him?

5. What should be the purpose of life, prosperity or general happiness and contentment? Write this in the context of what John tells the narrator about his career and progress during the last two years.

The Brook

CHAPTER 1

by Alfred Lord Tennyson

Introduction The poem 'The Brook' by Alfred Lord Tennyson deals with the journey of a brook from its place of origin to its final destination. The brook relates its own experiences as it cheerfully passes through many hurdles and difficulties in order to reach its ultimate destination, the brimming river.

Likewise, man's journey is also full of many ups and downs. Human beings must learn to face both joys and sorrows, and keep moving forward like the brook.

The poet has also contrasted the similarity of their journey with the difference in their nature. While the brook is eternal and everlasting, the life of man is temporary and short-lived.

Stanzawise Explanation

Stanza 1 (Lines 1-4)

I come from haunts of coot and hern;
I make a sudden sally
And sparkle out among the fern,
To bicker down a valley.

Explanation The brook (a small river) emerges in a distant place in the mountains, which is regularly visited by birds like the heron and the coot. Its rushing water touches all the plants growing on its banks and reflects the sunlight, thus creating a dazzling effect. The brook is flowing with a lot of noise to reach a valley. This noisy movement shows that the brook is in a hurry to reach its destination. Here, the brook may be compared to a man in his youth, full of enthusiasm and ready to face all the challenges that come in his way.

Stanza 2 (Lines 5-12)

By thirty hills I hurry down,
Or slip between the ridges,
By twenty thorpes, a little town
And half a hundred bridges.
Till last by Philip's farm I flow
To join the brimming river,
For men may come and men may go,
But I go on for ever.

Explanation The brook's journey is quite long and tiring. It passes through thirty hills, twenty villages and fifty bridges. It quickly moves between the mountain ranges. The brook also passes by Philip's farm and finally joins the brimming river, its ultimate destination.

In the last two lines, the brook comments on the transient nature of humans. Human beings have a short lifespan, which is subject to the continuous cycle of arrival (life) and departure (death). However, the brook, which represents nature, is immortal or permanent. It will never die but go on forever. This is also the message that the poet wants to give to the readers through this poem.

Stanza 3 (Lines 13-24)

I chatter over stony ways,
In little sharps and trebles,
I bubble into eddying bays,
I babble on the pebbles.
With many a curve my banks I fret
By many a field and fallow,

And many a fairy foreland set
With willow-weed and mallow.
I chatter, chatter, as I flow
To join the brimming river,
For men may come and men may go,
But I go on for ever.

Explanation In the early phase of its life, the brook has a very fast motion. It overcomes all the obstacles, stones and pebbles in its way. While rushing down the hills, the brook produces a tremendous noise as it passes the stony pebbles. This sound is compared to different musical notes.

The brook wanders through cultivated fields as well as wild and natural land. The poet describes the land as a fairyland because it is so beautiful with flowers and plants that it seems like an imaginary abode of fairies. There are many curves on its banks which affect the brook's flow (makes it fret). The brook also provides a home and breeding ground to willows and mallows. Thus, the brook keeps flowing with a lot of noise to join the river. The brook again comments on its being eternal and men being mortal.

Stanza 4 (Lines 25-36)

I wind about, and in and out,
With here a blossom sailing,
And here and there a lusty trout,
And here and there a grayling,
And here and there a foamy flake
Upon me, as I travel
With many a silvery waterbreak
Above the golden gravel,
And draw them all along, and flow
To join the brimming river
For men may come and men may go,
But I go on for ever.

Explanation Here, the brook mentions its movements. The brook does not follow a straight path. Sometimes it moves in a curved and winding manner, and is lively and energetic in its movement. The brook carries many things with its flow like the flowers that have fallen into it and the trout and graylings (types of freshwater fish) leaping on its journey. As the brook moves down the hills, it forms foam which gets collected at the banks where gravel gathers in plenty. As it passes over beds of sand with a tinge of golden colour, the brook sparkles like silver till it meets the river. Then, again the brook mentions its eternity against the short lifespan of the humans.

Stanza 5 (Lines 37-44)

I steal by lawns and grassy plots,
I slide by hazel covers
I move the sweet forget-me-nots
That grow for happy lovers.
I slip, I slide, I gloom, I glance,
Among my skimming swallows;
I make the netted sunbeam dance
Against my sandy shallows.

Explanation Sometimes the brook flows quietly and stealthily and covers more and more area of the grassy plots in the lawns. Here, the movement is silent and calm. The brook now gracefully moves on by hazelnut plants. As it advances, it moves the sweet forget-me-not plants and flowers that give joy to the lovers. The brook slips, slides, glides and dances. Swallows hunt for their food from the water of the brook. In the morning when the Sun starts shining, the brook's surface reflects the glare of the Sun.

Sandy shallows refer to the part of the brook which is not very deep and contains a lot of deposited sand and silt.

Here, the poet has drawn a comparison between the brook's journey and human life. As humans face difficulties and happiness throughout their life, the brook also sometimes faces curves and sometimes flows through flowery valleys.

Stanza 6 (Lines 45-52)

I murmur under Moon and stars
In brambly wildernesses;
I linger by my shingly bars;
I loiter round my cresses;
And out again I curve and flow
To join the brimming river,
For men may come and men may go,
But I go on for ever.

Explanation When night comes and total darkness covers the surroundings of the countryside, the flow of the brook changes from one with splashy noise into a gentle murmur under the light of the moon and stars. It appears as if the brook is talking softly to itself. The brook flows through the thorny bushes growing in deserted places. It moves on very slowly as it flows over bars of sand and pebbles. The effect of the brook on the shores in the daytime is as much as it is in the night. Thus, the brook curves and flow into the river. Finally, the brook again tries to convey that it is immortal and will continue to flow for ever, whereas men are mortal and will come and go.

Poetic Devices Used in the Poem

Personification In the poem, the brook has been personified and attributed human qualities.

Alliteration

- a sudden sally
- hills I hurry
- field and fallow
- fairy foreland
- with willow-weed
- foamy flake
- golden gravel
- skimming swallows
- sandy shallows
- By twenty thorpes, a little town
- I slip, I slide, I gloom, I glance,
- For men may come and men may go

Onomatopoeia

- To bicker down a valley
- I chatter over stony ways
- I babble on the pebbles
- I murmur under moon and stars

Repetition
- I chatter, chatter, as I flow
- For men may come and men may go, But I go on for ever

Rhyme
- The rhyme scheme of the poem is *abab*.

Metaphor
- The brook is used as a metaphor for the human life.

Refrain
- For men may come and men may go, But I go on for ever.

Imagery
- Silvery waterbreak
- I make the netted sunbeam dance

Word Meaning

Word	Meaning
Stanza 1	
haunts	places frequently visited by someone
coot	a water bird with blackish feathers, lobed feet, and a long bill that extends back on to the forehead
hern	heron, a kind of long-legged, long-necked water bird
sally	emerge suddenly
fern	a flowerless plant
bicker	flow or fall down with a lot of noise
Stanza 2	
ridges	mountain ranges
thorpes	small villages
brimming	overflowing, filled to capacity
Stanza 3	
chatter	make a series of short, quick, high-pitched sounds
sharps	a musical note raised above natural pitch, shrill and high-pitched sounds
trebles	high pitched tune
eddying	spiral movement of water
bay	a part of the river
babble	sound made when one talks gaily
pebbles	small stones made smooth and round by the action of water or sand
fallow	a piece of land left uncultivated in order to restore its fertility
foreland	a piece of land that extends into the sea
willow-weed	any one of the various plants of the primrose family with willow-like leaves
mallow	a plant with hairy stems and leaves, and pink, white or purple flowers
Stanza 4	
sailing	flowing
lusty trout	a big freshwater fish
grayling	a silvery grey freshwater fish
foamy	frothy, having a mass of small bubbles
flake	a small, flat, very thin piece of something
silvery	shiny and grey-white in appearance
waterbreak	a place in a stream where the surface of water is broken by irregularities at the bottom
Stanza 5	
steal by	move quietly or secretly
hazel	a small tree or bush with edible nuts
forget-me-nots	a low-growing ornamental plant, with blue flowers
gloom	look depressed
swallows	small migratory birds with dark, glossy blue back, red throat and a long tail
shallows	areas of a lake or river where the water is not very deep
Stanza 6	
brambly wildernesses	an area densely covered with trees and shrubs
linger	stay in a place longer than necessary
shingly	covered with small rounded pebbles
loiter	stand or wait around without apparent purpose
cresses	strong-smelling leaved plants like cabbages

Textbook FOLDER

Here, we have covered questions given in the CBSE Textbook along with their answer

ON PAGE 66

Q.4 After reading the poem answer the following questions.

The poet has used a number of words which indicate 'movement' and 'sound'. Working with your partner make a list of these words from the poem and complete the web chart.

(a)

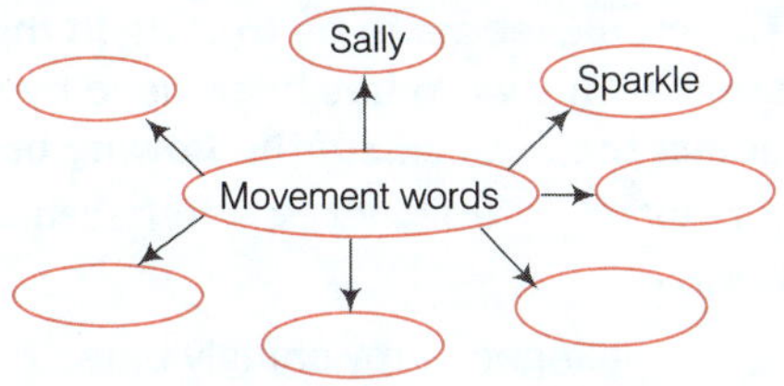

Ans.

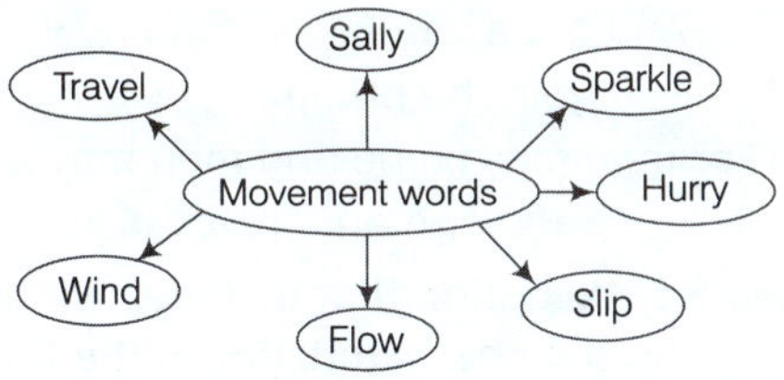

(b)

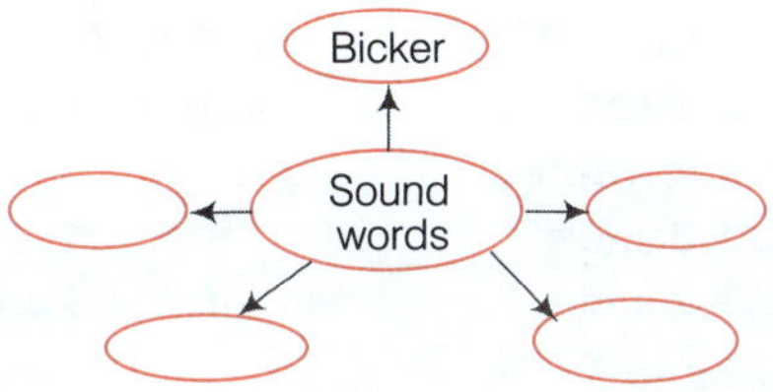

Ans.

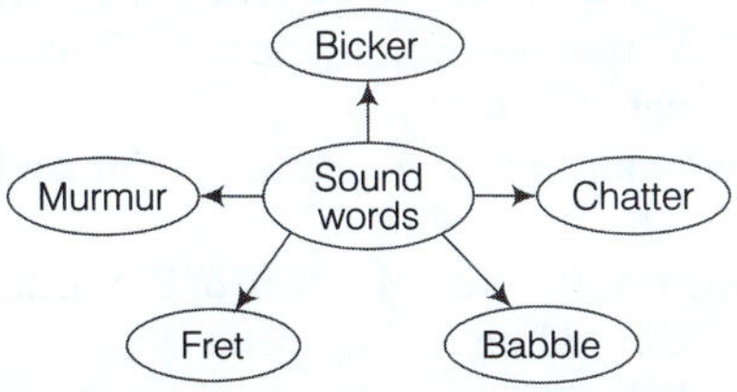

(c) A word or a combination of words, whose sound seems to resemble the sound it denotes (e.g. 'hiss', 'buzz' etc.), is called Onomatopoeia. From the words that you have filled in the blurbs above, point out these words.

Ans. The Onomatopoeic words are chatter, babble and murmur.

ON PAGE 67

Q.5 The following is a flow chart showing the course of the brook. Can you fill in the blank spaces with help from the phrases given below?

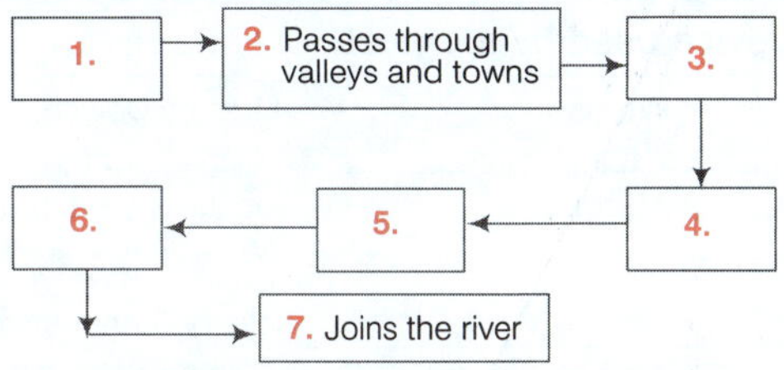

(a) Passes under fifty bridges;

(b) Comes from the place where coots and herons live;

(c) Passes lawns filled with flowers;

(d) Crosses both fertile and fallow land;

(e) Goes through wilderness full of thorny bushes.

Ans.

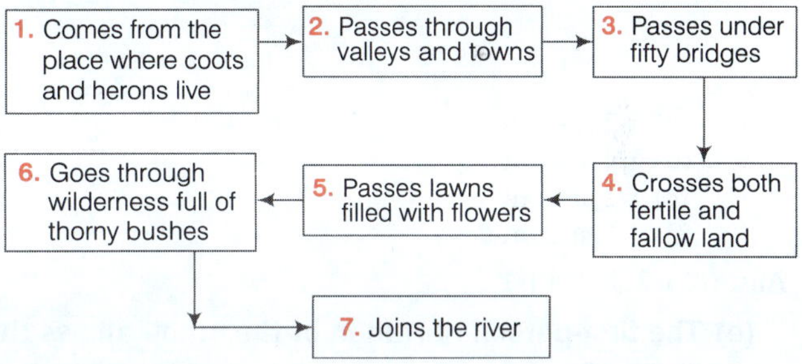

ON PAGE 67-68

Q.6 A. On the basis of your understanding of the poem, answer the following questions by ticking the correct choice.

(i) The message of the poem is that the life of a brook is

(a) temporary (b) eternal

(b) short-lived (d) momentary

Ans. (b) eternal

(ii) The poet draws a parallelism between the journey of the brook with

(a) the life of a man

(b) the death of man

(c) the difficulties in a man's life

(d) the endless talking of human beings

Ans. (a) the life of a man

(i) **In the poem, the below mentioned lines suggest that**

"And here and there a lusty trout,
And here and there a grayling"
suggest that

(a) the brook is a source of life.
(b) people enjoy the brook.
(c) fishes survive because of water.
(d) the brook witnesses all kinds of scenes.

Ans. (a) the brook is a source of life.

(d) **Select the option that matches the given words/phrases with the appropriate literary device used by the poet.**

	Words		Literary Device
(i)	Chatter; Babble; Murmur	1.	Alliteration- the occurrence of the same letter or sound at the beginning of adjacent or closely connected words
(ii)	Men may come and men may go but I go on forever	2.	Onomatopoeia-the formation of a word from a sound associated with what is named
(iii)	fairly foreland; with willow seed; foamy flake; golden gravel	3.	Inversion - reversal of the normal order of the words and phrases in a sentence
(iv)		4.	Refrain - a word, line or phrase that is repeated within the lines or stanzas of the poem itself.

(a) i-2, ii-1, iii-4
(b) i-4, ii-2, iii-3
(c) i-2, ii-4, iii-1
(d) i-1, ii-2, iii-3

Ans. (c) i-2, ii-4, iii-1

(e) **The first-person narration of the brook allows the reader to**

(a) appreciate Tennyson's use of symbols.
(b) realise the ultimate goal of the brook.
(c) experience the soothing effect of the sound of water.
(d) understand the brook's experience as a living organism.

Ans. (d) understand the brook's experience as a living organism.

ON PAGE 68-69

Q.6B Read the given extracts and answer the questions that follow by selecting the correct options.

A. With many a curve my banks I fret
By many a field and fallow,
And many a fairy foreland set
With willow-weed and mallow.

(i) **Choose the option that best describes the brook's journey in the given stanza.**
It is a journey full of ....

(a) comfort and luxury
(b) trials and tribulations
(c) sorrow and misery
(d) joy and laughter

Ans. (b) trials and tribulations

(ii) **The poet has used the pronoun 'I' to refer to the brook and thus employed a literary device in his depiction. Choose the option that uses the same literary device as used in the first line.**

(a) The magnitude of the bottomless ocean was divine.
(b) The angry walls echoed his fury.
(c) A mother is like a lioness protecting her cubs.
(d) I felt the power of the gushing stream.

Ans. (b) The angry walls echoed his fury.

(iii) **The brook seems to be fretting in the given stanza. This word has been used by the poet to depict the .... of the flowing brook.**

(a) force (b) kindness (c) silence (d) beauty

Ans. (a) force

B. I linger by my shingly bars;
I loiter round my cresses;
And out again I curve and flow
To join the brimming river,
For men may come and men may go,
But I go on forever.

(i) **Choose the option that includes words that best describe the characteristics of the brook, as revealed in the given extract.**

1. perpetual **2. silent**
3. twisted **4. unbound**
5. interrupted

(a) 1, 3 and 4
(b) 1, 2, 4 and 5
(c) 1, 2 and 3
(d) 1, 2 and 4

Ans. (c) 1, 2 and 3

(ii) **The line, 'men may come and men may go'**

(a) mocks the shortness of the brook's life as it goes through its journey.
(b) highlights the eternal nature of human life as opposed to its own.
(c) contrasts the eternal nature of brook against short-lived human life-span.
(d) highlights the eternal story of men that the brook comes across during its journey.

Ans. (c) contrasts the eternal nature of brook against short-lived human life-span.

(iii) **What do the words, 'linger and loiter' show about the brook?**

(a) Its continuity
(b) Its slow movement
(c) Its powerful force
(d) Its ultimate purpose

Ans. (b) Its slow movement

ON PAGE 70

Q.7 Answer the following questions.

(a) Why does the brook 'sparkle'?

Ans. The brook sparkles as it flows down in the midst of grass. The water in the brook is clear and transparent in the early part of its journey. When the bright sunbeam is reflected on the surface of water, it makes the brook seem to sparkle.

(b) 'Bicker' means 'to quarrel.' Why does the poet use this word here?

Ans. A quarrel is often quite noisy. The poet has used such a sense of sound to indicate that the brook flows down to the valley, creating different noises. The sound produced here is like that of children quarrelling playfully.

(c) Why has the word 'chatter' been repeated in the poem?

Ans. The word 'chatter' has been repeated quite a few times in the poem. It represents the sound made by the brook as it flows through stony ways. It also provides a flow and rhythm to the poem. Moreover, it gives a personified touch to the brook as it appears to be talking.

(d) "*I wind about, and in and out.*" What kind of picture does this line create in your mind?

Ans. Tennyson has used an imagery quite playfuly to enhance the lyrical quality of the poem. These lines create a picture of the water flowing freely in a zig-zag manner. It also creates an impression that sometimes the brook flows underground or inside the cracks in the rocks and then comes out again.

(e) What does the poet want to convey by using the words 'steal' and 'slide'?

Ans. By using the words 'steal and slide', the poet wants to convey that the brook quietly passes through small hurdles and slips through various obstructions in its flow like sandy banks, trees, wild bushes, etc. These words also suggest the quiet but swift movement of the brook.

(f) "*I make the netted sunbeam dance.*" What does 'the netted sunbeam' mean? How does it dance?

Ans. In the morning, the rays of the Sun fall on the flowing water of the brook. The rays appear to be netted as they pass through the trees. They are then reflected here and there due to the rippling water of the brook and hence they seem to 'dance'.

(g) What is the 'refrain' in the poem? What effect does it create?

Ans. The 'refrain' in the poem is, "For men may come and men may go, but I go on for ever." It tells us about the permanent nature of the brook and the temporary aspect of human life. It emphasises the central idea of the poem, which is maintained throughout the poem through repetition.

(h) Why has the poet used the word 'brimming' in the line 'to join the brimming river'?

Ans. The poet has used the word 'brimming' to indicate the amount of water in the river which the brook finally joins. It creates a picture of immense volume and abundance.

Q.8 Identify the rhyme scheme of the poem.

Ans. The rhyme scheme of the poem is *ab, ab, cd, cd, ef, ef* and so on.

Q.9 The poem is full of images that come alive through skilful use of words. List out any two images that appeal to you the most, quoting the lines from the poem.

Ans. The poet has described the movements of a brook in such a manner that words create a mental picture. The image of water coming out suddenly, water birds flying around and water moving down the valley making loud noise is presented in the first stanza.

I come from haunts of coot and hern;
I make a sudden sally
And sparkle out among the fern,
To bicker down a valley.

The second image is of zig-zag movement of the water. It moves, carrying on its surface many flowers and leaves. Freshwater fish like trout and grayling can be seen gliding at its bottom.

I wind about, and in and out,
With here a blossom sailing,
And here and there a lusty trout,
And here and there a grayling,

Q.10 The brook appears to be a symbol for life. Pick out examples of parallelism between human life and the brook from the poem .

Ans. The examples of parallelism in the poem are

(i) **Birth** The brook's emergence in the mountains is similar to human birth in this world.

(ii) **Youth** When one is young, one is strong and full of enthusiasm (energy). Similarly, the brook in its youth hurries down. It makes a huge noise and rushes forcefully towards its destination. It 'sallies', 'bickers' and 'chatters' while it flows.

(iii) **Support** Human beings are a source of support of life for each other by providing help to each other. In the same way, the brook also supports life of fish like trout and grayling. So, both man and the brook are similar.

(iv) **Old Age and Death** In old age, man becomes calm and wise. In the same way, the brook also slows down and starts moving slowly towards its destination. Man dies and the brook joins the brimming river.

REVIEW EXERCISE

Including Exam Pattern Practice Questions

Extract Based Questions

Read the following extracts carefully and answer the questions that follow.

1. I come from haunts of coot and hern;
I make a sudden sally
And sparkle out among the fern,
To bicker down a valley.

(a) Who is 'I' in these lines?

Ans. 'I ' refers to the brook.

(b) How does the poet describe the movement of 'I'?

Ans. The brook suddenly emerges and moves with great force and enthusiasm making a lot of noise.

(c) What does the phrase, 'coot and hern' mean?

Ans. The phrase 'coot and hern' are types of water birds.

(d) What do you mean by 'sally'?

Ans. The word, 'sally' means to emerge suddenly.

Or

(a) According to the stanza, where does the brook originate from?

Ans. The brook originates from the mountains, favourite haunts of birds like the coot and the heron.

(b) Bring out two characteristics of 'I' in the given stanza.

Ans. Two characteristics of 'I' are–The brook is sparkling and noisy. It is full of life and energy.

(c) The word..........in the extract means "to flow down with a lot of noise."

Ans. 'bicker'

(d) Which is the literary device used in these lines?

Ans. The poet has used personification and personified the brook. Alliteration is used in 'sudden sally'.

2. By thirty hills I hurry down,
Or slip between the ridges,
By twenty thorpes, a little town,
And half a hundred bridges.

(a) The brook passes by ....

Ans. hills and bridges, ridges and villages, towns and lands

(b) What is the brook's movement like?

Ans. The movement of the brook appears to be quite fast and steady.

(c) How is the journey of the brook similar to that of man?

Ans. The brook starts with a shrill sound and passes through a number of difficulties in its journey, like man.

(d) The number words symbolise ....

Ans. the length of the journey

3. Till last by Philip's farm I flow
To join the brimming river,
For men may come and men may go,
But I go on for ever.

(a) Where is Philip's farm situated?

Ans. Philip's farm is situated close to the brimming river in which the brook finally merges.

(b) What is the motive of the brook?

Ans. The motive of the brook is to join the brimming river.

(c) Which word in the extract is a synonym of 'always'?

Ans. The word 'ever' is a synonym of 'always'.

(d) Which poetic device is used here?

Ans. Personification and refrain have been used here.

4. I chatter over stony ways,
In little sharps and trebles,
I bubble into eddying bays,
I babble on the pebbles.

(a) What do you mean by 'I chatter'?

Ans. The brook makes a rapid clicking noise while it moves over stony paths and thus appears to be talking or chatting.

(b) Name the poetic devices used here.

Ans. Personification and onomatopoeia have been used here.

(c) Which line indicates that the brook is full of enthusiasm?

Ans. The fourth line, 'I babble on the pebbles', indicates the brook's enthusiasm.

(d) What is the mood of the brook as it flows towards the river?

Ans. The brook is cheerful and filled with joy.

5. With many a curve my banks I fret
By many a field and fallow,
And many a fairy foreland set
With willow-weed and mallow.

(a) Who is 'I' here?

Ans. 'I' here refers to the brook.

(b) What is the aim of the brook?

Ans. The aim of the brook is to merge with the brimming river.

(c) The rhyme scheme of the stanza is ....

Ans. *ab ab*

(d) Which word used in the extract tells us that it also flows by the piece of land that extends into the sea?

Ans. 'Foreland' indicates that the brook also flows by the piece of land that extends into the sea.

6. I chatter, chatter, as I flow
To join the brimming river,
For men may come and men may go,
But I go on for ever.

(a) Who is 'I' in the above lines?

Ans. 'I' in the lines is the brook.

(b) What is the relevance of 'brimming river'?

Ans. The brook originated in the mountains, undertook a difficult journey and would join the river full of water, its final destination.

(c) Why has the word 'chatter' been repeated?

Ans. The word has been repeated to emphasise the loud noise created by the brook. The repetition of the word also conveys the brook's joyous mood.

(d) The brook flows ....

Ans. over stones and pebbles, creating a lot of noise which appears to be like talking

7. I wind about, and in and out,
With here a blossom sailing,
And here and there a lusty trout,
And here and there a grayling.

(a) How is the brook moving at this time?

Ans. The brook is moving in a zig-zag way, encountering (coming across) twists and turns.

(b) What is the brook carrying with it?

Ans. The brook is carrying blossoms and fishes with it.

(c) Which figure of speech is used in the last two lines?

Ans. Repetition has been used in the last two lines; the phrase 'here and there' has been repeated.

(d) What do you mean by 'lusty trout' and 'grayling' ?

Ans. 'Lusty trout' and 'grayling' are kinds of fish.

8. And here and there a foamy flake
Upon me, as I travel
With many a silvery waterbreak
Above the golden gravel,

And draw them all along, and flow
To join the brimming river
For men may come and men may go,
But I go on for ever.

(a) Explain the first two lines of the extract.

Ans. The zig-zag water movement forms a foam of water in the brook.

(b) What do you mean by 'golden gravel'?

Ans. The 'golden gravel' refers to the sand which is golden in colour.

(c) This comparison reflects the poet's ....

Ans. respect for nature

(d) Explain, 'But I go on for ever'.

Ans. The poet contrasts the timelessness of the brook with the finite or transient nature of human existence.

9. I steal by lawns and grassy plots,
I slide by hazel covers
I move the sweet forget-me-nots
That grow for happy lovers.

(a) Explain the first two lines.

Ans. The brook flows silently through lawns and meadows and elegantly moves on by the small trees having nuts which can be eaten.

(b) How are the 'sweet forget-me-nots' moved by the brook?

Ans. As the brook passes by lawns or gardens filled with 'forget-me-nots', these flowers are moved by the brook. It may also be that the lovers throw them into the brook and they flow with it.

(c) What is the device used in the first three lines?

Ans. Personification is used in the first three lines.

(d) What does the phrase 'I steal' means here?

Ans. 'I steal' here is the reference to the brook's silent or stealthy movement.

10. I slip, I slide, I gloom, I glance,
Among my skimming swallows;
I make the netted sunbeam dance
Against my sandy shallows.
I murmur under moon and stars
In brambly wildernesses;

(a) **Which line suggests different movements and moods of the brook?**

Ans. The first line, 'I slip, I slide, I gloom, I glance', suggests the different movements and moods of the brook.

(b) **Identify the figure of speech used in the third line.**

Ans. Personification has been used in the third line.

(c) **What do you mean by 'skimming swallows'?**

Ans. 'Skimming swallows' refers to the swallow birds which are flying just above (skimming) the brook's water.

(d) **What does 'murmur' mean here?**

Ans. The word indicates a slow and gentle movement of the brook.

11.

I Linger by my shingly bars:
I loiter round my cresses
And out again I curve and flow
To join the brimming river,
For men may come and men may go,
But I go on for ever.

(a) **Explain "linger by my shingly bars".**

Ans. The brook is interrupted by the hurdles coming in its way. Therefore, its movement becomes a little slow or gentle.

(b) **Which lines reflect the importance of the destination?**

Ans. The first two lines reflect the importance of the destination. In spite of the obstacles coming in the brook's movements, it gets ready to join the brimming river.

(c) **Identify the poetic device, apart from personification.**

Ans. Refrain is the poetic device used here. It refers to repetition of the same verses.

(d) **The word .... in the extract means 'everlasting.'**

Ans. forever

Short Answer Type Questions

Answer the following questions in 30-40 words.

1. From where does the brook emerge and where does it go?

Ans. The brook emerges from the region that is inhabited by the water birds like coots and herons and passes through various valleys, towns and fields. Finally, it merges with the brimming river which is its final destination.

2. Why has the poet used the word, 'babble' for the brook?

Ans. When the brook flows down to meet the brimming river, it makes a cheerful sound when it hits the pebbles. The sound made is very similar to when one talks happily. Thus, the poet has used the word, 'babble' for the brook.

3. Give at least two similarities between the brook and the human beings.

Or **How is the journey of the brook similar to human life?**

Or **Mention briefly how we can relate the journey of a brook with that of human life.**

Ans. The similarities are that both, the brook and human beings, have to struggle to reach the final destination in life, irrespective of the hurdles and obstructions in their path.

Both face quite similar phases of life and go through happiness and difficulties alike.

4. What is the difference between man and brook?

Ans. Though the journey of the brook and man are quite similar, they are very different. The brook is eternal and everlasting, and will go on forever. However, man's life is temporary and short-lived. He will disappear from the face of earth after a short period as he is mortal.

5. Why have the lines, "For men may come and men may go, but I go on for ever" been repeated in the poem several times? What is the significance of these lines? Competency Based

Ans. These lines form the refrain in the poem and carry the central idea of the poem. They have been repeated for the sake of emphasis. Human beings are mortals while the brook is immortal. All of us will die one day, but the brook and nature is never-ending and will outlive humans.

6. Why has the poet introduced the poem in the form of the brook's autobiography rather than narrating it himself?

Or **Why do you think that the poet has let the brook describe its journey rather than describing it himself?** Competency Based

Ans. The brook has been personified throughout the poem and allowed to describe its own journey. The poet has done so because it sounds more lively and vivid, which it would not have been had the poet narrated it himself. The readers feel that the brook is talking to them and relating its own experiences; which is much more authentic (original).

Long Answer Type Questions

Answer the following questions in 120 words.

1. Imagine you are the brook. Having faced a number of obstructions, you have joined the brimming river. Write a diary entry about your thoughts highlighting the importance of a destination in life.

Ans. Wednesday, 11th March, 20XX 11 p.m.

Dear Diary

Today my joy knows no bounds. At last I have joined my destination, the brimming river.

When I originated in the mountains, I was happy to see myself in the lap of beautiful nature. I started my journey towards my goal. I crossed many bridges, hills and villages. I was interrupted by stones and pebbles and many more obstacles. However, I kept on going, through different moods and movements. I finally reached where I had to go.

Unlike man, I am immortal, but both of us have to undertake a journey that is quite difficult. However, we keep on going, fighting and struggling to our destination, as without it, our existence is hollow and meaningless. So, destination is a must in life.

Brook

2. Had the brook got exhausted midway, it would not have reached its destination. How far is this statement true about our life? Explain.

Ans. It is true that if the brook got exhausted midway, it would not have reached its destination. It is also true in the case of our life. Whatever hurdles the brook or we face in life must be overcome.

If we are tired, we can have a short rest but we should not stop under the pretext (excuse) of exhaustion. Life is meaningful only if we are moving. Still life is like stagnant (standing or still) water, which breeds lethargy, (laziness), monotony etc. Moreover, hurdles and obstacles that come in our way make us even stronger. We should never give up and be tough and go on, as tough times never last, but tough men do. Only then will we be able to reach our final destination.

3. Often we match our life with natural things, and sometimes we find them to be too close to our emotions. Taking ideas from the poem, 'The Brook', write a paragraph on the topic, 'Nature appears to be a symbol of life'. Competency Based

Ans. Nature is undoubtedly a symbol of life. In the poem 'The Brook' by Alfred Lord Tennyson, the brook represents nature. The poet has here drawn a very close parallel between man's life and the brook. The brook's journey from its origin till joining its final destination, the brimming river, is like man's journey of life from birth to death. Whatever hurdles the brook faces on the way, reflect what man faces all through his life.

The origin of the brook is similar to the beginning of human life. The brook's noisy flow is similar to man's struggling and fretting and fuming against the problems. The brook slips, slides, glooms and glances. Human beings do the same. The brook carries many things with it as it flows. So does man, as he meets people, builds relationships, carries memories and collects materialistic (worldly) things as he goes through life. The only difference between man and the brook is that man's life comes to an end, while the brook lives on and on for ever.

4. What are the values that one can learn through the journey of the brook?

Or **Life cannot be lived at one steady pace. Instead, it is a journey in which times can be joyous or tormenting. Justify the statement with reference to the poem, 'The Brook' and describe the values that we can learn from it .**

Ans. It is true to say that life cannot be lived at one steady pace. Instead, it is a journey in which times can be joyous or tormenting. This can be easily understood by the journey undertaken by a brook to meet the brimming river, Just like the brook, human life also passes through distant places and varying stages during its journey.

However, it is quite important to note here that while the human beings often become restless, impatient and pessimistic during certain unmanageable situations, the brook's attitude towards the various situations that it comes across is full of positivity and optimism. The brook's journey teaches us a number of lessons for our life.

It teaches us the value of giving. We learn to be generous and benevolent like the brook which selflessly serves all the creatures on earth. We should also learn to be selfless and serving all, like the brook. The brook's energy and determination inspire us to be lively and firm like the brook. It continues to flow towards its ultimate destination, the river, in spite of all the obstacles that come in its way. We should also constantly make efforts towards achieving our goal in life, in spite of the hurdles that we come across.

ASSESSMENT EXERCISE

Extract Based Questions

Read the following extracts carefully and answer the questions that follow.

1.

Till last by Philip's farm I flow
To join the brimming river
For men may come and men may go,
But I go on for ever.

(a) What do the first two lines describe – the beginning of the brook's journey or its end?

(b) The word .... in the extract has the same meaning as 'overflowing'.

(c) Explain the contrast between man's life and the life of the brook.

(d) What is the message of the poet?

2.

And draw them all along, and flow
To join the brimming river
For men may come and men may go,
But I go on for ever.

(a) Give an antonym of 'for ever.'

(b) What is the attitude of the poet towards life?

(c) What is the significance of the last two lines?

(d) What is the final destination of the brook?

Short Answer Type Questions

Answer the following questions in 30-40 words.

1. Why is the poem 'the Brook' narrated in the first person?
2. How does the brook slip between the ridges?
3. How many hills, thorpes and bridges does the brook pass during its journey? Do you think the poet has used exaggeration here? Why?
4. What is the brook's ultimate aim?
5. What are the different places the brook passes by?
6. Is the brook enthusiastic to meet 'the brimming river'? How can you say?
7. What are the different things that the brook draws along with it as it flows?
8. Bring out the contrast between the Brook's movement in the beginning and towards the end of its journey.

Long Answer Type Questions

Answer the following questions in 120 words.

1. The brook has different movements in different terrains. Do these different movements symbolise the varying moods of humans in different situations? Discuss.
2. Human life, like the brook, is a journey? What are the factors that make life successful?

The Road Not Taken

by Robert Frost

CHAPTER 2

Introduction The poem 'The Road Not Taken' by Robert Frost deals with the difficult situations that man faces in life. It talks about the choices that one has to make in life and the consequences of such choices. Many times, we regret the choice made by us but what is done once cannot be undone. Decisions are like steps; one takes us towards the other. Thus, whatever direction our life takes is determined by the choice made by us.

Moreover, having reached wherever our decisions take us, we can only look back and meditate on the consequences. However, we cannot go back and start all over again.

Stanzawise Explanation

Stanza 1 (Lines 1-5)

Two roads diverged in a yellow wood,
And sorry I could not travel both
And be one traveller, long I stood
And looked down one as far as I could
To where it bent in the undergrowth;

Explanation The poet has come to a forest in the autumn season when the leaves have turned yellow. The poet reaches a point where the two roads separated into two directions. The roads symbolise the two ways of life. The poet, as a traveller, knew that he had to make a choice as he cannot travel both the roads at the same time. So, he stood there for a long time and looked down on both the roads. The poet looked at the first road and found that it has a bent which was covered with small plants and bushes. Just like the poet, we also take decisions and make choices every day. Thus, we must analyse the situation to make the correct choice.

Stanza 2 (Lines 6-10)

Then took the other, just as fair,
And having perhaps the better claim,
Because it was grassy and wanted wear;
Though as for that the passing there
Had worn them really about the same,

Explanation The poet looked at the other road. According to him, this road seemed better and more impressive as it was covered with grass. It had not been walked over by many people. However, as the poet walked on the road for some distance he realised that both the roads have been walked over equally.

Stanza 3 (Lines 11-15)

And both that morning equally lay
In leaves no step had trodden black.
Oh, I kept the first for another day!
Yet knowing how way leads on to way,
I doubted if I should ever come back.

Explanation The poet now says that both the roads were similar on that morning as no one has travelled on any of the roads. The leaves were still green and fresh as they have not been crushed by anyone while walking. The poet decides to travel the second road and kept the first one for some other day. However, the poet had a doubt if he could ever come back again to walk on the first road. As the poet knew that once he made a choice, he will move ahead and take many more decisions. As a result, he would not be able to come back to change his choice.

Stanza 4 (Lines 16-20)

I shall be telling this with a sigh
Somewhere ages and ages hence;
Two roads diverged in a wood and
I took the one less travelled by,
And that has made all the difference.

Explanation In these lines, the poet talks about the consequences of the choice. The poet states that sometime in the future, he will remember the day he made the choice. He would be telling about his decision with a sigh either with relief or regret (relief of making the right choice or regret of making the wrong choice).

He would tell that from the two roads that went into the forest, he took the less travelled one and the choice had made a significant impact on his life.

Word Meaning

Word	Meaning
Stanza 1	
diverged	separated
yellow wood	the leaves on the trees are yellow, suggesting it is the autumn season
undergrowth	dense growth of plants and bushes
Stanza 2	
fair	good/beautiful
better claim	it seemed better and more impressive
grassy	full of grass
wanted wear	looked less worn out or used
passing	on walking down
Stanza 3	
equally lay	were equally covered
trodden black	turned the path black by crushing the leaves
way leads on to way	one thing leads to another.
Stanza 4	
sigh	A long deep breath here either of relief/satisfaction or regret.
ages and ages hence	many years in the future

Poetic Devices Used in the Poem

Personification Because it was grassy and wanted wear; the author has personified the path here. As a path cannot want, only humans can want.

Metaphor The poem on the whole is a metaphor. The roads represent choices in life. The poet, thus, compares the paths or roads to the choices one makes in life.

Alliteration wanted wear

Symbolism The two roads described by the poet are the symbols of challenges and choices that life has to offer.

Textbook FOLDER

Here, we have covered questions given in the CBSE Textbook along with their answer

ON PAGE 73

Q.7 On the basis of your understanding of the poem, answer the following questions by ticking the correct choice.

(a) In the poem, a traveller comes to a fork in the road and needs to decide which way to go to continue his journey. Figuratively, the choice of the road denotes

(i) the tough choices people make on the road of life.
(ii) the time wasted on deciding what to do.
(iii) life is like a forest.
(iv) one must travel a lot to realise his dreams.

Ans. (i) the tough choices people make on the road of life.

(b) The poet writes, "Two roads diverged in a yellow wood." The word diverged means

(i) appeared (ii) curved
(iii) branched off (iv) continued on

Ans. (iii) branched off

(c) The tone of the speaker in the first stanza is that of

(i) excitement (ii) anger
(iii) hesitation and thoughtfulness
(iv) sorrow

Ans. (iii) hesitation and thoughtfulness

(d) Select the quote that captures the central idea of the poem most appropriately.

(i) We often confuse what we wish for with what is.

(ii) I have always been much better at asking questions than knowing what the answers were.

(iii) You are free to make whatever choice you want but you are not free from the consequences of the choice.

(iv) To live a creative life, we must lose our fear of being wrong.

Ans. (iii) You are free to make whatever choice you want but you are not free from the consequences of the choice.

ON PAGE 73-74

Q.8 Answer the following questions briefly.

(i) Describe the two roads that the poet comes across.

Ans. While walking, the poet came across a path that split into two roads. The first road was the beaten path, where the grass has been worn out by people walking on it. The second road was grassy, which shows that not many people have walked down that road.

(ii) Which road does the speaker choose? Why does he choose that?

Ans. The poet chooses the second road, which is less frequently travelled upon as he feels it was more attractive and grassy. The second road looked much more promising to him.

(iii) Which road would you choose? Why? Give reasons for your choice.

Ans. I would perhaps choose the worn out road and not the grassy one as the well travelled path leads us to a certain destination. Maybe I would also have taken the grassy road if I wanted to reach a new or unknown destination. It is quite difficult to choose between two paths when we do not know where they will lead us.

(iv) Does the speaker seem happy about his decision?

Or **Was the poet satisfied with his decision of choosing the second road? Why/why not?**

Or **The final stanza in the poem 'The Road Not Taken' starts 'with a sigh'. Why?**

Or **Does the poet seem happy about his decision in 'The Road Not Taken'?**

Ans. We do not know whether the speaker is happy with his choice. He may be sorry or happy about his decisions or about the roads he took. His sighs might be a sigh of satisfaction or regret.

(v) The poet says, *"I took the one less travelled by, And that has made all the difference."* What is 'the difference' that the poet mentions?

Or **Explain the statement, *"And that has made all the difference"* with reference to the poem 'The Road Not Taken'.** **Competency Based**

Ans. 'The difference' indicates that the poet's decision and choice to do so has had a significant impact in his life/journey. In other words, our choices influence and shape our life.

(vi) Comment on Frost's use of nature to establish a connection with a human situation.

Ans. In the poem, Robert Frost has used natural imagery to present human situations o f making a choice that each individual faces in life. In the poem, the roads represent all those situations when we need to make a difficult choice. The two divergences represent the multiple options. Further, the poet's choice and his thoughts about the future tell us that in life when a choice is made, it leads to many other choices. These choices, cannot be undone and have a significant impact on one's life. Thus, we can say that 'The Road Not Taken' is a metaphor of life.

(vii) The poem carries a tinge of regret. Do you agree? Explain with a reason.

Ans. No, I do not agree that the poem carries a tinge of regret. The poem nowhere indicates that the poet is regretting his decision. He may be sorry or happy about his decisions or about the roads he took. His sighs might be a sigh of satisfaction or regret.

(viii) Establish a connection between the given quote and the poem.

If you want to achieve something you've never had, you have to move out of your comfort zone to travel towards it.

Ans. The given quote refers to making choices in life which are unusual and not very common. The quote signifies that extraordinary things can't be achieved by following ordinary paths or doing commonplace things. The poem also reflects on similar values. In the poem, the road less travelled appeals to the poet because it appears quite favourable to him. He was unwilling to stick to the tradition of using the same path that many other people had taken. He moves outside his comfort zone and takes the risk of choosing the less travelled path.

ON PAGE 74

9. Identify the rhyme scheme of the poem, 'The Road Not Taken'.

Ans. The rhyme scheme of the poem 'The Road Not Taken', by Robert Frost is *abaab.*

10. Fill in the blanks to complete the following paragraph that highlights the theme of the poem. Use the words given in the box below

decision sorry foresee choices pleasant direction fork trail rewarding chance wonder both

The poem 'The Road Not Taken' by Robert Frost is about the (i)(.........) that one makes in life. It tells about a man who comes to a (ii)(.........) in the road he is travelling upon. He feels (iii)(.........) that he can not travel (iv)(.........) paths as he must choose one. Frost uses this fork in the road to represent a point in the man's life where he has to choose the (v)(.........) he wishes to take in life. As he thinks about his (vi)(.........) he looks down one path, as far as he can see trying to what life will be like if he walks that path. He then gazes at the other and decides that the outcome of going down that path would be just as (vii)(.........). At this point he concludes that the (viii)(.........) that has been less travelled on would be more (ix)(.........) .... when he reaches the end of it. The man then decides that he will save the other path for another day, even though he knows that one path leads to another and that he won't get a (x)(.........) to go back. The man then says that he will be telling this story with a sigh, someday in the future suggesting that he will what life would have been like if he had chosen the more walked path even though the path he chose has made all the difference.

Ans. (i) choices, (ii) fork, (iii) sorry, (iv) both, (v) direction, (vi) decision, (vii) pleasant, (viii) trail, (ix) rewarding, (x) chance

REVIEW EXERCISE

Including Exam Pattern Practice Questions

Extract Based Questions

Read the following extracts carefully and answer the questions that follow.

1. Two roads diverged in a yellow wood,
And sorry I could not travel both
And be one traveller, long I stood
And looked down one as far as I could
To where it bent in the undergrowth;

(a) What do you mean by 'yellow wood'?

Ans. The poet is standing amidst a small forest, where the leaves of the trees have yellowed.

(b) The speaker is feeling sorry because ....

Ans. he can't travel both the roads

(c) Why is the poet confused?

Ans. The poet seems to be confused about which road he should take. He is not able to take a decision.

(d) State the word from the extract which means "a dense growth of plants."

Ans. 'Undergrowth'

2. Then took the other, as just as fair,
And having perhaps the better claim,
Because it was grassy and wanted wear;
Though as for that the passing there
Had worn them really about the same,

(a) Which of the two roads did the poet take?

Ans. The poet took the second road as it seemed less travelled upon and therefore, appealed to him.

(b) Which road according to the poet, had 'the better claim'?

Ans. The second road had the better claim, according to the poet. It was more grassy and less worn out than the other.

(c) The word/phrase .... in the extract means 'not used enough.'

Ans. 'wanted wear'

(d) What is the rhyme scheme of these lines?

Ans. The rhyme scheme of these lines is *abaab.*

3. And both that morning equally lay
In leaves no step had trodden black.
Oh, I kept the first for another day!
Yet knowing how way leads on to way,
I doubted if I should ever come back.

(a) Which morning is the poet talking about?

Ans. The poet is talking about the morning the speaker begins his journey on that road.

(b) Explain 'In leaves no step had trodden black'.

Ans. The expression suggests that the roads have been used by no one.

(c) What do you mean by 'trodden'?

Ans. The word 'trodden' means 'walked'.

(d) What does 'both' in the above lines refer to?

Ans. 'Both' refers to the two roads that diverged in different directions.

Or

(a) Whom does 'I' refer to?

Ans. 'I' refers to the poet, Robert Frost.

(b) Why would the speaker like to come back?

Ans. The speaker would like to came back to travel by the road that he had not chosen at the time. He was anxious to know where this other road would lead him.

(c) Which word in the above passage means the same as 'to be uncertain'?

Ans. The word 'doubted' means the same as 'to be uncertain'.

(d) The phrase 'way leads on to way' means ....

Ans. one decision would lead to another decision

4. I shall be telling this with a sigh
Somewhere ages and ages hence:
Two roads diverged in a wood, and I—
I took the one less travelled by,
And that has made all the difference.

(a) Identify the poetic device used in the first line.

Ans. 'Onomatopoeia' is the poetic device used in the first line.

(b) The speaker sighs, ...

Ans. thinking about his decision

(c) What do you mean by 'sigh?'

Ans. 'Sigh' is a long, deep breath expressing relief, sadness, etc.

(d) What does the poet want to say about the choice?

Ans. The poet appears to be thinking how the choice that he had made affected his life.

Short Answer Type Questions

Answer the following questions in 30-40 words.

1. What does the choice made by the poet indicate about his personality in the poem 'The Road Not Taken'?

Ans. Robert Frost chose the road which others avoided or seldom took. This indicates that the poet is brave and adventurous. He likes to take risks and make his own path rather than following others.

2. Describe the two roads that the poet finds. Which road did he choose?

Ans. The poet comes across a place at which two roads separated into two directions. One road is well used, whereas the other one did not appear to have been walked over. The poet chose the second road as it looked much more promising to him.

3. What is the significance of the fact that the road 'bent in the undergrowth'? **Competency Based**

Ans. The 'bent in the undergrowth' obstructs the vision of the traveller and he can't see where the road leads. This image expresses the significance that the future is unknown, mysterious and surprising; one can't know what it will bring.

4. The poet takes a long time to make his decision. What is he thinking about?

Ans. The poet takes a long time to make his decision because he wants to choose the road that is best for him. However, he is not sure which road would suit him the best as he couldn't see the road beyond a particular point. Thus, the poet stands there for a long time to make a choice.

5. Why did the poet think that the other road had a better claim?

Ans. The poet thought that the other road had a better claim because it was not much used. He is reluctant to follow the tradition of using the same road that other people have previously used.

6. What does the poet promise himself, although he knows he can't keep his promise?

Ans. The poet promises himself that he would come back after some time and then take the first road, even though he knew that he won't be able to keep his promise. It is because, once a choice is made and a decision is taken, he will move on and take many more decisions. As a result, he would not be able to come back and undo his choice.

7. Explain 'Way leads on to way'.

Ans. The phrase 'way leads on to way' means that the path chosen by the poet will lead on to many more paths. In other words, once a choice is made, one must move on and make other choices that will come in the journey of life. Therefore, it will be difficult for an individual to return to the past and undo his choice.

8. Why does the speaker say "he will be telling this with a sigh/somewhere ages and ages hence"?

Ans. The speaker said these words over the thought that when he looks back at his life and the decisions he made, he may be sorry or happy about his decisions or about the roads he took. These might be sighs of satisfaction or regret. He is thinking back and it reflects on his decisions in life.

9. "I took the one less travelled by, and that has made all the difference." What is the speaker saying here?

Ans. In the given lines the poet highlights the essential theme he wants to bring out through the poem. The poet here says that in future, he will remember that he took the less travelled road. His decision and choice to do so has had a significant impact in his life/journey. In other words, our choices influence and shape our life.

10. 'The Road Not Taken' is a metaphor of life. Justify this statement. **Competency Based**

Ans. In the poem 'The Road Not Taken', the poet Robert Frost presents a situation that each individual faces in life. In the poem, the roads represent all those situations when we need to make a difficult choice. The two divergences represent the multiple options. Further, the poet's choice and his thoughts about the future tell us that in life when a choice is made, it leads to many another choices. These choices cannot be undone and have a significant impact on one's life. Hence, it is true that 'The Road Not Taken' is a metaphor of life.

Long Answer Type Questions

Answer the following questions in 120 words.

1. Imagine yourself in place of the poet. You want to choose one of the roads. What values will you dwell upon while making your decision?

Ans. If there were two roads before me, I would choose the unused and not the worn out road. Though the worn out road appears more attractive and welcoming, I would avoid it. It is also certain that it will lead me to a definite place as people have already taken it before and have prepared the path for others.

However, we all know that a comfortable and smooth road can never lead to fulfillment of ambition. The path to success is always surrounded with obstructions and difficulties. So, I know that the grassy road is not easy to pass through, but if I want to be successful in life, I have to walk on this difficult path. My friends may convince me to choose the easy path, but I would hear the voice of my instinct, which would remind me of the troubles the legends had to face on the path to success.

2. Making choices seems to be a part of everyone's life. Yet, they need to be made. Elaborate in relation to the poem, 'The Road Not Taken'. **Competency Based**

Or "Our life is often governed by the choices we make." Do you agree with this statement? Justify your answer.

Ans. In our life, we often come across situations which present us options and we are required to make a choice. It is often difficult to choose amongst the multiple options that are available before us. Still, we have to take a decision, as we cannot avoid or escape from the truths or realities of life.

Making a choice depends upon several factors like circumstances, needs, family members, friends, etc. As we are guided by so many aspects which may sometimes even mislead us, we must be very sensible and careful about making the right decisions, because our life depends upon the choices we make. Besides, once we make a choice, we cannot go back, as one decision leads to another. This is exactly what Frost regrets in the poem, 'The Road Not Taken'. He chose the path less travelled by, instead of a road travelled upon by many people. However, he does not seem to be very happy about the decision, and he wishes that he could have gone back and started afresh.

Hence, it is our choices which make all the difference in our lives; they determine the quality of our life. While a right decision brings everlasting joy, a wrong one can ruin our life.

3. Suppose an important decision of yours has proved wrong and you want to change your decision, but you can't. Write a diary entry, expressing your regret and helplessness.

Ans. Wednesday, 12th March, 20XX 10:00 p.m.

Dear Diary

Today, I am shocked to see the negative consequences of my wrong decision. I chose the grassy road and deserted the other, which was worn out. The grassy road appeared to have good prospects. However, today, I realise that all that glitters is not gold.

I wish I could change my decision. But a decision is not a text that whenever we want, we can replace it with a new one. Every decision leaves a permanent impression on our life. It changes the course of our life. It makes us happy or sad.

But how could one predict the outcome of one's decision? I think it is destiny and not the decision which gets one success. I am quite helpless but I can't do anything but regret.

Kshitij

4. Do you agree that decision making is an important factor in people's life? Support your answer in the context of the poem 'The Road Not Taken'. Competency Based

Ans. Yes, I agree that decision making is an important factor in people's life. We need to take decisions and make choices even in the simplest of situations like buying a product. Each one of our decisions/ choices have far reaching consequences. It shapes our lives and makes us what we become in the future.

The poem 'The Road Not Taken' highlights exactly this point through a situation faced by the poet. The poet while travelling in the forest came across a point where the path divided into two roads going in different directions. He faced a dilemma of making a choice. After much thought, he chose the road that was less travelled. He knew that his choice will show its results in future. Therefore, he states that in future he would either be relieved or regretful because of his choice as it will have a significant impact on his life. Hence, when making a decision, it is very crucial to make the right choice.

5. Bring out the contrast and similarities between the two roads mentioned in the poem.

Ans. In the poem 'The Road Not Taken', the poet comes across two roads going in different directions in the forest. He cannot see much into the roads but finds that they have many similarities as well as contrasts. To the poet, both roads in the autumn season look equally inviting and puts the poet in a dilemma. He stands and observes both the roads to decide which road to take.

He first observes the first road. He finds that it bends after some distance and is covered with dense growth of plants and bushes. The other road, according to the poet, is as beautiful as the first road. It is grassy and it seems that it has rarely been used.

However, on that morning, both the roads had not been used as they were covered with leaves. For the poet, these roads symbolise two different choices that an individual has to make in life. Once a road/choice is taken/made, it must be stuck to as both lead to two different journeys.

ASSESSMENT EXERCISE

Extract Based Questions

Read the following extracts carefully and answer the questions that follow.

1.

Then took the other, as just as fair,
And having perhaps the better claim,
Because it was grassy and wanted wear;
Though as for the passing there
Had worn them really about the same,

(a) Why did the speaker take the 'other' road?

(b) What do you understand by 'grassy and wanted wear'?

(c) What does the speaker's choice of the road tell us about him?

(d) Explain—"And having perhaps the better claim".

2.

Two roads diverged in a yellow wood,
And sorry I could not travel both
And be one traveller, long I stood
And looked down one as far as I could
To where it bent in the undergrowth;

(a) What do you mean by 'diverged'?

(b) What does he see before him?

(c) What is his desire at this moment?

(d) Give an antonym of 'bent'.

Short Answer Type Questions

Answer the following questions in 30-40 words.

1. Describe the two roads that the poet finds in the wood one morning.
2. What does the divergence of roads signify in real life?
3. Why did the poet want to travel both the roads?
4. What dilemma is the poet in? How does he resolve it?
5. Do you think the poet is happy about his decision. Why?
6. What impression do you form of the speaker from the poem?

Long Answer Type Questions

Answer the following questions in 120 words.

1. Frost's 'The Road Not Taken' is about the importance of making the best use of time and opportunity. Comment.
2. Have you ever come across a situation where you found it difficult to make the right choice?
3. Describe the situation and your feelings when you were caught up in a dilemma. What decision did you finally take?

The Solitary Reaper

CHAPTER 3

by William Wordsworth

Introduction The poem, 'The Solitary Reaper', by William Wordsworth deals with the theme of the power of human imagination to see the transcendent (something extremely great and beyond the usual limits of human knowledge) in the everyday events. It celebrates the beauty of one of the forms of art and emphasises how a beautiful thing, such as a song of the solitary reaper, gives us an everlasting pleasure.

Stanzawise Explanation

Stanza 1 (Lines 1-8)

Behold her, single in the field,
Yon solitary Highland lass!
Reaping and singing by herself;
Stop here, or gently pass!
Alone she cuts, and binds the grain,
And sings a melancholy strain:
O listen! for the vale profound
Is overflowing with the sound.

Explanation While passing through a valley in the Scotland hills, the poet sees a young girl who belongs to the highland region of Scotland. The poet asks the passersby to look at her. She is so busy reaping the crop and singing to herself. So, he requests the passersby either to stop to hear her magical notes silently or to move on quietly without causing any disturbance. She is all alone reaping and binding the crop while singing her melancholy song in the field. The poet is totally fascinated as the whole valley is echoing with her beautiful song, which enters into the hearts of the listeners.

Stanza 2 (Lines 9-16)

No nightingale did ever chant
More welcome notes to weary bands
Of Travellers in some shady haunt.
Among Arabian Sands
A voice so thrilling ne'er was heard
In spring-time from the cuckoo-bird.
Breaking the silence of the seas
Among the farthest Hebrides.

Explanation The poet here lists the things that cannot equal the beauty of the girl's singing. Her melody greets the oppressed and lonely hearts. The poet says that no nightingale ever sang such melodious welcome songs to the group of tired travellers resting in shady places in the heated sands of the Arabian Desert. The poet means that the girl's song is more charming and wonderful than that of the nightingale.

The poet adds that the reaper's fascinating voice is more thrilling than even the sweetest song of the cuckoo bird that sings at the start of every spring. It can break even the silence of the farthest islands of the 'Hebrides.'

Stanza 3 (Lines 17-24)

Will no one tell me what she sings?
Perhaps the plaintive numbers flow
For old, unhappy, far-off things,
And battles long ago:
Or is it some more humble lay,
Familiar matter of to-day?
Same natural sorrow, loss, or pain,
that has been, and may be again?

Explanation The poet is unable to understand the actual meaning of the song. Perhaps he is not able to understand the dialect in which the reaper is singing. He asks if no one would tell him the meaning of her song. He guesses, from the sad melody that the song was about some old and unhappy events such as battles fought in the past. He further thinks that the song may be about some ordinary day-to-day matter or about some natural sorrow, loss or pain that may occur again. This sorrow is of a universal nature which man has always been experiencing and will keep on experiencing.

Stanza 4 (Lines 25-32)

Whate'er the theme, the maiden sang
As if her song could have no ending;
I saw her singing at her work,
And o'er the sickle bending;
I listen'd motionless and still
And, as I mounted up the hill,
The Music in my heart I bore,
Long after it was heard no more.

Explanation Though the poet cannot arrive at the theme of the maiden's song, this does not stop him from enjoying it. He stands there listening with rapt attention. The poet says that whatever the girl was singing about—it appeared as if her song was never ending. The poet sees her singing while bending over her sickle and harvesting the crop. The poet is spellbound by the song but he has to move on. As he climbed up the hill, he could hear its echo in his heart, even long after the song couldn't be heard.

The song leaves a permanent impression on his heart. Here, the meaning is that the girl's beautiful song remains a dear memory for him for a long time after he has left the place.

Poetic Devices Used in the Poem

Alliteration

- sings a melancholy strain
- Among Arabian Sands
- silence of the seas

Hyperbole

- Breaking the silence of the seas among the farthest Hebrides.
- O listen! For the vale profound is overflowing with the sound.

Metaphor

- Solitary reaper's song is compared to the sweet notes of the cuckoo bird and the nightingale.

Word Meaning

Word	Meaning
Stanza 1	
behold	(archaic or literary) see or observe
yon	that
solitary	lonely
highland	mountainous region in northern Scotland
lass	a girl or young woman
reaping	cutting or gathering a crop or harvest
melancholy strain	sad song
vale profound	broad deep valley
overflowing	echoing
sound	the sweet singing voice
Stanza 2	
chant	sing
notes	songs
weary	tired
bands	groups
haunt	a place frequented by a person
Arabian Sands	the deserts of Arabia
thrilling	exciting
farthest	most distant, remotest
Hebrides	islands that lie to the North-West of Scotland in the Atlantic
Stanza 3	
plaintive	sad
numbers	musical notes
humble	simple, ordinary
lay	song
Stanza 4	
sickle	an agricultural tool for cutting grass or crops
mounted	climbed
bore	carried

Textbook FOLDER

Here, we have covered questions given in the CBSE Textbook along with their answer

ON PAGE 78

Q.4 **Imagine that you are the poet, William Wordsworth. You continue on your walk, and when you reach home you tell a friend what you saw and felt. Which of the following best describes your experience? (Work in pairs, then have a class discussion.**

(a) "I was walking past some fields when I saw a young girl, a farm worker, harvesting grain by hand, with a sickle. She was so beautiful that I stood out of sight and watched her for a long time. I have never seen anyone more gorgeous! In fact, she reminded me of other beautiful experiences I've had - the song of the nightingale or the cuckoo, for instance. I'd certainly like to see her again"!

(b) "As I was standing on the hill top just now, I heard a very sad and plaintive song. I looked down, and saw a young woman reaping grain, singing as she did so. She seemed quite melancholy as she sang. But somehow her song brought great comfort and joy to me. In fact, I found it a very emotional experience. As I continued my walk along the hill top, I also heard a nightingale and a cuckoo. But the young farm worker's song affected me most deeply, even though I couldn't understand the words".

(c) "Just now, as I was walking in the valley, I saw a young farm worker in the field. She was singing to herself as she worked. I was so affected by her singing that I stopped and listened. She had a beautiful voice which seemed to fill the whole valley. The song was a sad one and I couldn't understand the words. But its plaintive tone and melancholy sound touched me greatly and its beauty reminded me of the song of a nightingale and a cuckoo. After some time, I walked up the hill, carrying the memory of the young woman's hauntingly beautiful song with me".

Ans. (c)

Q.5 **The poet could not understand the words of the song, yet he raised several possibilities about its theme. In the chart below are some of these possibilities. Read the third stanza again, and find the phrase that matches each. Complete the chart by writing a phrase in each of the empty boxes. Work in pairs.**

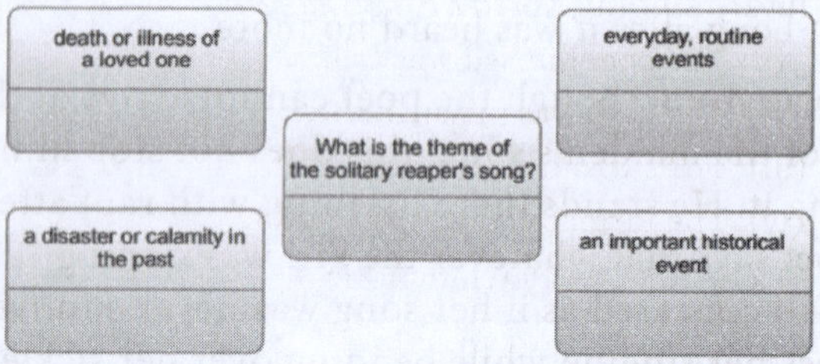

Ans.

- death or illness of a loved one- Same natural sorrow, loss, or pain
- everyday, routine events- is it some more humble lay, Familiar matter of to-day
- What is the theme of the solitary reaper's song?- Will no one tell me what she sings?
- a disaster or calamity in the past- For old, unhappy, far-off things
- an important historical event- - And battles long ago:

ON PAGE 80

Q.6A **On the basis of your understanding of the poem, answer the following questions by ticking the correct options.**

(a) The central idea of the poem 'The Solitary Reaper' is ......

(i) well sung songs give us happiness.
(ii) melodious sounds appeal to all.
(iii) beautiful experiences give us life-long pleasure.
(iv) reapers can sing like birds.

Ans. (iii) beautiful experiences give us life-long pleasure.

(b) In the poem 'The Solitary Reaper' to whom does the poet say 'Stop here or gently pass'?

(i) To the people cutting corn
(ii) To himself.
(iii) To the people who make noise
(iv) To all the passersby

Ans. (iv) To all the passersby

(c) 'The Solitary Reaper' is a narrative poem set to music. This form of verse is called a ....

(i) ballad (ii) soliloquy
(iii) monologue (iv) sonnet

Ans. (i) ballad

(d) The poet's lament in the poem 'The Solitary Reaper' is that ....

(i) he cannot understand the song
(ii) he did not know the lass
(iii) she stopped singing at once
(iv) he had to move away

Ans. (i) he cannot understand the song

(e) Why does the poet feel that the Reaper was most likely singing sorrowful songs?

(i) The poet himself was sad.
(ii) The tune was melancholic.
(iii) The surrounding was dismal.
(iv) The Reaper was weeping.

Ans. (ii) The tune was melancholic.

ON PAGE 81

Q.6B Read the given stanzas and answer the questions given below by selecting the correct option.

Alone she cuts and binds the grain,
And sings a melancholy strain;
O listen! for the Vale profound
Is overflowing with the sound.

1. The exclamation mark used in O listen! suggests

(a) a call for attention (b) a request to listen
(c) a sense of wonder (d) a warning to alert

Ans. (a) a call for attention

2. Select the option that illustrates the task done by 'she'.

(i) (ii) (iii) (iv)

(a) Option (i) (b) Option (ii)
(c) Option (iii) (d) Option (iv)

Ans. (b) Option (ii)

3. Select the option that displays lines with the same rhyme scheme as that of the given stanza.

(a) Clear sky, no clouds high up
The farmer looks and sighs
No monsoons yet, God why?
It will rain, it must.

(b) The farmer looks at the sky
Thankful for the monsoon days
I am sure it's going to rain, he says
Thankful for the clouds up so high

(c) Are any clouds visible?
No, none that I see.
How unfortunate, poor me.
Faith is my only reprieve.

(d) The farmer looks at the sky
Thankful for the clouds up so high.
I am sure it's going to rain, he says
Thankful for the monsoon days.

Ans. (d) The farmer looks at the sky
Thankful for the clouds up so high.
I am sure it's going to rain, he says
Thankful for the monsoon days.

ON PAGE 82

Q.7 Answer in detail.

(a) Do you think that the poet feels overwhelmed by the song of the Solitary Reaper? Why/Why not?

Ans. Yes, I think that the poet feels overwhelmed by the song of the Solitary Reaper as he was mesmerised by its sweetness. He could not understand the meaning of the words but he stood there motionless and charmed, enjoying the melodious song. It charmed him so much that he carried its melody in his heart for a long time.

(b) The use of imagery in the poem has a major impact on the reading experience. Discuss.

Ans. The use of imagery allows the reader to clearly see, touch, taste, smell and hear what the poet is referring to and even sympathise with the poet. In the given poem, the poet has described the feelings that come into his mind as he hears the solitary reaper's song. Hence, the poem becomes rich in visual imagery. The visual imagery of nightingales, Arabian Sands, bodies of water and the Hebrides trigger mental pictures in the mind of the readers.

The reader also gets to imagine all that has been described creating a wonderful effect. For example, "Reaping and singing by herself", "I saw her singing at her work" and " More welcome notes to the weary bands" gives a pictorial description of the young woman at work. The poet makes the readers visualise what he had seen and how he had felt.

(c) The language of music is universal. Justify with reference to The Solitary Reaper.

Ans. The language of music is universal and it doesn't require the listener to understand the words to appreciate the music. In the given poem, the highland girl was singing in her native language, which the poet wasn't able to comprehend. Despite his best efforts, he could not understand the meaning of her song. Still, the poet is mesmerised by the melody and follows the voice. He feels connected to the song and it brings about certain images as well as emotions in his mind.

This shows us that music has no language. He believes that it is a sorrowful song and listens with attention. The poet was so spellbound by the song that he could hear its echo in his heart, long after the song could not be heard. Hence, the song leaves a permanent impression on him even though he doesn't understand its theme.

ON PAGE 82

Q.8 **(a) Read the second stanza again, in which Wordsworth compares the solitary reaper's song with the song of the nightingale and the cuckoo. On the basis of your reading (and your imagination), copy and complete the table below. (Work in groups of four then have a brief class discussion.)**

	Place	Heard by	Impact on Listener
Solitary Reaper	Scottish Highlands	the poet	holds him spellbound
Nightingale	....	....	....
Cuckoo	....	....	....

Ans. (a)

	Place	Heard by	Impact on Listener
Solitary Reaper	Scottish Highlands	the poet	holds him spellbound
Nightingale	Arabian Desert, Oasis	tired travellers	travellers feel fresh
Cuckoo	Farthest Island of the Hebrides	sailors	breaks the silence

(b) Why do you think Wordsworth has chosen the song of the nightingale and the cuckoo for comparison with the solitary reaper's song?

Ans. Wordsworth has chosen the song of the nightingale and the cuckoo for comparison with the song of the reaper to highlight the incomparable sweetness of the reaper's song. The poet wants to convey that the voice of the solitary reaper is both sweeter and more wonderful of the birds which are known for their singing.

(c) As you read the second stanza, what pictures come to your mind? Be ready to describe them in your own words, to the rest of the class. (Do not be afraid to go beyond what the poet has written.)

Ans. The second stanza presents the scene of a lonely girl standing in the middle of the field, busy in cutting the grain and binding it. She is singing a sad song while doing her job and the grief of that song can be felt by all. The sadness of her song is so immense that no nightingale can be heard singing. It brings gloomy and sad pictures to our mind. We are forced to believe that some misfortune has struck the poor girl.

Q.9 **In the sixth line of the first stanza, we read:**

"......... and sings a melancholy strain ......"

This 's' sound at the beginning of sings and strain has been repeated. Poets often do this. Do you know why? Do you know what this 'poetic repetition' is called? Can you find other instances of this, in 'The Solitary Reaper'?

Ans. This poetic repetition is called 'Alliteration'. The poets often use this poetic device to give musical touch to their creations. The other instances are

- No nightingale did ever chant; 'n' sound
- Of Travellers in some shady haunt; 's' sound
- Among Arabian Sands; 'a' sound

ON PAGE 83

Q.10 **In the first stanza, some words or phrases have been used to show that the girl working in the fields is alone. Which are those words and phrases? What effect do they create in the mind of the reader?**

Ans. The words 'single' and 'solitary' and the phrase 'all by herself' reflect the solitude of the girl working in the fields all by herself. These words or phrases focus the readers' attention solely on the girl. They further invoke awe in the minds of the reader, as they enrich the scene with a feeling of romance.

REVIEW EXERCISE

Including Exam Pattern Practice Questions

Extract Based Questions

Read the following extracts carefully and answer the questions that follow.

1. Behold her, single in the field,
Yon solitary Highland lass!
Reaping and singing by herself;
Stop here, or gently pass!
Alone she cuts, and binds the grain,
And sings a melancholy strain:
O listen! for the vale profound
Is overflowing with the sound.

(a) Who is the poet asking to stop or gently pass?

Ans. The poet is asking the other passersby to stop and enjoy the moment quietly or pass by silently without disturbing the girl.

(b) What is the solitary reaper doing?

Ans. The solitary reaper is singing a song while reaping the crops.

(c) What do you mean by 'lass' as used in the extract?

Ans. The word 'lass' means a young girl.

(d) What is the meaning of the expression 'vale profound'?

Ans. The expression 'vale profound' refers to the vast deep valley.

2. No nightingale did ever chant
More welcome notes to weary bands
Of Travellers in some shady haunt.
Among Arabian Sands

(a) For whom did the nightingale sing the melodious songs?

Ans. The nightingale sang the melodious songs for the group of tired travellers who were resting in some shady places in the heated sands of the Arabian Desert.

(b) The speaker quotes the example of the nightingale as ....

Ans. he wants to establish that the girl's voice is more enchanting than that of the nightingale

(c) What do you understand by 'some shady haunt'?

Ans. The phrase refers to a shady resting place, probably an oasis in the deserts of Arabia.

(d) Identify the poetic device used in the last line.

Ans. The poet has used 'alliteration' in the last line.

3. A voice so thrilling ne'er was heard
In spring-time from the cuckoo-bird.
Breaking the silence of the seas
Among the farthest Hebrides.

(a) What wonderful quality does the voice of the solitary reaper have?

Ans. The voice of the solitary reaper reaches a very long distance and is heard in the midst of the silence of the seas as far as 'the farthest Hebrides'.

(b) The speaker compares the voice of the reaper with that of the cuckoo because ....

Ans. he wants to establish that her voice is more thrilling and enchanting than that of the cuckoo

(c) Identify the poetic device used in the last two lines.

Ans. Alliteration is used in the last two lines 'silence of the seas.'

(d) Why has the cuckoo bird been mentioned? What does the poet want to convey?

Ans. The cuckoo bird has been mentioned to draw a comparison between its voice and that of the solitary reaper.
The poet wants to convey that the voice of the solitary reaper is more melodious than that of the cuckoo.

(e) What are, the farthest Hebrides'?

Ans. The 'farthest Hebrides' refers to the remote group of 'islands that lie to the North-West of Scotland.

4. Will no one tell me what she sings?
Perhaps the plaintive numbers flow
For old, unhappy, far-off things,
And battles long ago:

(a) The poet speaks the first line because ....

Ans. the poet is unable to comprehend what the solitary reaper is singing

(b) The poet conjectures about the song that it may be about ....

Ans. an unhappy past, some sad happening or a war fought years ago

(c) **'Plaintive numbers' means ....**

Ans. the sad song of the reaper

(d) **What do the above lines convey about the poet?**

Ans. The poet, though mesmerised by the reaper's song, is unable to understand it.

5. Or is it some more humble lay,
Familiar matter of to-day?
Same natural sorrow, loss, or pain,
that has been, and may be again?

(a) **What does 'lay' here mean?**

Ans. The word 'lay' means the song.

(b) **Explain 'Some natural sorrow, loss, or pain'.**

Ans. The reaper could be singing about the loss or pain which has already occurred and may occur again. This sorrow is of a universal nature.

(c) **Who is singing and where?**

Ans. The solitary reaper is singing in the field.

(d) **What does 'humble lay' mean?**

Ans. 'Humble lay' here means the song of the reaper which may be about an ordinary thing.

6. Whate'er the theme, the maiden sang
As if her song could have no ending;
I saw her singing at her work,
And o'er the sickle bending;

(a) **What do you mean by 'whate'er the theme'?**

Ans. The phrase means that she is singing in an unknown dialect (form of the language) and the poet does not understand the theme of the song.

(b) **The speaker calls her song as having no ending because ....**

Ans. his heart was filled with the song even after he left the place.

(c) **Which line suggests that she is still harvesting?**

Ans. The last line, 'And o'er the sickle bending' suggests that she is still harvesting while singing.

(d) **Why cannot the poet understand the theme of the song being sung?**

Ans. The poet cannot understand the theme of the song as he is unaware of the native dialect (form of language) in which the girl is singing.

Short Answer Type Questions

Answer the following questions in 30-40 words.

1. What request does the poet make to the passersby and why?

Or **Why does the poet want the passersby to stop or gently pass?**

Ans. The reaper is so deeply engrossed in harvesting and singing that she is completely forgetful of her surroundings. According to the poet, such dedication and preoccupation need not be interrupted or she might stop singing. So, he requests the passersby to either pass silently or stop and listen to her song.

2. How does Wordsworth describe the song of the Highland lass in his poem, *The Solitary Reaper*?

Or **How does the poet describe the song of the solitary reaper?**

Or **How does Wordsworth bring out the sweetness of the solitary reaper's song?**

Ans. The poet is greatly fascinated by the sad tone of the solitary reaper. He feels that her voice and melody have outshone even the voices of the nightingale and the cuckoo. The song fills the farthest corner of the valley, entering into the hearts of the listeners.

3. How does the poet bring out the beauty in the song of 'The Solitary Reaper'?

Ans. The poet compares the song of the solitary reaper to the sweet notes of the nightingale and the cuckoo. The song of the nightingale is very welcoming to the tired travellers and the song of the cuckoo bird brings joy to the listeners. Similarly, the song of the reaper too arouses the same feelings of pleasure and joy in the poet.

4. Having failed to understand the lyrics of the song, what does the poet wish?

Or **Why did the poet ask someone to tell him what the solitary reaper was singing?**

Ans. As the solitary reaper belongs to the highland region of Scotland, she is singing in a language which the poet does not understand. Yet, his soul is delighted by her beautiful voice. He is greatly influenced and yearns that someone could explain to him the contents of her song.

5. What are the guesses the poet makes with regard to the solitary reaper's song?

Or **What are the probable themes of the song being sung by the solitary reaper?**

Or **Wordsworth did not understand the words of the song sung by the reaper. However, he raises a few possibilities. What are these?** Competency Based

Ans. The poet is not able to comprehend the dialect of the reaper's song. However, the song appears melancholic to him. He makes some guesses. According to him, she may be singing about some unhappy event of the past or about the war fought years ago. She may also be singing about some current familiar topic or some natural misfortunes.

6. What effect does the song of the reaper have on the poet?

Or **What is the effect of the solitary reaper's song on the poet William Wordsworth?**

Ans. The poet was captivated by the reaper's melancholic song. He stood motionless and heard it with rapt attention. The song left a long lasting impression in his heart. He bore her music in his heart for a long time afterwards even when he could not hear her singing.

7. Justify the title of the poem, 'The Solitary Reaper'.

Ans. The title of the poem is an apt one. The title indicates that the contents of the poem relate to a harvester who is all alone and who is the main character of the poem. The word 'solitary' also reflects her untold pain of loneliness and evokes our sympathy for the reaper.

8. In 'The Solitary Reaper', do you think that the poet had a special ability to see and sense things?

Competency Based

Ans. Yes, the poet certainly had a special ability to see and sense things. He has good observation skills and could notice a lonely highland girl harvesting and singing in the field. He has a good sense of music too as he can appreciate the girl's melodious song and waits for sometime to enjoy it. The poet could not understand the lyrics but could make out that it was a sad song. He also began to guess some of the themes the song could be about. Even after he leaves the scene, the song continues to echo in his mind, even when he can no longer hear it.

Long Answer Type Questions

Answer the following questions in 120 words.

1. Some beautiful experiences amidst nature become sweet memories to us. Reflecting upon William Wordsworth's poem 'The Solitary Reaper,' write your memories in the form of a diary entry.

Ans. Tuesday, 9th March, 20XX 9:30 p.m.

Dear Diary,

Natural experiences that man comes across, enhances his inner joy. They leave an everlasting impact on his mind and heart. I had a similar experience with nature. While passing through the hills of Scotland, a melodious song caught my attention. It was so captivating that I stood there motionless so as not to disturb the singer. The song was sweeter than the sweet notes of both nightingale and cuckoo. The music of the song made me spellbound. It touched my heart and soul. The song left such an everlasting impression on my mind that I still bear the memory of the melodious song in my heart.

Trisha

2. Music doesn't know boundaries. Wordsworth was not able to understand the dialect of the song of the reaper, and even though it was melancholic, it left a long lasting impression in his heart.

Describe, in your own words, how music can soothe the tired one even if one doesn't understand it.

Competency Based

Ans. Wordsworth was passing through the fields when he heard the 'melancholic strain' of the solitary reaper, which at once caught his attention and totally enchanted him. He was on his way to some place but he was so caught up by the melody, that he stopped for some time to listen to it. He was awestruck even though the song was a sad one and he could not understand the language in which the girl was singing.

This is what music does. It doesn't know boundaries. It affects all, and the source of the sound doesn't matter. In the desert, the nightingale's song comes as a blessing for the tired travellers. In spring time, the cuckoo bird breaks the silence.

Music is above the barriers of language and tones. It affects us and enchants us.

3. John Keats, another poet of English Romantic poems begins his poem Endymion with the lines "A thing of beauty is a joy forever." Does Wordsworth's 'The Solitary Reaper' echo the same idea? How does beautiful things tend to provide us with an everlasting joy?

Ans. Wordsworth's poem 'The Solitary Reaper' celebrates the beauty of one of the forms of art, that is music. Wordsworth is enchanted by the sweet and incomparable singing of the young girl, harvesting the grain in the field all alone. Her melodious voice charms the poet so much that he stops there for a while and listens to it with rapt attention. Then he decides to move on, but the song keeps echoing in his ears long after he has actually stopped hearing it. Wordsworth concludes the poem, writing that he will always cherish the memory of the reaper's beautiful melody in his heart.

This is where the poet emphasises the permanent effect of a beautiful work of art i.e. music. Wordsworth seems to agree with to Keats's idea, "A thing of beauty is a joy forever." A beautiful experience is sure to give us pleasure, even after our actual experience is over. The pleasant memory of the melodious singing of the reaper will continue to give the poet pleasure. Long after, he has gone away from the place and thus cannot hear the song anymore.

ASSESSMENT EXERCISE

Extract Based Questions

Read the following extracts carefully and answer the questions that follow.

1. No nightingale did ever chant
More welcome notes to weary bands
Of travellers in some shady haunt
Among Arabian Sands.

(a) Why does the poet refer to the nightingale's song?
(b) The word .... in the extract means the same as 'tired'.
(c) Whose song is more 'welcome' than the song of the nightingale?
(d) Write the synonym of 'haunt'.

2. I listen'd, motionless and still
And, as I mounted up the hill,
The Music in my heart I bore,
Long after it was heard no more.

(a) Why did the poet stand motionless?
(b) Give a synonym of 'motionless'.
(c) Where did the poet finally walk?
(d) What does the poet want to convey by 'Long after it was heard no more'?

Short Answer Type Questions

Answer the following questions in 30-40 words.

1. Why does the poet describe the reaper as 'solitary'?
2. How does the reaper's song affect the poet?
3. What does the poet want the passersby to do?
4. Why does the poet call the reaper's song as 'melancholy strain'?
5. To what does the poet compare the reaper's song?
6. Who are the 'weary band of travellers'? How does the nightingale's song affect them?
7. What guesses does the poet make about the reaper's song?

Long Answer Type Question

Answer the following question in 120 words.

1. For life to be worth living, there should be harmony between music in nature and music created by man. Discuss this statement in the light of Wordsworth's 'The Solitary Reaper'.

The Seven Ages

CHAPTER 4

by William Shakespeare

Introduction The poem 'The Seven Ages' is taken from William Shakespeare's famous play, 'As You Like It'. It describes the seven phases in a man's life from childhood to old age. These seven phases of man's life are that of infant (a new born baby), school boy, lover, soldier, judge, old man and finally death.

The poem contains classical description of human nature and behaviour. The poet makes a comparison between the world and a stage. He says that the world is like a stage, life is like acting, and men and women are like actors. After playing all seven roles of life, man departs from this world and stage.

Stanzawise Explanation

Stanza 1 (Lines 1-5)

All the world's a stage
And all the men and women merely players:
They have their exits and their entrances;
And one man in his time plays many parts,
His acts being seven ages.

Explanation In the opinion of the poet, the world is like a global stage wherein all men and women are acting the roles given to them. Just like in a drama wherein each actor has their own entrances and exits, in life all individuals make their entry with their birth and exit with their death. Every person in a lifetime has to play many roles. The poet has distinguished seven such roles that each and every individual has to go through.

Stanza 2 (Lines 6-10)

At first the infant,
Mewling and puking in the nurse's arms.
Then the whining schoolboy, with his satchel
And shining morning face, creeping like snail
Unwillingly to school.

Explanation The first stage of life of every human being is the stage of infancy. An individual enters in this world as a baby. He makes his presence felt by crying at the top of his voice. Many times, he vomits in the nurse's arms. During this period, he is absolutely helpless and dependent.

The second stage is that of the schoolgoing boy. Shakespeare describes him as a boy having a bright, and fresh well-washed face in the morning, with his bag hanging on his side. He does not want to go to school. He thinks that by walking in the speed of a snail (a small creature that moves very slowly), he will never reach school. His slow pace reflects his unwillingness to go to school.

Stanza 3 (Lines 11-13)

And then the lover,
Sighing like furnace, with a woeful ballad
Made to his mistress' eyebrow.

Explanation The third stage is his early youth, the peak of love and romance.

In this age, man is completely dominated by the moods of his lover. He has no time for himself. He truly and sincerely devotes himself to his beloved. Thus, he composes a song in praise of his beloved's eyebrow. The song describes his pain and agony.

Stanza 4 (Lines 14-18)

Then a soldier.
Full of strange oaths, and bearded like the pard,
Jealous in honour, sudden and quick in quarrel,
Seeking the bubble reputation.
Even in the cannon's mouth.

Explanation The fourth stage is that of a soldier, whose life is full of obligations, commitments, compliances, oaths and vows. He has a beard like that of a leopard. In this stage of life, his strength and courage is at its peak. He enjoys an energetic life with a fearfully quick-tempered nature. He is not contented with what he has and always looks at what others have. As he is quite emotional and warm-blooded, quarrels are part of his normal daily life.

He has always been a seeker of worldly name and fame, which is short-lived and transient like a bubble which disappears within a short time after its appearance. His thirst for honour and esteem is never quenched and he strives his best to gain status. He even foolishly puts his life at stake to earn a short-lived reputation.

Stanza 5 (Lines 19-23)

And then the justice,
In fair round belly with good capon lined,
With eyes severe and beard of formal cut,
Full of wise saws and modern instances;
And so he plays his part.

Explanation This is the fifth stage of man's life which the poet calls middle age or 'justice'. In this stage, a man tries to live a fair and justified life.

His stomach becomes bigger than normal. He looks serious and his beard is formally cut. He quotes maxims (proverbs) and gives many instances to show his wisdom as a judge is supposed to be wise.

Practically, he is a blend of custom, morality, religion and education. A visible authority can be seen in his manner. He has to take a lot of correct decisions to keep up with the ever changing times. So, this stage is the most powerful stage in life.

Stanza 6 (Lines 24-30)

The sixth age shifts
Into the lean and slippered pantaloon,
With spectacles on nose and pouch on side,
His youthful hose, well saved, a world too wide
For his shrunk shank; and his big manly voice,
Turning again toward childish treble, pipes
And whistles in his sound.

Explanation Here, the poet narrates the events that take place in the sixth stage of human life. This is when a man prepares himself for the next level in life, i.e. old age. He learns to relax from the struggles of life.

This man is gradually going thin with his skin hanging in folds and his clothes fitting loosely. His strength begins to reduce and he spends more time at home. He looks like an old fool in his old slippers. Even his voice begins to descend to a lower tone and there is a piping and whistling sound in it.

Stanza 7 (Lines 31-34)

Last scene of all,
That ends this strange eventful history,
Is second childishness and mere oblivion,
Sans teeth, sans eyes, sans taste, sans everything.

Explanation The seventh stage is the tragic end of man's life which started as a newborn and passed through various different stages. The last stage is old age where he enters his second childhood. In this stage, man loses control over all of his senses and strength, due to which his life truly becomes dependent on others as it was when he was a child. His memory weakens and all his faculties start diminishing. He loses his teeth, his eyes, his sense of taste and everything else. He finally departs from the world, leaving behind a story full of events.

Poetic Devices Used in the Poem

Alliteration
- plays many parts
- plays his part
- well saved, a world too wide
- shrunk shank
- turning again toward childish treble

Metaphor
- all the world's a stage
- and all the men and women merely players:
- they have their exits and their entrances;
- and one man in his time plays many parts,
- seeking the bubble reputation.
- last scene of all,

Personification
- cannon's mouth

Repetition
- sans teeth, sans eyes, sans taste, sans everything.

Rhyme
- with spectacles on nose and pouch on side,
  his youthful hose, well saved, a world too wide

Simile
- creeping like snail
- sighing like furnace
- bearded like the pard

Word Meaning

Word	Meaning
Stanza 1	
players	actors
exits	leaving the stage
entrances	entering the stage
ages	age groups
Stanza 2	
infant	a new-born baby
mewling	crying
puking	vomiting, being sick
whining	protesting
satchel	school bag
shining morning face	the boy's face is shining as he has taken a bath
Stanza 3	
woeful	very sad
ballad	song which tells a story
made to his mistress' eyebrow	sung to his lover's eyes
Stanza 4	
oaths	solemn promises
pard	leopard (a symbol of fierceness in Shakespeare's time)
bubble reputation	reputation which is temporary like a bubble
cannon	a big gun firing iron balls

Word	Meaning
Stanza 5	
justice	judge
in fair round belly	having a paunch
with good capon lined	fat like a chicken ready for eating
eyes severe	serious manner
saws	sayings or proverbs
modern instances	current examples
Stanza 6	
slippered	wearing slippers
pantaloon	foolish old man wearing baggy trousers
pouch	a soft fold of loose skin that hangs down
youthful hose	tight fitting leg covering of his younger days
saved	preserved
a world too wide	very loose
shank	part of leg from knee to ankle
treble	high pitched voice
pipes and whistles	whistling and piping voice due to missing teeth
Stanza 7	
last scene	last stage of life
childishness	dependency on others
oblivion	forgetting everything and being forgotten by everybody
sans	a French word meaning without

Textbook FOLDER

Here, we have covered questions given in the CBSE Textbook along with their answer

ON PAGE 85-86

Q.3 On the basis of your understanding of the poem, answer the following questions by selecting the correct choice.

(i) All the world's a stage is an extended metaphor for ....

(a) the life shown in well known plays
(b) seeing the well known plays
(c) life of well known actors
(d) life of man that comes to an end

Ans. (d) life of man that comes to an end

(ii) All 'have their exits and their entrances'. Exits and entrances refer to ....

(a) birth and death
(b) beginning and end of play
(c) coming and going of actors
(d) death and birth

Ans. (d) death and birth

(iii) The seven roles that a man plays correspond to his

(a) chronological age in life
(b) desires
(c) mental development through life
(d) idea of a perfect life

Ans. (a) chronological age in life

ON PAGE 86

Q.4 Having read this extract, identify the stages of a person's life as Shakespeare has done. Write down these stages in your notebook and sum up the characteristics of each stage in two or three words. e.g.

Stage Characteristic feature

Infancy Crying

Ans.

	Stage	Characteristic feature
1.	Infancy (infant)	crying, helplessness
2.	Childhood (schoolboy)	bright but reluctant
3.	Youth (lover)	sentimental, poetic
4.	Adult professional (soldier)	looking for glory, quarrelsome
5.	Middle age (justice)	mature, authoritative
6.	Old age	weak
7.	End of life	clueless, dependent

ON PAGE 86-87

Q.6 Read the given lines and answer the questions that follow by selecting the correct option.

(a) All the world's a stage

And all the men and women merely players:
They have their exits and their entrances;
And one man in his time plays many parts,
His acts being seven ages.

1. **And one man in his time plays many <u>parts</u>...... Replace the underlined word with the correct option which has the same meaning as used in the given lines.**

   (a) scenes (b) roles (c) jobs (d) tasks

Ans. (b) roles

2. **The word 'merely' reveals that the poet regards/views human life as ....**

   (a) impressive (b) inconsequential
   (c) magnificent (d) uninspiring

Ans. (b) inconsequential

3. **Pick the option that does not match with the poetic device used in the phrase 'All the world's a stage'.**

   (a) A thing of beauty is a joy forever.
   (b) The lightning was fireworks in the sky.
   (c) Heavy is the heart that wears the crown.
   (d) The movie was a roller coaster ride of emotions.

Ans. (c) Heavy is the heart that wears the crown.

(b) The sixth age shifts

Into the lean and slippered pantaloon,
With spectacles on nose and pouch on side,
His youthful hose, well saved, a world too wide
For his shrunk shank; and his big manly voice,
Turning again toward childish treble, pipes
And whistles in his sound.

1. **The tone of the poet in line 'His youthful hose, well saved, a world too wide/ For his shrunk shank' is largely**

   (a) nostalgic
   (b) humorous
   (c) pessimistic
   (d) regretful

Ans. (c) pessimistic

2. **Select the option that displays the changes very old age witnesses.**

   i. Round belly **ii. Full of wisdom**
   iii. Loss of vigour **iv. Lean and bony**
   v. Hoarse voice

   (a) i, iii, iv (b) ii, iii, v
   (c) ii, iii, iv (d) iii, iv, v

Ans. (d) iii, iv, v

ON PAGE 88

Q.7 You already know the two literary devices generally used by writers and poets for comparison, i.e. metaphor and simile. e.g.

(a) He was a lion in the battle. (metaphor)

(b) He fought like a lion. (simile)

In (a) the writer talks of the soldier in terms of a lion. The comparison is implied. In (b) the writer compares the soldier to a lion with the use of the word like, (as may also be used for such comparisons).

Read the poem again and note down the metaphors and similes. Complete the following chart.

Reference	Metaphor	Simile
world	all the world's a stage	
men, women		
school-boy		
lover		
soldier		
reputation		
voice		

Which comparison(s) do you find most interesting? Why?

Ans.

Reference	Metaphor	Simile
world	all the world's a stage	
men, women	all the men and woman merely players	
school-boy		creeping like snail
lover		sighing like a furnace
soldier		bearded like a pard
reputation	the bubble repuation and his big manlyvoices turning again to word childish treble	
voice	childish treble	

Which comparison(s) do you find most interesting? Why?

Ans. Do it yourself.

Q.8 In this poem, life is compared with a play. Just as in a play, a man acts many parts, so also in life, a man plays many roles. Can you think of some other comparison for life? (For example, life could be compared with the seasons in nature, the days of the week, the lessons in a school day.) Select one of these comparisons (or choose one of your own), and write about the similarities that life has with it. (80-100 words)

Ans. Life can be compared with the seasons in nature as it is very similar to the manner of their occurrence. Like the spring season, when plants sprout and bloom, man takes birth and enters the first stage of his life. Like nature, man is growing, which can be compared to blooming. Then, comes the summer season, bringing heat. Man, likewise, grows, falls in love and is passionate about everything. Then, comes the autumn season, when the trees shed their leaves. Likewise, man enters old age. His strength begins to weaken and his voice begins to change. Winter comes, and everything is frozen. Similarly, man also enters the last stage of his life and makes his exit from the world when he dies.

REVIEW EXERCISE

Including Exam Pattern Practice Questions

Extract Based Questions

Read the following extracts carefully and answer the questions that follow.

1.

All the world's a stage
And all the men and women merely players:
They have their exits and their entrances;
And one man in his time plays many parts,
His acts being seven ages.

(a) 'All the world's a stage' is an extended metaphor for ....

Ans. life of a man

(b) What does exits and entrances refer to ?

Ans. Exits and entrances refers to death and birth respectively.

(c) What do the seven roles that a man plays in the poem correspond to ?

Ans. The seven roles that a man plays in the poem correspond to the seven chronological ages in life.

(d) Which poetic device is used in the given lines?

Ans. Metaphor

2.

At first the infant,
Mewling and puking in the nurse's arms.
Then the whining schoolboy, with his satchel
And shining morning face, creeping like snail
Unwillingly to school.

(a) The stage(s) of human life described in these lines is/are ....

Ans. the first two stages of life i.e. the infant and the schoolgoing boy are described in these lines.

(b) Which word in the extract is a synonym of 'vomiting'?

Ans. The word 'puking' is the synonym of vomiting.

(c) The schoolboy 'creeps like snail' because ....

Ans. he is reluctant to go to school

(d) What is the meaning of the word 'mewling'.

Ans. The word 'mewling' means to cry feebly.

3. And then the lover,
Sighing like furnace, with a woeful ballad
Made to his mistress' eyebrow.

(a) Which stage is described here?

Ans. The stage of youth is described here.

(b) How does the lover spend his time?

Ans. The lover spends his time by thinking about his beloved's looks, writing poetry for his beloved and expressing his frustration in love by sighing.

(c) Which word in the extract means the same as 'very sad'?

Ans. The word 'woeful' means very sad.

(d) Name the poetic device used in 'sighing like furnace'.

Ans. The poetic device used in 'sighing like furnace' is simile.

4. Then a soldier.
Full of strange oaths, and bearded like the pard,
Jealous in honour, sudden and quick in quarrel,
Seeking the bubble reputation.
Even in the cannon's mouth.

(a) Describe the characteristics of a soldier.

Ans. The soldier is a foul mouthed and short-tempered man. He picks up quarrels for the smallest reasons and is willing to die for the sake of his honour.

(b) Why has reputation been described as 'bubble'? What is ironical about a soldier dying for it?

Ans. Reputation is just like a bubble because it is transitory in nature. The irony is that the soldier does not survive to enjoy the reputation he has defended.

(c) What does the poet mean by 'pard'?

Ans. 'Pard' means 'leopard'.

(d) What is the rhyme scheme of the given lines?

Ans. There is no rhyme scheme in the lines

5. And then the justice,
In fair round belly with good capon lined,
With eyes severe and beard of formal cut,
Full of wise saws and modern instances;
And so he plays his part.

(a) Describe the man presented in the given extract.

Ans. The man gains both stature as well as experience in this stage of life. He grows fat, severe and shares his preaching.

(b) How does a man perform in the justice age?

Ans. In the justice age, man grows critical of everything. He keeps quoting sayings and instances. He is more experienced and indulges in overeating.

(c) The word 'saws' used in the extract means ..... .

Ans. sayings

(d) What does 'good capon lined' mean?

Ans. The phrase 'good capon lined' means 'fat like a chicken'.

6. The sixth age shifts
Into the lean and slippered pantaloon,
With spectacles on nose and pouch on side,
His youthful hose, well saved, a world too wide
For his shrunk shank; and his big manly voice,
Turning again toward childish treble, pipes
And whistles in his sound.

(a) Which is the stage of man's life that the poet describes here?

Ans. It is the sixth stage of life, wherein a man is quite old.

(b) Give the meaning of 'shrunk shank'.

Ans. The phrase means that the calf muscles of the legs have weakened and shrunk due to old age and the legs have become thin and weak.

(c) Why does his voice again turn 'toward childish treble'?

Ans. Due to old age, the vocal chords also weaken considerably and the manly voice turns into a childish shriek.

(d) What does 'youthful hose' mean?

Ans. 'Youthful hose' means the tight fitting leg covering of the youthful days.

7. Last scene of all,
That ends this strange eventful history,
Is second childishness and mere oblivion,
Sans teeth, sans eyes, sans taste, sans everything.

(a) Why is this stage called a 'second childishness'?

Ans. This stage is called a 'second childishness' because the man in this stage is completely dependent on others, just like when he was a child.

(b) What is meant by 'that ends this strange eventful history'?

Ans. The phrase means that this is the end of life which has passed through seven eventful stages different from each other.

(c) What is meant by the word, 'oblivion'?

Ans. The word, 'oblivion' means 'the state of being forgotten'.

(d) What does 'sans' mean?

Ans. 'Sans' means 'without'.

Short Answer Type Questions

Answer the following questions in 30-40 words.

1. Explain 'All the world's a stage' with reference to the poem 'The Seven Ages'.

Or What is the significance of the words, 'entrances and exits' in the poem, 'The Seven Ages'?

Ans. Shakespeare compares life to a drama in which an individual person plays many parts as he progresses through life from early childhood to old age, the last stage of life. He enters the world at birth just like an actor enters the stage when he has to play his part and plays different roles throughout his life. He finally exits from this world just like an actor who has completed his role and exits from the stage.

2. Bring out the parallels between the life of man and actors on a stage.

Or How can you compare human life to a drama?

Ans. The world is a stage and all human beings are actors on that stage. Like actors, we too have our entrances and exits; that is, we are born and we die and like them we play different roles from the day that we are born to the time that we die. The stage, thus, stands for life and the actors can represent all of us at different stages or ages in our lives.

3. Why does the schoolboy whine when he goes to school?

Ans. The poet says that in the second stage of life, the schoolboy whines while going to school because he doesn't want to go to school. He shows his unwillingness by whining and walking slowly to school.

4. What does man do at the lover's stage of life in the poem, 'The Seven Ages' ?

Ans. In the lover's stage of life, the lover pines for his beloved. He sighs like a burning furnace and sings sad ballads of romance. He craves for his love and writes sad songs in praise of his beloved's beauty.

5. Explain, 'Made to his mistress' eyebrow'.

Ans. The expression refers to the song composed by the lover in praise of his beloved's eyebrow. To a lovesick lover, even as insignificant a thing as the eyebrow of his beloved is a worthy subject for writing a song in her praise.

6. How does man behave in the 'soldier' stage of life according to Shakespeare in the poem, 'The Seven Ages'? Competency Based

Ans. In the 'soldier' stage of life, man swears all the time. The soldier is sensitive about his honour and is always ready to defend it. He is short-tempered and ambitious. He is willing to even risk his life for his reputation.

7. The soldier and the justice have contrasting appearance and nature. Justify the statement.

Ans. The soldier has a clumsy looking appearance as he wears a leopard-like beard. Very sensitive about his reputation, this aggressive, short-tempered young man doesn't mind laying down his life to save his honour.

The judge, on the other hand, sporting a beard of a formal cut, goes about quoting wise sayings. This well-fed gentleman with a round belly faces the world with a serious expression on his face. Thus, they are both contrasting in appearance and nature.

8. How does a man look and behave in the sixth stage of life?

Or How does Shakespeare describe man in his sixth age?

Or What becomes of man in his sixth stage?

Ans. In this stage of life, man's voice becomes childlike and loose skin hangs in folds from his thin and bony body. As the body grows thin and weak with age, the trousers that he used to wear as a young man becomes too loose for him. As he moves about in slippers with his spectacles on his nose, he looks quite funny.

9. When does a man fall into 'a world too wide for his shrunk shank'?

Ans. In the sixth stage of life, man has entered into old age and he begins to lose his charm. He does not look physically or mentally appealing. He shrinks in stature and personality. He becomes thin, wears spectacles and the skin around him hangs loosely. His clothes do not fit him and hang on his frame while his once manly voice turns into a childish one.

10. What are the similarities between the last and the first stages of life?

Ans. Just as a child in his infancy is absolutely helpless and totally dependent on others, similarly man in the last stage of life also becomes totally dependent on others. Weak and sick, with all his senses failing, he is not able to do anything himself. Toothless like an infant, at this stage of life, he stands at the door of death.

11. What is 'second childishness' ?

Ans. The last stage of extreme old age has been called second childishness. It has been called so, because man loses control over his senses and becomes as dependent on others as he was when he was a child.

Moreover, just as a child is unaware of everything around him, an old man also dwells in 'mere oblivion' and his memory starts fading.

12. Explain any two metaphors used in the poem, 'The Seven Ages'.

Ans. Following two metaphors are used in the poem

(i) 'They have their exits and their entrances;' means that just like actors in a drama enter and exit the stage, in the same way, man enters the drama of life at birth and exits it at death.

(ii) 'Seeking the bubble reputation' means that the reputation that the soldier is seeking is transient and temporary, just like a bubble which breaks soon after its appearance.

Long Answer Type Questions

Answer the following questions in 120 words.

1. "All the world's a stage, all men and women merely players." Inspired by the quote, write about the moral value that is imparted through the above lines. Competency Based

Ans. Man is born into this world to go through distinct stages of his life with altogether different features and activities. A player has to understand the surroundings to do his best at each stage of his life. At every stage, like the acts of a play, man's character undergoes a radical change.

The message is quite clear that during the short span of life, one must be a 'hero' in strife. Man can become immortal through his good deeds.

One should gladly accept the departure from any stage of life and believe in the power of the Almighty, who has the right to give and take life.

2. What, according to Shakespeare, are the personality traits of a soldier? Which one impresses you the most?

Or **Which stage of a man's life depicts him as an egoistic person? What's the reason behind his ego? Discuss the values a man should possess to become selfless in life.**

Ans. According to Shakespeare, a soldier is as ferocious as a leopard. He is aggressive and short-tempered. He picks up quarrels for the smallest reasons and is willing to die for the sake of his honour. This stage of life depicts him as an egoistic person. The reason behind his ego is his feeling of wanting to protect his reputation at all costs, even his life. To become selfless, the values a man must possess are totally the reverse — he should be even-tempered, calm and of an endearing nature. Like a soldier, I too want to be courageous. The soldier's willingness to put his life at stake for his country's honour impresses me the most.

ASSESSMENT EXERCISE

Extract Based Questions

Read the following extracts carefully and answer the questions that follow.

1.
All the word's a stage
And all the men and women merely players :
They have their exits and their entrances;
And one man in his time plays many parts,
His acts being seven ages.

(a) His acts being seven ages means every man ....

(b) The term 'players' in the above lines refers to ....

(c) What does the poet mean by 'exits' and 'entrances'?

(d) What parellelism has the poet drawn between the stage and the world?

2.
And then the lover,
Sighing like furnace, with a woeful ballad
Made to his mistress' eyebrow.

(a) What is the poetic device used in the second line?

(b) Explain 'woeful ballad'.

(c) Give one characteristic trait of the lover as perceived by the poet.

(d) What is the theme of the poem?

Short Answer Type Questions

Answer the following questions in 30-40 words.

1. Justify the title of the poem 'The Seven Ages'.
2. Bring out the analogy between the world and the stage.
3. What does the poet reflect through the schoolboy?
4. Why is the soldier willing to die?
5. In reality, how do the last two stages in life overlap?
6. Why has life been called an 'eventful history'?

Long Answer Type Questions

Answer the following questions in 120 words.

1. 'Youngsters seek bubble reputation.' Correlate the quote on the basis of the poem, 'The Seven Ages'.
2. According to the poet, men and women are only players in a drama. Do you agree? Justify.

Oh, I Wish I'd Looked After Me Teeth

by Pam Ayres

CHAPTER 5

Introduction The poet Pam Ayres regrets neglecting her teeth during her childhood. She wishes that she had controlled herself better at the time when she had all her teeth, but couldn't control her bad habits. She also realises how she had mocked her mother's false teeth earlier and now, she had become an object of mockery herself. Since she ate too many sweets, she has to now visit the dentist frequently and bear the pain of drilling and injections. While lying in the dentist's chair, she would keep looking up miserably at the nose of the dentist in the fear of his drill causing her pain.

Stanzawise Explanation

Stanza 1 (Lines 1-5)

Oh, I wish I'd looked after me teeth,
And spotted the perils beneath.
All the toffees I chewed,
And the sweet sticky food,
Oh, I wish I'd looked after me teeth.

Explanation The poet wishes that she had looked after her teeth well. She also regrets that she did not realise in time the damage that was being done to her teeth by toffees and sticky food. Chewing of toffees and consumption of sticky food proved to be injurious to her teeth. She faced 'perils' i.e. the threat of tooth decay and cavities. The poet regrets her careless attitude towards her teeth.

Stanza 2 (Lines 6-10)

I wish I'd been that much more willin'
When I had more tooth there than fillin'
To pass up gobstoppers.
From respect to me choppers,
And to buy something else with me shillin'.

Explanation The poet talks about the time when she did not have so many cavities in her teeth and did not require so much filling. The poet wishes that when her teeth were free from any cavities, she should have been more willing to protect her teeth by giving up the habit of eating gobstoppers. Showing more respect for her teeth, she should have purchased something better and different with her money. She now wishes she had resisted the temptation and paid more attention to the damage they could have caused to her teeth.

Stanza 3 (Lines 11-15)

When I think of the lollies I licked,
And the liquorice all sorts I picked,
Sherbet dabs, big and little,
All that hard peanut brittle,
My conscience gets horribly pricked.

Explanation The poet's love for sweet things tempted her to think about the sweet lollies, liquorice, sherbet dabs and peanut brittle she had eaten. Nothing could stop her from eating these sweet and sticky candies.

When she remembers that all these things have caused her tooth decay, she feels guilty and remorseful (sorry). Her foolishness, immaturity and lack of self-control made the poet eat so many lollies and sweets that she now has many cavities.

Stanza 4 (Lines 16-20)

My mother, she told me no end,
'If you got a tooth, you got a friend.'
I was young then, and careless,
My toothbrush was hairless,
I never had much time to spend.

Explanation The poet remembers that her mother used to tell her that having a tooth is equal to having a friend. This is because if we lose a tooth we can never get it back naturally. The narrator did not take her mother's advice as she was a young child. She never spared enough time to take care of her teeth or her toothbrush.

Stanza 5 (Lines 21-25)

Oh I showed them the toothpaste all right,
I flashed it about late at night,
But up-and-down brushin'
And pokin' and fussin'
Didn't seem worth the time-I could bite!

Explanation The poet did brush her teeth late at night but she performed this ritual hurriedly and carelessly without properly brushing up and down and cleaning all nooks and corners. She felt that the thorough brushing of teeth would be complete wastage of time. Now, she regrets it because her teeth have been badly damaged by excessive intake of sweets.

Stanza 6 (Lines 26-30)

If I'd known, I was paving the way
To cavities, caps and decay,
The murder of fillin's
Injections and drillin's,
I'd have thrown all me sherbet away.

Explanation The poet didn't know that consumption of too many sweets would cause irreparable damage to her teeth. The poet says that had she been aware that her carelessness and unhealthy eating habits would result in damaging her teeth, she would have thrown away her sweets like sherbet dabs. This would have saved her from unnecessary drilling and filling in the dental cavities.

Stanza 7 (Lines 31-35)

So I lay in the old dentist's chair,
And I gaze up his nose in despair,
And his drill it do whine,
In these molars of mine.
"Two amalgum," he'll say, "for in there."

Explanation The poet had to pay the price of eating toffees and candies excessively. As she ate too many sweets, she eventually had to lie in the dentist's chair for her teeth to be drilled. While lying there, she would keep looking up miserably at the nose of the dentist as he leant over her mouth to carry out the dental procedure.

The very idea of the dentist's drill digging and poking her teeth makes the poet shiver in pain. As the dentist drilled her damaged teeth, she looked at him helplessly and he declared that two of her molars needed fillings.

Stanza 8 (Lines 36-40)

How I laughed at my mother's false teeth,
As they foamed in the waters beneath.
But now comes the reckonin'
It's me they are beckonin'
Oh, I wish I'd looked after me teeth.

Explanation As a child, the poet used to ridicule her mother's false teeth. Her mother had false teeth which she would put sometimes in a bowl of water. On seeing bubbles coming up in the water, she would laugh and feel quite amused.

Little did she realise at that time, that her carelessness would damage her teeth and a stage might come in her life when she too would need false teeth.

The poet feels that it was time for her to face the consequences of her actions-irresponsible eating and carelessness.

She realised that very soon she too will have false teeth because the natural teeth are all decayed and gone. So, she feels that she should have looked after her teeth.

Poetic Devices Used in the Poem

Alliteration

- sweet sticky
- much more
- there than
- them the
- cavities, caps

Elision (replacement of a letter in a word by an apostrophe sign – in the words given below, the letter 'g' has been replaced by an apostrophe sign)

- brushin', fussin', willin', fillin', shillin', reckonin', beckonin', pokin'

Inventive spelling

- me (instead of *my*)
- amalgum (instead of *amalgam*)

Personification

- respect to me choppers
- Oh, I showed them the toothpaste all right,

Repetition

- Oh, I wish I'd looked after me teeth.

Rhyme

- Every group of 5 lines (i.e. each stanza) has the rhyme scheme *aabba*.

Word Meaning

Word	Meaning
Stanza 1	
me teeth	my teeth
spotted	found out
perils	problems
Stanza 2	
fillin'	fillings to replace missing teeth
gobstoppers	large hard sweets
choppers	teeth
me shillin'	my pocket money
Stanza 3	
lollies	lollipops
liquorice	candy made from the dried root of the liquorice plant
sherbet dabs	tiny sweets
peanut brittle	hard candy made with peanuts, sugar and corn syrup
Stanza 4	
no end	many times

Word	Meaning
to spend	to spare for these activities
Stanza 5	
showed them	hurriedly brushed the teeth
pokin' and fussin'	carefully checking
Stanza 6	
caps	capping on decayed teeth
sherbet	tiny sweets
Stanza 7	
whine	shrill sound made by a drill
molars	large teeth at back of mouth for crushing and chewing food
amalgum	mixture of silver and mercury used for making fillings in teeth
for in there	required there
Stanza 8	
foamed	gave out foam
reckonin'	accounting
beckonin'	calling

Textbook FOLDER

Here, we have covered questions given in the CBSE Textbook along with their answer

ON PAGE 91

Q.3 On the basis of your understanding of the poem, complete the following table.

Stages in the life of the poet	Activities	Consequences
(a) Youth	eating toffees	
(b) Adulthood		gazing at the dentist in despair

Ans.

Stages in the life of the poet	Activities	Consequences
(a) Youth	Eating toffees, gobstoppers, sherbet dabs, liquorice, peanut brittle and other sweet sticky food as well as licking lollies. Brushing the teeth carelessly	Cavities, tooth decay, fillings and caps
(b) Adulthood	Going to the dentist due to tooth decay and sitting in the dentist's chair	Gazing at the dentist in despair Facing injection and drilling of the teeth

Q.4 On the basis of your understanding of the poem, answer the following questions by ticking the correct choice.

(i) The title 'Oh, I wish I'd looked after me teeth' expresses ....

(a) regret (b) humour

(c) longing (d) pleasure

Ans. (a) regret

(ii) The conscience of the speaker pricks her as she has ....

(a) been careless (b) been ignorant

(c) been fun loving (d) been rude

Ans. (a) been careless

(iii) The speaker says that she has paved the way for cavities and decay by ....

(a) eating the wrong food and not brushing

(b) not listening to her mother

(c) laughing at her mother's false teeth

(d) not listening to the dentist

Ans. (a) eating the wrong food and not brushing

(iv) The tone of the narrator is one of ....

(a) joy (b) nostalgia

(c) regret (d) sorrow

Ans. (c) regret

ON PAGE 92

Q.5 Answer the following questions.

(a) "......... But up-and-down brushin'

And pokin' and fussin'

Didn't seem worth the time-I could bite!"

What do these lines convey?

Ans. The given lines convey that the poet did not realise the importance of regular brushing and proper dental hygiene when she was a child. She did not care for her teeth regularly. She thought it was useless and worthless to clean her teeth after eating anything.

(b) Why did the poet go to the dentist? How could she have avoided it?

Ans. The poet went to the dentist to get her teeth examined. She had developed cavities in her teeth due to unhealthy eating habits and irregular brushing of teeth. She could have avoided this visit if she had taken proper care of her teeth during childhood by brushing them properly and regularly.

(c) *"If you got a tooth, you got a friend"*; what do you understand from the line?

Ans. A tooth is like a friend. As a lost friend can never come back, a lost tooth never grows again. It cannot be regained or made naturally.

(d) With reference to the poem, how can you look after your teeth?

Ans. With reference to the poem, we can look after our teeth by

(i) brushing our teeth properly twice a day and rinsing our mouth after each meal,

(ii) avoiding sweet and sticky food for better oral hygiene

(iii) getting a regular dental checkup to maintain healthy teeth.

(e) Give an appropriate proverb that conveys the message that this poem carries.

Ans. An appropriate proverb that conveys the message that this poem carries is "Prevention is better than cure."

Q.7 Read the following statement and imagine you are Jack.

"I can't afford to, after what Jack's done to his teeth." What is it, you think you can't afford and why? Write a diary entry in not less than 125 words.

(in-class activity; not to be set up as homework).

Ans. Tuesday, 13th Feb, 20XX 11:00 pm

Dear Diary,

Today I overheard some people make stupid remarks about me and my teeth. They said, "I can't afford to, after what Jack's done to his teeth." I think they were talking about going to drink chocolate shakes and icecream together. I would also love to drink a tasty chocolate shake. However, I have been forbidden to eat those things by my parents and the dentist. You already know that I am stupidly fond of chocolates. That fondness has ruined my teeth. I also didn't brush my teeth well because apparently I'm stupid. So four of my teeth had cavities. Mother took me to the dentist. I am telling you dear diary, that dentist was definitely a demon because he smiled at the ruined state of my teeth. Nothing is scarier than being strapped to a dentist's chair and being unable to move while he happily brings out his drilling machine. From now on, what I can't afford to do is eating chocolates and not brushing my teeth.

Jack

Q.8 In line 35, the poet has misspelt the word as 'amalgum'. Why do you think she has done that? Discuss.

Ans. The word has been misspelt deliberately to create a pun (word having double meaning) with the word 'gum'. On one hand, the word 'amalgam' refers to the mixture of mercury and silver used by the dentist to make fillings, while the word 'gum' refers to chewing-gums which are definitely bad for the teeth. It is done to add humour.

REVIEW EXERCISE

Including Exam Pattern Practice Questions

Extract Based Questions

Read the following extracts carefully and answer the questions that follow.

1. Oh, I wish I'd looked after me teeth,
And spotted the perils beneath.
All the toffees I chewed,
And the sweet sticky food,
Oh, I wish I'd looked after me teeth.

(a) Why does the poet wish that she had taken better care of her teeth?

Ans. The poet wishes that had she taken better care of her teeth, she wouldn't have to face the problems she is facing now.

(b) What caused perils/ decay beneath the poet's teeth?

Ans. The poet used to chew a lot of toffees and sweet sticky food which caused the decay beneath her teeth.

(c) What were the pleasures the poet had enjoyed before?

Ans. The pleasures the poet had enjoyed earlier were eating varieties of sweets and not brushing her teeth properly.

Ans. The word 'spotted' is a synonym of 'noticed'.

(d) The conscience of the author pricks her as she has been ....

Ans. eating the wrong kinds of food and not brushing properly.

2. I wish I'd been that much more willin'
When I had more tooth there than fillin'
To pass up gobstoppers.
From respect to me choppers,
And to buy something else with me shillin'.

(a) What does the word 'gobstoppers' mean?

Ans. 'Gobstoppers' are large hard sweets.

(b) What happened to the poet's teeth when she continued eating all kinds of sweets?

Ans. When she continued eating all kinds of sweets, her teeth decayed and needed fillings.

(c) Explain, 'From respect to me choppers'.

Ans. This line suggests that she should have paid more attention to her teeth by reducing her eating of sweets.

(d) What is the tone of the extract?

Ans. The tone of the extract is 'regret'.

3. When I think of the lollies I licked,
And the liquorice all sorts I picked,
Sherbet dabs, big and little,
All that hard peanut brittle,
My conscience gets horribly pricked.

(a) Why does the poet feel her conscience horribly pricked?

Ans. Having lost almost all her teeth due to eating too many sweets and not brushing the teeth earlier, the poet feels guilty about them and thus her conscience is horribly pricked.

(b) What is responsible for the poet's present state of pain, suffering and guilt feelings?

Ans. The poet's love for a number of lollies, liquorices, sherbets and peanut brittle is responsible for her present pain, suffering and guilt.

(c) Which word in the extract means the same as 'troubled'?

Ans. The word 'pricked' means the same as troubled.

(d) How is the speaker feeling?

Ans. The speaker is feeling guilty.

4. My mother, she told me no end,
'If you got a tooth, you got a friend.'
I was young then, and careless,
My toothbrush was hairless,
I never had much time to spend.

(a) What does the mother mean when she says that teeth are like friends?

Ans. The mother means that if we lose a tooth we can never get it back naturally. The same happens with a friend.

(b) Why did the poet not have time to spend?

Ans. The poet did not spend time on brushing her teeth or replacing her toothbrush when it was worn out because she felt that these things were not important.

(c) **What is meant by the phrase, 'no end'?**

Ans. This phrase means 'many times' or 'repeatedly'.

(d) **What is the opposite of 'spend'?**

Ans. The opposite of 'spend' is 'earn'.

5. Oh I showed them the toothpaste all right,
I flashed it about late at night,
But up-and-down brushin'
And pokin' and fussin'
Didn't seem worth the time-I could bite!

(a) **What do you mean by 'pokin' and 'fussin'?**

Ans. 'Pokin' and 'fussin' means checking carefully.

(b) **What does the line 'Didn't seem worth the time' mean?**

Ans. The line means that as a child she felt brushing her teeth was a wastage of time as she could bite comfortably.

(c) **What trait of the poet's personality is highlighted by her casual approach to her teeth?**

Ans. Her casual approach to her teeth brings out the poet's foolishness, laziness and carelessness.

(d) **Explain 'showed them the toothpaste.'**

Ans. The phrase means that she brushed her teeth casually and hurriedly without much care.

6. If I'd known, I was paving the way
To cavities, caps and decay,
The murder of fillin's
Injections and drillin's'
I'd have thrown all me sherbet away.

(a) **How did the poet pave the way for cavities in her teeth?**

Ans. The poet cleared the way for cavities in her teeth by eating a large amount of sweets, gobstoppers, lollies, candies and by not brushing her teeth properly.

(b) **What is the meaning of sherbet?**

Ans. Sherbet means sweets.

(c) **What had the poet not known?**

Ans. The poet had not known that eating all kinds of sweets would result in tooth decay and she would need fillings in her teeth.

(d) **What does 'paving the way' mean?**

Ans. 'Paving the way' means to make something easier.

7. So I lay in the old dentist's chair,
And I gaze up his nose in despair,
And his drill it do whine,
In these molars of mine.
"Two amalgum", he'll say, "for in there."

(a) **Why was the poet lying in the dentist's chair in despair?**

Ans. The poet was lying in the dentist's chair waiting for the dentist to use his drill to remove the decayed teeth. The poet was 'in despair' because she expected a lot of pain when the dentist drilled her teeth.

(b) **Explain the lines, "And his drill it do whine, In these molars of mine." What does the word 'whine' tell us about the speaker's experience?**

Ans. These lines means that the dentist's drill makes a whining sound when it drills out the decayed molar teeth of the poet. The noise (whining) made by the drill shows that the speaker is having a painful experience.

(c) **What does 'amalgum' mean?**

Ans. The word is actually 'amalgam', which is an alloy of mercury and silver used as a filling in teeth.

(d) **Is the poet happy?**

Ans. No, the poet is not happy.

8. How I laughed at my mother's false teeth,
As they foamed in the waters beneath.
But now comes the reckonin'
It's me they are beckonin'
Oh! I wish I'd looked after me teeth.

(a) **Explain "But now comes the reckonin', It's me they are beckonin."**

Ans. The poet has to pay for making fun of and laughing at her mother's false teeth as now she also needs false teeth.

(b) **What do you mean by 'reckonin', here?**

Ans. 'Reckonin' here means settlement of account.

(c) **When did the poet laugh at her mother's false teeth?**

Ans. The poet laughed at her mother's false teeth when her own teeth were in a good condition during her childhood.

(d) **How do the speaker's emotions change in the above stanza?**

Ans. The speaker goes from being happy to being regretful.

Short Answer Type Questions

Answer the following questions in 30-40 words.

1. **What are the perils the poet talks about in the poem "Oh I Wish I'd Looked After Me Teeth" and how have they been caused?**

Ans. The 'perils' refer to the cavities and tooth decay that the poet is suffering from. They have been caused by eating too many sweets as a child and not brushing her teeth properly.

2. What did the poet recall after spotting the perils beneath?

Ans. After spotting the perils beneath her teeth, the poet recalled all the toffees she had chewed and all the sweet sticky food she had eaten during her childhood.

3. What did the poet wish when she had all her teeth and no fillings?

Ans. The poet had all her teeth and no fillings in her childhood but she didn't care at all for the health of the teeth at that time. Later, she regretted not caring about them. Now, she wished that she should have skipped eating hard sweets and brushed her teeth properly.

4. What does the speaker mean when she says, "my conscience gets horribly pricked"? Why does she feel like this?

Ans. The phrase means that the speaker is feeling very guilty because she realises that she herself is responsible for her tooth decay. She also feels guilty at the thought of the number of sweets she has had in the past.

5. Why didn't the poet brush her teeth properly before sleeping?

Ans. Having a casual approach towards her dental hygiene, the poet brushed her teeth late at night hurriedly. It was more of a ritual of brushing rather than taking good care of her teeth by brushing them thoroughly up and down. She thought brushing teeth was a waste of time.

6. Write some linguistic variations in the poem.

Ans. Some linguistic variations in the poem are

(i) 'Me teeth' for 'my teeth'.

(ii) 'Me choppers' for 'my choppers'.

(iii) 'Me shillin' for 'my shillings'.

(iv) 'All me sherbet' for 'all my sherbets'.

7. How does the poet feel while lying in the 'old dentist's chair'?

Ans. The very idea of the dentist's drill digging and poking her teeth makes the poet shiver in pain. While lying in the dentist's chair, she feels very helpless and miserable. Owning the responsibility of ruining her own teeth, she is full of regret and blames herself for her misery, but it is too late.

8. What had happened to the poet's mother's teeth and how had she (the poet) behaved at that time?

Ans. The poet's mother had false teeth. As a child, the poet had all her teeth intact, sound and healthy; hence her mother's 'teeth' in a bowl amused her. She used to ridicule her mother's false teeth.

9. Explain the line "It's me they are beckonin" in the last stanza.

Ans. The poet saw her mother's false teeth foaming in the water in which they were kept so as to be kept clean. She laughed while looking at them, but now she is terrified. It means that she is afraid because the fun she used to make of her mother has become a reality for her now.

10. Justify the title "Oh, I Wish I'd Looked After Me Teeth." Competency Based

Ans. The title is apt as it conveys the poet's regret at having damaged her teeth due to her negligence. The poet, Pam Ayres, has deliberately used a clause rather than a phrase to explicitly underline her sense of remorse at her irresponsible approach and carelessness. The use of 'Oh' brings out the sense of helplessness of the poet.

Long Answer Type Questions

Answer the following questions in 120 words.

1. What key message does the poet, Pam Ayres want to give us through the poem, 'Oh, I Wish I'd Looked After Me Teeth'? Give instances from the poem to support your answer. Competency Based

Ans. The poet, Pam Ayres wishes to give us the message, 'Prevention is better than cure' through the poem. According to the poem, teeth need to be cared for with diligence from a young age. Children should set limits to eating sweets including chocolates, toffees, sweet food, hard sweets, liquorice and pickled sweets. Taking care of the teeth also involves daily brushing of teeth with care. Thus, we should take preventive measures in every aspect of life so that problems could be prevented or not allowed to increase.

2. Imagine you are Pam Ayres. As a child, despite your mother's scolding, you ate a lot of chocolates. Today your teeth have decayed and it's too late. Write a diary entry expressing your guilt and regret at your wrongdoings and how you could have avoided it.

Ans. Wednesday, 10th May, 20XX 10 : 00 p.m.

Dear Diary

Today, when I sat in the dentist's chair to get my teeth filled, I remembered incidents from my childhood. I used to laugh at my mother's false teeth foaming in the water! Little did I know that later on I would face a similar problem!

I used to avoid brushing my teeth properly and regularly. In addition, I used to spend all my pocket money on buying sweets and chocolates, as I loved eating them. Now, I regret all those incidents, as the dentist says my teeth have decayed.

Oh, how I wish I had looked after my teeth during my childhood!

Pam

3. Disobeying elders/parents can result in serious problems. The stubborn and negligent attitude of the poet Pam Ayres led to serious dental problems. Explain. Competency Based

Ans. Our elders and parents always advise us how to live our lives successfully and without any troubles because they have got the experience to give us such advice. When the poet's mother advised the poet to brush her teeth regularly and properly as well as not to eat sweets and other sweet sticky food, she wanted the poet's teeth to last a long time. However, the stubborn attitude of continuing eating what she liked caused her teeth to decay. Her negligent attitude of not brushing her teeth properly also added to their decay.

ASSESSMENT EXERCISE

Extract Based Questions

Read the following extracts carefully and answer the questions that follow.

1.

Oh I showed them the toothpaste all right,
I flashed it about late at night,
But up-and-down brushin'
And pokin' and fussin'
Didn't seem worth the time-I could bite!

(a) What does 'them' mean in the first line?

(b) How did the poet clean her teeth?

(c) Why didn't she brush her teeth methodically and meticulously?

(d) Explain the first two lines.

2.

So I lay in the old dentist's chair,
And I gaze up his nose in despair,
And his drill it do whine,
In these molars of mine.
"Two amalgum," he'll say, "for in there."

(a) What is the meaning of the last line?

(b) What led the poet to the dentist's chair?

(c) What was her mind's state while lying in the dentist's chair?

(d) What does 'two amalgum' mean?

Short Answer Type Questions

Answer the following questions in 30-40 words.

1. What are the two main reasons for the poet's decaying teeth and cavities?
2. Although the poet brushed her teeth every night, she could not save them. Why?
3. How did the poet spend her pocket money and how should she have spent it?
4. What does the poet feel about her dental problems?

Long Answer Type Questions

Answer the following questions in 120 words.

1. What Do's and Don'ts have you learnt from the poet's experience of poor dental health?
2. Write an article for your school magazine in about 120 words discussing the role of parents, schools, the media and dentists in spreading awareness about the need for dental hygiene.

Song of the Rain

by Kahlil Gibran

CHAPTER 6

Introduction The poem 'Song of the Rain' by Kahlil Gibran presents the beauty of nature. In the poem, the poet has personified rain as it tells its story in the first person. He tells us how raindrops are formed, how they fall upon the thirsty Earth to satisfy the thirst of the trees and plants. Finally, the rain ends and the rainbow in the sky marks the end of rain.

Stanzawise Explanation

Stanza 1 (Lines 1-35)

I am dotted silver threads dropped from heaven
By the gods. Nature then takes me, to adorn
Her fields and valleys.

Explanation The poem begins with the rain comparing itself to silver threads. The rain droplets are silver in colour and while it comes down in a line, it appears to be a thread. It states that it is sent from heaven by the gods. Once it reaches the ground, it is put to use by Mother Nature in order to beautify the fields and valleys.

Stanza 2 (Lines 4-6)

I am beautiful pearls, plucked from the
Crown of Ishtar by the daughter of Dawn
To embellish the gardens.

Explanation The rain is so beautiful that it looks like pearls pulled out from the crown of Ishtar, the Goddess of fertility, love and war, by the daughter of Dawn (early in the morning) to decorate the gardens.

In other words, the dew drops are like the pearls which add to the beauty of the gardens.

Stanza 3 (Lines 7-9)

When I cry the hills laugh;
When I humble myself the flowers rejoice;
When I bow, all things are elated.

Explanation When the rain falls, the hills are cheerful because it gives life. It will revive everything on the hills. The word 'cry' here suggests that it rains heavily on the hills. The echo of the rain sounds like the laughter of the hills. When the rain falls moderately the flowers feel happy. Here, 'humbles' means falling moderately i.e., neither heavily or lightly. When the rain falls lightly, it gives immense joy to everything on Earth. The rain is, thus, a source of rejuvenation and renewal.

Stanza 4 (Lines 10-13)

The field and the cloud are lovers
And between them I am a messenger of mercy.
I quench the thirst of the one;
I cure the ailment of the other.

Explanation The field refers to Earth and the cloud refers to the clouds in the sky. The field and the clouds, though far away from each other, are personified as lovers. The rain, as a messenger of mercy, connects the field with the clouds in the sky. It fills the void between the sky and the Earth.

Raindrops quench the thirst of the Earth and cure the ailments (disease) caused by the heat of summer. This heavenly blessing works as a cure for many problems. The clouds are also relieved of their weight of water vapours. Thus, it makes both of them comfortable and suggests that both the Earth and clouds need each other and they both depend on rain.

Herein, the quality of mercy indicates the benefits that the rain droplets bring. It saves earth from drought and does provide necessary nourishment.

Stanza 5 (Lines 14-18)

The voice of thunder declares my arrival;
The rainbow announces my departure.
I am like earthly life which begins at
The feet of the mad elements and ends
Under the upraised wings of death.

Explanation In this stanza the poet compares the life cycle of the rain to that of humans. Besides, the poet artistically presents the scientific phenomenon of rainbow. The news of the arrival of rain is brought by thunder and its departure is marked by the presence of the rainbow.

Further, the rain draws a parallel between 'earthly life' and its own life. As a human has the main phases of life birth-maturity and death, rain also has the same cycle of life-birth (Evaporation), maturity (Condensation), and death (Showering of rainfall). The rain is said to begin at the feet of 'mad elements' which is a combination of many gases and vapor. Then, the rain dies under the upraised wings of death which indicates the strong wind which blows the cloud away when the cloud becomes light after rainfall.

Stanza 6 (Lines 19-22)

I emerge from the heart of the sea and
Soar with the breeze. When I see a field in
Need, I descend and embrace the flowers and
The trees in a million little ways.

Explanation In this stanza, rain talks about how it originates in the form of water vapour from the depths of the sea and is lifted to the sky by the breeze. The water vapour then collects in the clouds. These fall down on the Earth in the form of rain droplets. Thus, rain falls in millions of droplets and thereby, refreshes the trees and helps the plants in their healthy growth.

Stanza 7 (Lines 23-26)

I touch gently at the windows with my
Soft fingers, and my announcement is a
Welcome song. All can hear, but only
The sensitive can understand.

Explanation The rain falls gently and its sound is an announcement of its arrival on Earth. Its arrival is like a welcome song. The inner music of the song of the falling rain is audible to all but only a few sensitive people can enjoy and appreciate it.

Stanza 8 (Lines 27-29)

I am the sigh of the sea;
The laughter of the field;
The tears of heaven.

Explanation The rain is bound to the different elements of nature-sea, land and sky. The water evaporating from the sea has been referred to as the sigh of the sea. As water vapour rises from the sea, it appears as if it is taking deep breaths. As the rain restores the greenery and freshens, the land, it seems to be laughing wholeheartedly. In other words, when the rain falls on the Earth, it spreads joy as it is a blessing particularly for the farmers in the field. So, the laughter refers to the happiness due to rain. The raindrops fall from the sky as tears fall from the eyes. Thus, the poet calls rain as the tears of heaven.

Stanza 9 (Lines 30-32)

So with love–
Sighs from the deep sea of affection; Laughter
from the colourful
field of the spirit; Tears from the endless heaven
of memories.

Explanation The rain spreads laughter through the colourful fields. The crops, which are the spirit of the field, flourish with rain. Therefore, the fields appear to the poet as if they are laughing. The raindrops fall like tears from the heaven to Earth and give new life to it. The rain connects the link between Earth and heaven.

Thus, in the end, rain wishes the inhabitants of the world a lot of love, laughter and delightful recollections from the storehouse of sweet memories.

Poetic Devices Used in the Poem

Alliteration

- pearls, plucked
- daughter of Dawn
- messenger of mercy
- under the upraised
- sigh of the sea

Allusion

- (reference to another work of art)
- I am beautiful pearls, plucked from the Crown of Ishtar...

Hyperbolic expression

- Embrace the flowers and the trees in a million little ways

Imagery

- sigh of the sea
- laughter of the field
- tears of heaven

Metaphor

- I am dotted silver threads
- I am beautiful pearls

Personification

(some examples are given; there are many others)

- When I cry, the hills laugh;
- When I humble myself the flowers rejoice;
- When I bow, all things are elated.
- Lines 10 to 29 contain many other examples of personification

Simile

- I am like earthly life

Word Meaning

Word	Meaning
Stanza 1	
dotted silver threads	threads looking like silver connecting heaven and earth
adorn	decorate or add beauty to
Stanza 2	
Ishtar	Goddess of fertility, love and war in Babylon
daughter of Dawn	starting early in the morning
embellish	decorate
Stanza 3	
cry	pour heavily
humble myself	fall in moderate quantity
bow	fall as a drizzle
elated	very happy and excited
Stanza 4	
quench	satisfy thirst
cure the ailment	relieve the burden
Stanza 5	
at the feet of the mad elements	from the elements
upraised	lifted or raised upwards
Stanza 6	
heart	depths
embrace	cover
Stanza 7	
welcome song	the rain feels welcomed
Stanza 8	
sigh	sound expressing relief
Stanza 9	
colourful field of the spirit	crops growing in the field

Textbook FOLDER

Here, we have covered questions given in the CBSE Textbook along with their answer

ON PAGE 96

Q.4A On the basis of your understanding of the poem, answer the following questions by ticking the correct choice.

(i) The rain calls itself the 'dotted silver threads' as ....

(a) the shimmering drops fall one after the other
(b) it ties heaven and Earth
(c) it dots the Earth with shimmering water
(d) it decorates the fields

Ans. (a) the shimmering drops fall one after the other

(ii) The tone and mood of the rain in the poem reflect its ....

(a) love for the Earth
(b) desire to take revenge
(c) merriment as it destroys
(d) desire to look beautiful

Ans. (a) love for the Earth

(iii) Choose the option that lists the examples of 'elated'.

1. Asmi is convalescing from her ailment.
2. Gurdeep and Sanvi met each other after a decade.
3. Damehi heard the news that he had been nominated for an award.
4. Sohrab has witnessed a burglar in the dark.

(a) 1, 3 (b) 2, 3
(c) 3, 4 (d) 1, 4

Ans. (b) 2, 3

(iv) Antithesis is a figure of speech which brings out a contrast in the ideas by placing opposing words, clauses or sentences within a parallel grammatical structure.

For example

- **"To err is human; to forgive divine." – Alexander Pope**
- **Hope for the best; prepare for the worst.**
- **Keep your friends close; keep your enemies closer.**

From the following phrases in the poem, select the option that correctly lists the examples of Antithesis.

1. When I cry the hills laugh; When I humble myself the flowers rejoice;
2. And between them I am a messenger of mercy.
3. When I bow, all things are elated.
4. The voice of thunder declares my arrival; The rainbow announces my departure.
5. I am dotted silver threads dropped from heaven
6. I touch gently at the windows with my Soft fingers

(a) 1, 3, 4, 6 (b) 1, 3, 4
(c) 1, 3, 4, 5 (d) 1, 3, 5

Ans. (b) 1, 3, 4

ON PAGE 97-99

Q.4B Read the given extracts and answer the following questions by selecting the correct option.

(a) I am dotted silver threads dropped from heaven
By the gods. Nature then takes me, to adorn
Her fields and valleys.
I am beautiful pearls, plucked from the
Crown of Ishtar by the daughter of Dawn
To embellish the gardens.

(i) Select the option that DOES NOT include a visual connected to the given lines.

(i)

(ii)

(iii) 

(iv) 

(a) Option (i) (b) Option (ii)
(c) Option (iii) (d) Option (iv)

Ans. (c) Option (iii)

(ii) Read the definitions given below

Allusion Reference to a famous person, place, or historical event, either directly or through implication.

Alliteration Repetition of same consonant sound at the initial position in two or more neighbouring words.

Select the option that correctly includes examples of i) allusion and ii) alliteration from the extract.

(a) (i) Ishtar (ii) daughter of Dawn
(b) (i) Dawn (ii) dotted silver threads
(c) (i) Nature (ii) pearls, plucked from the Crown

Ans. (a) (i) Ishtar (ii) daughter of Dawn

(iii) Choose the option containing a statement that is NOT conveyed through the extract.

(a) The rain calls itself the shimmering drops sent by gods.
(b) The rain is the daughter of Dawn born to decorate the gardens.
(c) Nature has adopted rain to decorate her fields and valleys.
(d) The rain is beautiful pearls plucked from the crown of the goddess of fertility.

Ans. (b) The rain is the daughter of Dawn born to decorate the gardens.

(iv) Ishtar is a Mesopotamian goddess and signifies diverse things in different cultures.

Select which symbol of Ishtar is relevant in the extract with the most appropriate reason.

(a) The poet utilised the symbol of 'Love' to represent Ishtar because the rain brings love and peace to the world.
(b) Ishtar signifies 'War' as her power arises from her connection with storms.
(c) Ishtar here represents 'Fertility' because she is responsible for all life and so is the relevance to the rain.
(d) The poet meant to associate the symbol of 'Beauty' to Ishtar as the rain makes the world beautiful.

Ans. (d) The poet meant to associate the symbol of 'Beauty' to Ishtar as the rain makes the world beautiful.

(b) The voice of thunder declares my arrival;
The rainbow announces my departure.
I am like earthly life, which begins at
The feet of the mad elements and ends
Under the upraised wings of death.

(i) The rain says, 'I am like earthly life'. Select the option with the most suitable explanation of the expression.

(a) The rain undergoes the same phases as that of earthly beings.
(b) Most of the rain's life is on the Earth.
(c) The fate of earthly life is dependent on the rain.
(d) Rain has a concern for earthly life.

Ans. (a) The rain undergoes the same phases as that of earthly beings.

(ii) The tone and mood of the rain in the extract reflects ....

(a) its merriment as it destroys
(b) rain's desire to reach its destiny
(c) its objective and realistic manner
(d) the rain's pride at its might

Ans. (b) rain's desire to reach its destiny

(iii) Read statements 1 and 2 given below and choose the option that correctly assesses these statements.

1. Rainbow declares the rain's parting.

2. Rainbow causes the end of the rain.

(a) Both statements 1 and 2 are false.
(b) Statement 1 is true but 2 is false.
(c) Statement 1 is the reason for statement 2.
(d) Statement 2 is the cause of statement 1.

Ans. (c) Statement 1 is the reason for statement 2.

ON PAGE 99

Q.5A Answer the following questions.

(a) Why is the rain divine?

Ans. The rain appears to be divine because it comes down from heaven. The shimmering drops of rain look like silver threads dropped from heaven by God. Moreover, it is a life-giving force that elates all flowers, fields and valleys.

(b) In this universe, rain performs many functions. What are those?

Ans. Rain adorns the fields and valleys. It makes hills laugh and embraces the flowers and trees. It quenches the thirst of Earth and makes the land fertile. It relieves the clouds overloaded with water vapour. It produces sweet music as it beats against windows and the leaves of trees. It provides joy to everybody and everything in nature.

(c) *"When I cry the hills laugh;*
When I humble myself the flowers rejoice;
When I bow, all things are elated."

***Cry, humble* and *bow* indicate different intensities with which the rain falls. Explain the three in context.**

Ans. The rain falls with different intensities and these are suggestive of its varying moods. Its cry indicates heavy rainfall which makes the hills green. When the rain is humble, it falls down moderately making flowers rejoice. And when the rain bows, it drizzles and makes everyone happy.

(d) The poem invokes beautiful imagery built around 'sigh of the sea', 'laughter of the field' and 'tears of heaven'. Explain the three expressions in the context of rain.

Ans. The poet has used vivid imagery throughout the poem to express the moods and nature of the rain. When the poet calls the rain 'sigh of the sea', there is a sigh of relief expressed in the lines. The sea is relieved that some water has evaporated from it. Then, the poet calls the rain 'laughter of the field' because when it rains, the fields are nourished and it is a sign that there will be fertility. It brings greenery and prosperity, and raises productivity. So, the fields are happy and they laugh. The rain is also called 'tears of heaven' as when those silver threads pour down from the sky, it feels as if the heaven is crying, and those drops are delivered to the nature on Earth by God.

(e) Define the role of the rain as the "Messenger of Mercy".

Ans. The rain, as a 'messenger of mercy', connects the fields with the clouds high in the sky. It mercifully establishes a link between the two. It fills the void between the sky and the Earth.

(f) Contrast the arrival of the rain with that of its departure.

Ans. The deafening voice of thunder announces the arrival of rains on Earth. However, the rain departs from Earth quietly. The rainbow sprinkling a handful of seven different colours across the blue surface of the sky after clouds disappear declares the departure of rain from Earth.

ON PAGE 100

Q.5B Answer in detail

(a) Shakespeare's 'Seven Ages' designates different stages of human life. Draw a parallel between the two poems to elicit the different stages of rain's life.

Ans. Shakespeare's poem 'Seven Ages' describes seven stages of life infant, school boy, lover, soldier, justice, pantaloon and old age. Similarly, in the poem 'Song of the Rain' the poet Kahlil Gibran has referred to various stages of a rain's life. The life cycle of the rain has been compared to humans: birth (evaporation), maturity (condensation) and death (rainfall). The rain talks about its origination in the form of vapour from the depths of the sea and lifted to the sky by the breeze. The water vapour then collects in the form of rain droplets. It, then, falls on the Earth in different phases- heavily, moderately and lightly. Later, it departs as the rain falls and the rainbow is formed.

(b) Imagery evokes a mental image or other kinds of sensual impressions in literary writings.

"I am beautiful pearls...", "dotted silver threads", "laughter of the field" , etc.

Now, observe auditory images created by the words "sighs", "thunders", "laughter", etc.

Critically appreciate the poem, explaining the effect these techniques create in the mind of the reader.

Ans. The poem 'Song of the Rain' is rich in visual and audio imagery that creates a beautiful image in the minds of the reader. The usage of words like I am beautiful pearls...', 'dotted silver threads', 'laughter of the field' , etc. increases the beauty of the poem.

Even the auditory images created by the words 'sighs', 'thunders', 'laughter', etc helps create the rhythm in the poem.

(c) "When I see a field in need, I descend and embrace the flowers and the trees in a million little ways".

Write an imaginary conversation between a flower, a tree and the field, discussing the role of rain in their lives.

You may begin like this:

Tree: My life began as a seed. I came to life only after the rain drops embraced me.

Field: My survival, thereby the survival of all mankind depends on me. And only rains can help me thrive...

Flower: ....

Ans. Tree My life began as a seed. I came to life only after the rain drops embraced me.

Field My survival, thereby the survival of all mankind, depends on me. And only rains can help me thrive.

Flower I was merely a bud, very small and delicate, until the rain fell and helped me blossom into a beautiful flower that is joyful to watch. How does the rain help you, Field, to ensure the survival of all mankind?

Field I am infertile and too poor to produce anything until the rain water helps me rejuvenate. It gives life to all the seeds sown in me and helps them thrive. Humans won't have many things to eat if the rain didn't help crops, fruits and vegetables to grow. Am I right, Tree ?

Tree Yes, you are completely right. Had it not been for the rain, I would not have been able to grow as big as I am, providing shelter from the Sun, fresh air and food products for humans to eat. It would all be impossible. Life on earth would soon come to an end if the rain stops its cycle.

Flower I wish that day never comes, Tree. None of us would survive without rain. My petals would dry and I would eventually fall off from the plant. No one would be able to take joy in my beauty and soon all life on Earth would perish.

REVIEW EXERCISE

Including Exam Pattern Practice Questions

Extract Based Questions

Read the following extracts carefully and answer the questions that follow.

1. I am dotted silver threads dropped from heaven
By the gods. Nature then takes me, to adorn
Her fields and valleys.

(a) Who is 'I'? Why is 'I' being compared to silver threads?

Ans. 'I' refers to the rain. It is being compared to silver threads as it looks silvery in colour and connects heaven and Earth like a thread when it falls from the clouds.

(b) Why does the rain call itself dotted silver threads?

Ans. When raindrops fall apart from one another, in a line of succession, brightened by the sunlight, they appear like dotted silver threads.

(c) For what does nature take the rain once it falls from heaven?

Ans. Once rain falls, nature beautifies its fields and valleys.

(d) Which word in the extract is a synonym of 'beautify'?

Ans. The word 'adorn' is a synonym of beautify.

2. I am beautiful pearls, plucked from the
Crown of Ishtar by the daughter of Dawn
To embellish the gardens.

(a) Who plucks the pearly rain from the crown of Ishtar?

Ans. The daughter of Dawn plucks the pearly rain from the crown of Ishtar.

(b) What is the significance of Ishtar in the poem?

Ans. Ishtar is the Goddess of fertility. Ishtar is significant in the poem because rain helps the nature by adding to its fertility.

(c) 'The word 'embellish' in the extract means ....

Ans. 'decorate'

(d) What is being compared to beautiful pearls?

Ans. The drops of rain are being compared to pearls.

3. When I cry the hills laugh;
When I humble myself the flowers rejoice;
When I bow, all things are elated.

(a) When do flowers make merry?

Ans. The flowers make merry when the rain comes gently in the form of a drizzle.

(b) What is the connection between 'I' crying and the hills laughing?

Ans. When 'I' cries i.e., when rain falls in heavy showers, it is very noisy. When its sound echoes in the hills they seem to be laughing. Moreover, the hills feel very happy and 'laugh' because their greenery is restored.

(c) Explain the line 'When I bow, all things are elated'.

Ans. The phrase means that when rain falls in all its humility and grace, meaning lightly, all hearts are gladdened. There is an atmosphere of joy and happiness all over.

(d) Which word in the extract is a synonym of 'happy'?

Ans. The word 'elated' is a synonym of 'happy'.

4. The field and the cloud are lovers
And between them I am a messenger of mercy.
I quench the thirst of the one;
I cure the ailment of the other.

(a) Explain "I quench the thirst of the one; I cure the ailment of the other".

Ans. The two lovers, the fields and the cloud, need the rain. The field is thirsty for the cloud's mercy while the cloud suffers because it is overburdened with water vapour. When rain pours down, both the lovers are satisfied.

(b) How is the rain a messenger of mercy?

Ans. Rain is a messenger of mercy between the field and the cloud as it reduces the cloud's load of water (its ailment) while watering the field (satisfying its thirst), thus showering mercy on both.

(c) What do you mean by the word 'quench' as used in the extract?

Ans. 'Quench' means to satisfy thirst.

(d) What is the rhyme scheme of the given lines?

Ans. The given lines do not have a rhyme scheme.

5. The voice of thunder declares my arrival;
The rainbow announces my departure.
I am like earthly life, which begins at
The feet of the mad elements and ends
Under the upraised wings of death.

(a) How is rain similar to earthly life?

Ans. The rain is short-lived, as is man's life on Earth. It comes and goes just as man is born and dies. Thus, both rain and earthly life are similar.

(b) State the contrast present in the given lines.

Ans. A contrast has been presented in the given lines in the way rain comes and goes away. Rain comes with a lot of noise and thunder but goes away calmly.

(c) What are the upraised wings of death for rain?

Ans. The upraised wings under which rain dies are the wings of the wind that blows the clouds away.

(d) What is the opposite of 'earthly'?

Ans. 'Heavenly' is opposite to 'earthly'.

6. I emerge from the heart of the sea and
Soar with the breeze. When I see a field in
Need, I descend and embrace the flowers and
The trees in a million little ways.

(a) What does rain mean by its million ways of embracing flowers?

Ans. Rain falls down in various ways. All the million drops that fall down are different in size, speed and many other qualities. They reach the Earth at various times, creating various sounds.

(b) What is a field in need?

Ans. A field in need is a dry, dehydrated summer field that awaits rain.

(c) Which word in the extract means the same as 'envelop'?

Ans. The word 'embrace' means the same as 'envelope'.

(d) What is the opposite of 'descend'?

Ans. The opposite of 'descend' is 'ascend'.

7. I touch gently at the windows with my
Soft fingers, and my announcement is a
Welcome song. All can hear, but only
The sensitive can understand.

(a) How is I's arrival taken by everyone?

Ans. I's arrival brings joy to every heart. Hence, it is welcomed by one and all.

(b) What do you mean by the word 'sensitive' here?

Ans. Sensitive here refers to those who have an understanding mind.

(c) Pick out an instance of personification from the stanza.

Ans. The word 'touch' in line 1 is personification. The rain says that it touches the windows just like a person.

(d) Why can only 'the sensitive' people understand the rain?

Ans. 'The sensitive' people are those with aesthetic sensibilities; thus they can understand the rain and appreciate it.

8. I am the sigh of the sea;
The laughter of the field;
The tears of heaven.
So, with love-
Sighs from the deep sea affection; Laughter from the colourful
field of spirit; Tears from
the endless heaven of memories.

(a) How is rain the sigh of the sea?

Ans. The rain is the sigh of the sea because the sea heaves a sigh of pain at the evaporation of water vapour but at the same time, it gives another sigh of relief with the thought that it would return in the form of rain.

(b) How is rain the laughter of the fields?

Ans. Rain is the laughter of the fields because its arrival gives the fields new life and joy.

(c) Which word in the extract means the same as 'unending'?

Ans. The word 'endless' means the same as unyielding.

(d) Which word in the passage means the same as 'fondness'?

Ans. The word 'affection' means the same as 'fondness'.

Short Answer Type Questions

Answer the following questions in 30-40 words.

1. Why is the rain sent to Earth from heaven?

Ans. The rain is sent to Earth from heaven to decorate the fields, valleys and gardens. It embraces the flowers and trees in a million little ways.

It acts as a messenger of mercy between the two lovers, the field and the cloud.

2. Explain the lines 'I am dotted silver threads dropped from heaven' and 'I am beautiful pearls, plucked from the crown of Ishtar'.

Ans. The rain is divine. When it falls from the sky, it appears to be like silver threads. It calls itself silver threads as it connects heaven and Earth. The poet has compared raindrops to the pearls in the crown of the Babylonian mother Goddess Ishtar. The raindrops falling makes the poet feel as if nature has plucked pearls from the crown to decorate the Earth.

3. What are the different intensities with which the rain falls and what do all indicate?

Or **When I cry the hills laugh;**

Where I humble myself the flowers rejoice;

When I bow, all things are elated.

Cry, humble and bow indicate different intensities with which the rain falls. Explain the three in context. **Competency Based**

Ans. The rain falls with different intensities and these are suggestive of its varying moods. A cry indicates heavy rainfall which makes the hills green. When the rain is humble, it falls down moderately making flowers rejoice. And when the rain bows, it drizzles and makes everyone happy.

4. Explain how rain is a messenger of mercy between the two lovers.

Or **The field and the cloud are lovers. How does the rain act as a messenger of mercy for them?**

Ans. The field and the cloud are lovers and between them the rain is a messenger of mercy. The rain quenches the thirst of one and cures the ailment of the other. As the Earth is dry, it needs water. Therefore, when the clouds burst into rainfall not only does it quench the Earth's thirst but it also relieves itself of the burden.

5. Explain the line ' The voice of thunder declares my arrival; The rainbow announces my departure'.

Or **How does thunder declare the arrival of the rain?**

Ans. The poet wants to say here that the deafening sound of thunder announces the arrival of rains on Earth. Similarly, when the rain ends, a rainbow appears, sprinkling seven different colours across the sky. The clouds then disappear, signalling the departure of rain from Earth.

6. The rain is content in satisfying others. Do you agree? Give two reasons.

Ans. The rain is content in satisfying others because

(i) it quenches the thirst of the field and cures the sickness of the cloud and

(ii) it makes the flowers, trees and hills happy in countless ways.

7. What is the cyclic movement of rain that is brought out in the poem?

Ans. Rain rises from the sea and is carried to the sky by the wind. It forms clouds and when clouds become heavy with water, rain falls to the Earth and in the sea. This cycle repeats, which brings out the cyclic movement of rain.

8. How do you think the song of the rain is the song of the soul?

Ans. The song of the rain is the song of the soul as it portrays the rain as divine. It is shown as a messenger of mercy between two lovers – the field and the cloud. The rain is called divine as it gives life to all the objects of nature.

Long Answer Type Questions

Answer the following questions in 120 words.

1. What key message is the poet trying to give through his poem 'Song of the Rain'?

Ans. The poet conveys a key message through the poem 'song of the Rain'. It states that rainfall should not be taken as just a common- place phenomenon of nature. Its occurrence is a wonder of nature and a boon to the Earth and mankind. It deserves to be admired and appreciated as something divine. However, to sense its divinity one needs to have refined sensibilities. One should thus recognise its significance and understand how important it is for Earth.

The poet through the poem also reveals how nature makes rain an instrument to enhance its beauty and to decorate it. The rain, in other words, rejuvenates Earth and fills joy in every being.

2. The poem 'Song of the Rain' begins on a single autobiographical descriptive note but ends on a philosophical note. Do you agree with this description or not? Give a reason in support of your answer. **Competency Based**

Ans. I agree with this description that the poem begins on a autobiographical note but ends on a philosophical one. The poem traces the journey of rain. It starts with its celebration and then, continues with its various benefits and functions like decorating the fields, gardens and valleys, satisfying the thirst of the Earth, becoming a messenger of mercy between the cloud and the field and so on. Then, the poem shifts into a philosophical mode when the poet says that rain makes the spirit of man rejoice and laugh. It finally bids farewell to all when it departs with love.

3. In 'Song of the Rain', the poet Kahlil Gibran celebrates rain as the life-giving force of the Earth. If you were the field that benefited from the rain, write a diary entry of your appreciation of the rain.

Ans. Wednesday, 10th July, 20XX 10:00 p.m.

Dear Diary

What a blessing the rain was today! It fell softly at first, as if it was tickling me, nudging me to wake up from deep sleep. Soon, the intensity increased and brought freshness and energy in my soil. I have lost the parched look now and look green and fertile. It has been really a gift from heaven! It beautifies everything that it falls on! It is a life-giving force which makes crops planted in me grow and the flowers bloom.

May the rain continue to spread happiness and cheerfulness!

Field

4. 'Song of the Rain' is an autobiographical poem. The narrator of the poem is the rain itself. It is very much upset to see that man has disturbed nature with his thoughtless actions like industrialisation and deforestation. He has disturbed the whole pattern of rainfall. Describe in your own words how man is disturbing the ecological balance. **Competency Based**

Ans. 'Song of the Rain' highlights the divine nature of rain, which enhances the beauty of the biosphere. It decorates and cools the plants and trees. It also restores the greenery and refreshes the vegetation. But man in his greed has disturbed the whole cycle of rain. He is cutting down trees. He has stripped the green cover of the hills and mountains. The underground water table is reducing. Summers are getting hotter and longer than ever before. Natural disasters like earthquakes, famines, droughts, floods and cyclones are occurring frequently. Global warming is increasing due to pollution and deforestation. In this way man has disturbed the ecological balance.

ASSESSMENT EXERCISE

Extract Based Questions

Read the following extracts carefully and answer the questions that follow.

1. I am the sigh of the sea;
The laughter of the field;
The tears of heaven.

(a) Who is 'I' in the above lines and why does it call itself 'the sigh of the sea'?

(b) Why does the field laugh?

(c) The word 'sigh' as used in the extract means ....

(d) Explain the first line.

2. I am dotted silver threads dropped from heaven
By the gods. Nature then takes me, to adorn
Her fields and valleys.

(a) The poetic device used in these lines is ....

(b) 'To adorn' means ....

(c) Song of the rain is a / an .... poem.

(d) Who does 'I' refer to in these lines?

Short Answer Type Questions

Answer the following questions in 30-40 words.

1. Why does the 'daughter of Dawn' pluck 'pearls' from 'Ishtar's crown'?

2. Who is Ishtar? In what context has this name been used here?

3. Why have the field and the cloud been called lovers?

4. "Earthly life which begins at the feet of the mad elements". What are these mad elements? How does earthly life begin at their feet?

5. Who all benefit from the rain falling?

6. What message does 'Song of the Rain' convey?

7. The rain is conscious of its beauty. Comment.

8. Why has this poem been called a song?

Long Answer Type Questions

Answer the following questions in 120 words.

1. Life, love and blessings are the virtues in rain that make it so desirable and lovable. How do these values bring joy in one's life?

2. Many efforts have been made by man to bring about artificial rain. Do you think human interference in the phenomena of nature is justifiable? Give reasons to support your views.

CHAPTER 1

Villa For Sale

by Sacha Guitry

About the DRAMA Villa for Sale is an interesting one-act play written by Sacha Guitry. The play is set in France. The action revolves around the sale of a villa. Juliette, the owner, wishes to sell her villa but is really disappointed as no likely buyers walked that way. When she is ultimately able to dispose of the villa, it turns out that the customer has actually duped her by selling it at a much higher price even before he actually purchased it from her. The play is not only a source of amusement, but also a beautiful literary work. It brings out the conflict between social classes and cultures, and also the cunningness of some people who thrive on cheating and dishonesty which they call shrewd business sense.

Important Characters

- **Juliette** The main character of the drama, Juliette is a proud lady and the owner of the villa. She is very impatient though she is polite and well-behaved. She is quite money minded and uses all her business tactics to sell the villa at the highest price possible. She is not shrewd enough to see through Gaston's change of mind and is easily duped by him.
- **Gaston** Gaston is a true opportunist. He is quite cunning and impolite. He is always observed as making critical or insulting remarks at others. He also seems more of a male chauvinist and is sarcastic towards his wife and her family. Gaston is quite calculative as a businessman and manages to sell the villa while Juliette, its real owner, is not around.
- **Jeanne** Jeanne is Gaston's wife. She is a simple lady, who is quite sensible and understanding. She loves her parents and is very keen to buy a villa for them. She is rather childlike and is easily duped by Gaston.
- **Mrs. Al Smith** Mrs. Al Smith is an American filmmaker and a prospective buyer of the villa. She is very proud and thinks highly of herself. She keeps on ridiculing the French. She is not good at business and lacks the sense of getting the full worth of her money. She is also a poor judge of people's character.
- **Maid** She is Juliette's domestic help. She is quite clever and knows how to make money. She sympathises with Juliette, who is going through hard times and suggests that she could also take up acting like herself if she was in urgent need of money.

Summary of the Drama

The Opening Scene — Villa for Sale

The play opens in a salon (a room for receiving guests) of a small villa located near Nogent Sur-Marne.

Juliette, (the owner of the villa) has put up her villa for sale due to financial crisis. She does not want to part with her villa as she is very fond of it but she has no option except selling it. She has been trying to sell it off for over a month but in vain. Some customers see the villa but do not show any interest in buying it. She has grown tired of their attitude and her crisis has filled her with so much disgust about the place that she is prepared to get rid of it even at a low price.

Villa's Proximity to Joinville — The French Hollywood

The villa is quite close to Joinville. So, quite a number of people in the locality are taking up acting in movies.

Juliette's maid requests her to give her a day off as she too has been offered the role of a maid in a movie and has to go for the shoot. Moreover, she'll be paid a hundred francs for just a few hours of work. The maid also suggests Juliette to try for a role in the cinema to handle her financial crisis. The role is of a cook and Juliette would have to do nothing but peel potatoes or make an Omelette. However, Juliette refuses the offer.

A French Couple Comes to See the Villa

Juliette receives a call from the agency saying that a lady will come to buy the villa. A French couple Gaston and Jeanne are passing by and after seeing the signboard that the villa was meant for sale, they come in to take a look at it. Juliette thinks that they are the buyers sent by the agency. She is reluctant to display her curiosity about the buyers, so she goes upstairs, making the visitors feel that she is quite busy. While waiting for the owner of the villa, the couple gets busy in a heated discussion regarding the purchase of the villa.

Gaston and Jeanne's Disagreement

Gaston shows disinterest in buying the villa. While Jeanne expresses her desire to buy it, as her parents and her sister's children are planning to come to spend the period between April to September with them. Gaston is very clever and he doesn't show much interest in making any investment for his wife's family. According to Gaston, it is a costly affair and he is doubtful about buying the villa. He criticises the defects of the villa without a break. He accuses Jeanne of taking him on such villa inspections when he has never said that he wanted to buy one. After a rather furious argument between the couple, both decide not to buy the villa and are about to leave when Juliette enters.

Juliette Praises her Villa

Juliette enters and narrates a complete description of her villa. She expresses her pride in the villa and even calls it 'a most delightful place.' She is a clever business women who flatters the young couple, calls them 'exceptional' and says that the villa perfectly suited their personality. The place is so dear to her that she wouldn't sell it to some ordinary customer but they have something special about them.

Juliette and Gaston Clash

Gaston keeps on making small insulting remarks between the talks. He also keeps on asking the price of the villa. Juliette quotes the price as two hundred and fifty thousand francs with the exception of a painting signed by Carot. Gaston says that the price is too high to accept and he gives the price of a mere sixty thousand francs.

After much bargaining, Juliette quotes the final price of two hundred thousand francs. Gaston doesn't agree and is about to leave when Jeanne expresses a desire to have a look around the villa. She wishes to see the upper floor, though Gaston doesn't join her. Both Jeanne and Juliette go upstairs.

Mrs. Al Smith Arrives as Another Customer

While Gaston is waiting for his wife to return, the maid ushers in the lady who is the customer the agency has actually spoken of. She is Mrs. Al Smith, an American film star, who is interested in purchasing the villa, as it is near the French Hollywood, Joinville. She is in a hurry and asks the maid about the price of the villa. The maid replies that she has no idea about it.

Americans vs. The French

Mrs. Al Smith doesn't seem to have a very high opinion about the French. She remarks that any delay makes her sick when she wants something.

Mrs. Al Smith mistakes Gaston to be Juliette's husband and the real owner of the villa. Gaston tries to explain the situation but the lady gets so impatient that she is ready to write a cheque without even bothering to inspect the villa at all. She informs him that she plans to replace the villa with a bungalow.

In the meantime, she keeps on criticising the French who, according to her, lack business sense and are always busy thinking about their past. On the other hand, the Americans are always planning about the future.

The Trickery of Gaston

Gaston, an opportunist, soon realises that Mrs. Al Smith is in a hurry to make the purchase and leave. He doesn't try to reveal his true identity. Thereafter, he sells her the villa for three hundred thousand francs and Mrs. Smith, as she is, takes the deal willingly. She hands over the cheque of the decided amount, saying that her lawyer will complete all the formalities. She further asks them to vacate the villa by the next morning. Gaston promises to vacate the villa by the next evening.

Villa Resold at a Handsome Profit

Jeanne returns with Juliette after inspecting the top floor. She has dropped the idea of buying the villa as she is not much impressed with it because it is not very big. However, to the amazement of the ladies, Gaston is now full of appreciation for the villa and expresses his desire to buy the villa for two hundred thousand francs.

Juliette says that there are many things to be discussed, but Gaston interrupts her and says that he wants the painting as a souvenir; Juliette agrees. Despite Jeanne's protests, he buys the villa for two hundred thousand francs and asks Juliette to vacate it before the evening of the next day. When he writes the check, he puts down twenty third as the date of sale. In truth, the date was twenty fourth. The reason for Gaston's sudden interest in buying the villa remains a mystery to Jeanne. Juliette is still unaware that Gaston had already 'sold' the villa to Mrs. Al Smith and has made a profit of a hundred thousand francs. Gaston's inventiveness is later discovered by Jeanne.

Word Meaning

Word	Meaning
discovered	seen on the stage as the curtain is raised
mind you	a phrase introducing something that should be taken into consideration
sell	a disappointment, especially one arising from being deceived with regard to the merits of something
wretched	very bad or unpleasant
paltry	a very small or meagre amount
engagement	appointment
hard up	short of money
looked up to	have a great deal of respect for
slicked	made flat, smooth and glossy by applying water, oil or gel to it
Greta Garbo	a Swedish film actress during Hollywood's silent and classic periods
cretonne	a heavy printed cotton fabric, used for upholstery
annexe	attachment
aggravating	annoying
tribe	family group
made a fortune	acquired great wealth by one's own efforts
pastel	a painting made with pastels which are crayons made of powdered pigments
exceptional	uncommon, extraordinary

Word	Meaning
assurance	satisfaction
furnished	containing furniture or containing furniture of a particular type
fixtures	attachments; here, furniture
decidedly	undoubtedly, certainly
excessive	more than normal or desirable
awkward	embarrassing
philanthropic	a person seeking to promote the welfare of others; generous and benevolent
shanty	a small crudely built hut
betcha	bet you (American slang used to express confidence that something will happen)
exception	different from the standard or rule
imitations	things intended to copy something else
parodies	imitations of the style of a particular writer or artist, with deliberate exaggeration for comic effect
architect	a person who design buildings or supervises their construction
driving at	what someone is really trying to say
unhooks	takes away from the hook
souvenir	a memento or token of remembrance which we keep as a memory of a person or place

Textbook FOLDER

Here, we have covered questions given in the CBSE Textbook along with their answers.

ON PAGE 115

Q.4 Complete the following paragraph about the theme of the play using the clues given in the box below. Remember that there are more clues than required.

sell, buying, house, enthusiastic, comes, 200 thousand francs, taking, favour, get, sleeps, money, 200 thousand francs, unhappy, in-laws, walks in, strikes, keep

Juliette, the owner of a villa wants to (a) .... it as she is in need of (b) .... Moreover, she is not in (c) .... of the house. Jeanne and Gaston, a couple visit her with the aim of (d) .... the Villa. While Jeanne is (e) .... about buying, Gaston detests the idea as he does not want his (f) .... in that house. Also, he finds the asking price of (g) .... to be expensive. When Jeanne and Juliette go around the house, another customer (h) .... and starts talking to Gaston (i) .... him to be Juliette's husband. Gaston (j) .... a deal with the customer by which he is able to give (k) .... to the owner and (l) .... one hundred thousand francs for himself.

Ans. (a) sell (b) money
(c) favour (d) buying
(e) enthusiastic (f) in-laws
(g) 200 thousand francs (h) walks in
(i) taking (j) strikes
(k) 200 thousand francs (l) keep

ON PAGE 115-116

Q.5 Read the following extracts and answer the questions that follow by choosing the correct options.

A. But the sign has been hanging on the gate for over a month now and I am beginning to be afraid that the day I bought it was when I was the real fool.

(i) Why is Juliette disappointed?

(a) She is unable to get the role of a cook in the films.
(b) Her maid is leaving as she has got a role in the films.
(c) She is unable to find a suitable buyer for her villa.
(d) Gaston is offering a very low price for the villa.

Ans. (c) She is unable to find a suitable buyer for her villa.

(ii) Why does she call herself a fool?

(a) She has decided to sell her villa.
(b) There are no buyers for the villa.
(c) She had bought the villa for more than it was worth.
(d) The villa was too close to the film studios.

Ans. (c) She had bought the villa for more than it was worth.

B. 'But your parents would take possession of it, every year from the beginning of spring until the end of September. What's more they would bring the whole tribe of your sister's children with them.'

(a) What does Gaston mean by 'take possession'?

(a) Her parents would stay with them for a long time.
(b) Juliette's sister has many children.
(c) Gaston does not like children.
(d) Juliette's sister's children are badly behaved.

Ans. (a) Her parents would stay with them for a long time.

C. 'While you were upstairs, I have been thinking a lot about your Papa and Mamma.

(i) What is the discrepancy between what Gaston said earlier and what he says now?

(a) Earlier he did not want Jeanne's parents to stay with them but now he is showing concern for them.
(b) Earlier he wanted Jeanne's parents to stay with them but now he does not want them to come over.
(c) Earlier he wanted to buy a house for them but now he wants them to come and stay in their villa.
(d) Earlier he stayed in Jeanne's parents' villa but now he wants them to stay with him and Juliette.

Ans. (a) Earlier he did not want Jeanne's parents to stay with them but now he is showing concern for them.

(b) What does the above statement reveal about Gaston's character?

(a) He is selfish. (b) He is an opportunist.
(c) He is a caring person. (d) He is a hypocrite.

Ans. (b) He is an opportunist.

ON PAGE 117

Q.6A Answer the following questions briefly.

(a) Why does Jeanne want to buy a villa?

Or Why was Jeanne interested in buying the villa?

Or Why was Jeanne so desperate to buy a villa in the play 'Villa for Sale'?

Ans. Jeanne wants to buy the villa for her parents and her sister's children who would spend time there from the month of April to September.

(b) Why is Gaston not interested in buying the villa in the beginning?

Or Why was Gaston not interested in buying the villa?

Ans. Gaston knows that Jeanne doesn't want to buy the villa for them. Instead, she wants to buy the villa for her parents. Gaston thinks that Jeanne's parents along with her sister's children would occupy it for most of the year. Hence, he was opposed to the idea of buying the villa. Moreover, he found the deal quite expensive.

(c) Mrs. Al Smith makes many statements about the French. Pick out any two and explain them.

Or How does Mrs. Al Smith comment on the French people?

Ans. Mrs. Al Smith makes the following statements about the French people.

1. "Frenchmen usually have to consult about ten people before they get a move on."
2. "You folk are queer. You think about the past all the time."

According to Mrs. Al Smith, French people lacked business sense. She insulted them for not possessing any decision-making power and having to consult over ten people before deciding on something. She also criticised them for always thinking about the past instead of focusing on the future.

(d) Juliette says "..... now I have only one thought that is to get the wretched place off my hands. I would sacrifice it at any price". Does she stick to her words? Why / Why not?

Ans. Juliette was quite frustrated at not being able to sell her villa. She needed the money desperately. As far as the sale of the villa at any price is concerned, Juliette fails to keep her word at the time of actual sale. She uses all sorts of tactics to convince Gaston and his wife to buy the villa at the price quoted by her.

(e) Who is better in business- Juliette or Gaston? Why?

Ans. Gaston appears to be better at business. Gaston is an opportunist who doesn't spend even a single penny and yet makes a profit of a hundred thousand francs. Juliette is also a good business woman as she tries every tactic to sell the villa.

(f) The ending of the play was a win-win situation approach for Gaston, Juliette and Mrs. Al Smith. Explain.

Ans. The play ends with a win-win situation approach for Gaston, Juliette and Mrs. Al Smith. Gaston not only acts as an opportunist in front of Mrs. Al Smith and pretends to be owner of the villa, but also manipulates to write the date of selling the villa to him at two hundred thousand francs a day before, i.e. 23rd while it was the 24th of the month.
So, Mrs. Al Smith has the villa to start her work, Gaston earns a hundred thousand francs and Juliette is finally able to sell her villa at the desired cost. However, Gaston is above her as he is cunning, smart and much more calculative.

Q.6B Answer in detail.

(b) Social Satire is a style of fictional representation that uses humour, irony, exaggeration, or ridicule to expose and criticise people's behaviour, particularly in a social context. Substantiate how Villa for Sale reflects this style. Competency Based

Ans. A Villa for Sale is indeed a satire that lays bare the human nature and ridicules people and their practices. The conversation between Juliette and her maid is not only comical but it also makes a mockery of the system. The maid suggests Juliette to work to earn extra as she was hard pressed for money. However, Juliette refuses further, Juliette desperate to sell the villa at a very low price but when Gaston and Jeanne come to see the villa, she ironically asked them to pay two hundred fifty thousand francs. Gaston doesn't want to spend money to buy the villa for Jeanne's parents, but when he made a deal with Mrs. Al Smith, he was ready to buy the villa.

The conversation between Gaston and Mrs. Al Smith also satirises the attitude of the capitalist countrymen and how they ridicule the outlook of people from France. "Europeans go to America to earn money and Americans come to Europe to spend money" and "Frenchmen usually have to consult about ten people before they get a move on..." reveal the prejudice the French and the Americans harbour.

(c) Passive characters are often considered 'weak' and 'uninteresting,' but can also be the true driving force of a story. Do you feel that the maid and Jeanne were the driving force of this play? Rationalise with evidence from the play.

Ans. It is true that passive characters are often considered weak and uninteresting. However, they can also be the true driving force of a story. The maid and Jeanne were the driving force of the play because they make it lively. Both the characters had a positive spirit, were determined and hard-working. They remain the same which brings stability to the otherwise over dramatic characters of Juliette and Gaston.

Q.7 **Select words from the box to describe the characters in the play as revealed by the following lines. You may take the words from the box given below.**

	Lines from the Play	Speaker	Quality Revealed
(a)	One hundred thousand francs if necessary and that's only twice what it cost me.	....	greedy
(b)	If you don't want the house, tell me so at once and we'll say no more about it.	....	....
(c)	No! I am very fond of your family, but not quite so fond as that.	Gaston	....
(d)	Quite so. I have, but you haven't.	....	....
(e)	I have never cared much about anybody's opinion.	....	....
(f)	On the principle of people who like children and haven't any can always go and live near a school.	....	....
(g)	The garden is not very large, but you see, it is surrounded by other gardens.	Juliette	....
(h)	I will be philanthropic and let you have it for two hundred thousand.	....	....
(i)	I have been thinking a lot about your papa and mamma. You see, I am really unselfish.	....	clever

cunning, clever, witty, smart, innocent, humorous, haughty, overbearing, critical, domineering, disapproving, materialistic, dishonest, practical, greedy, cruel, boastful.

Ans.

	Speaker	Quality Revealed
(a)	Juliette	greedy
(b)	Jeanne	practical
(c)	Gaston	disapproving, cruel
(d)	Gaston	domineering, overbearing
(e)	Gaston	haughty, boastful
(f)	Gaston	witty
(g)	Juliette	smart, witty, boastful
(h)	Juliette	practical, cunning
(i)	Gaston	clever

ON PAGE 118
LISTENING TASK

Q.8 **You are Jeanne. After coming home, you realise that the Villa was not actually bought and your husband has fooled both you and the landlady of the villa. You are filled with rage, disgust and helplessness because of your husband's betrayal. Write your feelings in the form of a diary entry.**

Ans. Wednesday, 12th March, 20XX 10:00 pm

Dear Diary

Today, I am shocked to learn about the trick my husband played on me and Juliette, the landlady of the villa.

I did not want to buy the villa, as I found it very small and thought that Gaston was right about it. However, later his promptness to buy the villa puzzled me greatly. At that time I was too confused to guess about Gaston's manipulations.

He had actually sold the villa to Mrs. Al Smith at a higher price than what Juliette had asked. He cheated all three of us. I would have been happy had he first bought it and then, sold it. However, he duped Mrs. Al Smith, then Juliette and finally me, his wife.

I don't trust him anymore. He has shown disrespect to our sacred matrimonial bond. I will never forgive him for this deception.

Jeanne

REVIEW EXERCISE

Including Exam Pattern Practice Questions

Extract Based Questions

Read the following extracts carefully and answer the questions that follow.

1. Mind you, if someone had bought it on the very day I placed it for sale, then I might have felt sorry because I would have wondered if I hadn't been a fool to sell at all.

(a) Who does 'you' stand for in the first line?

Ans. 'You' in the first line stands for Juliette's maid.

(b) How long ago had the speaker put up her villa for sale?

Ans. The speaker had put up her villa for sale about a month ago.

(c) Why would she have considered herself a fool if she had managed to sell it on the day she put up the notice?

Ans. If the speaker had managed to sell it on the day she put up the notice, it would mean that the villa was a much-coveted property and her decision to sell it was a mistake.

(d) What is the speaker feeling in the extract?

Ans. The speaker is feeling frustrated in the extract.

2. Oh! I'm fed up with the place. Because nobody really wants it! What time did those agency people say the lady would call?

(a) What do you mean by 'fed up' here?

Ans. The phrase 'fed up' means sick and tired.

(b) What do you think may be the reason that nobody wants it?

Ans. Nobody is interested in that villa because it is very small and the price quoted by Juliette is much higher than the actual rate.

(c) Identify the context about which the lady would call.

Ans. The lady would call to see the villa that Juliette was going to sell and to buy it if she was happy with the place.

(d) What do you understand by 'the agency people'?

Ans. 'Agency people' means brokers and agents.

3. But still... even so ... it would be funny if I couldn't manage to sell a place here, a stone's throw from Joinville, the French Hollywood, when all I'm asking is a paltry hundred thousand!

(a) Identify the speaker and the listener.

Ans. Juliette is the speaker and her maid is the listener.

(b) Where is the villa situated?

Ans. The villa is situated very near to Joinville, the French Hollywood.

(c) What does 'paltry' mean?

Ans. The word 'paltry' means an amount too small to be considered important or useful.

(d) Why did the speaker think that he/she would not be able to sell the villa?

Ans. The speaker thought so because nobody seems inclined to buy the villa which is near to Joinville, the French Hollywood.

4. You see, Madame, film acting is rather looked up to round here. Everybody wants to do it. Yesterday the butcher did not open his shop, he was being shot all the morning. Today, nobody could find the four policemen, they were taking part in Monsieur Milton's fight scene in his new film.

(a) Who liked to act in films?

Ans. Everybody, regardless of their profession, liked to act in films.

(b) Why did the butcher not open his shop?

Ans. The butcher did not open his shop as he was busy in the shooting of a film.

(c) What does the phrase, 'looked up to' mean?

Ans. The phrase 'looked up to' means to hold something in high regard.

(d) Explain – film acting is rather looked up to round here.

Ans. Due to handsome money being paid, everybody in the locality was eager to do a role acting in the film.

Or

(a) Identify 'it'.

Ans. 'It' refers to acting in films.

(b) Why does everybody want to do 'it'?

Ans. Everybody wants to act in films as the studio people pay a handsome amount of money for it.

(c) Give an antonym of 'Monsieur.'

Ans. 'Madame' is an antonym of 'Monsieur.'

(d) Why could the four policemen could not be found?

Ans. The four policemen were not found because they might be busy acting in the film.

5. "I am going upstairs for a moment. If that is the lady, tell her I will not be long. It won't do to give her the impression that I am waiting for her."

(a) What do you mean by 'I will not be long'?

Ans. The phrase 'I will not be long' means she won't take a long time.

(b) "It won't do to give her the impression", what impression is the speaker talking about?

Ans. The speaker doesn't want to give the impression that she had been desperately waiting for buyers.

(c) What character traits of the speaker are revealed in the above passage?

Ans. The speaker is revealed as a clever and calculative woman.

(d) Who is the 'lady' here? Why is she expected to visit the speaker?

Ans. The lady in question is Mrs. Al Smith. She is a possible buyer of the villa. However, the lady who comes in now is Jeanne who was just passing by and came in to see the villa.

6. Gaston and they call that a garden! Why, it's a yard with a patch of grass in the middle.

Jeanne But the inside of the house seems very nice, Gaston.

Gaston Twenty-five yards of Cretonne and a dash of paint...you can get that anywhere.

Jeanne That's not fair. Wait until you've seen the rest of it.

Gaston Why should I? I don't want to see the kitchen to know that the garden is a myth and that the salon is impossible.

Jeanne What's the matter with it?

Gaston Matter? Why you can't even call it a salon.

(a) What is Gaston trying to do?

Ans. Gaston is pointing out the shortcomings of the villa.

(b) What do you think may be the reason of this attitude?

Ans. He does not want Jeanne to buy the villa as it is a costly affair. Besides, he is not quite happy with the idea of his in-laws coming and living with them in the villa.

(c) What is the meaning of 'Cretonne'?

Ans. 'Cretonne' is a heavy cotton material in colourfully printed designs, used especially for drapery and slip covers.

(d) What is the synonym word of 'fair'?

Ans. The synonym of 'fair' is 'just'.

7. Gaston I told you before we crossed the road that I didn't want it. As soon as you see a sign '*Villa for Sale*', you have to go inside and be shown over it.

Jeanne But we are buying a villa, aren't we?

Gaston We are not.

Jeanne What do you mean: 'We are not'? Then we're not looking for a villa?

(a) What do you mean by 'we are not'?

Ans. 'We are not' means that Gaston and Jeanne are not buying any villa.

(b) Do you really think that they are not buying the villa?

Ans. Jeanne wants to buy it but Gaston doesn't seem to be at all interested.

(c) Did Gaston stick to his decision till the end?

Ans. Yes, because he had already sold it before buying it, making a profit of one hundred thousand francs.

(d) What do you understand by the phrase 'be shown over it' ?

Ans. The phrase 'be shown over it' means that she wanted to go inside the villa and see it.

8. You are an exception. Frenchmen usually have to consult about ten people before they get a move on. Listen! Do you or don't you want to sell this house?

(a) What do you mean by 'exception'?

Ans. The word 'exception' means different from standard.

(b) What is the opinion of the speaker about Frenchmen?

Ans. Mrs. Al Smith, the speaker, thinks that the French people have no decision-making power. They usually consult about ten people before making a decision.

(c) Why is the listener an exception?

Ans. She calls Gaston an exception because he doesn't consult his wife before taking decisions.

(d) Write the meaning of 'consult'.

Ans. The word 'consult' means to discuss.

9. Copies are not always good. We could only imitate you and imitations are no better than parodies. We are so different. Think of it ...

(a) What does the speaker mean by 'we' and 'you'?

Ans. 'We' refers to the Europeans, particularly the French, while 'you' refers to the Americans.

(b) What context are they talking in?

Ans. Mrs. Al Smith is ridiculing the French while Gaston is denying her claims.

(c) What do you mean by 'parodies'?

Ans. Parodies are an imitation of the style of a particular writer, artist or genre with deliberate exaggeration for comic effect. Here, it means copying the lifestyle.

(d) **In the opinion of the speaker, why are copies not always good?**

Ans. Copies are not always good because it resembles parodies which mocks or ridicules the original document.

10. **Jeanne** What on Earth have you done?
Gaston I? Made a hundred thousand francs and a Carot!

(a) **How has Gaston made a hundred thousand francs?**

Ans. Gaston had sold Juliette's villa for three hundred thousand francs to Mrs. Al Smith. After this, he bought it from Juliette for two hundred thousand francs, thus making a profit of a hundred thousand francs.

(b) **Mention any two characteristics displayed by Gaston when he made a hundred thousand francs.**

Ans. Gaston appears as an opportunistic and calculative person when he made a hundred thousand francs.

(c) **What do you mean by Carot in these lines ?**

Ans. Carot is a painting made by a French landscape painter who is named JC Carot.

(d) **What does 'made' mean here?**

Ans. The word 'made' here means earn a profit.

Short Answer Type Questions

Answer the following questions in 30-40 words.

1. Who hung the sign 'For Sale' and for how long had the sign been hanging?

Ans. Juliette, the owner of the villa, herself hung the sign 'For Sale'. When the signboard was brought, she waited until it was night and then, she hung it herself. She felt that as people could not read the sign in the dark, the house would belong to her for one more night. The sign had been hanging for over a month.

2. Why does Juliette put up her villa for sale?

Or Despite her ardent love for the villa, Juliette had to sell it. Why?

Ans. Juliette loved her villa very passionately. Yet, she had to put up it for sale as she was going through a financial crisis. Business was not doing well and the only possible source of money was through the sale of the villa.

3. How can you say that Juliette was very fond of her villa?

Ans. Juliette did put up the 'For Sale' sign on the villa gate, but only after it was dark. She put up the sign in the dark so that no possible buyer would be able to read it and she would have a chance to live in her villa or feel that it belonged to her for one more night. By this, we can say that she was very fond her villa.

4. Describe Juliette's relationship with her maid.

Ans. Juliette and her maid share quite a friendly relationship. Juliette is very kind towards her and listens to what she has to say. The maid also cares about her mistress and when she realises that she is in trouble, she advises her to take up an acting assignment. Though Juliette doesn't find the suggestion agreeable, she is still not annoyed with or rude towards her maid.

5. What mistake was made by Mrs. Al Smith on seeing Gaston at Juliette's villa? What is the result of this mistake?

Ans. Mrs. Al Smith mistook Gaston as Juliette's husband when she saw him at the villa. As a result, Gaston, being an opportunist, took advantage of the situation. He sold the villa that did not even belong to him at a much higher price, thereby making a huge profit.

6. Why was Mrs. Al Smith not interested in going over the house?

Ans. Mrs. Al Smith was not interested in going over the house because she was in a hurry and had no time to waste. Moreover, she planned to knock down the villa and build a bungalow there. She was, thus, not interested in the villa but in the land.

7. What impression of Mrs. Al Smith do you form as she buys the villa without any loss of time?

Or Do you agree that Mrs. Al Smith is the representative of American outlook. How?

Ans. Mrs. Al Smith is a haughty lady who thinks very highly of herself. She does not have a high opinion of the French people and often criticises them. She is always in a hurry and does things unthinkingly. She is upset by hold-ups and delays and gets annoyed at the relaxed attitude of the French. In all this, she is certainly a representative of American outlook. The Americans too have a high idea of themselves, look down upon others and are highly critical of them. Besides, they too pretend to be very busy, with no time to waste.

8. Gaston's serious interest in buying the villa was a surprise. Why?

Or How did Jeanne react to Gaston's decision to purchase the villa?

Ans. Initially, Gaston was not at all interested in buying the villa and continuously kept belittling it. However, when Juliette and Jeanne came back, they were shocked to see that Gaston was actually very keen to buy the villa. His sudden change was a mystery to them.

9. Why does Gaston agree to buy the villa?

Or **Describe how the villa was sold.**

Or **In the end, Gaston has changed his views of buying the villa. Give reasons to support your answer.** Competency Based

Ans. Gaston was initially reluctant to buy the villa. He was waiting for his wife when Mrs. Al Smith arrived and mistook him to be the owner of the villa. Gaston tricked her into buying the villa for three hundred thousand francs. It was for this reason that he seemed to have changed his view. He then bought the villa from Juliette for two hundred thousand francs and hence, made a huge profit.

10. At Juliette's house, Gaston acquires two things by taking advantage of the situation. Which are the two things he gets?

Ans. Gaston is an opportunist who very well knows how to use any situation to his advantage. At Juliette's house, he first manages to sell the villa to Mrs. Al Smith for three hundred thousand francs, and then, buys it from Juliette at the price of two hundred thousand francs. He, thus, makes a profit of a hundred thousand francs.

Second, he insists on keeping a the Carot painting as a souvenir, pretending not to know its real worth. He knew that it was the work of a famous French artist and perhaps wanted to use it later to gain more benefit out of it.

11. Does Sacha Guitry's 'Villa For Sale' define human behaviour through the character of Gaston? Give reasons.

Ans. 'Villa for Sale' defines human behaviour through the character of Gaston. It shows how cunning and manipulative humans can be. In real life too, there are people like Gaston, who are thorough opportunists and take advantage of innocent people. It shows how mean and money-minded people can be.

Long Answer Type Questions

Answer the following questions in 120 words.

1. Do you think that our strong desire to own material things is making us less aware of important personal qualities such as loyalty, kindness and concern for others? Express your views by taking examples from the play 'Villa for Sale'. Competency Based

Ans. The world we live in today has become extremely materialistic. All of us are guided by a strong desire to possess material things and forget the important moral values like loyalty, kindness and concern for others.

In the play 'Villa for Sale', all the characters except Jeanne run after worldly things. Juliette is a vain woman who tells blatant (shockingly obvious or open) lies to sell her villa. She even flatters her possible buyers. Her only aim is to sell off the place at the highest price she can get. Juliette's maid too wants leave from work so that she can earn a little extra money by acting.

Gaston is cunning, greedy and deceptive to the core. His success and wealth have made him so arrogant that he shows no concern either for his wife or for other women like Juliette or Mrs. Al Smith.

He is rude to Juliette, cheats both her and Mrs. Al Smith, and also betrays his wife's trust in him.

Mrs. Al Smith is a snobbish lady who is too proud of her riches and American identity to care for the feelings of others. Thus, the play shows how man's desire for material things has made him less aware of important human values.

2. In what way can ignorance lead one into a trap and cause losses beyond one's imagination? What values should one imbibe in oneself to be able to escape such traps? Give your answer in reference to 'Villa for Sale'.

Ans. Ignorance and innocence are often valued as qualities one must possess. However, there are times when these can lead a person into a trap and result in serious losses.

Jeanne, in the play 'Villa for Sale', is a simple lady ignorant of the ways of the world. She wants to buy a villa, apparently for her parents and is at once impressed by Juliette's villa.

She is also easily taken in by Juliette's attempts to flatter her. However, on a closer inspection of the villa, she decides not to buy it. She does show some good sense in taking an independent decision.

However, we also see how Jeanne is easily fooled by Gaston, her husband. Gaston has spent all her dowry and now refuses to part with his own money for her family. He does not respect her feelings and also betrays her trust when he makes a profit of a hundred thousand francs by trading in the villa without telling her anything about it.

In order to escape such traps of worldly-wise people, one must possess qualities like keen sense of observation and good judgement, ability to read between the lines and an acute understanding of human character.

3. You are Juliette. You feel duped and cheated by Gaston. You decide to take legal action against him. Write a letter to your friend in 80-100 words, sharing this incident and the action you plan to take against him.

Ans. 12, Victoria Street, Paris

27th November, 20XX

Dear Samantha

I feel so annoyed at my own foolishness. In my desperation to sell off the villa, I have allowed that cheat to outsmart me. Gaston's behaviour has indeed shocked me. It was just yesterday I discovered the deception.

Gaston never appeared a gentleman with his rude and insulting behaviour. But who could ever think that he would rob me like this? That day, when I had been waiting for Mrs. Al Smith, Gaston and his wife Jeanne walked in. Jeanne seemed a pretty little soul and showed much interest in buying the villa. While I was upstairs showing the villa to the lady, Mrs. Al Smith walked in. I still cannot believe that he sold my villa to Mrs. Al Smith for a shocking three hundred thousand francs. No wonder he readily purchased it from me for two hundred thousand francs, a price he earlier found too excessive. Little did I realise how cunning he had been!

I will meet a lawyer tomorrow morning and see if I can challenge him in the court and get my money back. I will teach him a lesson he will never forget. Please suggest me a good lawyer if you know one.

Your loving friend

Juliette

4. Both Jeanne and Juliette were duped by Gaston in the play 'Villa for Sale'. How could this have been prevented? Describe the values Gaston should have possessed, that would have shown him in a positive light.

Ans. Both Jeanne and Juliette were duped by Gaston in the play 'Villa for Sale'. On one hand, Gaston was successful in selling off Juliette's villa to Mrs. Al Smith without her knowledge; on the other hand, he pretended to purchase the villa from Juliette thereby pleasantly surprising Jeanne.

Gaston could have been stopped from taking advantage of the situation if the maid would have clarified to Mrs. Al Smith about the identity of the man.

Moreover, had Jeanne not expressed her desire to be shown the villa, they would have encountered Mrs. Al Smith and probably, Juliette would have sold her villa at a better price. Gaston appears to be a mean and money-minded man. He should have possessed positive qualities in order to win the appreciation of the readers. He should have been polite towards his wife as well as Juliette.

Moreover, he should not have committed the unethical act of selling Juliette's villa. He should have honestly informed her of Mrs. Al Smith's visit and made his exit at the same time as he had no intention of buying the villa.

5. You are Gaston. Write a diary entry expressing your joy of having made a huge profit by selling the villa. Also, share your feelings of regret for cheating your unsuspecting wife.

Ans. Tuesday, 12th April, 20XX 10:30 pm

Dear Diary

On Jeanne's insistence, I went to Juliette's villa. I was not at all interested in buying the villa. However, when Jeanne went with Juliette to see the villa, Mrs. Al Smith entered and was in a great hurry. She mistook me to be the owner of the villa. I took advantage of the situation and struck a deal with her, thereby making a huge profit of a hundred thousand francs. Jeanne was pleasantly surprised when I purchased the villa. I was too happy with the unexpected money but at the same time I regret cheating on my wife. She did not suspect my actions, however, I shall tell her the reality very soon. I hope she would forgive me. I pledge not to cheat her again in future. It was immoral and unethical to indulge in such an act. I shouldn't have betrayed her confidence in me.

6. Gaston has proved his cunningness in business matters, but as far as moral ethics are concerned, there is a definite lack of it in him. Discuss the values he should have possessed with reference to 'Villa for Sale.' Competency Based

Ans. Gaston is a shrewd and cunning opportunist who possesses much business sense. This is evident from the way he manages to sell Juliette's villa at a much higher price than she demanded, even before having bought it himself. He thus earns a profit of a hundred thousand francs, without having to invest anything at all. Thus, he proves his cunningness in business matters. Though Gaston has shrewd business sense, he lacks business and moral ethics. To sell something which belongs to somebody else is certainly unethical. Besides, there are more important values in life which Gaston lacks and should actually have possessed to come out as a lovable character in the play.

Gaston is a male chauvinist (a man who believes that men are more important and intelligent than women) who does not have any respect for his wife or her family and often criticises her openly. He suspects that Jeanne wants to buy the villa for her own parents. He has spent all her dowry, has made plenty of money for himself and is still reluctant to spend it for his wife's happiness. This shows that he is quite mean and money-minded.

Gaston lacks courtesy and is quite impolite in his behaviour towards ladies. He keeps interrupting Juliette as she describes her villa to him and his wife. His conversation with the American customer, Mrs. Al Smith, also speaks of his arrogance. Had Gaston been more polite, courteous, considerate and gentlemanlike, he would have perfectly complemented his wife Jeanne, and also won the hearts of the readers or the audience.

7. "A successful business deal cannot be made without sacrificing ethics." Do you agree with this statement? Give reasons to support your answer.

Ans. A successful business deal need not always require a sacrifice of ethics or morals. There are many upright businessmen who thrive on honesty and the practice of business ethics. This does not mean that they are less successful or make less profits than those shrewd, calculative, business-minded opportunists who thrive on cheating and the practice of unethical means, which they term as shrewd business sense.

In the play 'Villa for Sale', we come across two business-minded characters, Juliette and Gaston. Juliette wishes to sell her villa at a high price. When she meets Gaston and Jeanne who show a little interest in her property, she presents her villa in an over-positive light and tries to psychologically blackmail the couple into buying her villa. However, she lacks the business acumen required to make a successful deal. Her villa was near the French Hollywood, and that was the most positive attribute she could have used to her advantage.

The other character is Gaston, who is certainly better at business than Juliette. However, he is pretentious, mean, money-minded and selfish. He too makes profit but through unethical means. He sells the villa to Mrs. Al Smith when it still belonged to Juliette. The money he made should rightfully have gone to Juliette.

He could have made the deal once he had bought the villa and it belonged to him, or he could have shared his profit with Juliette. Both the characters sacrifice their morals to make profit.

ASSESSMENT EXERCISE

Extract Based Questions

Read the following extracts carefully and answer the questions that follow.

1. That was a month ago and now I have only one thought, that is to get the wretched place off my hands. I would sacrifice it at any price.

(a) Identify the speaker and the listener.

(b) What did the speaker want to sacrifice and why?

(c) What does 'wretched' mean?

(d) In this context, what is the meaning of 'sacrifice'?

2. If you would go and see them with your hair slicked back the way you do when you are dressing, Madame, I am sure they would engage you right away.

(a) What do you mean by 'dressing' here?

(b) Who are 'they'? How can they engage Madame?

(c) Did 'Madame' go to seek work from 'them'?

(d) Who is the speaker of these lines and to whom does he/she speak?

Short Answer Type Questions

Answer the following questions in about 30-40 words each.

1. Why did Juliette put up the 'For Sale' signboard on the villa gate after it was dark?

2. Why was Juliette annoyed every time she passed the 'For Sale' signboard?

3. Juliette was of the view that her villa had a wonderful location. Why did she think so?

4. Why did Juliette's maid request her for half a day's leave?

5. Why and what did the maid suggest to Juliette? What was Juliette's reaction?

6. Give a brief description of the villa.

7. Why did Juliette go upstairs as Gaston and Jeanne arrive at the villa and ring the doorbell?

8. What does Juliette say in order to flatter the couple?

9. Why did Gaston quote a price as low as sixty thousand francs for the villa? For how much did he sell the villa?

10. What is Mrs. Al Smith's plan as she buys the villa?

Long Answer Type Questions

Answer the following questions in about 120 words.

1. "Material things can't give us true happiness." Comment with reference to the play 'Villa For Sale'.

2. Some cunning people have both their hands full, thanks to some presence of mind,
some trickery and a dash of good luck. Comment with reference to the play 'Villa for Sale'.

3. Do you approve of Gaston's manner of conducting business?
Had you been in Gaston's place, what would you have done on Mrs. Al Smith's arrival?

CHAPTER 2

The Bishop's Candlesticks

by Norman Mckinnell

About the DRAMA The play 'The Bishop's Candlesticks' by Norman Mckinnell is built on a very simple plot involving characters like the Bishop, the Convict, the Bishop's sister-Persome, the maid-Marie and others. The play starts with a dialogue between Persome and Marie, regarding the whereabouts of the Bishop. The play dramatically depicts how the love and compassion of the Bishop brought about a change of heart in a convict and turned him into a man who promised to lead a good life.

Important Characters

- **The Bishop** He is a very noble and simple person, who is always ready to help anyone in distress. He treats the Convict like a friend even after the Convict stole his silver candlesticks and helps him to start a new life.
- **The Convict** He was leading a normal life before he turned into a criminal due to poverty. He had no faith in religion. He became heartless and soulless after being given severe punishment for a minor crime. However, the Bishop's compassion changed his character totally.
- **Persome** She is the Bishop's sister. She was very materialistic and behaved rudely with the oppressed (poor and helpless) people. She felt that people misuse the simplicity and goodness of the Bishop.
- **Marie, The Maid** She is a simple maidservant in the Bishop's house.

Summary of the Drama

The scene opens in the kitchen of the Bishop's cottage. It is a plain and slightly furnished house. There is a fireplace with heavy mantelpiece on right. There is also an oak settee with cushions behind left curtain and a table next to a window with writing materials and crucifix (wood) near the right curtain. On the left hand side, there is a kitchen dresser with cupboard to lock, oak dinner-table, chairs, books, etc. on the right. On the mantel piece are two very handsome candlesticks which look strangely out of place with their surroundings.

The Opening Scene

The drama opens in the kitchen of the Bishop's house. The two ladies Marie and Persome appear on the stage. Marie works as a maid in the Bishop's house. She was stirring soup on the fire while Persome was upset as she did not know where her brother (the Bishop) had gone.

Marie told Persome that the Bishop had gone to her mother's house because she was ill. Persome, then asked Marie to put the salt-cellars on the table. Marie informed her that the Bishop had sold the salt-cellars to help Mere Gringoire because she could not pay her rent. Persome ignored her and thought that the Bishop would sell everything for the sake of others.

Bishop Enters the House

The Bishop entered the home and gave his muffler to Marie as it was very cold outside. He informed Marie that her mother was feeling better now. He tells Marie to run back home to care for her recovering mother since the doctor had paid a visit. He cautions her to make no noise to disturb her sleeping mother.

Persome, angry with her brother, remarked that any clever person could cheat him. However, the Bishop answered that he was ready to sacrifice everything to help the needy people. He felt sorry that he could do so little, whereas the world had endless suffering.

Persome Taunts her Brother

Persome did not like that her brother lived for others and not for himself. She thought that people would take unfair advantage of his charitable nature. His door was never shut; it was open for everybody. At this, the Bishop was taunted by Persome that one day, he would sell the candlesticks which were given by his mother. The Bishop, however, replied that he never wanted to sell them. She made him promise not to give away the candlesticks to anybody in future. Then, she went to sleep.

A Convict Enters the House

At night, when the Bishop was about to go to bed, a Convict entered the house. At knife-point, he demanded food from the Bishop. The Bishop called Persome and asked her to give some food to the Convict. The Convict wondered why the Bishop kept his doors and windows open even at night. He asked the Bishop if he wasn't afraid of thieves.

The Bishop told him that he was not afraid, rather he felt sorry for them as they were poor sufferers. He treated the Convict with love and respect. He regarded him as a friend. Thus, the Convict started talking to the Bishop and told him his story.

The Convict's Story

The Convict told the Bishop that once he stole food for his ill and starving wife as he had no money. However, he was caught and sentenced to ten years in prison. His wife died as well.

The authorities regarded him as a hard-core criminal and treated him like an animal. Then one day, he escaped, but society treated him no better. As he was a Convict, nobody would give him a job and the police was hunting for him. He was starving and so, he stole again.

Thus, society, with its wrong attitude, did not give him a chance to lead a good life. He entered the house of the Bishop as he was hungry. After hearing his tale, the kind Bishop was touched and gave him food and a bed to sleep on. When the Convict noticed the silver candlesticks. The Bishop informed him that they were the last gift from his late mother. Seeing that the Bishop was offering him kindness, the Convict was angry. He felt that the Bishop was trying to convert him into a religious and law abiding man. The Bishop refused it and went to sleep.

Silver Candlesticks Stolen

During the stay in the Bishop's house, the Convict saw the silver candlesticks on the mantlepiece (a shelf over a fireplace). Left alone on his bed, the Convict could not stop himself from stealing the silver candlesticks. So, he took them and quietly left the house. As he went out, the door shut loudly.

Persome got up at the sound and found that the Convict had stolen the silver candlesticks and fled. The Bishop was devastated to lose the candlesticks. However, he felt that the candlesticks might be of some use to the Convict. Persome insisted that they must inform the police about the robbery but the Bishop forbade her from doing so.

Convict Brought Back by the Police

The Convict was caught by the Police Sergeant before he had gone very far. The Sergeant and three policemen came to the Bishop's house with the Convict. The Sergeant told them that they found him walking on the road with the candlesticks.

They arrested him on the basis of doubt. They identified the Bishop's candlesticks, so they brought the Convict there. However, the Bishop told them that the accused was his friend and he himself had presented the candlesticks to the Convict. He had invited him to dinner last night and given him those silver candlesticks as a gift.

Consequently, the police Sergeant released the Convict and went away. The Convict was deeply affected by this deed of the Bishop.

Convict's Transformation into a True Christian

The Convict was overwhelmed by the love of the Bishop and was convinced that the Bishop was kind and loving. He requested the Bishop to bless him. He had regained the faith that there can be goodness in men. He was sorry for stealing the candlesticks. He felt that he was once again a human being and not an animal.

The kind Bishop told him of the secret road that led to Paris and gifted him the candlesticks. The Bishop asked him to remember that "The body of man is the Temple of the living God". The Convict was already a changed man and he promised to remember the Bishop's advice and went away to begin a new life.

Word Meaning

Word	Meaning
settee	sofa or couch
crucifix	image of Jesus on the cross
eight-day clock	a floor standing long wooden case clock requiring winding once a week only
dresser	a large wooden furniture item for storing utensils
candlesticks	a metal holder for candles
discovered	seen when the curtain opens
Monseigneur	My Lord (expression of respect for a high-ranking person)
Mon Dieu	French expression for 'My God'
nincompoop	idiot or fool
pray	please
feeling poorly	not feeling well
do you put	is it not your duty to put
salt-cellars	containers for salt and pepper kept on the dining-table
ahem	a short coughing sound to avoid saying something embarrassing
bailiff	an officer of the Court
dot	dowry
disgracefully dirty	very dirty
presently	soon; shortly
let yourself in	go inside your house
comforter	muffler
charity begins at home	you should help and care for your own family before helping others
dupe	a person who is easily cheated
scamp	a rascal/vagabond
parish	an area or population covered by a church
mend	fix
minx	a clever girl
china	utensils made from white clay
send	send a message for you to visit her
talking to	scolding
dispose of	sell
incorrigible	incurable
set such store by	to treasure; to value greatly
trims	adjusts
too old a bird to be caught with chaff	too experienced to be fooled
rouse the house	wake everyone in the house
wolf	hunger
entrails	intestines (actually meaning stomach)
play me false	fool;cheat me

Word	Meaning
as sure as there are devils in hell	definitely
pretty	odd or unusual
to be at the beck and call of	to obey
ne'er-do-well	a good-for-nothing person
favour this gentleman with	give
stand below	away from
starts	expresses surprise
ushuttered	open
unbarred	not locked
voraciously	greedily
holy virgin	Mary, Mother of Jesus
may escape that	may avoid swearing
lived in hell	been given very bad treatment in prison
set them	put them
vines	climbing plants that produce grapes
prison hulks	ships used as prisons
gaoler	jailor
lashed	whipped
coverings	blankets or sheets to cover you while sleeping
handsome	high-class
hundreds	hundreds of Francs (local currency)
I'll warrant	I'm sure
start me fair	help me to get a good start in life
collaring the plunder	gathering the stolen stuff
hard	difficult to bear
about	around / in the open
scoundrelly	dishonest and immoral
slinking	moving quietly and secretly
isn't he strong	he is very strong
securing	tying him up
dogged	stubborn
sup with me	had dinner with me
loose	release
given me them	given them to me
fed and warmed	given comfort and food
blackguard	dishonest villain
had come into	has happened
body is the temple of the Living God	God lives in us

Textbook FOLDER

Here, we have covered questions given in the CBSE Textbook along with their answers.

ON PAGE 135

Q.3. Complete the following paragraph with suitable words/phrases highlighting the theme of the play. You can do it in pairs.

The play deals with a **(i)** .... and **(ii)** .... Bishop who is always ready to lend a **(iii)** .... hand to anyone in distress. A **(iv)** .... breaks into the Bishop's house and is **(v)** .... and warmed. The benevolence of the Bishop somewhat **(vi)** .... the Convict, but, when he sees the silver candlesticks, he **(vii)** ...... them and runs away. However, he is **(viii)** .... and brought back. He expects to go back to jail, but the Bishop informs the police they are a **(ix)** .... The Convict is **(x)** .... by this kindness of the Bishop and before he leaves, he seeks the priest's blessing.

Ans. (i) kind (ii) charitable (iii) helping (iv) convict
(v) fed (vi) confounds (vii) steals (viii) arrested
(ix) gift (x) moved

ON PAGE 135-136

Q.4. (a) Working in pairs, give antonyms of the following words.

kind-hearted	unscrupulous	forgiving	stern	benevolent	credulous	generous	pious
suspicious	sympathetic	understanding	wild	innocent	penitent	clever	brutal
protective	honourable	cunning	caring	sentimental	trusting	concerned	embittered

(b) Select words from the above box to describe the characters in the play as revealed by the following lines from the play.

	Lines from the play	Speaker	Quality revealed
1.	You told him she was feeling poorly, did you? And so my brother is to be kept out of bed, and go without his supper because you told him she was feeling poorly.		
2.	.... take my comforter, it will keep you warm.		
3.	If people lie to me they are poorer, not I.		
4.	You are like a child. I can't trust you out of my sight. No sooner my back is turned than you get that minx Marie to sell the silver salt-cellars.		
5.	My dear, there is so much suffering in the world, and I can do so very little.		
6.	My mother gave them to me on - on her death bed just after you were born, and ....and she asked me to keep them in remembrance of her, so I would like to keep them.		
7.	I am too old a bird to be caught with chaff.		
8.	You have your soul to lose, my son.		
9.	Give me food or I'll stick my knife in you both and help myself.		
10.	... they have made me what I am, they have made me a thief. God curse them all.		
11.	Why the devil are you kind to me? What do you want?		
12.	I - I - didn't believe there was any good in the world. . .but somehow I - I - know you're good, and – and it's a queer thing to ask, but could you, would you bless me before I go?		

Ans. (a)

Word	Antonym	Word	Antonym
kind-hearted	cruel	innocent	guilty
unscrupulous	principled	penitent	unrepentant
forgiving	merciless	clever	stupid
stern	friendly	brutal	gentle
benevolent	unkind	protective	destructive
credulous	incredulous	honourable	dishonourable
generous	stingy	cunning	guideless
pious	faithless	caring	uncaring
suspicious	trusting	sentimental	unsentimental
sympathetic	unsympathetic	trusting	untrusting
understanding	indifferent	concerned	unconcerned
wild	tame	embittered	endeared

(b)

	Lines from the play	Speaker	Quality revealed
1.	You told him she was feeling poorly, did you? And so my brother is to be kept out of bed, and go without his supper because you told him she was feeling poorly.	Persome	stern
2.	…….. take my comforter, it will keep you warm.	Bishop	kind, concerned
3.	If people lie to me they are poorer, not I.	Bishop	benevolent, understanding
4.	You are like a child. I can't trust you out of my sight. No sooner my back is turned than you get that minx Marie to sell the silver salt-cellars.	Persome	distrustful
5.	My dear, there is so much suffering in the world, and I can do so very little.	Bishop	kind, concerned
6.	My mother gave them to me on - on her death bed just after you were born, and ….and she asked me to keep them in remembrance of her, so I would like to keep them.	Bishop	sentimental
7.	I am too old a bird to be caught with chaff.	Convict	clever, cunning
8.	You have your soul to lose, my son.	Bishop	sympathetic, concerned
9.	Give me food or I'll stick my knife in you both and help myself.	Convict	brutal, wild
10.	... they have made me what I am, they have made me a thief. God curse them all.	Convict	embittered
11.	Why the devil are you kind to me? What do you want?	Convict	suspicious
12.	I - I - didn't believe there was any good in the world. . .but somehow I - I - know you're good, and – and it's a queer thing to ask, but could you, would you bless me before I go?	Convict	penitent, sentimental

ON PAGE 136

Q.5 Read the following extracts and answer the questions that follow by choosing the correct options.

(A) "Monseigneur the Bishop is a ... ahem!"

(i) Why does Persome not complete the sentence?

(a) She used to stammer while speaking.
(b) She was about to praise the Bishop.
(c) She did not wish to criticise the Bishop in front of Marie.
(d) She had a habit of passing such remarks.

Ans. (c) She did not wish to criticise the Bishop in front of Marie.

(ii) Why is she angry with the Bishop?

(a) The Bishop has sold the salt-cellars.
(b) The Bishop has gone to visit Mere Gringoire.
(c) He showed extra concern for Marie.
(d) She disliked the Bishop.

Ans. (a) The Bishop has sold the salt-cellars.

(B) "She sent little Jean to Monseigneur to ask for help."

(i) Who sent little Jean to the Bishop?

(a) Mere Gringoire (b) Marie
(c) Persome (d) Marie's mother

Ans. (a) Mere Gringoire

(ii) Why did she send Jean to the Bishop?

(a) So that he could pray for her.
(b) As she knew that he was a generous person.
(c) As she was a greedy woman.
(c) As she was a poor woman.

Ans. (b) As she knew that he was a generous person.

(C) "I offered to take her in here for a day or two, but she seemed to think it might distress you."

(i) The Bishop wanted to take Mere Gringoire in because ....

(a) she was sick
(b) she had no money
(c) she was unable to pay the rent of her house
(d) she was a close friend of Persome

Ans. (c) she was unable to pay the rent of her house

(ii) Persome would be distressed on Mere Gringoire's being taken in because ....

(a) she did not want to help anyone
(b) she felt that Mere Gringoire was taking undue advantage of the Bishop
(c) she was a self-centred person
(d) she would be put to a great deal of inconvenience

Ans. (b) she felt that Mere Gringoire was taking undue advantage of the Bishop

ON PAGE 137-138

Q.6A Answer the following questions briefly.

(a) Do you think the Bishop was right in selling the salt-cellars? Why/Why not?

Ans. Yes, the Bishop was right in selling the salt-cellars. This shows that people mattered more to him than worldly things. Moreover, the Bishop was a kind-hearted man, who always helped needy people.

(b) Why does Persome feel the people pretend to be sick?

Or **Why did Persome feel that people pretend to be ill?**

Ans. Persome is not as kind-hearted as the Bishop. She thinks that people pretend to be sick, so that the Bishop can help them financially or they can extract money from him.

(c) The Convict says, *"I am too old a bird to be caught with chaff."* What does he mean by this statement?

Ans. The Convict meant that he had spent a long period of his life in jail. He had learned all the tricks and now, he could not be cheated by any softness of words, which may hide some deception. He was too experienced to be fooled.

(d) Why was the Convict sent to prison? What was the punishment given to him?

Ans. The Convict was sent to prison for ten years for stealing. He was chained like an animal and beaten like a hound. He was not given proper food and had insects on his body. He was further beaten mercilessly when he complained about the food.

(e) Do you think the punishment given to the Convict was justified? Why/Why not?

Ans. The punishment given to the Convict was definitely not justified. The Convict had only stolen food for his ill wife. At the most, the law should have fined him or imprisoned him for a short time. However, severe imprisonment for ten years was too much for a man who has stolen only for buying food to eat.

(f) Before leaving, the Convict asks the Bishop to bless him. What brought about this change in him? Competency Based

Or **How was the Convict transformed into a man again?**

Ans. The Bishop's love, large-heartedness, care and kindness brought about a change in the Convict. The Bishop had saved him from the police. The Convict changed into a gentleman from an animal and started believing in religion again. Therefore, he asked the Bishop to bless him so that he could stay like this forever.

(g) **What did Persome mean by, 'charity begins at home'?**

Ans. The idiom "charity begins at home" means that people should prioritize their family and close neighbors before helping others who are further away. It's often used to encourage people to focus on their own responsibilities and obligations, and to remind them that small acts of kindness can have a big impact. By making this statement, Persome wants the Bishop to stop giving away all the things for the benefit of others and think about himself too.

(h) **What is the reason behind the convict quoting a number as his identity?**

Ans. The convict quotes a number as his identity because he was treated as a number, not a person, in prison. He says, "I am not a man, but a number: number 15,729". This shows that he has lost his sense of self and dignity after spending ten years in prison.

(i) **The role of a 'mother hen' aptly fits Persome. Comment.**

Ans. The role of a mother hen is a metaphor that describes someone who is nurturing, protective, and caring, similar to how a mother hen cares for her chicks. This metaphor can be applied to the character of the Persome in regard to her nurturing and protective actions for her brother. If we look at Persome as a mother hen for anyone else, we would be completely wrong.

ON PAGE 138

Q.6B Answer in detail.

(a) **The Convict goes to Paris, sells the silver candlesticks and starts a business. The business prospers and he starts a reformatory for ex-Convicts. He writes a letter to the Bishop telling him of this reformation and seeks his blessings. As the Convict, Jean Valjean, write the letter to the Bishop.**

Ans. Dear Bishop,

I trust this letter finds you well. I wish to express my heartfelt gratitude for the immense kindness you showed me. The silver candlesticks you gave me that night have become symbols of redemption and hope, guiding me away from the darkness of my past. Your faith in my goodness has inspired a profound transformation within me and I strive daily to be deserving of the compassion you showed. Your impact resonates in the choices I make and I am committed to paying forward the grace you generously extended. With this thought in mind, I have started a reformatory for ex-Convicts. In my efforts to pull these tortured souls away from their darkness, I have realised that one must be a man of great patience and compassion. While I do try to follow your example, I know that I fall terribly short. Still, I remember your kindness on that cold and hungry winter night. For the miracle of turning this animal into a man again, I shall forever be in your debt.

With sincere gratitude,

Jean Valjean

(b) **People say that the smallest change in perspective can transform a life. What facts from the play would you select to justify the above statement with reference to the Bishop?**

Ans. "The play 'The Bishop's Candlesticks' underscores the power of a subtle shift in perspective. The Convict, hardened by a decade of suffering, viewed himself as a beast, detached from human emotions. Despite stealing the Bishop's silver candlesticks, a memento from his deceased mother, the Convict's life takes a transformative turn. The Bishop's kindness and compassion gradually remove the Convict's hatred for the world, revealing the goodness in a world he once deemed inherently evil. This portrayal elegantly exemplifies how the Bishop's minimal change in perspective profoundly transforms the Convict's life, emphasising the significant impact even small acts of kindness can have."

(c) **Evaluate the roles of Persome (from The Bishop's Candlesticks) and the 12 year old Sudha Murty (from How I taught my grandmother to read) in the light of the given quote. "I feel the capacity to care is the thing which gives life its deepest significance." – Pablo Casals** Competency Based

Ans. Pablo Casals touched upon a deep idea when he said that 'the capacity to care is the thing which gives life its deepest significance.' The characters of Persome and the 12-year-old Sudha Murty stand on opposite ends of the spectrum in the context of the given quote. Persome is a miserly woman who shies away from showing even the smallest bit of care for others. She is rude to Marie and doesn't care that Marie's mother is sick. Nor does she care for the cold outside and would rather send her in the freezing cold without the comfort of a muffler. Similarly, she didn't care that the Convict was starving. On the other hand, Sudha Murty cared deeply for the pains of her grandmother. That is why she took the time and effort to teach her old grandmother how to read and write. With her ability to care for her grandmother, Sudha Murty changes her life in the most significant way possible.

ON PAGE 138-139

Q.7 **The term irony refers to a discrepancy or disagreement of some sort. The discrepancy can be between what someone says and what he or she really means (verbal irony). The discrepancy can be between a situation that one would logically anticipate or one that would seem appropriate (situational irony).**

The discrepancy can even be between the facts known to a character and the facts known to us, i.e. the readers or the audience (dramatic irony).

Working in groups of four complete the following table. Find instances of irony from the play and justify them.

Extract	Justification
I believe you want to convert me; save my soul, don't you call it? Well, it's no good ...... see? I don't want any damned religion	Later, the convict say, it's a queer thing to ask, but-could you would you bless me before I go.
....	....
....	....
....	....
Why the devil do you leave the window unshuttered and the door unbarred so that anyone can come in?	If the door had been parred the convict could't have entered the house.
....	....
....	....
....	....
My mother gave them to me on ... on her death bed just after you were born, and ... and she asked me to so I would like to keep them	Later he hands the convict the candlesticks and tells him to start a new life.
....	....
....	....
....	....

Ans.

Extract	Justification
I believe you want to convert me; save my soul, don't you call it? Well, it's no good—- see? I don't want any damned religion.	Later, the Convict says, "it's a queer thing to ask, but - could you, would you bless me before I go."
Why the devil do you leave the window unshuttered and the door unbarred so that anyone can come in?	If the door had been barred the Convict couldn't have entered the house.
My mother gave them to me on – on her death bed just after you were born, and – and she asked me to keep them in remembrance of her, so I would like to keep them.	Later he hands the Convict the candlesticks and tells him to start a new life.
Stop! Neither of you shall leave this room till I do.	What's that? Leave us. Yes, yes, leave us. Good night.
Play me false and as sure as there are devils in hell, I'll drive my knife through your heart.	I believe you, but damn me if I knew why.
I have a wolf inside me, tearing at my entrails, tearing me.	You made me feel that.... As if I were a man again and not a wild beast.

ON PAGE 139

Q.8 **Identify the situations which may be termed as the turning points in the Convict's life.**

Ans. The situations which may be termed as the turning points in the Convict's life were

(i) The Convict was arrested for stealing money to buy food for his sick wife. He was sent to jail and treated inhumanely. This treatment turned him from a normal man into an animal.

(ii) The Convict was treated with kindness and given food and shelter by the Bishop. The Bishop was kind towards him, which softened him a little.

(iii) The Convict was alone with the candlesticks and could not stop himself from stealing them. In spite of the Bishop's hospitality and kindness, he stole them and fled away, becoming a criminal again.

(iv) The Convict was arrested by the police and produced in front of the Bishop. However, the Bishop forgave him and called him his friend. He even gifted his candlesticks to him. This changed him and he sought the Bishop's blessings.

REVIEW EXERCISE

Including Exam Pattern Practice Questions

Extract Based Questions

Read the following extracts carefully and answer the questions that follow.

1. 'Did Monseigneur the Bishop leave any message for me?'
'No, madam.'
Did he tell you where he was going?"
'Yes, madam.'
'Yes, madam! Then why haven't you told me, stupid!'
'Madam didn't ask me.'
'But that is no reason for your not telling me, is it?'

(a) Why is Persome angry with Marie?

Ans. Persome is angry with Marie because Marie had not told her that the Bishop had gone out.

(b) The word 'Monseigneur' in the extract means ....

Ans. My lord

(c) Who is Marie?

Ans. Marie is the maid in the Bishop's house. She is by nature a little foolish.

(d) In which sense 'reason' has been used?

Ans. The word 'reason' is synonymous to 'excuse'.

2. Monseigneur, the Bishop is a–ahem! But-but what can he have wanted with the money!

(a) Why does Persome not complete the sentence?

Ans. Persome did not complete the sentence because she did not wish to criticise the Bishop in front of Marie.

(b) Why is she angry with the Bishop?

Ans. She is angry with the Bishop because he has sold her silver salt-cellars.

(c) The word 'ahem' used in the extract is ....

Ans. a short coughing sound made to avoid saying something embarrassing.

(d) Who is known as 'Bishop'?

Ans. A Christian priest with a high rank who is the head of all the churches in an area is known as Bishop.

3. Madam, it was for rent. The bailiff would not wait any longer and threatened to turn her out today if it were not paid, so she sent little Jean to Monseigneur to ask for help.

(a) Who sent little Jean to the Bishop?

Ans. Mere Gringoire sent little Jean to the Bishop.

(b) Why did she send Jean to the Bishop?

Ans. She sent her because she knew that he was a generous person.

(c) How did the Bishop help her?

Ans. He sold his silver salt-cellars to give her money to pay her rent.

(d) Who has been referred as 'little'?

Ans. Here, 'little' is indicative of the young girl Jean.

4. Ah! How nice and warm it is in here! It is worth going out in the cold for the sake of the comfort of coming in.

(a) Who is the speaker and where had he been?

Ans. The Bishop is the speaker and he had been to see Marie's mother as she was ill.

(b) Which word in the extract means 'pleasant sensation'?

Ans. The word 'comfort' means pleasant sensation.

(c) Who had been waiting for the speaker?

Ans. Persome, the Bishop's sister, had been waiting for the speaker.

(d) How far do you agree with the statement? Give reason.

Ans. I agree with this statement because the Bishop felt relieved when he came in. His relief was physical as well as mental for the deed he had done.

5. You are like a child. I cannot trust you out of my sight. No sooner is my back turned than you get that little minx Marie to sell the silver salt-cellars.

(a) Why did the listener get Marie to sell the silver salt-cellars?

Ans. The listener got Marie to sell the silver salt-cellars as Mere Gringoire needed the money to pay her rent.

(b) The word 'minx' as used in the extract means ....

Ans. clever girl

(c) Why did the speaker not want the salt-cellars to be sold?

Ans. The speaker did not want the salt-cellars to be sold because they had been in their family for years.

(d) Justify the speaker's calling the little Marie 'a minx.'

Ans. The speaker was wrong in calling little Marie 'a minx' because the girl was not the reason behind the sale of the salt-cellars.

6. You have your soul to lose, my son, it is of more value than my heart.

(a) Explain 'my son'.

Ans. 'My son' was uttered by the Bishop to address Convict. It was said in a fit of compassion and generosity. This was a token of love from the Bishop.

(b) What has the person being spoken to just threatened to do?

Ans. The Convict has just threatened to drive his knife through the Bishop's heart. The Convict says that he has nothing to lose.

(c) How did the speaker save the listener's soul?

Ans. He saves the Convict's soul by making him believe by his action that there is still hope for him and that there is still good in the world.

(d) Which word in the extract can be replaced by 'significance'.

Ans. The word 'value' can be replaced by 'significance'.

7. What, at this time of night? A pretty business truly. Are we to have no sleep now, but to be at the beck and call of every ne'er-do-well who happens to pass?

(a) What is the speaker talking about?

Ans. The speaker, Persome, is talking about having to play host to passing travellers in the middle of the night.

(b) How does the speaker feel on coming there?

Ans. The speaker is upset because she has been woken up in the middle of the night by her brother. She is irritated with the idea of feeding a passing traveller at that hour.

(c) What is meant by 'beck and call'?

Ans. The phrase 'beck and call' means 'to obey'.

(d) Explain the contrast involved in the use of 'pretty'.

Ans. 'Pretty' has been said in utter dismay. This was sarcastic for none love to cook food or serve it at midnight to a passing traveller.

8. Tell you about it? Look here, I was a man once. I'm a beast now, and they made me what I am. They chained me up like a wild animal, they lashed me like a hound. I fed on filth, I was covered, with vermin, I slept on boards and I complained. Then they lashed me again. For ten years, ten years. Oh God! They took away my name, they took away my soul and they gave me a devil in its place. But one day they were careless, one day they forgot to chain up their wild beast and he escaped. He was free. That was six weeks ago. I was free, free to starve.

(a) What is 'it' in the above lines?

Ans. 'It' here means the duration of the imprisonment of the Convict which the Bishop wants to know more about.

(b) What has been done to the Convict?

Ans. The prison authorities made the Convict a wild animal by treating him inhumanely.

(c) Which word in this extract means the same as 'regarding'?

Ans. The word 'about' means 'regarding'.

(d) Why does the speaker say that I'm a beast now?

Ans. The speaker said that he was a beast because there was no mercy, no sympathy and no human consideration left in him.

9. Yes, to starve. They feed you in Hell, but when you escape from it you starve. They were hunting me everywhere and I had no passport, no name.

(a) Who is the speaker? Who are 'they'?

Ans. The speaker is the Convict who has escaped from prison. 'They' are the police and the jailers.

(b) What is the mental state of the speaker in the above extract?

Ans. The mental state of the speaker in the above extract is one of desperation.

(c) What is meant by the word 'starve'?

Ans. It means 'to die of hunger'.

(d) Explain—'feed you in Hell'.

Ans. 'Feed you in Hell' reflects the food items served to the prisoners while they are in the jail.

10. Ah, you are admiring my candlesticks, I am proud of them.

They were a gift from my mother. A little too handsome for this poor cottage perhaps, but all I have to remind me of her. Your bed is ready.

(a) What gift is being referred to here?

Ans. The gift being referred to here is the two silver candlesticks which were a gift to the Bishop from his mother.

(b) **Why does the speaker say the above lines?**

Ans. The Bishop says these lines because he was very poor and nothing much of value was left in the cottage.

(c) **The word 'handsome' as used in the extract means ....**

Ans. princely or high class

(d) **What does 'poor cottage' imply?**

Ans. The 'poor cottage' implies that the living place of the Bishop has been in a poor state for the lack of the household items.

11. Yes, my friend. He did me the honour to sup with me to-night and I– I have given him the candlesticks.

(a) **To whom did the Bishop say these words?**

Ans. The Bishop said these words to the Sergeant when he brought the Convict to him.

(b) **Which word in this extract means the same as 'dinner'?**

Ans. The word 'sup' means 'dinner'.

(c) **How did the Sergeant react to the Bishop's statement?**

Ans. The Sergeant found it difficult to believe the Bishop's statement.

(d) **Explain your views on the usage of 'honour.'**

Ans. The Convict had not been under the honour but the Bishop had the intention of saving him from the cops. So, he urged that there was an 'honour' in supper with him.

12. I-I-didn't believe there was any good in the world;...... but somehow you're good, and-and it's a queer thing to ask, but-could you, would you bless me before I go? I-I think it would help me.

(a) **Why does the speaker feel there is no good in the world?**

Ans. The speaker feels this way because he had been sentenced to ten years imprisonment for a small theft and was ill-treated during his imprisonment.

(b) **What has made him change his opinion?**

Ans. The kindness and generosity shown by the Bishop, even though he threatened to kill the Bishop, made him change his opinion.

(c) **Find the word in the extract which is the antonym of 'normal'.**

Ans. The word 'queer' is an antonym of 'normal'.

(d) **Explain – 'It (blessings) would help me'?**

Ans. When the Convict said 'it (blessings) would help me' he meant it. He knew that the blessing of the Bishop would prove to be a milestone in his life.

Short Answer Type Questions

Answer the following questions in 30-40 words each.

1. **Why did the Bishop sell the silver salt-cellars?**

or **How did the Bishop extend help to Mere Gringoire?**

Ans. The Bishop was a kind-hearted man who always helped the needy. He sold his silver salt-cellars in order to help Mere Gringoire who was unable to pay her house rent. He used the money that came from selling the salt-cellars to pay off the poor woman's house rent.

2. **Why did the Bishop give his comforter to Marie?**

Ans. The Bishop was a kind and helpful person. He believed that charity was a way of reaching closer to God. Marie, their maid, was going home for the night and the weather outside was very cold. So, the Bishop gave her his comforter (muffler) for protection against the cold.

3. **How does Persome treat Marie?**

Ans. Persome is a strict mistress. She calls Marie lazy and disorderly. She treats her authoritatively and scolds her in an undignified manner. She scolds her for being so talkative and when she becomes quiet, she again scolds her for being quiet. She finds fault with anything that Marie does.

4. **Why does Persome call the Bishop, 'the dupe of every idle scamp'?**

or **In what ways do the parishioners take advantage of the Bishop's kindness?**

Ans. Persome calls the Bishop, 'the dupe of every idle scamp' because she felt that the Bishop was easily taken advantage of by his parishioners. She thought that people exploited the Bishop's goodness and humility by fooling him. She was in fact hurt to see the Bishop sacrificing his joys and comfort for the sake of others.

5. **Why does Persome call her brother 'a child'?**

Ans. Persome feels 'her brother' is simple and innocent. He bears no ill will against anyone. He is always ready to help others and is sincere in his efforts. He gave away his precious possessions for the sake of the poor. His childlike behaviour makes him neglect himself and so he needs to be looked after like a child.

6. **Persome refers to her brother as incorrigible. Why?**

Ans. The Bishop was in the habit of selling everything he could lay his hands on to help other people. He sold off his estate and spent his savings in bits and pieces to help the poor. Recently, he sold the silver salt-cellars too. Persome was, thus, fed up with her brother's generosity and called him incorrigible.

7. **Why were the doors and windows of the Bishop's house always left open?**

Ans. The doors and windows of the Bishop's house were always left open as he was a simple man who did not suspect that anyone would steal any of his possessions. Moreover, he left the doors open so that anyone who needed help could come in his house at any time of the day.

8. **"I think one who has suffered much." About whom is the Bishop talking? Why has he suffered?**

Ans. The Bishop is talking about the Convict. He has suffered because his wife died due to starvation and then, he was imprisoned for ten years for a small crime. Further, he was given bad and stale food in prison, made to sleep on hard boards, kept chained and beaten up when he complained.

9. **The Convict says "I have lived in hell for ten years". What does he mean? Explain.**

Ans. The Convict's experience in prison was horrifying. He was imprisoned for a minor crime and was kept chained like an animal. He was tortured and beaten up, besides being served bad and stale food. It was indeed hell for him.

10. **What does the Convict tell the Bishop about his life before imprisonment?**

Ans. The life of the Convict before imprisonment was not going well. He had a cottage covered with vines. He had a wife, Jeanette but she was ill. They had a bad year and there was no food to eat. He had to steal to buy food for his wife but was caught and sentenced to ten years imprisonment.

11. **What effect did the inhuman treatment in prison have on the Convict?**

Ans. The Convict received very inhuman treatment in prison, as the jailers whipped him, fed him with bad and stale food, made him sleep on cold hard boards, etc. The Convict felt hurt and afraid by this. Soon, his spirit was broken by this inhumanity. He became just a number and forgot his early life. He even lost the ability to pray for he says that he lost his soul. This inhuman treatment turned him into a beast.

12. **"I was a man once. I am a beast now". What circumstances turned the man into a 'beast' in 'The Bishop's Candlesticks'?**

Ans. The circumstances which turned the Convict into a 'beast' were the unjustifiable prison sentence of ten years awarded to him for a minor theft and the inhuman treatment he suffered in prison, where he was served bad and stale food and beaten mercilessly when he complained about it.

13. **What kind of treatment does the Convict get at the Bishop's house?**

Ans. The Convict got the same treatment at the Bishop's house as any other guest. He was served food and the Bishop asked the Convict to sleep in his room for the night and assured him that no harm would come to him. He also brought coverings for him so that the Convict could sleep comfortably.

14. **"The man with the hungry eyes has gone and he has taken your candlesticks". Who had taken the candlesticks and why?** **Competency Based**

Ans. Persome informed the Bishop that the Convict had taken his candlesticks with him. This was because the Convict had no money and could buy food with the money he would get by selling the silver candlesticks. So, he stuffed the candlesticks in his coat and escaped.

15. **How did the Bishop and Persome react when they learned that the candlesticks are stolen?**

Ans. Persome reacted violently; she shouted and was very upset. She even started a heated argument with the Bishop, only to hear from him that the Convict was in more need of the candlesticks than them.

The Bishop was sorry to lose the candlesticks, as they were given to him by his mother. However, he felt sorry that he was responsible for the Convict's behaviour by keeping them before him, which led him into temptation.

16. **What does the Bishop tell the Sergeant?**

Ans. The Sergeant saw the Convict moving stealthily and arrested him. He brought the Convict along with the stolen candlesticks to the Bishop's house. However, the Bishop told him that the Convict was his friend and the silver candlesticks were a gift from the Bishop to him.

17. **Why did the Bishop give the candlesticks to the Convict ?**

Ans. The Bishop gave the candlesticks to the Convict because of his kind nature. He did so in order to reform the Convict and provide him an opportunity to start life afresh by selling his prized silver candlesticks. He does not want the Convict to go back to prison and live the life of an animal.

18. **What significant role did the Bishop's candlesticks play?**

Or **What was the significance of the silver candlesticks?**

Ans. The candlesticks were a gift from the Bishop's dying mother to him. They reminded him of her. However, when the Convict received them as a gift, they became symbols of hope and life. The Convict could now believe in the goodness of life and lead an honest life.

19. **The Bishop tells Persome that there is so much suffering in the world and he can do so little to lessen it. What suffering did the Bishop talk about and what did he do for that?**

Ans. By suffering, the Bishop means all the hardships that people face in this world. No one in the world is happy because poverty, sickness, financial problems, depression, etc can be seen everywhere. The Bishop wants to help people overcome this suffering. He tries his best to help the poor people by giving them money, his possessions and anything else that he can. He also tries to help the sick people of his parish but he says that it is not enough.

20. 'One must do a great deal for the devil in order to do a little for God.' The Bishop's concern for the Convict was nothing but a reflection of his own belief. Comment.

Ans. It is true that the Bishop's concern for the Convict was nothing but a reflection of his own belief. He treated the Convict with love and kindness. He provided the Convict food and drink as well as arranged for his comfort and sleep. He even saved the Convict from the police even though the Convict was a criminal and had stolen his candlesticks. Thus, he proved that he did a great deal for the devil (personified by the Convict) in order to do a little for God (by reforming the Convict).

21. How did the Bishop react on learning about the betrayal by the Convict? What does it reflect about him?

Ans. The Bishop was heartbroken when he realised that the Convict had stolen his candlesticks. Despite the candlesticks being his mother's last memory, he refused to inform the police as he thought that the candlesticks now belonged to the Convict and would help him to start afresh in life. He didn't want to push the Convict back to a miserable life in the prison.

This speaks highly of his good and sympathetic character, besides his sacrificing nature in letting go of the last memory of his mother. It also shows that he had forgiven the Convict for stealing his candlesticks.

22. Why does the Bishop refer to the Convict as his friend? What do we learn from this behaviour of the Bishop?

Ans. This reference to the Convict as his friend was in front of the Sergeant and Gendarmes because he did not want the Convict to be arrested and imprisoned again. He knew that if he told the Sergeant that the Convict had broken into his house to steal food and had taken his candlesticks the Convict would have again been imprisoned and ill-treated just like before. This shows that the Bishop was a very helpful and kind person and wanted to reform the Convict.

Long Answer Type Questions

Answer the following questions in 120 words each.

1. Persome quoted, "Charity begins at home." With reference to 'The Bishop's Candlesticks', do you feel that the Bishop was doing the same? Reflect on the values that are highlighted through the Bishop's character. Competency Based

Ans. The saying, "Charity begins at home" means that you should take care of your family and the people close to you before you worry about helping others.

However, in the case of the Bishop, it is just the reverse. Persome says this ironically because the Bishop had donated everything he had to help others in need, but not thought of keeping anything for himself or his sister. Persome feels that he should also think about his own survival before donating things to others.

However, the Bishop has highlighted the values of being helpful to others and being selfless by selling the silver salt-cellars to pay Mere Gringoire's rent, giving his comforter to Marie and gifting the silver candlesticks to the Convict.

2. "So, I stole to buy food for my wife. They caught me, I pleaded to them, they laughed at me". Do you think the Convict should have been given a second chance? Which values are being overlooked by the Convict?

Ans. Yes, I think the Convict should have been given a second chance. This is because he was not a professional thief. The circumstances forced him to steal. He had stolen food for his ill wife who ultimately died. This act can be seen as a noble act from the humanitarian point of view.

Had he gotten a chance, he could have changed his ways and worked hard to earn the food that he was forced to steal. He would also have been able to save his wife's life. However, honesty and responsibility towards society are being overlooked by the Convict.

3. "They have made me what I am, they have made me a thief. God curse them all!" This was the Convict's opinion in the play, 'The Bishop's Candlesticks.' Is the Convict justified? Give reasons. Competency Based

Ans. The Convict was a product of unfortunate circumstances and an indifferent society. He was caught and sent to prison for stealing food for his sick wife.

He was inhumanly treated there. His name and soul were taken away from him. This inhuman treatment changed him into a beast. The insensitivity of society and law as well as persistent and prolonged suffering in jail turned him into such a hardened criminal that he did not hesitate to kill, rob and steal. He lost faith in God and religion. Thus, the Convict is indeed justified in his statement. The unfortunate circumstances, violence, ill-treatment and torture that he had gone through in his life made him what he was.

4. The prison is meant for reformation, not punishment. Justify this statement with reference to the play 'The Bishop's Candlesticks'.

Ans. Prisons are meant for reforming criminals but in actual fact this is not the case in most prisons. The treatment given out to Convicts is very harsh and this converts them into hardened criminals.

This is also true for Convicts who have committed minor crimes. Due to this, they lose their trust in the justice system and commit more crimes when released. In 'The Bishop's Candlesticks', the Convict has turned into a hardened criminal due to the torture that he underwent in prison. If the justice system was more tuned towards reforming criminals, probably the Convict would not have tried to escape and would have become a good man once he was released.

5. From your understanding of the play 'The Bishop's Candlesticks', do you agree that it is a human quality to deceive one's benefactors? Justify your statement.

Ans. Deception is a human quality but it is not true for all. Some people, in their greed, end up hurting or cheating people who help them. However, there are others, like the Convict, who learn from their mistakes and regret making them. The Convict regretted stealing the Bishop's candlesticks when the Bishop supported him by saying that he himself had given the candlesticks to the Convict as a gift. Thus, judging all humans based on a single incident is unfair.

There are many people in this world who return the good deeds done to them. Humans have different reactions to the same situation and they will not all react similarly to the same situation.

6. The Bishop gives the same candlesticks to the Convict that he had stolen. Do you think it was right on his part to gift it to the Convict. Why?

Or **The Bishop's philanthropic nature is highlighted by his act of selling his salt-cellars for Mere Gringoire, giving the candlesticks to the Convict and the comforter to Marie. What is your opinion of him as a benefactor?** Competency Based

Ans. The Bishop was indeed right on his part to gift the same candlesticks to the Convict that he had stolen. He saved the Convict from the police and gave his prized silver candlesticks so that the Convict could begin his life afresh. Further, he sold the salt-cellars for paying Mere Gringoire's rent and gave his comforter to Marie. Thus, he was a benefactor to all three of them, enabling them to carry on their lives or start living a new life. These little gestures of the Bishop helped them greatly.

In the beginning, the Convict was an innocent man. However, circumstances turned him into a criminal lacking any human compassion or feelings. It was the Bishop's act of kindness and generosity that transformed him from an animal into a human being. The Bishop's compassion revived his faith in the church, religion and life itself. The urge to once again become a man and start a new life stirred his heart.

7. Kindness and compassion can change lives for the better. Justify the statement with reference to 'The Bishop's Candlesticks.'

Ans. The play conveys the message that goodness dwells in all human beings and no one is born a criminal or sinner. Unfortunate circumstances and an indifferent society turn one into a criminal. Also, it is kindness, generosity and compassion rather than violence, that can change a man for the better.

Provision of a respectable life for everyone and an understanding approach can contribute towards bringing down the crime rate and provide a healing touch to all criminals. The world can become a better place to live in if we have a loving, caring and a respectable attitude towards each other.

8. "Nobody is born a criminal. It is the circumstances which turn a person into a criminal". Elaborate with reference to the play. What qualities should the authorities have to humanely deal with criminals?

Ans. It is rightly said that nobody is born a criminal. It is the circumstances which turn a person into a criminal. In the play, the Convict himself accepted that he had changed from a man to a wild animal. Earlier, the Convict was a normal man. It was extreme poverty that forced him to steal money to buy food for his ill wife.

For this, he had to spend ten years in prison. He had to go through different types of tortures in jail which changed him into an animal. Thus, an innocent man became a hardened criminal because of circumstances, an indifferent society and the law. The authorities should have patience, kindness, benevolence and compassion to humanely deal with criminals.

9. After the Convict left, the Bishop, was very happy that he was able to redeem the Convict and that he went back happy. Put down the feelings of the Bishop in the form of a diary entry expressing his state of happiness. Discuss the values reflected through the Bishop's action of kindness.

Ans. Friday, 27th December, 20XX 10:00 p.m.

Dear Diary

Yesterday, I was able to redeem a soul. The Convict had lost all of his goodness when I met him. After hearing about the unfortunate circumstances, violence, ill-treatment and torture that he had gone through in his life, I developed sympathy for him. I decided to restore his faith in life as he was a good soul. My little act of kindness and generosity changed the Convict.

He was full of gratitude when I called him my friend and saved him from being arrested. I gave my silver candlesticks to him so that he could start a new life. I believe that goodness dwells in all human beings and no one is born a criminal or sinner. I was happy to provide him a start as a respectable person. I can now sleep in peace.

Bishop

10. Imagine you are the Convict. You have just come back from the house of the Bishop as a changed person. Put down your feelings in the form of a diary entry expressing what values helped in bringing about a change in your personality.

Ans. Sunday, 29th December, 20XX 10:00 p.m.

Dear Diary

Today, I'm a free man, free from hell. The Bishop living outside Paris has been my saviour. I'm thankful that I broke into the Bishop's house. He helped me to escape the clutches of the Gendarmes by pretending to be my friend. He has restored my faith in humanity. I have realised now that God resides within me. His compassion and love for me, his kindness towards all, his helpful nature and above all, his faith in God has transformed me. Now, I want to start a new life and follow these values in my own life.

Jean

ASSESSMENT EXERCISE

Extract Based Questions

Read the following extracts carefully and answer the questions that follow.

1. "Madam, it was for the rent. The bailiff would not wait any longer, and threatened to turn her out today ...."

(a) Identify the speaker.

(b) Find the word in the extract which is opposite to 'helped'.

(c) Is the victim rescued finally? Who comes to her rescue?

(d) What do you understand by the word 'baliff'?

2. "But certainly, my son, you shall have food. I will ask my sister for the keys of the cupboard."

(a) Who is hungry and asking for food? Why?

(b) How does the speaker change the stranger's attitude?

(c) Find the word in the extract which is opposite to 'indefinitely'.

(d) Explain the significance of the word 'my son'.

3. "Worth hundreds I'll warrant. If I had these turned into money they'd start me fair. Humph! The old boy's fond of them too, ..."

(a) Who is the speaker and what was worth hundreds?

(b) Why was the 'old boy' fond of them?

(c) What is the meaning of "they'd start me fair"?

(d) What does 'Humph' mean or express?

4. "That is why they are left open."

(a) Who speaks this line to whom?

(b) What does 'they' here stand for and why are 'they' left open?

(c) What does the above statement tell us about the speaker's character?

(d) For whom are 'they' left open?

Short Answer Type Questions

Answer the following questions in 30-40 words each.

1. Persome is a very caring sister to the Bishop. Give three instances to prove this statement.

2. "But you had no right to do so without asking me." Why is Persome angry with Marie?

3. "Why, what is the matter? You have been crying." Why was Persome crying?

4. How does Persome react when she sees the Convict?

5. Do you think the Convict is correct in holding society responsible for his current state? Why?

6. Who is Mere Gringoire and why is she in distress?

Long Answer Type Questions

Answer the following questions in 100-120 words each.

1. Justice is flawed if it is not mingled with mercy and intent to reform. Discuss on the basis of your understanding of the play, 'The Bishop's Candlesticks'.

2. Describe some values observed in the character of the Bishop. How far can these values be practised in actual life?

3. What values should the Convict have learned from his act of stealing to buy food for his ill wife, his torture in jail and finally. his stealing of the candlesticks and arrest by the gendarmes? Why was he reformed after meeting the Bishop?

4. If a man has been a recipient of another person's sacrifice and compassion, the receiver must live upto the expectations of the doer. In what way do you think the Convict could have thanked the Bishop?

ASL

Assessment of Speaking and Listening Skills

CBSE has clearly outlined the significance of Speaking and Listening Skills as a part of co-scholastic areas of achievement by every learner and also stressed the clear integration of Assessment of Speaking and Listening Skills as a part of the curriculum.

As good communication skills raise the self-esteem of a student, CBSE essentially desires that the students acquire proficiency in it by the time they leave school. In the present day global markets, speaking and listening are considered to be the essential skills of real life. So, it has been felt for a long time that CBSE must focus on assessing speaking and listening skills for qualification in examination.

Considering this, CBSE has proposed to give 20% weightage in the Assessment of Speaking and Listening Skills. Therefore, the Assessment of Speaking and Listening Skills will be done formally at the term-end examination. Schools may conduct ASL themselves as per the guidelines provided by the CBSE.

The overall purpose of the test is to help improve and standardise student's communicative skills. Thus, in keeping with the international standards, the CBSE has put this assessment in place.

Listening Skills

The **Listening Comprehension** section tests the student's ability to listen for basic interpersonal, instructional and academic purposes. A number of sub-skills need to be developed in the everyday classroom transaction. Given below are some of the sub-skills of listening which need to be assessed in the formative and summative assessments.

(i) Listening for specific information
(ii) Listening for general understanding
(iii) Predictive listening
(iv) Inferential listening
(v) Listening for pleasure
(vi) Intensive listening
(vii) Evaluative listening

Role of Examiner

Here the Examiner is assigned the job of assessing a candidate's performance in any of the skills that is to be assessed.

It is extremely important to keep in mind the factors listed below as they can significantly influence the expected outcome of the Listening Test.

- Size of the room
- Seating arrangements
- Acoustics of the room
- Equipment used
- Quality of the recording of the listening input
- Quality of the oral rendering of the listening input (in case it is to be read aloud by the Examiner), in terms of volume, clarity, enunciation, intonation, pace, etc.

Test Administration *For the Examiner (Teacher)*

- Select the time and date of the assessment.
- Plan the seating arrangement in advance.
- Decide exactly as to how much time is to be reserved for instructions or any possible interaction regarding clarifications, etc and for the actual test.
- Make the announcement giving general instructions directed to the candidates before the recording is played or before the reading of the text.
- Adhere strictly to the time specified for each of the three phases of the Test (Pre-listening, While listening and Post-listening)
- The general instructions given below should be followed while conducting the test.

The Listening Assessment

The Listening Assessment comprises a variety of tasks. These tasks are graded according to the length of the task and the difficulty level. Schools may download the sample tasks and reorganise them in two parts - transcripts and the marking scheme for the examiner and the worksheets for the students on which students will write answers.

General Instructions for Students

- You are not allowed to ask questions or interrupt the Examiner at any point.
- You are being tested on your Listening Skills.
- You will hear a set of recordings of the Listening Input or listen to a reading of the Listening Input.
- Each of the recordings will be played twice. In case there is an oral rendering of the Listening Input, it shall take place twice.
- You are required to answer a set of questions based on each of the Listening Inputs.
- The assessment consists of 4 sections.
- You are required to attempt all 4 sections of the assessment.
- Familiarise yourself with the questions on the worksheet. It will help you to answer them later on.
- After you have listened to the input, you will be given specified minutes to answer the questions on your worksheet.
- You may answer the questions on your worksheet while listening.
- Do not interact/comment until you have moved out of the Examination room.

PRACTICE ASSIGNMENT

> ***Instructions***
>
> The test comprises four tasks which have been divided into twenty questions.
>
> Each question carries 1 mark.
>
> Each of the tasks is based on a transcript which may be in the form of a speech, conversation, or a short extract conveying some useful information.
>
> Answer the questions as you listen to the transcripts.

☑ TASK 1

Questions

You will hear some tips on improving memory. Read the notes below, then listen to the teacher's tips and complete the notes using one or two words only. You will hear the recording twice.

1. **Use games to .... your brain.**
2. **Make an effort to reduce .... in your daily life.**
3. **Say things you need to learn .... more than once.**
4. **Put things in .... to help remember them.**

Transcript

Teacher Now I know you are all trying to prepare for the examinations, so let me give you some tips on how to improve your memory! Ready?

Use crossword puzzles and chess and so on to exercise your brain.

Worry makes you forget things, so try to reduce stress in your day-to-day life.

Create memorable images in your mind to help you remember the important facts.

Repeat things you need to learn out loud several times.

When you need to remember things, it can help if you try to put them altogether into groups.

Try meditation.

If you follow these simple tips, you will improve your memory and do better in your examination.

☑ TASK 2

Questions

You will hear four short extracts about the advantages of the internet. Read the statements given below, then listen to the extracts and match each statement A-F to each speaker 1-4. There are two statements you do not need. You will hear the recordings twice.

A. Online library access makes studying easier.

B. Online courses let you study in your own house.

C. Books can be downloaded easily.

D. Search engines are a faster way of finding information.

E. Shopping online is not boring.

F. A means of communication available day and night.

Transcript

Speaker 1 In the past I would have had to spend hours in the library and live in the town where I was doing my degree, but I'm a busy housewife with three small children to bring up and that's just not practical. Now, over the internet, I have access to the documents I need from any university library in the world. So I can continue my studies and look after my family at the same time.

Speaker 2 I work in a busy press office, and in the past I had to search through paper after paper for relevant articles. It was very boring. But nowadays, it's so much easier, as I just use the search engines of the national daily newspapers, and the article or news item I am looking for comes up immediately.

Speaker 3 I never imagined five years ago that I'd be doing this, but it's wonderful. You know, when something breaks down in Germany, or Poland , or somewhere, they e-mail me. It can be at any time of the day or night, and I simply send them instructions over the internet so that they can put it right and get back to work. Managing business in a foreign country has become so much easier.

Speaker 4 I live in a small town and I am taking a course in English Language. It's really not practical for me to travel into a city, just for a couple of lessons a week. I mean, the journey's not very easy. Anyway, luckily, I heard about these online courses run by the university, and it's such a pleasure to be able to do everything from home.

TASK 3

Questions

You will now listen to a conversation where a girl is talking to her father about yoga. Read the questions below, then listen to the talk and write your answers. You will hear the recording twice.

1. **State whether the following statements are True or False.**
   (a) Meera tells her father that the yoga method is similar to the warmth of sunlight.
   (b) Meera's father has heard of hot yoga before.
   (c) Jonathan was a yogi before becoming a lawyer.
2. **Fill in the blanks with appropriate words or phrases.**
   (a) The most popular version of hot yoga is called ....
   (b) Some of the major benefits of hot yoga are increased .... and reduced ....

Transcript

Father You said you were going for a yoga class today. Tell me about your experience.

Meera My friends in class said they heard of a new yoga method that warms the body the same way sunlight does.

Father This sounds so interesting. And what is it actually known as?

Meera It's called hot yoga.

Father Is it a new concept? I don't recall reading or hearing about this.

Meera Hot yoga is not a new concept. The most well-known version is called Bikram.

Father That's an Indian name.

Meera Yes indeed, it was founded in California in 1976 by a living yoga master Bikram Choudhury.

Father Tell me more about the technique. Does it have many poses?

Meera Imagine, Dad, it consists of 26 poses. They are called *asanas*. His original series of 26 poses are now practised in studios around the world.

Father And what happens? Does the body temperature rise?

Meera Yes, the human body gets heated to a sweltering 40 degrees Celsius with 40% humidity.

Father That is very high heat to deal with–I would find it very uncomfortable.

Meera Yes, Dad, we were told that while the health benefits of Bikram are widely recognised, some find the heat too much and complain of feeling dizzy or sick during the class.

Father I read of another place today called Triyoga Chelsea.

Meera That sounds so unique, please tell me about it.

Father Triyoga Chelsea is a beautiful, clean and airy space opened by lawyer-turned-yogi Jonathan Sattin.

Meera He must be very passionate about yoga.

Father I suppose so. He creates a warm space with infrared panels on the ceiling that heat up your body rather than just the air around you—much like the feeling of lying in the Sun.

Meera What would the temperature be, Dad?

Father I guess about 34 degrees Celsius.

Meera That seems more comfortable for the human body.

Father It seems you do an hour of poses ranging from breathing exercises to static postures. And in that time you will work up a sweat and leave feeling balanced and recharged.

Meera I'm told that yoga has many natural benefits for the human body.

Father Yes, of course—hot yoga benefits are amazing–they are able to offer benefits like increased flexibility, reduced stress, weight loss and the release of toxins.

Meera I recall reading that hot yoga also leaves you with glowing skin. In a way, you could even think of it as a facial and workout in one.

☑ TASK 4

Questions

You will hear a speech about joint families. Read the questions given below, then listen to the extracts and choose A or B or C for each question. You will hear the recording twice.

1. **People prefer nuclear families because**
   (a) there is more freedom
   (b) there are fewer members
   (c) it is the latest trend in many countries
2. **According to the speaker, young people don't listen to elders because they**
   (a) don't want to be restricted. (b) think they know better. (c) learn from their mistakes.
3. **In a joint family, you don't have to ask for help from outsiders as**
   (a) you are smart enough to make decisions.
   (b) your children are able to take care of themselves.
   (c) your family members are there to support you.
4. **Joint families follow the concept of sharing as**
   (a) the clothes are shared among family members.
   (b) all family members are collectively responsible.
   (c) the finances are distributed equally.
5. **Joint families do not depend on outside help for children because**
   (a) grandparents take care of them.
   (b) mothers stay at home.
   (c) children care for each other.
6. **The best way to create a good joint family is to**
   (a) be open to differences in opinion.
   (b) listen to elders all the time.
   (c) not voice your views on anything.

Transcript

A nuclear family consists of husband, wife and their children. The concept of joint family where all the family members like aunt, uncle, cousins and grandparents live together contrasts with the idea of a nuclear family. There are many countries where you would traditionally find many joint families but at the same time the concept of nuclear families is catching on. We often forget that there are many advantages of a joint family.

The most important advantage that attracts people to nuclear families is that the couple can have their privacy in their own home. People can live their own way and can do whatever they want to. There are no boundaries set by the elders to follow. In a joint family, the elders restrict youngsters not to do certain things because they think it is not good for them. But today's generation is very smart. They know what is good and bad for them and have enough analytical power so they don't like to restrict themselves. Instead, they want their freedom so that they can do and achieve whatever they want in their life.

The advantages of joint families are many. You get the complete support of family members whenever needed. You don't have to ask for help from others, if all family members are living together. Your children will not be left alone at home when you go to a job. Many burglaries take place during the daytime because nobody is present in the home, so if there is a joint family, burglary cases also decrease. You can share your joys and sorrows with them. Each and every member of the family shares his/her opinions and the family takes a decision together. One member is not burdened with the responsibility of decision-making and it becomes a joint responsibility. The basic pillar of a joint family is to have healthy and selfless moral values for all members.

In a joint family, one always gets guidance from older people. They are more experienced. They can take care of grandchildren rather than depending on outside help. In a joint family, the elders are always there to guide and encourage us in every decision we take and their experiences make us grow wiser and become a better person. But again, it revolves around how considerate we are–how we listen to others' points of view before considering our own. Keeping an open mind, accepting our faults and moving ahead is the best way to make a joint family an ideal family.

Answers

Task 1

1. exercise **2.** stress **3.** out loud **4.** groups

Task 2

1. A **2.** D **3.** F **4.** B

Task 3

1. (a) True (b) False (c) False **2.** (a) Bikram (b) flexibility, stress

Task 4

1. (a) there is more freedom.
2. (a) don't want to be restricted.
3. (c) your family members are there to support you.
4. (b) all family members are collectively responsible.
5. (a) grandparents take care of them.
6. (a) be open to differences in opinion.

Speaking Skills

The speaking skill has acquired a very important place as a communication skill. Like listening skill—a number of sub-skills of speaking need to be consciously developed among students. Some of the sub-skills which can be assessed are as follows:

- Speaking intelligibly using appropriate word stress, sentence stress and intonation patterns.
- Narrating incidents and events, real or imaginary in a logical sequence.
- Presenting oral reports or summaries; making announcements clearly and confidently.
- Expressing and arguing a point of view clearly and effectively.
- Taking active part in group discussions, showing ability to express agreement or disagreement, summarising ideas, eliciting the views of others and presenting own ideas.
- Expressing and responding to personal feelings, opinions and attitudes.
- Participating in spontaneous spoken discourse in familiar social situations.

General Instructions

The total administration time for the speaking assessment is approximately 10-12 mins.

The speaking assessment will be conducted for two students at a time.

There will be a single teacher to function as the examiner.

The examiner should be a qualified English teacher.

Role of Examiner

- The examiner should ensure that the room is quiet and has good acoustics.
- The tone, manner and body language of the examiner should be relaxed, encouraging and pleasant. Care should be taken to make the candidates feel at ease.
- Students must not be discouraged from making a fresh start in case they are unable to do so at the first attempt.
- The examiner needs to be flexible, sympathetic and reassuring in her/his demeanour.
- The examiner should also be a proficient user of the language in order to conduct the speaking assessment successfully. For example, the examiner should be skilled in elicitation techniques, so that questions such as... "Explain how"/"Why"..."Tell me what you think of " .... may be asked. Yes/ No questions should generally be avoided.
- Ideally, the examiner should award marks after the candidates have left the examination room. If necessary, notes can be made discreetly to be used later in the scoring, so that it does not make the candidates unduly tense and self-conscious.

The Speaking Assessment is divided into three stages

Stage 1 General Introduction

The aim of this introductory task is to put the candidate at ease through some general, open-ended questions, thereby creating a space for the candidate to respond with personal feelings and opinions. Simple warm up questions based on the candidate's names, place of residence, leisure preferences, etc. are asked.

Stage 2 Topic Presentation

This can take the form of PowerPoint/OHP presentations, book reviews, debates, speech, etc. The focus of this task is to assess a candidate's ability to sustain a straightforward, subjectwise description, mapped out in a fluent and cohesive style.

In this section, the examiner gives each candidate the choice to pick up a Role Card or a Cue Card with a topic written on it. The candidates are given 1 min to prepare. The examiner should be ready with sheets of paper and a pencil. Candidates may organise their thoughts and ideas. Prior to the day of the speaking assessment, as an assistance to students to prepare for the presentations, the teacher can give a choice of 20 to 30 topics in class to students so that they can prepare presentations based on the topics and organise their ideas. Similar topics can be given in the formal assessment. Please note that students are not allowed to write full length answers. They may jot down points only in the sheets given by the examiner. Therefore, a pencil and sheet of paper should be provided on the table. Students are not allowed to carry pen, paper or mobile phone to the examination room. After a minute, each student will be given 2 mins each to present his/her ideas. In case, a student is unable to speak during/for the allotted time, the Examiner may ask some rounding off questions.

Stage 3 Problem Solving (Pair Interaction)

The third section of the test is for 3 mins. Both students are given a verbal or visual stimulus and asked to respond to it. Both the students are given a total of 3 mins to interact. Both of them will talk together. After 2 mins the examiner can ask questions based on their discussion.

Closing

The closing is for 1 min duration only. In case a students has not been able to speak or has been unable to speak owing to nervousness, the dominance of the second candidate or any other factor, then the examiner may use the 1 min to give a fresh opportunity to that student.

CBSE Assessment of Speaking and Listening (ASL) Descriptors for Assessment of Speaking

Interactive Competence	5	4	3	2	1
Task Management	Contributions are highly effective and fulfil the task. Can fulfil the communicative functions of the level with spontaneity.	Contributions are effective and fulfil the task. Can fulfil the communicative functions of the level.	Contributions are adequate and fulfil the task. Can fulfil functions of the level but may not do so consistently.	Contributions are limited and there is some attempt at the task which is not fulfilled and/or may be repetitive.	There is almost no contribution and/or contributions may not be related to the task.
Initiation and Turn-taking	Is prompt to initiate discussions on the themes/ functions at the given level appropriately. Contributes spontaneously to keep the interaction going; takes turns appropriately.	Is easily able to initiate discussions on the themes/ functions at the given level appropriately. Contributes effectively to keep the interaction going and takes turn appropriately.	Is able to initiate discussions on the themes/ functions at the given level. Makes an effort to keep the interaction going; takes turns.	Struggles to initiate discussions on the themes/functions at the given level. Makes little effort to keep the interaction going;	Does not initiate discussions. Makes no effort to keep the interaction going.
Appropriacy and Relevance	Speaks with a clear sense of purpose and audience in both formal and informal situations. Contributions are always appropriate to the context/ situation.	Speaks with a fair sense of purpose and audience in both formal and informal situations. May be less confident in normal situations.	Speaks with an awareness of purpose and audience may not adapt register effectively. Contributions are appropriate to the context/situation.	Has unclear sense of purpose and may be unable to adapt register. Contributions may be unconnected to the context/ situation.	Has hardly any sense of purpose and cannot adapt to register.

Fluency	5	4	3	2	1
Cohesion and Coherence Speed of Delivery	Presents information in a logical sequence of linked utterances with a clear connection between ideas, arguments and statements. Uses a range of cohesive devices. Speak fluently with minimal hesitation. Intelligible speed of delivery.	Presents information in a logical sequence of linked utterances with a connection between ideas, arguments and statements. Uses with ease some cohesive devices. Speaks fluently with some hesitation. Intelligible speed of delivery.	Presents information generally in a logical order but overall progression may not always be clear. Uses a range of cohesive devices but some over/under use. Coherence may be affected by hesitancy or rephrasing. Intelligible speed of delivery.	Presents information but without clear progression. Uses limited cohesive devices repetitively. Severe hesitation may impede communication. Speed of delivery impedes understanding.	Presents information with no progression and/or little control of organisational features. May use only isolated words and phrases.

Pronunciation	5	4	3	2	1
Pronunciation, Stress and Intonation	Has clear, natural pronunciation that can be easily understood by the listener. Varies stress and intonation in keeping with the task, content and meaning.	Has pronunciation that can be easily understood by the listener. Varies stress and intonation in keeping with the task, content and meaning.	Is intelligible though there are examples of some mispronunciation. Tries to speak, varying stress and intonation according to task, content and meaning.	Is not always intelligible and the listener may have to ask for repetition from time to time Flat intonation and/or inappropriate stress for the task, content or meaning	Is not intelligible...

Language	5	4	3	2	1
Accuracy	Uses a range of grammatical patterns with accuracy, including some complex forms. Makes only negligible errors.	Uses a range of grammatical patterns with accuracy, including few complex forms and makes only noticeable errors.	There may be some mistakes which affect meaning but there is an attempt to correct most of these mistakes.	There are mistakes which affect meaning but there is hardly an attempt to correct these mistakes.	Communicates with fragments of words and structures but does not manage to bridge the gaps or correct his/her mistakes.
Range	Uses an expressive and appropriate range of structures, words and phrases on topics appropriate to the level and to deliver an effective message.	Uses an expressive and appropriate range of words and phrases on topics appropriate to the level. These may be repetitive.	Can use the language of the level but is repetitive. May search for words with the risk of the message becoming weaker.	Uses basic, simple words and phrases for the level. There may be an effort to find suitable words, which may hamper the message.	Uses simple, isolated words for the level. There is little effort to find words.

AN OVERVIEW OF SPEAKING TEST

STAGE 1

1. Introduction (1 min)

Section Time	Procedure
10 secs	Examiner Hello, please sit down. My name is X. What's your name? *(to Candidate A)* And what's your name? *(to Candidate B)* So your names are *(name and serial number A)* and *(name and serial number B).*
25 secs	*(Candidate A), tell me something about (e.g. where you live).* Candidate A responds
25 secs	*(Candidate B), tell me something about (e.g. your school).* Candidate B responds

STAGE 2

2. Topic Presentation (4 min)

Section Time	Procedure
5 secs	Examiner Now *(Candidate A)*, you are going to tell us about your topic. When you have finished, *(Candidate B)* will ask you a question and then I will ask you some more questions. Would you like to begin please?
1 min	Candidate A speaks
15 secs	Examiner Thank you. *(Candidate B)* can you ask *(Candidate A)* a question please? Candidate B asks question ; Candidate A responds
40 secs	The examiner asks 2 or 3 follow-up questions as appropriate from the topic prompt list. *Stage 2 example follow-up questions* How often do you .... ? Why? When you .... do you .... ? Why do you think .... is important?
5 secs	Examiner Thank you. Now *(Candidate B)*, you are going to tell us about your topic. When you have finished, *(Candidate A)* will ask you a question and then I will ask you some more questions. Would you like to begin please?
1 min	Candidate B speaks
15 secs	Examiner Thank you. *(Candidate A)* can you ask *(Candidate B)* a question please? Candidate A asks a question; Candidate B responds.
40 secs	The examiner aks 2 or 3 follow-up questions as appropriate from the topic prompt list.

STAGE 3

3. Problem Solving (3 min)

Section Time	Procedure
25 secs	Examiner Thank you. Now let's go to the next task.
	I'm going to give you a card which has information about a problem.
	I'd like you to read the information and then discuss together how you are gong to solve the problem.
	You have 2 mins to do this. Here is your problem.
	Stage 3 sample problem solving card
	Your classmates have not been keeping the school tidy. After lessons there is litter in the classrooms and in the halls.
	With your partner, discuss this problem and decide what you can do to make the school a nicer, cleaner place for everyone.
	Candidates read the given card (20 secs) and then the examiner asks them to start speaking.
2 min	Candidates discuss the problem and a solution.
35 secs	Examiner OK, can you stop now please.
	Option A (for candidates who have not reached a solution):
	Thank you. *(Move straight on to a question)*
	Option B (for candidates who have not reached a solution):
	Can you agree on a solution? What is it?
	Candidates explain
	Then the examiner asks 1 or 2 follow-up questions as appropriate from the list of problem solving prompts.
	Stage 3 example follow-up questions
	Do you think your solution will be effective enough? Why?/Why not? What role do you think .... plays in this problem? Why? .... sounds interesting. Could you tell me more about that/this?
	Please stop there. That's the end of the test.
	Thank you and go

PRACTICE ASSIGNMENT

Instructions

The speaking assessment will be conducted for two students at a time.

Students should not have pen, paper, mobile phone, etc.

The teacher will be both an examiner and an assessor.

STAGE 1

1. **General Introduction (1 min)**

The examiner makes the students feel comfortable

Examiner	Good morning, I am ...... Hope you are looking forward to this brief interaction.
Student A	Yes .... / I am ....
Examiner	And what about you? *(Looking at Student B)*
Student B	....
Examiner	What do you do in your spare time? *(To Student B)*
Student B	....
Examiner	And how about you? *(To Student A)*
Student A	....
Examiner	What makes you special? *(To Student A)*
Student A	....
Examiner	What about you? *(To Student B)*
Student B	....
Examiner	What do you admire in other people? *(To Student A)*
Student A	....
Examiner	How about you? *(To Student B)*
Student B	....
Examiner	Thank you. This is the end of the first part of the test.

STAGE 2

2. **Mini Presentation (1 min Preparation + 2 mins each for the students = 5 mins)**
Now, in this part of the test, candidates are given a topic with some points. They have a minute to prepare on the given topic and two minutes for the presentation.

Students are given the following sets of inputs on cards or sheets of paper. Three options are given. Only one option has to be used at a time.

Examiner *(To both A and B)* Here is your topic. Both of you prepare your presentation on it. You are given one minute for preparation. Please use the pencil and paper for writing points. After one minute, I ask you to present your views on the topic. I can ask either one of you first. So be prepared and get ready. *(Examiner hands over one card with cues to both A and B)*

Mobile phones in school

- Security
- Multiple uses
- Distraction

If the student is not able to speak at length, the teacher could ask rounding off questions.

- Do you think mobile phones should be allowed in school?
- Give two advantages of carrying a mobile phone to school.
- Do you think advantages outweigh the disadvantages?

2. Changing concepts and methodologies of teaching-learning in India
   - Examination pattern
   - Variety of subjects
   - Assessment parameters

If the student is not able to speak at length, the teacher could ask rounding off questions.

- Do you like this present system of evaluation?
- Do you learn better when you are stress free?
- Do you think some students take this system very casually?

3. An incident/person/book that changed my life.
   - What it is?
   - What it is about?
   - How it affected me?

If the student is not able to speak at length, the teacher could ask rounding off questions.

- What was that specific quality that remained with you?
- What did you learn?
- How would you like to be now?

STAGE 3

3. Pair Interaction (3 mins)

Examiner In this part of the test, the candidates A and B will discuss the given topic together. The examiner can refer to the assessment scale while the candidates are discussing together.

Students respond to visual/verbal stimulus.

1. **Changing roles of women— a multi-tasker, works in office, answers phone calls and is always under pressure of work. Working at home is additional.**

2. **Growing Pollution—all kinds of pollution, water, air and tourism pollution.**

3. **Discipline issues in schools are now becoming a serious concern. As responsible citizens discuss**
   (i) Kinds of indiscipline issues
   (ii) Reasons for growing indiscipline
   (iii) Advice/solutions for your fellow students.
4. **Closing (1 min)**
   Thank you very much. That was the end of your test. The examiner retrieves the pencil and paper.

Suggested Topics for Presentation

1. Women Empowerment
2. Child Abuse in India
3. Speaking English is the ladder to success
4. Does Science hold the key to the future?
5. Corruption cannot be eradicated from India
6. Crime against women
7. Biodiversity
8. Effects of pollution on historical monuments
9. Social networking has made us antisocial
10. Is Delhi a home away from home for North-Eastern students?
11. Female Foeticide
12. Effects of Advertisement on children
13. Keeping pets is a violation of animal rights
14. Science is a threat to humanity
15. Parents should let teens make their own decisions
16. Reality Television does more harm than good
17. Juveniles should be tried as adults
18. Mercy Killing
19. Value-based politics is the need of the hour
20. Global climate change is man-made.

Suggested Questions for Problem Solving Task

1. Some of your classmates are under-confident in speaking English. They are also a little shy and do not know how to get help. They simply do not know how to improve their spoken English. With your partner, discuss what could be done to help them.
2. Your school's basketball team has been performing badly for a few months and has not won any matches. The morale of the team is also very low. With your partner, discuss how the situation could be handled, and the performance of the team could be improved.
3. You have a friend in your class who wants to learn swimming, but also confesses that he/she is scared of water. With your partner, discuss how this fear can be overcome.

Sample Question Paper 1 (Solved)

A Highly Simulated Sample Question Paper for CBSE Class IX

English Communicative

Time : 3 hrs	M.M. : 80

General Instructions

1 This question paper is divided into four sections.
2 All questions are compulsory.
3 Separate instructions are given with each section and question, wherever necessary. Read these instructions very carefully and follow them.
4 Do not exceed the prescribed word limit while answering the questions.

Section A (Reading Skills) [20 Marks]

1. Read the following passage carefully. (10)

1. It was the city's first indoor play park of its kind. Like a good mother, I was sceptical of virtually every aspect of it. How could it succeed? Why should it succeed? How would a set of contraptions in a room hold the attention of today's children? Don't call me paranoid: I stood with dozens of mothers in similar states of quandary, while the cheerful staff whisked away the curious kids for an hour. "I thought she blew the whistle after 15 minutes," huffed the pre-teen when she returned.
2. The manager came up to me. "I told you, the child would have a blast," she laughed. And explained, "There are hardly any parks in our cities." She meant, hardly anywhere children can be themselves and like a Maria in 'The Sound of Music', where they could climb a tree, scrap their knees and tear their dresses. Most of the recreation now is limited to electronic activity and given half a chance, children would jump for something more physically explorative. Even if it is simple stuff like climbing, whizzing down and jumping on a trampoline.
3. Latest research shows that computer games slow down brain development. The 'in' thing till yesterday, they are 'out' today. Says Nandita Sharma, parent of a well-adjusted teenager, "Any mother can tell that standing at a console, juggling a joy-stick isn't conducive to physical relaxation. I rationed Karan's hours at the video games and made sure he spent evenings with his friends in the little space outside the house." Nandita was also afraid that the bright lights of computer games could hurt young eyes. Nor did she like the topic most of the games are based on. "There's just too much violence and fast activity. I know my kid can't lag behind in today's world and computer games certainly sharpen reflexes, but I wish the games would be more interactive and socially inclusive."
4. Indeed, apart from making a zombie out of the child, research indicates that computer games only stimulate activity in the parts of the brain associated with vision and movement. It can also lead the child to be more violent. The lack of mental calisthenics curbs their agility in controlling their response to an unsavoury situation.
5. Moreover, most electronic games isolate the child from the group fun of playing outdoors. Playing with peers and taking a toss or two appreciably strengthens the child's tolerance of others. This behaviour is governed by the frontal lobe, which continues to develop in humans till about 20 years. The more this lobe is exercised during moments of restraint, the more the fibres connecting the neurons in this part of the brain thicken, improving the individual's control of reactions. Playing electronic games, research shows does not encourage the development of this lobe.

6. So now, the parents know what to do-put away the placebos. After school and home assignment hours, the best thing they could do for their kid is invite his friends home and roll the carpet away!

Based on your understanding of the passage, answer the questions given below.

(i) Pick out the option that correctly lists the author's opinion towards gaming. **(1)**

(a) Supportive (b) Disapproving (c) Satisfying (d) Illogical

(ii) The writer would agree with the given statements, based on Paragraph 4, EXCEPT **(1)**

(a) Computer games make a child more violent.

(b) A child becomes a zombie if he plays computer games.

(c) Computer games aid a child's agility in controlling their response to an unsuitable situation.

(d) Computer games stimulate activity in the brain associated with vision and movement.

(iii) Complete the sentence appropriately. **(1)**

The author was paranoid about the indoor play park because ....

(iv) Substitute the underlined word in the given sentence with a word from the passage which means the same. **(1)**

The evidence provided by Jaya made me <u>doubtful</u> of the new employee.

(v) The given passage posits that the indoor play park was a hit. Based on your understanding, state the reasons of this success. **(1)**

(vi) Suggest a suitable title for the above passage. **(1)**

(vii) Comment on the writer's reference to computer games in Paragraph 3, as a health problem for children. (30-40 words) **(2)**

(viii) List two reasons why parents prefer outdoor physical activity for their children in comparison to video games. Answer in 30-40 words. **(2)**

2. Read the following passage carefully. **(10)**

1. Schizophrenia is a chronic and severe mental disorder affecting more than 20 million people worldwide which is characterised by distortions in thinking, perception, emotions, language, sense of self and behaviour. Common psychotic experiences include hallucinations and delusions which involve having fixed, false beliefs.

2. The treatment planning of schizophrenia has three goals which are to reduce or eliminate symptoms, to maximise quality of life and adaptive functioning and to promote and maintain recovery from the debilitating effects of illness to the maximum extent possible. Medications are invaluable in the management of patients with mental illnesses. Pharmacists are therefore indispensable in improving the quality of service rendered to patients with mental illnesses such as schizophrenia which contributes to reduction of the numerous problems associated with and faced by such patients.

3. Management of patients with such conditions is generally a collaborative effort which encompasses incorporation of skills of a myriad of health care professionals involved in patient care. Clinical pharmacists have been instrumental in several roles such as being educators, consultants and providers. They are authorities in pharmaceutical care; they also apply their complementary skills and knowledge in managing these patients together with other health care professionals in the multidisciplinary team. They contribute to patient care by playing a vital role in the detection, resolution and prevention of medication-related problems. In ensuring the safe and efficacious use of medications, clinical pharmacists are also pivotal. In addition, pharmacists are available to provide comprehensive drug information to patients, the patient's relatives and other health care professionals involved in patient management. Pharmacists spearhead medication adherence and are involved in education on primary prevention of mental illnesses, health promotion and lifestyle modification.

Based on your understanding of the passage, answer the questions given below.

(i) Complete the given sentence appropriately. **(1)**

Patients with .... require a collaborative effort encompassing incorporation of skills of multiple health care professionals.

(ii) Complete the following analogy correctly with a word/phrase from the above passage. **(1)**

Perception : Awareness :: .... : False belief

(iii) Select the option listing the objectives of treatment of schizophrenia. **(1)**

(a) Reduce symptoms
(b) To increase the quality of life
(c) To promote recovery
(d) All of these

(iv) Which of the following statements is True in the context of the passage? **(1)**

(a) The treatment planning of schizophrenia has four goals.
(b) Schizophrenia is a chronic and severe mental disorder.
(c) Neurosurgeons contribute to patient care by playing a vital role in the detection, resolution and prevention of medication-related problems.
(d) Schizophrenia is irreversible and incurable.

(v) Complete the following statement by choosing an appropriate option. **(1)**

Pharmacists are available to provide comprehensive drug information to patients, the patient's relatives and other health care professionals involved in patient management. This statement is ....

(vi) What should be title of the report? What is the purpose of this passage? **(1)**

(vii) Infer one reason for the following statement, based on information in Paragraph 2. (30-40 words) **(2)**

Pharmacists are integral to provide quality service to the patients of schizophrenia.

(viii) What are the clinical pharmacists involved in addition to making sure that medication is strictly followed? Answer in 30-40 words. **(2)**

Section B (Writing Skills) **[24 Marks]**

3. **You are Amar, the Secretary of Environment Club of Dharmik Sandhya Public School. Write a notice to invite students of Class IX to the Tree Plantation Drive organised by the club on the World Environment Day.** **(4)**

4. **Two friends, Ram and Shyam, are talking about the hazards of smoking. Write the dialogue between them in about 100 words.** **(5)**

5. **Write a letter to your younger brother advising him to take part in evening games in about 120 words.** **(7)**

6. **Write a paragraph on the visual clue given below.** **(8)**

Or **Write a paragraph on the adventure sport paragliding. You can use the following clues.**

Adventure sport – lightweight, free-flying, foot-launched glider aircraft – pilot sitting in harness – air pressure entering vents in front of the wing – no engine used – cover many hundreds of kilometers – 1-2 hour flight is more common

Section C (Grammar) [10 Marks]

7. Fill in the blanks with the most grammatically appropriate words. **(3)**

Rain *(a)* .... (come/comes/came) as a welcome relief after the heat and dust of the summer. Rain is *(b)* .... (a/an/the) wonderful gift of nature to all mankind. If there is no rain, all the vegetation *(c)* .... (will/would/could) wither away.

8. In the passage that follows, one word has been omitted in each line. Write the missing word along with the word that comes before and the word that comes after it in your answer sheets. **(4)**

	Word Before	Word Missing	Word After
The Theory of Evolution states that the plants and animals			
(a) in the world today developed in natural way from earlier	....	....	....
(b) forms that simpler. These earlier forms developed from	....	....	....
(c) still simpler ancestors and process goes back to millions of	....	....	....
(d) years ago to the very beginning, when life was in simplest form,	....	....	....
merely a tiny mass of jelly-like protoplasm.			

9. (i) Rearrange the following jumbled words/phrases in the given information to form a meaningful sentence. **(3)**

The tiger population stands at a slim 1411 in India today. The Indian authorities are really concerned. The population of tigers is falling sharply.

considered/was/tigers,/Sariska,/for/sanctuary/a/which/tigers left/have/any/does not

(ii) Report the given dialogue to complete the paragraph that follows.

Swara Hey, Ruchi! How are you? Did you enjoy during the holidays?

Ruchi Yes, I had a lot of fun with my family. We all went to Kerala for ten days and it was an amazing experience.

Swara exclaimed as she met Ruchi and asked her how she was. Further, she asked her

(a) .... Ruchi answered in affirmative and said that she

(b) .... family. She added that they all had gone to Kerala for ten days and that it was an amazing experience.

Section D (Literature Textbook) [26 Marks]

10. Read the given extracts and answer the questions that follow. (attempt any two) **(4 + 4 = 8)**

(i) In 1953, Hooper was a favoured young man. A big genuine grin civilised his highly competitive nature. Standing six-foot-one, he'd played on the university football team. He was already a hard-charging Zone Sales Manager for a chemical company.

(a) Who was Hooper?

(b) What do you mean by a 'favoured young man'?

(c) Write three adjectives that have been used for Charles Hooper.

(d) What is the opposite of 'genuine'?

(ii) Two roads diverged in a yellow wood,
And sorry I could not travel both
And be one traveller, long I stood
And looked down one as far as I could
To where it bent in the undergrowth;

(a) What do you mean by 'yellow wood'?

(b) Why is the speaker feeling sorry?

(c) Why is the poet confused?

(d) The word .... in the extract means 'a dense growth of plants.'

(iii) Gaston I told you before we crossed the road that I didn't want it. As soon as you see a sign 'Villa for Sale', you have to go inside and be shown over it.
Jeanne But we are buying a villa, aren't we?
Gaston We are not.
Jeanne What do you mean 'We are not'? Then 'we're not' looking for a villa?

(a) What do you mean by 'we are not'?

(b) Do you really think that they are not buying the villa?

(c) Did Gaston stick to his decision till the end?

(d) What do you understand by '.......' be shown over it?

11. Answer any six of the following questions in about 30-40 words each. **$(6 \times 2 = 12)$**

(a) What guesses does the poet make with regard to the solitary reaper's song?

(b) Why was Sudha Murty surprised when her grandmother touched her feet?

(c) Why does everyone resent Private Quelch?

(d) Where was Pescud going by train and why?

(e) Why was Charles Hooper a favoured young man in 1953?

(f) Why was Harold's father's profession kept a secret from him?

(g) From where does the brook emerge and where does it go?

12. Answer any one of the following questions in about 120 words. **(6)**

How was the sale of the villa a battle of wits between Gaston ans Juliette in the play 'Villa for Sale'? Discuss the values Gaston should have possessed with regard to moral ethics.

Or Is there any difference between the two roads as the poet describes them

(i) in stanzas two and three? (ii) in the last two lines of the poem?

Answers

1. (i) (b) Disapproving

(ii) (c) Computer games aid a child's agility in controlling their response to an unsuitable situation.

(iii) it could never provide the feeling of playing in a real park

(iv) Skeptical

(v) The indoor play park was a hit among parents as well as children because it not only kept the children away from computer games but also made sure that children play with their peers in the middle of nature.

(vi) (a) A suitable title of the passage can be 'The Indoor Park'.

(vii) As per the writer, computer games slow down brain development. There is a lot of violence in computer games which adversely affects the children. Apart from this, the bright light of these games also hurts the eyes of the young children.

(viii) Parents prefer outdoor physical activity in comparison to video games because
- Most of the games are full of violence.
- The computer games slow down brain development.

2. (a) (i) Schizophrenia (ii) Delusion

(iii) (d) All of these

(iv) (b) Schizophrenia is a chronic and severe mental disorder.

(v) an important piece of information

(vi) The title of the report should be 'Schizophrenia'. The purpose of this passage was to study schizophrenia and its treatment.

(vii) It is true to say that pharmacists are integral to provide quality service to the patients of schizophrenia because medications are invaluable in the management of patients with mental illness.

(viii) The clinical pharmacists are involved with, in addition to making sure that medication is strictly followed, education on preventing the mental illness, promoting a healthy life and modifying lifestyle in accordance with treatment.

3.

Dharmik Sandhya Public School

NOTICE

25th May, 20XX

Tree Plantation Drive

All the students are hereby informed that the Environment Club of the school is organising a Tree Plantation Drive on the occasion of World Environment Day on 5th June, 20XX. The club needs volunteers to make the drive meaningful and successful. Interested students of Class IX may register their names with the undersigned by 2nd June, 20XX.

For further details, contact the undersigned.

Amar
(Secretary, Environment Club)

4. **Ram** : Hello Shyam, where are you going?

Shyam : I am going to buy cigarettes.

Ram : You must not smoke so many cigarettes. Smoking is injurious to health and it is mentioned on the packets too.

Shyam : I know, Ram. It's a difficult habit to give up though.

Ram : Smoking not only spoils your health but also harms the people around you, such as your friends and family. It causes cancer and is the root cause of many other problems.

Shyam : I completely understand what you are saying. I just don't know how I can stop smoking.

Ram : You can join a support programme for people who want to quit smoking and you will see a change in yourself soon.

Shyam : Thanks for your advice. I will definitely try.

Ram : You are welcome. If you are successful, I will organise a party for you.

Shyam : I will give it up from today itself, I promise.

Ram : I wish you are successful.

5. 12, South West Block
Alwar

15th February, 20XX

Dear Tapan

How are you? I am good here and hope that you are hale and hearty. I have written to talk to you about something. I had a talk with your class teacher yesterday. He told me that you got first place in the class. I was glad to hear it. But he also told me that you have become a bookworm. You don't take part in any kind of games. That is not good and it will effect your health.

I suggest you to take part in evening games. Do not study at the cost of your health. Play badminton, cricket or football, even if it is just for an hour. It will refresh your mind and keep you physically fit. This will also help you in your studies. Do study hard, but do take time out to play for a while. Work, while you work and play, while you play; that is the way to be happy and healthy.

Yours affectionately

Prakash

6. Sunita Williams, a US Navy Captain, is a veteran of two long-duration space flights and has spent a total of three hundred and twenty two days in space. Sunita Williams holds a record for total cumulative space walk time by a female astronaut which covers fifty hours and forty minutes. She has been selected by NASA for commercial flights to the International Space Station from the US soil. Sunita is a US Navy Captain and she received her commission in the Navy in May 1987. Then she became a helicopter pilot, logging more than 3000 flight hours in more than thirty different aircraft. She now ranks sixth on the all time US endurance list and second all-time for a female astronaut. Being an Indo-American, Sunita Williams said about Kalpana Chawla in a talk that she had to continue Kalpana's dream.

Or Paragliding is an adventure sport: lightweight, free-flying, foot-launched glider aircraft with no rigid primary structure. The pilot sits in a harness suspended below a fabric wing comprising a large number of interconnected cells. Wing shape is maintained by the suspension lines, the pressure of air entering vents in the front of the wing, and the aerodynamic forces of the air flowing over the outside. Despite not using an engine, paragliders flight can last many hours and cover many hundreds of kilometres though flights of one to two hours and covering some tens of kilometres are more the norm. By skilful exploitation of sources of lift, the pilot may gain height, often climbing to altitudes of a few thousand meters.

7. (a) comes (b) a (c) will

8.

Word before	Missing word	Word after
(a) in	a	natural
(b) that	were	simpler
(c) and	this	process
(d) in	the	simplest

9. (i) Sariska, which was considered a sanctuary for tigers, does not have any tigers left.
(ii) (a) if she had enjoyed during the holidays
(b) had a lot of fun with her

10. (i) (a) Hooper was a tall and smart young man with a cheerful and competitive disposition. He worked as a Zone Sales Manager for a chemical company.
(b) The phrases indicates that Charles Hooper was living his life to the fullest, and there were no obstacles in his life.
(c) 'Favoured', 'competitive' and 'hard-charging' are the three adjectives that have been used to describe Hooper.
(d) The opposite of 'genuine' is 'fake'.

(ii) (a) The poet is standing amidst a small forest, where the leaves of the trees have yellowed.

(b) The speaker is feeling sorry because he can't travel both the roads.

(c) The poet is confused about which road he should take. He is not able to make a decision.

(d) 'undergrowth'

(iii) (a) 'We are not' means that Gaston and Jeanne are not buying any villa.

(b) Jeanne wants to buy it but Gaston doesn't seem to be at all interested.

(c) Yes, Gaston stuck to his decision till the end. We can say so because he had already sold it before buying it, making a profit of one hundred thousand francs.

(d) 'be shown over it' means that she wanted to go inside the villa and see it.

11. (a) The guesses that the poet makes regarding the solitary reaper's song is that it is either about things of the past like wars, the death or illness of a loved one, a natural calamity or disaster or some day to day routine matter.

(b) Sudha Murty was surprised when her grandmother touched her feet because younger people touch the feet of their elders, but her grandmother was touching hers. She was doing so because Sudha was her teacher and students should touch their teacher's feet out of respect.

(c) Everyone resented Private Quelch because of his bad manners. It was true that he was a knowledgeable person, but the show of knowledge he indulged in was not required. He even interrupted his seniors, which was certainly obnoxious.

(d) Pescud was going to Coketown to collect some blossoms (flowers) and cuttings of petunias growing in Coketown as his wife Jessie wished to grow them like the ones she had at her Virginia home.

(e) Hooper was a favoured young man because he had a good life. He was tall, handsome young man who worked as a Zone Sales Manager for a chemical company. He had a happy married life and always had a big, genuine smile on his face. He was a competitive person as well as an energetic sportsman.

(f) Harold's father was a professional boxer while Harold was an intellectual genius. He was very sensitive. At that time, boxing was not considered a respectable profession and his parents thought that it might be difficult for Harold to accept that his father was such a person. Hence, his father's profession was hidden from him.

(g) The brook emerges from the region that is inhabited by the water birds like coots and herons and passes through various valleys, towns and fields. Finally, it merges with the brimming river, which is its final destination.

12. Initially, Juliette decided to sell her villa at only double the price she had bought it. However, later she changed her mind on seeing her prospective customers, Gaston and Jeanne. She quoted a price of two hundred and fifty thousand francs which was really higher than its actual worth. Gaston too was not interested in buying the villa initially but eventually changed his mind on meeting Mrs. Al Smith.

When we compare these two businessmen, Juliette did business ethically and did not harm anyone. The villa belonged to her and she had the right to demand a desired amount. On the contrary, Gaston was unethical, manipulative, unscrupulous and opportunistic. He did not bother about social or moral values. He cheated all the three ladies. He should have possessed moral standards, righteousness and truth.

Or (i) In stanza two, the poet explains that the only difference between the two roads was that the road that he took had a better claim or looked more impressive because it was covered with grass and looked as if it had not been much walked over. However, at the end of the stanza, he says that both roads had been almost equally worn down by people walking on them. In stanza three, the poet says that on that morning, both the roads were equally covered with leaves and that no person had stepped on them.

(ii) In the last two lines of the poem, the poet says (probably many years later in future that there was a difference between the two roads, because he took the road that was less travelled and that made all the difference to his journey and in his life.

Sample Question Paper 2 (Solved)

A Highly Simulated Sample Question Paper for CBSE Class IX

English Communicative

Time : 3 hrs	M.M. : 80

General Instructions

1 This question paper is divided into four sections.
2 All questions are compulsory.
3 Separate instructions are given with each section and question, wherever necessary. Read these instructions very carefully and follow them.
4 Do not exceed the prescribed word limit while answering the questions.

Section A (Reading Skills) [20 Marks]

1. Read the following passage carefully. **(10)**

1. Even international students whose first language is English can find themselves struggling to understand an alien academic culture. The problems are very familiar. Students' first problem is often with listening skills. They may feel nervous about this and it is certainly a steep learning curve. They need a structured listening experience, for instance how to pick out the main ideas. They also need help with academic reading – how to approach an article or book, how to skim, read and make notes.
2. However, while a student's confidence in listening skills grows, it is in the area of academic writing where more serious cultural differences become apparent. Much of British education is based on essay writing, but this may be a demanding task for students from other cultures. Suddenly, they are faced with the need to express their own ideas, develop their opinions and evaluate different issues, all in polished English. For some, the concept of originating this kind of written discourse can prove problematic and they may find themselves scoring low marks because of plagiarism or reproducing someone else's ideas. In Britain, plagiarism is regarded as academic theft, though this is not always the case in other countries. Students are expected to do research in a library before tackling an assignment and simply regurgitating lecture notes is also not acceptable.
3. The best way to overcome these hurdles is to be prepared. The first step is to take a test to assess the English language skills needed to cope with the issues of academic culture.
4. If an accredited test indicates that a student's language skills are not sufficient to embark on a university degree, the next step is to consider pre-sessional courses, generally at the university where the student will take a degree. These can last from three weeks to an academic year, so it is wise for students to be realistic about their needs. It is generally accepted that approximately 200 hours of study are needed to improve on one bad score on some tests. Some of the 'new' universities that formed from polytechnics in 1992 are experimenting with new styles of pre-sessional and foundation courses. Elspeth Jones, Director of the Centre for Language Study at Leeds Metropolitan University explains, "Our courses are monthly and so students from parts of the world with a different academic year can enrol at any time."
5. She feels that language training in new universities is generally more flexible than in older institutions. "Universities like ours can take students with lower language test grades and can put them through a programme that will bring them up to the required standard, though we cannot guarantee how long it will take."

Based on your understanding of the passage, answer the questions given below.

(i) What does academic writing include? **(1)**

(a) How to approach an article
(b) How to read a work
(c) How to make notes
(d) All of these

(ii) Which of the following will be the most appropriate title for the passage? **(1)**

(a) Overcoming Language Hurdles
(b) Language Training
(c) British English-Ways to Cope
(d) Emergence of New Kinds of Courses

(iii) Complete the following appropriately.

Essay writing is a demanding task because ……… **(1)**

(iv) Identify the words/phrases that incorrectly state the meaning of 'accredited' as used in the passage. **(1)**

(a) To credit
(b) To thank
(c) Officially recognised or authorised
(d) To give license
(e) Of quality
(f) To give an appointment

(v) Complete the following appropriately.

What is British education based on? **(1)**

(vi) What does the writer project with reference to the following? Answer in one word. **(1)**

Much of British education is based on essay writing, but this may be a demanding task for students from other cultures.

(vii) What according to the author causes international students to score low marks? State any one reason in about 40 words. **(2)**

(viii) Based on your reading of the text, list any one benefit of pre-sessional courses in about 40 words. **(2)**

2. Read the following passage carefully. **(10)**

1. Right from literacy, accessibility to schools and household expenditure on education, the rural-urban gap remains significant. There is a digital divide, too, with just 4% of rural households having access to computers as compared to 23% in urban areas. These and other trends on a rural-urban gap in education are revealed in the details of a survey conducted by the National Statistical Office (NSO).
2. The report on 'Household Social Consumption: Education' surveyed 1.13 lakh households spread across over 8,000 villages and 6,000 urban blocks between July 2017 and June 2018. The study involved 1.52 lakh students across different levels of study.
3. On accessibility, while 92.7% of the rural households have a primary school within 1 km as compared to 87.2% in urban areas, the situation gets skewed as only 38% of the rural households have access to secondary school as compared to 70% in the urban areas on similar parameters.
4. While accessibility to a neighbourhood school at the primary level is not an issue in rural areas, the gross attendance ratio is also satisfactory with nearly 100% of boys and girls in rural as well as urban areas attending classes. However, in sync with reduced accessibility, there is a gap at the secondary level between rural and urban settings. The all-Indian literacy rate among persons aged 7 years and above is 77.7%. However, for the same age group, rural literacy is 73.5% and for urban areas, it is, 87.7%.
5. The digital divide between rural and urban households is stark with just 4% of the rural population having access to computers. The report highlighted that while only 15% surveyed population in the rural cluster has internet access, 42% of the students in the urban areas have access to the internet.
6. At the school level while the majority of the urban households had shown a preference for private schools, it's the opposite for rural households. The report highlights that 76.1% of the rural children are attending a primary and middle school run by the government, while only 38% of the urban children attend government schools. However, for graduate and above studies, 49.7% of rural students are attending classes in government institutions as compared to 41% of their urban counterparts in government institutions.

STARK DIVIDE IN SECONDARY EDUCATION

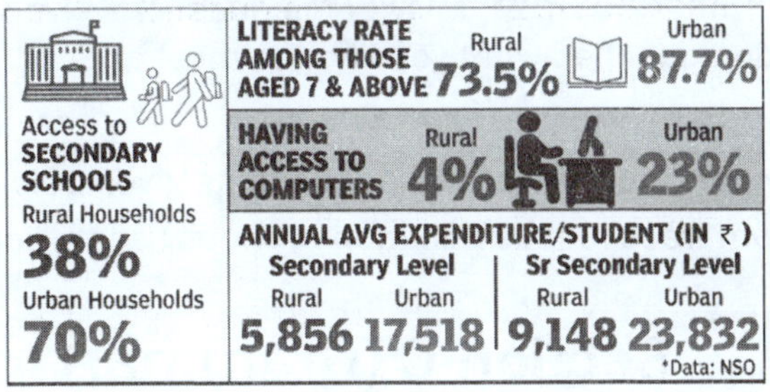

Based on your understanding of the passage, answer the questions given below.

(i) Fill in the blank. **(1)**

The majority of urban households show preference to ....

(ii) Fill in the blanks with the appropriate option from those given in the brackets, based on your understanding of passage. **(1)**

Rural areas have .... (more/less) primary schools .... (within/without) a km as compared to that in urban areas.

(iii) What does the Household Social Consumption: Education focus on? **(1)**

(a) Rural-urban gap in education

(b) Backtracking of online education.
How the digital divide is more evident in education.

(c) Need for making technology more affordable
Rural-urban gap in education

(d) How the digital divide is more evident in education.

(iv) Based on your understanding of the passage, choose the option that lists the factors that indicate the rural-urban gap. **(1)**

1. Right to literacy
2. Accessibility to schools
3. Household expenditure
4. Digital divide
5. Employment opportunities
6. Infrastructure development

Codes

(a) 1 and 2 (b) 3 and 4

(c) 5 and 6 (d) All of these

(v) In which aspect is the condition of education in the urban and rural households equal? **(1)**

(vi) What did the survey conducted by the NSO cover? **(1)**

(vii) What data shows that the rural-urban gap is visible at the secondary level of education? **(2)**

(viii) What did the 'Household Social Consumption: Education' survey found out? **(2)**

Section B (Writing Skills) **[24 Marks]**

3. You are Shiv, School Captain of Delhi Public School, Daryaganj, Delhi. Write a notice informing the students of Class IX about a guest lecture by Mr. Rajiv, an environmentalist on the topic 'Conservation of water'. (4)

4. Rajani's teacher, Mrs. Khanna has invited her mother Mrs. Sharma, to talk about her daughter. Write a dialogue between Mrs. Khanna and Mrs. Sharma in about 100 words. (5)

5. Write a letter to your friend, apologising for not being able to keep an appointment with them in about 120 words. (7)

6. Write a paragraph about your favourite cartoon character based on the hints given below.

Name of character-description-qualities-what you like the most about it **(8)**

Or

Write a paragraph on the importance of trees using the hints given below in about 150 words.

Green gold - useful items from trees-reduce pollution - various uses - friends to humans.

Section C (Grammar) [10 Marks]

7. Fill in the blanks with the most grammatically appropriate words. **(3)**

William Shakespeare is considered to be *(a)* .... (a/an/the) unparalleled literary genius of the Elizabethan age. He wrote for *(b)* .... (a/an/the) contemporary Elizabethan stage in simple lyrical language which the court and public *(c)* .... (can/could/will)enjoy.

8. The following passage has not been edited. There is an error in each of the lines against which a blank is given. Identify the error and write it along with the correction in the answer sheet. The first one has been done for you as an example. **(4)**

	Incorrect	Correct
e.g. Scotland has the rich cultural heritage.	the	a
(a) Part of this are reflected in the thousands	....	....
(b) of castles that are scatter around the length	....	....
(c) and breadth of the country. Most of a	....	....
(d) castles is now in ruins.	....	....

9. (i) Rearrange the following jumbled words/phrases in the given information to make a meaningful sentence. (3)

have been/by/infuriated/I/of/etiquette/lack/people's

Freedom of speech cannot be taken away from one. Yet one cannot keep on speaking all the time.

(ii) Report the dialogue to complete the paragraph that follows.

Rahul Do you know that Ranjit met with an accident and is in hospital ?

Samar Oh! I don't. Is he badly hurt? Which hospital is he in?

Rahul The doctors say that there is nothing to worry. He is admitted to Beach Hospital.

Rahul asked Samarif he knew that Ranjit had met with an accident and was hospitalised. Samar expressed his ignorance and enquired (a).................. . He also asked (b) .... Rahul told him that according to the doctors there was nothing to worry and said that he was admitted to the Beach Hospital.

Section D (Literature Textbook) [26 Marks]

10. Read the given extracts and answer the questions that follow. (Attempt any two) **(4 + 4 = 8)**

(i) "And day in and day out, he lectured to us in his droning, remorseless voice on every aspect of human knowledge. At first we had a certain respect for him, but soon we lived in terror of his approach. We tried to hit back at him with clumsy sarcasms and practical jokes."

(a) "At first we had a certain respect for him, but soon we lived in terror of his approach." What does this tell us about the narrator and his friends?

(b) What made the narrator and his friends live in terror of Private Quelch's approach?

(c) What does the word 'remorseless' indicate about Private Quelch?

(d) What does 'droning' indicate in the extract?

(ii) Alone she cuts, and binds the grain,
And sings a melancholy strain:
O listen! for the vale profound
Is overflowing with the sound.

(a) Identify 'she' in the current stanza.

(b) What is she doing?

(c) Give a synonym of 'melancholy'.

(d) What is the meaning of the expression 'vale profound'?

(iii) What, at this time of night? A pretty business truly. Are we to have no sleep now, but to be at the beck and call of every ne'er - do - well who happens to pass?

(a) What is the speaker talking about?

(b) How does the speaker feel on coming there?

(c) What is meant by 'beck and call'?

(d) Explain the contrast involved in the use of 'pretty'.

11. Answer any six of the following questions in about 30-40 words each. **(2 × 6 = 12)**

(a) Why couldn't Sudha Murty's grandmother get educated in her childhood?

(b) What special qualities made Duke an extraordinary dog?

(c) What were the 'perils' that the narrator spotted in her teeth?

(d) What did the Major do to convince Mr. Bramble to give up boxing?

(e) What was John A. Pescud's opinion about bestsellers?

(f) Why was the poet in the poem 'The Road Not Taken' in a dilemma?

(g) Why has William Wordsworth compared the Solitary Reaper's song with the song of a nightingale and cuckoo?

12. Answer any one of the following questions in about 120 words.

"The narrator felt happy that her student, her grandmother had passed with flying colours." Comment. **(6)**

Or Comment upon the following extract and draw a parallel to the fate of the rain and the fate of man.

'I am the sigh of the sea;

The laughter of the field;

The tears of heaven':

Answers

1. (i) (d) All of these

(ii) (b) Language Training

(iii) one needs to develop ideas, evaluate issues in polished English and research in the library.

(iv) (c) Officially recognised or authorised and (d) To give license

(v) British education is primarily based on essay writing, where students need to express their own ideas, develop their opinions and evaluate different issues, all in polished English.

(vi) Concern

(vii) British education is focused on essay writing. International students who are not accustomed to essay writing then find it difficult to assess, create and formulate their ideas and opinions. They plagiarise, thus end up scoring low marks.

(viii) Pre-sessional courses assess and prepare the students who find difficulty in their ongoing courses. They equip them with the necessary skills needed for their course.

2. (i) private schools

(ii) more, within

(iii) (a) Rural-urban gap in education

(iv) (d) All of these

(v) On the accessibility of primary schools

(vi) The survey covered over 8,000 rural and 6,000 urban households.

(vii) The fact that only 38% households in rural areas have access to secondary schools and more than 70% of households in urban areas have access to secondary schools, shows that the rural-urban gap is visible at the secondary level of education.

(viii) 'Household Social Consumption Education Survey' found out that there is a stark divide in the secondary education received by children vis-a-vis rural-urban divide.

3.

Delhi Public School, Daryajanj, Delhi

NOTICE

3rd October, 20XX

Guest Lecture by Environmentalist

All the students of Class IX are informed that a guest lecture on the topic 'Conservation of Water' by a renowned environmentalist, Mr. Rajiv, is being organised by the school. The lecture will be held on Saturday, i.e. 3rd November in the school auditorium from 11:00 A.M. to 1 : 00 P.M. It is mandatory for Class IX students to attend the lecture. For more information, contact the undersigned.

Shiv
(School Captain)

4. Mrs. Sharma : Good morning, Mrs Khanna. I am Rajni's mother, Shilpa Sharma. You wanted to tell me something about Rajani.

Mrs. Khanna : Yes, Mrs. Sharma. Please have a seat. Rajani is an intelligent girl, she got good grades in all subjects except English. She has been doing quite poorly in English.

Mrs. Sharma : Yes, I have seen her report card. I discussed the matter with her as well. Actually, Rajani used to study at a Hindi-Medium School prior to taking admission in this school. I am also very worried about this matter. Do you have any suggestions?

Mrs. Khanna : I can suggest that you get an English tutor for Rajani. I know a good teacher, Mrs. Sangeeta Jhalani. I can ask her to speak with you, I believe she would be able to help you out.

Mrs. Sharma : Thanks a lot, Mrs. Khanna. You have solved my problems. Will the teacher cover the entire course taught in school?

Mrs. Khanna : Yes, she would teach her everything she needs for school as well as clarify things for her. She would be able to explain the basics with which Rajani Suffers. Many students have improved after her lessons.

Mrs. Sharma : Thank you so much. Have a nice day.

Mrs. Khanna : You are welcome, Mrs. Sharma. Good bye.

5. 29, Janta colony

Jaipur

19th June, 20XX

Dear Pradeep

I am sorry I couldn't join you for dinner last night. You must have been waiting for me and feeling bad that I couldn't keep the appointment. This lapse on my part was due to the fact that I met with an accident while coming over to your place.

As I was walking towards your house, a motorcycle came towards me from the opposite direction. Its head lights were not on. It hit me, making me fall to the ground. My left arm was badly injured. I was taken to the hospital by some people who had seen the accident.

I was allowed to leave the hospital only after midnight. I hope you will excuse my absence and forgive me.

Yours sincerely

Ashok

6. I like to watch cartoons and there are many cartoon characters I like. Some of them are Tom, Doremon, He-Man, Mickey Mouse etc. however, the cartoon character that I like the most is Jerry. Jerry is a mouse that appears in my favourite cartoon show, Tom and Jerry Show. I have been watching Jerry in the Tom and Jerry Show since I was a kid. He is portrayed in the cartoon series as a small mouse which is brown in colour. The other character in the show is Tom, the cat. Tom is much bigger than Jerry and is always after it. This is so because Jerry is habitual of teasing Tom. Jerry plays a lot of pranks on Tom and is not fearful of the big-sized cat at all. It is a lot of fun watching both of them running after each other. It seems obvious to viewers that Tom would be able to get hold of Jerry but that doesn't happen. It is the prankster Jerry that wins in the end and steals the show. I enjoy this show so much and am always in awe of Jerry.

Or

Trees are called 'GREEN GOLD'. It means trees are as valuable as gold. We get wood from trees. Wood is used in making furniture, houses and other useful things. Trees give us fruits, spices, timber and many useful medicines and fodder to animals. Trees breathe out oxygen which we breathe in to survive. Trees help in reducing air-pollution soil erosion and help to prevent natural disasters such as floods and landslides. Trees attract clouds and clouds bring rain. They are useful in many ways.

In reality, trees are the valuable gifts of nature to man. We should honour and preserve trees.

7. (a) an (b) the (c) could

8.

Incorrect	**Correct**
(a) are	is
(b) scatter	scattered
(c) a	the
(d) is	are

9. (i) I have been infuriated by people's lack of etiquette.

(ii) (a) if he was badly hurt

(b) which hospital he was in

10. (i) (a) This tells us that the narrator and his friends started disliking Private Quelch.

(b) Private Quelch's habit of showing off his knowledge and publicly correcting the mistakes of his colleagues, so that they were embarrassed made them live in terror of Private Quelch's approach.

(c) The word remorseless means 'unpleasantly unafraid or non-regretful'. This indicates that private Quelch had no regrets because he considered himself as superior to others.

(d) The word droning indicates the continuous lectures given by Private Quelch.

(ii) (a) 'She' refers to the solitary reaper.
(b) She is harvesting the crop and singing a sad song.
(c) 'Sad' is a synonym of 'melancholy'.
(d) The expression 'vale profound' refers to the deep vast valley.

(iii) (a) The speaker, Persome is talking about having to play host to passing travellers in the middle of the night.
(b) The speaker is upset because she has been woken up in the middle of the night by her brother. She is irritated with the idea of feeding a passing traveller at that hour.
(c) It means 'to obey'.
(d) 'Pretty' has been said in utter dismay. This was sarcastic as no one loves to cook food or serve it at midnight.

11. (a) The grandmother couldn't study because she was very young when she lost her mother, and only her father remained. At that time, education was not considered important for girls. The grandmother got married at an early age and got busy with household duties for the rest of her life. She could not attend school.

(b) Duke was an extraordinary dog in that he had an incalculable enthusiasm, extraordinary intelligence and sincerity. He could sense Chuck's changed needs due to his accident and acted accordingly. He was patient and understanding, as he helped Chuck Hooper recover step by step.

(c) The 'perils' that the narrator spotted in her teeth refer to the cavities and tooth decay that she was suffering from. They were caused as a result of her complete disregard for dental hygiene and continuous gobbling of sweets in her younger days.

(d) Major Percy was adamant that Mr. Bramble should give up boxing. He scared Mr Bramble that the match would be extensively reported. There was every chance of his photograph appearing in the newspaper and Harold could easily stumble upon it.

(e) John was of the opinion that all best sellers had a hero who was a wealthy American man who loved a royal princess from Europe. He strongly felt that these novels were far from reality and purely fictional because in actual life, a man would marry a woman from a similar background.

(f) The poet was in a dilemma because he couldn't decide which road to take. One road seemed to be used abundantly, while the other one was grassy and not used as much. He decided to choose the grassy one, but both of the roads appeared equally attractive to him and he had to make a decision.

(g) The poet finds the voice of the Solitary Reaper to be better than that of the nightingale and cuckoo. He finds it more melodious than that of the nightingale, which can soothe the weavy travellers in the Arabian desert and better than the sweetest song of the cuckoo that sings at the break of every spring.

12. Krishtakka proved to be a wonderful student. She read, repeated, wrote and recited all her lessons with great enthusiasm and concentration. Despite her age, the amount of work the grandmother did was amazing. On the day of the Dussehra festival, when she gifted her teacher (the narrator) with a frock material, the narrator also gave the grandmother a copy of 'Kashi Yatre' which by that time had been published in the form of a novel. When the grandmother read the novel, 'Kashi Yatre' and the author's name, Triveni as well as the publisher's name; the narrator's joy knew no bounds and she knew that her student had passed with flying colours.

Or

In the poem 'Song of the Rain', the poet deals with the autobiographical elements of the rain. The rain, in an autobiographical manner, narrates some of the functions that it performs. It falls down on the earth from the sky. It decorates the fields, valleys and gardens.

The fate of the rain is like the fate of man. The child is born. He grows up into a young man and then an old man and then dies in the end. Similarly, the rain is born in the form of a cloud in the sky. When the cloud bursts, it dies.

The rain is glorified as a welcome song. When it falls gently, softly and tenderly on the windows, it announces its arrival with a sound. That sound becomes a welcome song for those who have the aesthetic sensibility to comprehend it. The rain, thus, becomes the sigh of the sea, the laughter of the field and the tears of the sky.

Sample Question Paper 3 (Unsolved)

A Highly Simulated Sample Question Paper for CBSE Class IX

English Communicative

Time : 3 hrs	M.M. : 80

General Instructions

1 This question paper is divided into four sections.
2 All questions are compulsory.
3 Separate instructions are given with each section and question, wherever necessary. Read these instructions very carefully and follow them.
4 Do not exceed the prescribed word limit while answering the questions.

Section A (Reading Skills) **[20 Marks]**

1. Read the following passage carefully. **(10)**

1. An urgent problem is now threatening libraries throughout the world. Their collections, which are crucial for diverse purposes as economic development, educational research and recreational pursuits are in danger of disintegration.
2. The problem is mainly due to one cause—the type of paper on which books have been printed for the past one and a half centuries. Until the 1850s, paper was produced from linen or cotton rags and proved to be relatively long-lasting. In the mid-19th century, however, the popular demand for paper and the commercial need for an economic method of production led to the use of mechanically ground wood pulp. Paper manufactured from wood pulp is highly acidic and therefore, inherently unstable. It contains lignin which causes paper to discolour and disintegrate.
3. Programmes are now being developed with two main aims in mind: on one hand, to improve the physical condition of library collections, especially by the process called 'mass deacidification' (to eliminate acid from the paper of published books and insert a buffer compound that will provide protection against future) and on the other, to transfer the contents of existing books to another medium.
4. Libraries will only be able to carry out these special tasks with the assistance of experts such as book conservators and high technology specialists. But, there is another group whose cooperation will be crucial, if the problem of decaying collections is to be arrested: the printing and publishing industries. The existing problem that of book collections already assembled in libraries is of vast proportions. It is intensified by the continuing use of acid-based paper in book publishing. The key issue is, how to preserve the books of the future, not simply those of the past.
5. If the future dimensions of the conservation problem are to be curbed, there will be a necessity of widespread adoption of paper which is of archival quality.
6. This change does not relate to a narrowly perceived need because the long-term preservation of library collections is important both for the overall social benefits they bring as well as for the special advantages they bestow on the printing and publishing industries.
7. In the first place, libraries are of critical importance to the well-being of citizens, since they provide the knowledge base of society. They contain the record of humanity, the accumulation of ideas and insights and discoveries on which social effort and progress are possible. The destruction of libraries would represent an immense cultural loss, a form of amnesia, which would affect every member of society.

Based on you understanding of the passage, answer the questions given below.

(i) Libraries can save their collections by .... **(1)**

(a) storing them in air-conditioned rooms (b) laminating the pages

(c) creating a dust-free atmosphere in their premises (d) widespread adoption of paper of archival quality

(ii) The writer would agree with the given statements based on Paragraph 2, EXCEPT **(1)**

(a) The paper produced from wood pulp is not everlasting.

(b) The paper produced from wood pulp is acidic in nature.

(c) The paper produced from wood pulp is still being produced.

(d) The paper produced from wood pulp is prone to discoloring.

(iii) Complete the given sentence appropriately. **(1)**

There was a need to produce mechanically ground wood pulp during the mid-nineteenth century because of ....

(iv) Which word conveys the opposite of 'complicate', from words used in Paragraph 4? **(1)**

(v) How can the tone of the passage be best described? **(1)**

(vi) According to the passage, linen or cotton rags were used as paper until the 1850's. Based on your understanding of the passage, state whether you promote going back to using them as paper. Give reason for your answer. **(1)**

(vii) Comment on the importance of libraries referred to in Paragraph 1. (30-40 words) **(2)**

(viii) List the two ways in which a book by Robert Frost could be saved from deterioration and loss. Answer in 30-40 words. **(2)**

2. Read the following passage carefully. **(10)**

1. I saw 'Jaws', the popular shark movie, the summer it came out, in 1975 and became paranoid about sharks. Though I kept swimming after Jaws, it was always with the vague fear that a shark's teeth could tug on my leg at any moment. Never mind that there'd been only two shark bites since 1900 on the Connecticut coast, where I lived.

2. So, when I got thisassignment for the National Geographic magazine, I decided to accept and do what I'd never wanted to do: swim with the sharks. I had to go to a place in the Bahamas known as Tiger Beach and dive with tiger sharks, the species responsible for more recorded attacks on humans than any shark except the great white. It was to be my first dive after getting certified—which meant it would be my first dive anywhere other than a swimming pool or a quarry—and without a diver's cage. Most people who got wind of this plan thought I was either very brave or very stupid.

3. But I just wanted to puncture an illusion. The people who know sharks intimately tend to be the least afraid of them, and no one gets closer to sharks than divers. The divers who run operations at Tiger Beach speak lovingly of the tiger sharks the way people talk about their children or their pets. In their eyes, these sharks aren't man-eaters any more than dogs are.

4. The business of puncturing illusions is never just black and white. My fellow divers had hundreds of dives under their belt and on the two-hour boat ride to the site in the morning of our first dive, they kept saying things like, "Seriously, I really can't believe this is your first dive." All this was okay with me until I reached the bottom and immediately had to fend off the first tiger shark, I had ever laid eyes on. However, when I watched the other divers feeding them fish and steering them gently, it became easy to see the sharks in a very benign light.

5. I think it would be unfair not to mention that though tiger sharks are apex predators. They act as a crucial balancing force in ocean ecosystems, constraining the numbers of animals like sea turtles and limit their behaviour by preventing them from overgrazing the sea grass beds. Furthermore, tiger sharks love warm water, they eat almost anything, have a huge litter and are the hardiest shark species. If the planet and its oceans continue to warm, some species will be winners and others will be losers, and tiger sharks are likely to be winners.

Based on you understanding of the passage, answer the questions given below.

(i) Complete the sentence appropriately. **(1)**

The author of the given passage, wants the reader to ....

(ii) Substitute the underlined word/phrase in the sentence with a word/phrase from the passage which means the same. **(1)**

Some academicians think that reward, as a form of discipline, is a simple right or wrong issue.

(iii) What do the tiger sharks love? **(1)**

(a) Eating turtles
(b) Harming people who bother them
(c) Warm water
(d) Sea grass

(iv) What does the use of the phrase 'benign light' suggest in the context of the writer's viewpoint about the tiger sharks? **(1)**

(a) Friendly nature of sharks
(b) Baseless fear of shark
(c) Incorrect quality associated with shark
(d) All of these

(v) Why does the writer say that people who know sharks intimately tend to be least afraid of them? **(1)**

(vi) Which traits of the writer is evident from lines 5-10? **(1)**

(vii) Cite a point in evidence, from the text, to suggest that the writer's post-Jaws fear was not justified. (30-40 words) **(2)**

(viii) People thought the writer was 'either brave or very stupid'. Why did some people think that he was 'very stupid'? Answer in 30-40 words. **(2)**

Section B (Writing Skills) [24 Marks]

3. **You are Rahul, Secretary, PL International School Football Association. It has been decided that a meeting has to be organised for all members of the school football team to discuss the plan for the upcoming state level tournament. Write a notice informing the members of the team about the meeting and requesting them to attend.** **(4)**

4. **Sandhya is visiting her family doctor because she is unwell. Write a conversation between the doctor and Sandhya.** **(5)**

5. **You are Ravi, living in Delhi. Your father has not been well in Jaipur for the past week. Write a letter to him asking about his health in not of more than 120 words.** **(7)**

6. **Write a paragraph on the mysterious Bermuda Triangle. You can use the clues given below.** **(8)**

Or **Write a paragraph based on the visual clue given below.**

Section C (Grammar) [10 Marks]

7. Complete the following paragraph by filling in the blanks. **(3)**

Dr. Diesel was *(a)* .... (a/an/the) gifted engineer. He *(b)* .... (is/was/were) highly practical and persevering in *(c)* .... (give/gave/giving) shape to his ideas.

8. The following paragraph has not been edited. There is one error in each line. Identify the error and write its correction against the correct blank number. Remember to underline the correction. The first one has been done for you as an example. **(4)**

	Error	Correction
e.g. Enid Blyton books are, of course, of primary	of	for
(a) school children. Many were suitable for old	....	....
(b) primary school children, but any are	....	....
(c) especially write for new readers	....	....
(d) in an early primary school years.	....	....

9. (i) Rearrange the jumbled words/phrases in the given information to create a meaningful sentence. **(3)**

Ashoka tree is a tall evergreen tree. It reaches a height of 15 m and even more. It is prized for its beautiful foliage.

Indian subcontinent / sacred / it / throughout / is considered / the

(ii) Report the dialogues to complete the paragraph that follows.

Mother Why are you looking so worried?

Daughter My exams are approaching.

Mother When will they start?

Daughter Next month, Mother.

Mother asked her daughter (a) .... The daughter replied that her exams were approaching. Mother further asked (b) .... The daughter told her mother that they would start in the following month.

Section D (Literature Textbook) [26 Marks]

10. Read the given extracts and answer the questions that follow. (Attempt any two) **(4 + 4 = 8)**

(i) "When people in real life marry, they generally hunt up somebody in their own station. A fellow usually picks out a girl who went to the same high-school and belonged to the same singing society that he did."

(a) Who is speaking and to whom?

(b) Can you call the lines ironic? Justify your stance.

(c) What do you understand by 'in their own station'?

(d) Comment on the tone of the given lines.

(ii) And then the justice,
In fair round belly with good capon lined,
With eyes severe and beard of formal cut,
Full of wise saws and modern instances;
And so he plays his part.

(a) What differentiates the justice age from other ages?
(b) How does a man perform in the justice age?
(c) The word 'saws' used in the extract means ....
(d) What does 'good capon lined' mean?

(iii) Oh I'm fed up with the place. Because nobody really wants it! What time did those agency people say the lady would call?

(a) What do you mean by 'fed up' here?
(b) What do you think may be the reason that nobody wants it?
(c) Identify the context about which the lady would call.
(d) What do you understand by 'the agency people'?

11. Answer any six of the following questions in about 30-40 words each. **($2 \times 6 = 12$)**

(a) Why did Robert Frost choose the road less travelled?
(b) How does Mrs Al Smith comment on the French people?
(c) What was 'intelligent reading' according to the 'Professor'?
(d) Why was the convict sent to prison? What was the punishment given to him?
(e) When did the grandmother realise that she wanted to learn to read?
(f) How does man behave in the 'Soldier' stage of life according to Shakespeare in the poem 'The Seven Ages'?
(g) What does the poet, Pam Ayres, regret about her teeth and why?

12. Answer any one of the following questions in about 120 words. **(6)**

Do you think that our strong desire to own material thing is making us less aware of important personal qualities such as loyalty, kindness and concern for others? Express your views by taking examples from play 'Villa for Sale' and 'Bishop's Candlesticks'.

Or

Express your views on the statement "When people in real life marry, they generally hunt up somebody in their own station," in about 120 words in the context of 'Best Seller'. Do you agree? Do you think now-a-days marriage is a relation of convenience and not a bond of two souls?

Sample Question Paper 4 (Unsolved)

A Highly Simulated Sample Question Paper for CBSE Class IX

English Communicative

Time : 3 hrs	M.M. : 80

General Instructions

1 This question paper is divided into four sections.
2 All questions are compulsory.
3 Separate instructions are given with each section and question, wherever necessary. Read these instructions very carefully and follow them.
4 Do not exceed the prescribed word limit while answering the questions.

Section A (Reading Skills)

[20 Marks]

1. Read the following passage carefully. **(10)**

1. Peer pressure is a phenomenon wherein we tend to get influenced by the lifestyle and the ways of thinking of our peers. Peer pressure can prove beneficial but it is most often observed to have negative effects.

2. The thought, behaviour and taste in fashion, music, television and other walks of life of the masses are often seen to have a deep impact on society. We tend to get influenced by the lifestyle of our peer group. The changing ways of life of our peers often force us to change our ways of looking at life and leading it. It's a human tendency to do what the crowd does. Few have the courage to resist peer pressure and be their own selves rather than being one among the lot.

3. Peer pressure is bound to affect most of us both positively and negatively. The distinction between positive and negative peer pressure lies in a thoughtful analysis of the views of the masses. Following your peers blindly leaves a negative impact on your life while an analytical approach to looking at peer behaviour can help you act positively.

4. Peer pressure is not always bad. It can help you analyse yourself and contemplate your ways of life. Some of the practices that the masses follow may actually teach you the way of living. You may be able to change yourself for the better. Looking at what others do, can help you bring about a positive change in your way of thinking. If you can pick selectively, peer pressure can actually result in a positive change in your way of life.

5. Teenage is that phase of life when you are exposed to the world outside. These are the years when you spend most of your time with your friends. Teenage is the phase of beginning to become independent in life; the years of forming your ideals and principles, the years that shape your personality and the years that introduce you to your own self. As adolescents you often spend most of your daily time with friends and owing to this, you tend to imitate your friends. The people around you are bound to influence you. However the effect of the influences of the masses is greater during your teen years. Parents have a vital role to play during this phase of your life.

6. Parents and teachers need to be careful while dealing with teenagers, as they are most susceptible to succumbing to peer pressure during these years of their life. Teenage individuals need to be taught to distinguish between the good and the bad, the right and the wrong and should be taught to be thoughtful in life.

7. A strong support from family, an ability to differentiate between the positive and the negative and a skill to choose friends from among peers this three-pronged strategy is the best way to keep away from negative peer pressure.

Based on your understanding of the passage, answer the questions given below.

(i) Evaluate the Appropriate reason for the effect of peer pressure in teenage years. **(1)**

(a) Teen years are always unmanageable.
(b) Teenagers spend more time with their peers and friends.
(c) Teenagers spend more time with their parents and old people.
(d) It is impossible to convince them.

(ii) Select the option that corresponds to the following relation below.

Peer pressure can prove beneficial but it is most often observed to have negative effects. **(1)**

(a) Beginnings and ends are easier to remember than middles.
(b) Sleep is good for memory but too much sleep can also be linked to health problems.
(c) Food tastes better when someone else makes it.
(d) Some people enjoy seeing anger in others.

(iii) Complete the following suitably.

The writer means .... by 'the way of living'. **(1)**

(iv) The writer says Teenage is that phase of life when you are exposed to the world outside.

Identify the words that correctly state the meaning of the term 'exposed' as used in the passage. **(1)**

(a) Visible (b) Vulnerable
(c) Public (d) Introduce
(e) Reveal (f) Displayed

(v) Why can changing ways of life of our peers can affect us? **(1)**

(vi) What does the writer project with reference to the following? **(1)**

Parents and teachers need to be careful while dealing with teenagers, as they are most susceptible to succumbing to peer pressure during these years of their life.

(vii) Justify the following in about 40 words. **(2)**

Parents and teachers need to be careful while dealing with teenagers, as they are most susceptible to succumbing to peer pressure during these years of their life.

(viii) The writer mentions The people around you are bound to influence you. (Paragraph 5) **(2)**

Mention one reason from the passage that supports the above statement. (40 words)

2. Read the following passage carefully. **(10)**

1. India is home to an estimated 10% of the global Snow Leopard population spread across five Himalayan states of Jammu and Kashmir, Himachal Pradesh, Uttarakhand, Sikkim and Arunachal Pradesh which is only 5% of the available global habitat for the animal.
2. Project Snow Leopard was introduced in India by the Project Snow Leopard Committee instituted by the Ministry of Environment and Forests, Government of India, in the year 2009 to safeguard and conserve India's unique natural heritage of high-altitude wildlife populations and their habitats by promoting conservation through participatory policies and actions.
3. Project Tiger and Project Elephant are prevalent in India with the former introduced in 1973 garnering worldwide attention.
4. The Snow Leopard usually occurs at an altitude of >2700m above sea level and is the apex predator in the Himalayan Region along with the Tibetan Wolf. The project is not only to protect the Snow Leopard but as with Project Tiger, it is considered an umbrella species and with its protection, comes the protection of other species and the habitat of which they are all a part.

5. Top 3 National Parks in India where the Snow Leopard can likely be seen

   (i) Kibber Wildlife Sanctuary - Himachal Pradesh

   (ii) Ulley Valley - Ladakh

   (iii) Hemis National Park - Himachal Pradesh

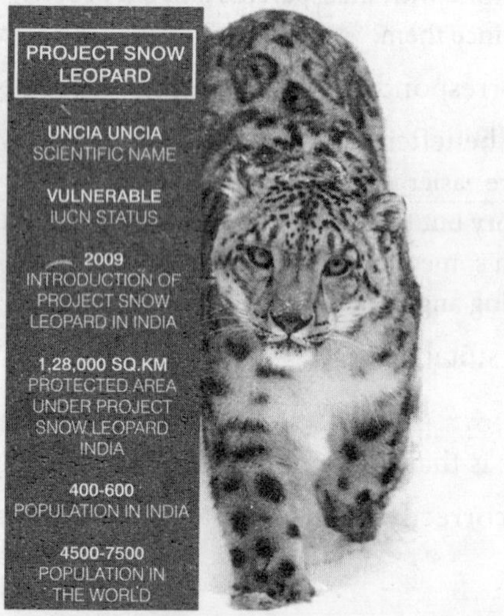

6. The reasons for the introduction of Project Snow Leopard are as follows.

   (i) High altitudes of India > 3000m including the Himalayan and Trans-Himalayan biogeographic zones support a unique wildlife assemblage of global conservation.

   (ii) There has been relatively less attention on the region from the viewpoint of wildlife conservation.

   (iii) The region represents a vast rangeland system supporting important traditional pastoral economies and lifestyles.

   (iv) The region provides essential ecosystem services and harbours river systems vital for the nation's food security.

   (v) India has ratified international agreements promoting the conservation of high-altitude wildlife species such as the snow leopard.

   (vi) The region is important for the country's national security as well as international relations.

   (vii) The high-altitude wildlife in India today faces a variety of threats.

   (viii) The existing high-altitude protected areas in India require considerable strengthening.

   (ix) Wildlife Management in the region needs to be made participatory.

Based on your understanding of the passage, answer the questions given below.

(i) Complete the following sentence. **(1)**

The reason for the introduction of Project Snow Leopard in high altitudes is that ....

(ii) Fill in the blank from Paragraph 4. **(1)**

The '................' (Snow Leopards/Arctic Fox) which usually occur at an altitude of >2700m, are the apex predators in the Himalayan Region.

(iii) Which of the following is True about the passage? **(1)**

(a) Wildlife Management in the region need not be made participatory.

(b) High altitudes of India > 3000m including the Himalayan and Trans-Himalayan biogeographic zones support a unique wildlife assemblage of global conservation.

(c) Project Tiger and Project Elephant are prevalent in India with the latter introduced in 1973 garnering worldwide attention.

(d) Project Snow Leopard was introduced in India by the Project Snow Leopard Committee instituted by the Ministry of Science and Technology.

(iv) Select the option that titles Paragraphs 1-3 appropriately, with reference to information in the text. **(1)**

(a) Project Snow Leopard Preserving India's Wild Protecting India's High-altitude Ecosystem	(b) Project Elephant Project Tiger High-altitude Wildlife
(c) Project Tiger Man in the Wild Wildlife in India	(d) Tibetan Wolf Project Tiger Project Snow Leopard

(v) Project Tiger and Project Elephant are prevalent in India with the former introduced in 1973. What has the former gathered? **(1)**

(vi) Infer the meaning of the phrase 'snow leopard is considered an umbrella species' from the passage. **(1)**

(vii) List any one reason why Project Snow Leopard was introduced in India. **(2)**

(viii) List any two reasons for the introduction of Project Snow Leopard in high altitudes. **(2)**

Section B (Writing Skills) **[24 Marks]**

3. **You are Rakesh, Secretary of the Book Club of Happy Public School, Delhi. Your club is organising a Book Fair for the students of your school. Write a notice giving all the relevant information about the event in not more than 50 words.** **(4)**

4. **Write a dialogue between a father and a son who are discussing going for jogging every morning in about 100 words.** **(5)**

5. **You are Abhishek, living in Jabalpur. Write a letter to your friend in Delhi, congratulating him on his success in the university examinations.** **(7)**

6. **Write a paragraph on a social figure you admire the most based on the clues given in the box. (150 words)** **(8)**

Name of personality - Physical features - birth place date- reason for being famous - his/her struggles - major achievements - qualities that you admire most about him/her.

Or **Write a paragraph based on the visual clue given below (150 Words).**

Section C (Grammar) [10 Marks]

7. Fill in the blanks with the most grammatically appropriate words. **(3)**

For centuries, the giant squid *(a)*.......... (has/have) filled many people with wonder. The Maori people in New Zealand *(b)*.......... (share/shares) great legends about the creature. Squids also *(c)*.......... (appear/appears) in Norwegian mythology, where they *(d)*.......... (is/are) named Kraken. The word Kraken *(e)*.......... (mean/means) 'a tree stump with its roots attached'.

8. The following paragraph has not been edited. There is one error in each line. Identify the error and write its correction against the correct blank number. **(4)**

	Incorrect	Correct
(a) Any people came to the site where the	....	....
(b) revolutionary general were to be hanged. When asked if	....	....
(c) he had any desire, the smile ran	....	....
(d) on him dry lips and he nodded his head.	....	....

9. (i) Rearrange the following jumbled words/phrases in the given information to create a meaningful sentence. **(3)**

Extremely/a/grief/it/is/that matter/unkindly/animals/are/of exploited.

They are beaten, chained, trained and killed mercilessly. But nobody hears and pays heed to their cries. Animals are our friends, auxiliaries and necessary for our survival. Our vision should be a world where animal welfare matters.

(ii) Read the conversation between a doctor and a patient and complete the passage that follows.

Doctor Your body temperature is dangerously high. Since when are you suffering from headache?

Patient The first time that I felt it was in the morning yesterday during my walk.

The doctor told the patient that his body temperature was dangerously high and asked him (a) .... from headache. The patient answered that the first time that (b) .... during his walk.

Section D (Literature Textbook) [26 Marks]

10. Read the given extracts and answer the following questions. (Attempt any two) **(4 + 4 = 8)**

(i) In the silence that followed, a dark flush stained the tan of Corporal's face. "Here", he said at last, "you give this lecture". As if afraid to say any more, he tossed the grenade to the Professor. Quite unabashed, Private Quelch climbed to his feet and with the air of a man coming into his birth-right gave us an unexceptionable lecture on the grenade.

(a) Why did the Corporal ask Private Quelch to give the lecture?

(b) Why was there a silence?

(c) On the basis of the extract, characterise Private Quelch.

(d) Do you think the professor was happy with private Quelch?

(ii) When I think of the lollies I licked,
And the liquorice all sorts I picked,
Sherbet dabs, big and little,
All that hard peanut brittle,
My conscience gets horribly pricked.

(a) Why does the poet feel that her conscience is horribly pricked?

(b) Will the speaker stop eating sugar now? Justify your position.

(c) **What message/moral does the poem from which the extract is taken give?**

(d) **Which word is the opposite of 'pleasantly' in the above lines?**

(iii) You folk are queer. You think about the past all the time. We always think about future.

(a) **Who speaks these lines?**

(b) **What do you mean by the word 'folk' here?**

(c) **What do the given lines tell about the speaker?**

(d) **Who thinks about the past; and who, about future?**

11. Answer any six of the following questions in about 30–40 words each. **($2 \times 6 = 12$)**

(a) Which suggestion of the maid surprised Juliette?

(b) What is the effect of the solitary reaper's song on the poet William Wordsworth?

(c) What was Pescud's opinion about best sellers?

(d) How is rain like earthly life?

(e) Why was 'Kashi Yatra' favourite story of the grandmother?

(f) Which incident left Chuck Hooper with subdural haemorrhage?

(g) Did Private Quelch's day-to-day practices take him closer towards his goal ?

12. Answer any one of the following questions in about 120 words. **(6)**

Imagine you are Robert Frost. You have chosen the desired path and now you are very happy and successful. Write an article expressing your sense of satisfaction and values you have learnt.

Or

Gaston clinched a deal with Mrs. Al Simith and made a good profit. Will you call his deed a businessman's skill or an unethical practice? Discuss the values Gaston lacked. What would you have done if you had been Gaston?

Sample Question Paper 5 (Unsolved)

A Highly Simulated Sample Question Paper for CBSE Class IX

English Communicative

Time : 3 hrs	M.M. : 80

General Instructions

1 This question paper is divided into four sections.
2 All questions are compulsory.
3 Separate instructions are given with each section and question, wherever necessary. Read these instructions very carefully and follow them.
4 Do not exceed the prescribed word limit while answering the questions.

Section A (Reading Skills) [20 Marks]

1. Read the following passage carefully. **(10)**

1. A large majority of the elderly in India does not get long-term and palliative care, revealed a study conducted for the United Nations. The survey of more than 10,000 respondents across Northern, Southern, Western, Eastern and Central India during May-June 2018, showed that 62.1% of the elderly did not get such care. More than half of these people, 52.4%, said they primarily need traditional family support, says a study by Age well Research and Advocacy Centre.

2. Older people in India often face problems such as disability, restricted mobility, loneliness, poverty and lack of awareness on accessing old-term care. With a fast growing population of older people, the ever-increasing gap between generations and the fast and demanding lifestyle of young people, for a majority of older people, life is still a struggle for independence.

3. "According to 64% of elderly respondents, loneliness, marginalisation and isolation are the most critical issues faced by bedridden, elderly patients as they cannot visit, meet or interact with their relatives, friends and neighbours," said Himanshu Rath, founder of Agewell Foundation.

4. The elderly have to compromise and make adjustments in their lifestyle according to the wishes of the younger members of their families to ensure they are cared for, the study revealed. It highlighted that 67.6% of the elderly being taken care of their family members have to look after the children of the families. They have to perform tasks such as babysitting in return for proper care and support.

5. "Around 73.7% said they have to take care of the house and other properties of their younger family members to ensure long-term and palliative care in old age," the study report said. "Over 75% of respondents have to limit their personal social interactions as their family members direct them to do so, otherwise their family members can avoid providing their basic needs of food and medicines."Most elderly respondents (68.5%) said breaking up of the joint family system is one of the biggest factors for the challenges they face in getting long-term, palliative care.

6. Healthcare equipment such as wheelchairs, relief material such as adult diapers and care-giving service should be provided on a regular basis to destitute older people, who are bedridden and suffering from acute mobility issues, the report said. "Though providing long-term and palliative care to older persons comes in the purview of family responsibilities in India, it is observed that older persons, who are financially independent, have a high net worth or hold property entitlements, are treated comparatively well by their family members" said Rath.

7. "Managing home care for the elderly is a massive challenge as multiple service providers—nursing agencies, physiotherapists and medical suppliers—are small scale and unorganised and, therefore, provide incomplete care," he said. "In India, health insurance coverage is essentially limited to hospitalisation. The concept of geriatric care has remained a neglected area of medicine so far in the country."

Based on you understanding of the passage, answer the questions given below.

(i) Select the option that displays the most likely reason for stating that older people who live with family are no better. **(1)**

(a) They also suffer from loneliness
(b) They have no one who loves or cares for them
(c) They have additional burden of responsibility
(d) All of these

(ii) Complete the given sentence by selecting the most appropriate option. **(1)**

Elderly limit their social interaction because ....

(a) family member told them too
(b) they cannot speak properly
(c) of their medical conditions
(d) they become anti-social

(iii) Complete the sentence appropriately. **(1)**

The problem with palliative healthcare for the elderly is that it is ....

(iv) Substitute the underlined word in the sentence with a word from the passage which means the same.

He is in a <u>bad</u> condition after the accident. **(1)**

(v) List two essential requirements for older people suffering from mobility issues. Answer in 30-40 words. **(1)**

(vi) Why are financially independent elderly called better off? **(1)**

(vii) After reading the passage, what do you think is the primary need of all the elderly people in India? **(2)**

(viii) Based on the reading of the text, state a point to challenge the given statement. (30-40 words) **(2)**

Joint Family System along with the need for private space has brought challenges to the long term elderly care.

2. Read the following passage carefully. **(10)**

1. Even international students whose first language is English can find themselves struggling to understand an alien academic culture. The problems are very familiar. Students' first problem is often with listening skills. They may feel nervous about this and it is certainly a steep learning curve. They need a structured listening experience, for instance how to pick out the main ideas. They also need help with academic reading—how to approach an article or book, how to skim, read and make notes.

2. However, while a student's confidence in listening skills grows, it is in the area of academic writing where more serious cultural differences become apparent. Much of British education is based on essay writing, but this may be a demanding task for students from other cultures. Suddenly, they are faced with the need to express their own ideas, develop their opinions and evaluate different issues, all in polished English. For some, the concept of originating this kind of written discourse can prove problematic and they may find themselves scoring low marks because of plagiarism or reproducing someone else's ideas. In Britain, plagiarism is regarded as academic theft, though this is not always the case in other countries. Students are expected to do research in a library before tackling an assignment and simply regurgitating lecture notes is also not acceptable.

3. The best way to overcome these hurdles is to be prepared. The first step is to take a test to assess the English language skills needed to cope with the issues of academic culture.

4. If an accredited test indicates that a student's language skills are not sufficient to embark on a university degree, the next step is to consider pre-session courses, generally at the university where the student will take a degree. These can last from three weeks to an academic year, so it is wise for students to be realistic about their needs. It is generally accepted that approximately 200 hours of study are needed to improve on one bad score on some tests. Some of the 'new' universities that formed from polytechnics in 1992 are experimenting with new styles of pre-session and foundation courses. Elspeth Jones, Director of the Centre for Language Study at Leeds Metropolitan University explains, "Our courses are monthly and so students from parts of the world with a different academic year can enrol at any time."

5. She feels that language training in new universities is generally more flexible than in older institutions. "Universities like ours can take students with lower language test grades and can put them through a programme that will bring them up to the required standard, though we cannot guarantee how long it will take."

Based on you understanding of the passage, answer the questions given below.

(i) Complete the sentence appropriately. **(1)**

In the field of .... serious cultural differences become apparent.

(ii) Complete the following suitably. **(1)**

Much of British education is based on essay writing, but this may be a demanding task for students from other cultures. Here, the writer projects ....

(iii) Why is 'essay writing' a demanding task? **(1)**

(a) One needs to develop ideas and evaluate issues in polished English
(b) One needs to research in the library
(c) One cannot rewrite lecture notes
(d) All of the above

(iv) Select the most suitable title for the above passage. **(1)**

(a) Overcoming Language Hurdles
(b) Language Training
(c) British English- Ways to Cope
(d) Emergence of New Kinds of Courses

(v) What is British education primarily based on? **(1)**

(vi) Substitute the underlined word in the given sentence with a word from the passage which means the same. **(1)**

The organisation has <u>officially registered</u> him as a writer of the thesis.

(vii) Based on your reading of the text, list any one benefit of pre-sessional courses. **(2)**

(viii) What according to the author causes international students to score low marks? State two reasons. **(2)**

Section B (Writing Skills)

[24 Marks]

3. You are Mahesh, Secretary of the Music Club of your school. Write a notice inviting students to give their names for participation in an inter-class singing competition organised by your club. (4)

4. Raj has lost his phone and has come to the police station to seek the help of police. Write a dialogue between Raj and the police officer in about 100 words. (5)

5. You recently visited your friend's house. Write a letter to him/her explaining why you enjoyed the stay with their family in about 120 words. (7)

6. Write a paragraph on the celebration of Children's Day in your school based on the clues given below. (150 words) (8)

Combined assembly of all wings - principal gave speech on importance of the day - followed by fancy dress competition - sweets distributed in lunch time - fun activities and games organised by teachers in class.

Or **Write a paragraph based on the visual clue given below (150 words).**

Section C (Grammar) [10 Marks]

7. Fill in the blanks with the most grammatically appropriate words.

History often ......*(a)*...... (seem/seems/seemed) like a story about the never-ending struggle for control over land. People ......*(b)*...... (has/have/had) travelled great distances for land. They have fought in bloody battles and wars to claim their ......*(c)*...... (own/none/a) little corner of Earth. **(3)**

8. The following passage has not been edited. One word is missing from each line. Identify the missing word and write it in your answer sheet along with the word that comes before and after it. Remember to underline the missing word. **(4)**

	Before	Missing	After
(a) The sudden accident of dear	....	....	....
(b) ones me reflect	....	....	....
(c) on human desire for safety.	....	....	....
(d) But unfortunately, we not follow traffic rules ourselves.	....	....	....

9. (i) Rearrange the jumbled words/phrases in the given information to create a meaningful sentence. **(3)**

health care / experience / villagers / many difficulties / services / accessing / in

Healthcare is a big challenge in rural India. Mortality rate in rural India is very high. This is mainly due to inadequate healthcare facilities.

(ii) Report the dialogues to complete the paragraph that follows.

Mother Rita, finish your food.

Rita I don't want to have this food. You never give me a pizza or burger.

Mother told Rita (a)............................ Rita replied that (b)...........................and told her mother that she never gave her a pizza or burger.

Section C (Literature Textbook) [26 Marks]

10. Read the given extracts and answer the following questions. (Attempt any two) **(4 + 4 = 8)**

(i) The little man's face became a battlefield on which rage, misery and a respect for the decencies of social life struggled for mastery.

(a) Who is the little man referred to?

(b) What does the expression 'face became a battlefield' mean?

(c) What did the decencies of social life demand from 'the little man'?

(d) What is the opposite of 'misery'?

(ii) I am beautiful pearls, plucked from the

Crown of Ishtar by the daughter of Dawn

To embellish the gardens.

(a) Is 'I' imagined or a real figure in the poem? Justify your answer.

(b) How does 'I' perceive itself? Can you call it vain?

(c) Explain 'Crown of Ishtar by the daughter of Dawn'.

(d) How does 'I' embellish the gardens?

(iii) I-I-didn't believe there was any good in the world;...... but somehow you're good, and-and it's a queer thing to ask, but-could you, would you bless me before I go? I-I think it would help me.

(a) Why does the speaker feel there is no good in the world?

(b) What has made him change his opinion?

(c) Find the word in the extract which is the antonym of 'normal'.

(d) Explain – 'It (blessings) would help me'?

11. Answer any six of the following questions in about 30-40 words each. **(2 × 6 = 12)**

(a) How is the journey of human life different from the journey of the Brook?

(b) Do you think Chuck was a duty conscious man? How can you tell?

(c) How does Persome react to the loss of the salt-seller?

(d) What does rain do for the Earth and Clouds?

(e) Why was Harold called a 'prodigy'?

(f) What did John Pescud say when the narrator asked him about his company and his work?

(g) What is 'second childishness' according to Shakespeare's poem 'The Seven Ages'?

12. Answer any one of the following questions in about 120 words. **(6)**

You are Krishtakka. Write a letter to Triveni, the popular writer, telling her why you like *Kashi Yatra* and how it motivated you to learn to read. Mention the values that helped you to overcome your weaknesses.

Or

Persome's eccentric behaviour is the result of her love and concern for her brother. Comment. Do you appreciate this kind of a character trait? Do you think such behaviour affects the people around us?